Refugees and Asylum Seekers

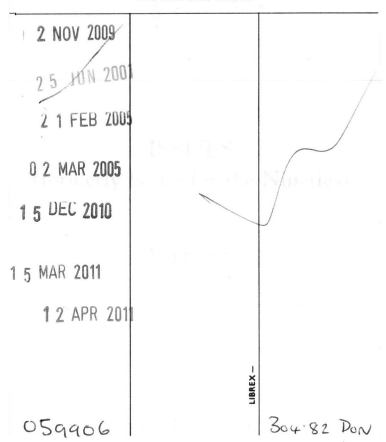
 **Independence**

Educational Publishers
Cambridge

First published by Independence
PO Box 295
Cambridge CB1 3XP
England

British Library Cataloguing in Publication Data
Refugees and Asylum Seekers – (Issues Series)
I. Donnellan, Craig II. Series
362.8'7

ISBN 1 86168 102 X

Printed in Great Britain
The Burlington Press
Cambridge

Typeset by
Claire Boyd

Cover
The illustration on the front cover is by
Pumpkin House.

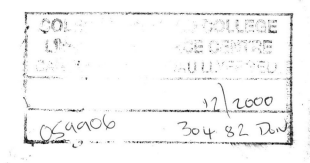

CONTENTS

Introduction

Refugees and Asylum Seekers is the fifth volume in the **Issues** series. The aim of this series is to offer up-to-date information about important issues in our world.

Refugees and Asylum Seekers looks at what is being done by governments, relief agencies and international bodies to alleviate the suffering of refugees and asylum seekers.

The information comes from a wide variety of sources and includes:
Government reports and statistics
Newspaper reports and features
Magazine articles and surveys
Literature from lobby groups
and charitable organisations.

It is hoped that, as you read about the many aspects of the issues explored in this book, you will critically evaluate the information presented. It is important that you decide whether you are being presented with facts or opinions. Does the writer give a biased or an unbiased report? If an opinion is being expressed, do you agree with the writer?

Refugees and Asylum Seekers offers a useful starting-point for those who need convenient access to information about the many issues involved. However, it is only a starting-point. At the back of the book is a list of organisations which you may want to contact for further information.

*****

The invisible generation

They've been killed and exploited in their millions, but until recently no one appeared to be listening

The statistics are almost un-imaginable. Two million slaugh-tered and six million injured or permanently disabled in the last decade alone. Many more millions dead of starvation and disease. Untold numbers raped, tortured, brutalised and abused. The centre of this world, according to one report, is 'a desolate moral vacuum devoid of the most basic human values' in which 'nothing is spared, held sacred or protected'. This is a place inhabited by children, many of them refugee children.

The global community has often been ambivalent towards babies, adolescents and teenagers. While many societies have nurtured and protected their young, children for centuries have also been exploited and abused. In recent decades, especially in the frightening world of peoples ripped from their homes and trying to reach a safe haven, this unstable balance has tilted even further against the young. Especially in regions gripped by war, the exercise today is 'to target the population, mainly women and children, to displace them, humiliate them, destroy them', says Olara Otunna, special UN representative for Children in Armed Conflict.

By Maya Ameratunga

'I joined the armed struggle to make things change so children would not be hungry. I found that girls were obliged to have sex "to alleviate the sadness of the combat-ants". They abused me. They tramp-led my human dignity' – a former girl soldier

---

The majority of refugees in the world are children. In an 'average' refugee population anywhere in the world, at least 50 per cent are youngsters

---

Governments and international institutions have, at last, begun to grapple with this crisis. In late 1996 the United Nations issued a devasta-ting report on the *Impact of Armed Conflict on Children* which for the first time pulled together in one comprehensive study the complex nightmare world in which millions of children live. Using the report as a base, humanitarian organisations

such as UNHCR have begun re-orientating policies they admit have been inadequate, and placing more emphasis on programmes specifically targeting the young.

The majority of refugees in the world are children. In an 'average' refugee population anywhere in the world, at least 50 per cent are youngsters, a figure which rises to 70 per cent in some situations. The number of child refugees is increasing by an estimated 5,000 per day, swelling the overall population of more than 22 million people UNHCR already cares for.

But while they number in the millions, children have been largely ignored as a specific group. 'The underlying explanation of our failures toward refugee children is that we simply do not see them,' says Iain Levine, who has worked with chil-dren in emergency situations for many years. 'Children are invisible, unconsulted, unheard.' Human-itarian agencies tended to see chil-dren as simply dependants without any special needs and consequently lack the programmes and the expertise in such fields as health, nutrition and education to care adequately for adolescents, Levine said. And while the 1989 Con-

vention on the Rights of the Child is the most comprehensive of any international legal document in existence, its provisions are often not enforced, he said

When 17-year-old Sam Kemoki clambered aboard a rusting freighter to escape the heavy artillery ripping Monrovia apart, he thought his troubles were over. They had just begun. For nine days, the ship limped from port to port along the West African coast. It was crammed with 3,500 people, there was virtually no food or water and gunboats opened fire to warn the ship away. No country wanted the refugees. 'I never thought I would leave that boat alive,' says Sam, who now lives in a refugee camp in Ghana.

High Commissioner Sadako Ogata has instructed all UNHCR field offices to draw up individual action plans covering five key areas: the needs of children, sexual violence and exploitation of minors, education, recruitment of child soldiers and the problems of separated minors. The agency has deployed six special senior advisers for children to Africa, Europe, Central Asia and countries of the former Soviet Union to help reshape UNHCR's overall approach. In coöperation with the Save the Children Alliance, training programmes for humanitarian, government and NGO personnel are being expanded.

The United States, Nordic and other countries are providing seed money for some of these activities. The US Congress earmarked $5 million for new refugee children's programmes and Washington has made it clear efforts in these areas should be progressively expanded. Sweden, a long-time champion of children's rights, made international protection for young people a top priority this year.

Norway has traditionally supported education and will soon devote 20 per cent of all its foreign aid to this field. Such support is vitally needed. Only 25 per cent of refugee children receive any meaningful education, causing grave concern that millions of deprived youngsters will eventually become not only an 'invisible generation' but also a 'lost generation' without the educational skills to survive in an increasingly complex and demanding world.

Four-year-old Kou Ya and six-year-old Sia Ya were leading their water buffalo to pasture when they noticed a 'ball' in a ditch. Sia Ya threw it to her brother. The bomb exploded, killing the two youngsters and wounding a passing cyclist.

'Children are dropping out of childhood. We must envision a society free of conflict, where children can grow up as children, not weapons of war'

If refugees are the most vulnerable group among the world's downtrodden, then refugee children and their mothers are the most vulnerable of the vulnerable. During flight, they are often the first to die on the road, victims of disease and exhaustion. They are sexually exploited and many young girls are forced into prostitution. An estimated 250,000 youngsters have been dragooned into becoming fighters in civil wars across the globe. Children in at least 68 countries live amidst the threat of 110 million landmines.

Says Olara Otunna, 'Value systems are being destroyed everywhere and an ethical vacuum created.' In many areas of the world 'anything goes . . . women, children, crops, stories, livestock, everything goes'. Adds Devaki Jain, who helped draft the UN report: 'Children are dropping out of childhood. We must envision a society free of conflict, where children can grow up as children, not weapons of war.'

• The above is an extract from Universal Declaration of Human Rights 50th Anniversary – *Refugees Magazine*, Issue 111, published by the United Nations High Commission for Refugees (UNHCR), from the UNHCR web site, which can be found at http://www.unhcr.ch
© United Nations High Commission for Refugees (UNHCR)

10 facts you should know about refugees

1 The United Nations High Commission for Refugees (UNHCR) says there are 27 million people in the world who are 'of concern' to them.

2 Of these, at least 15 million people are entitled to international protection because they are refugees.

3 25 to 30 million people are displaced within their own countries.

4 80 per cent of the world's refugee population live outside Europe and North America.

5 Most refugees are women and children.

6 The majority of asylum seekers to Europe and North America are men.

7 More than half the world's refugees live in Africa and the Middle East.

8 1 in every 115 people on earth has been forced into flight.

9 People flee their homes and countries because they fear being victims of human rights violations.

10 Amnesty International's 1997 theme campaign will call for more effective international protection of refugees.

© Amnesty International

Governments callous about fate of refugees

Governments increasingly show a callous disregard for the impact of policies deliberately designed to prevent people who are genuinely fleeing persecution from reaching safety in their countries, Amnesty International said today as it launched a global campaign on refugees.

'The new battery of techniques aimed at keeping refugees at bay mean that countless people never get a real chance to escape from torture or death threats or are sent back to countries where they run a real risk of getting thrown in jail or handed over to executioners,' Amnesty International said.

The organisation said there are more than 15 million men, women and children refugees and a further 20 million people internally displaced because they have been forced to leave their homes but have not crossed an international border.

'The vast majority are women and children – with women particularly at risk before, during and after they flee,' Amnesty International said.

'Rape is increasingly used to torture and terrorise women into flight, especially in conflicts such as in Afghanistan, Rwanda and the former Yugoslavia.'

With the scale of human rights violations that force people into exile continuing unabated, the number of those displaced is likely to grow in coming years, as shown most recently by the political crisis which has been unfolding in Albania in the past month.

At this stage it appears that the Italian authorities are admitting Albanian asylum seekers. Amnesty International is monitoring the current crisis and urging all governments to fulfil their obligations toward these asylum seekers.

'While the number of people needing international protection continues to grow, governments seem more concerned with keeping refugees away from their borders,' Amnesty International said. 'They should at least have the decency to protect refugees when human rights tragedies unfold.'

In 1951, in the aftermath of the Second World War, states formulated the Refugee Convention in order to deal with the mass outpourings of people.

'The increasingly restrictive approach that more and more governments take towards refugees makes a mockery of their international and national obligations'

One of the key principles spelled out in the Convention and general international law is that of *non-refoulement* – that no one should be forcibly returned to a country where his or her life or freedom would be at risk .

'Yet nearly half a century after the Convention was drafted, there is more than ample evidence that this principle is simply not respected and that people are in fact sent back to countries where their life or liberty is at risk,' Amnesty International said.

In one case, a Zairean woman escaped from a military prison where she was tortured and sought asylum in Sweden. The Swedish authorities rejected her claim on several grounds, including their view that the president does not control the military and therefore torture by soldiers does not constitute state persecution.

In another case in July last year, the Belgian authorities deported Bouasria Ben Othman to Algeria after refusing his asylum application.

Despite repeated efforts, Amnesty International received no information from the Belgian authorities about his location, until 19 November when they said the Algerian authorities said he had been arrested upon arrival in Algeria, released and rearrested. On 26 November Bouasria appeared on Algerian television saying he was well and that people should stop asking about him. A week later Algerian police told his family that he had thrown himself out of a

---

Refugees and Asylum Seekers World-wide

This map includes statistics on two categories of uprooted people: refugees, who are unwilling or unable to return to their home countries because they fear persecution or armed conflict there and who lack a durable solution; and asylum seekers who are awaiting a refugee status determination.

Europe
2,020,000

The Americas and the Caribbean
616,000

East Asia and the Pacific
535,000

Middle East
5,708,000

South and Central Asia
1,743,000

Africa
2,944,000

World total: 13,566,000

As of December 31, 1997

Source: U.S. Committee for Refugees

window and died. However, there are allegations that he died as a result of torture.

'Governments have made the rules on the refugees and they should now play by those rules,' Amnesty International said. 'The increasingly restrictive approach that more and more governments take towards refugees makes a mockery of their international and national obligations.'

This restrictive approach includes limiting access to their countries, harshly applying asylum criteria, detaining asylum seekers, temporarily protecting or forcibly repatriating refugees, and fining airlines and shipping companies if they carry people who do not have travel documents.

For example, after the military coup in Haiti in September 1991, most Haitian refugees tried to reach the USA and more than 38,000 risked their lives at sea. In June 1992 the USA intercepted Haitian boat people at sea and summarily returned them, without any examination of their asylum claims.

'While governments may have the right to control their borders, they do not have the right to refuse people access to asylum procedures,' Amnesty International said.

In Bosnia-Herzegovina alone, more than half the population was uprooted by the war with an estimated 1.3 million people displaced inside the country and another million or more refugees abroad.

Since November 1996, the massive repatriation of refugees in the Great Lakes region without clear guarantees of safety on their return has been marked by a shocking disregard for the rights, dignity and safety of hundreds of thousands of people. Disparate groups from Rwanda, Zaire and Burundi are in grave danger of human rights abuses, and they are not getting the protection they deserve from the international community.

'If the repatriation solution is needed, it must be defined in terms that give human rights considerations the highest priority at every stage,' Amnesty International said.

The human rights organisation is calling on the world's governments to fulfil their international obligations for the protection of refugees.

They must support the efforts of the UNHCR and other international organisations who work to protect and help refugees. They must remind their communities that refugees need protection, they are not abusing the asylum system for their own gain, they are not economic migrants, they are not moving *en masse* for illegitimate reasons.

• For further information, you can also access the Refugee Campaign Web site on: http://www.refuge.amnesty.org/

© Amnesty International

You've got 10 minutes to get out

What would you take that could save your life?

If you were one of the world's 15 million refugees, you'd need some survival tips. Death threats or violent encounters with local security forces will have probably made you fear for your life.

Take a few minutes to calm yourself, then, if you're not already at home, get there, get packed and get out.

Mementos
Family snap shots may not seem like a priority when the police or army want to gun you down, but you may never see your loved ones again. Photographs are easily carried but if folded or allowed to get wet, they easily perish.

Cooking implements
Most refugees have no idea how long they will be on the road. If you are cold, or if you are supplied with raw cereal rations from aid agencies, you will need an old can or biscuit box in which to cook.

Tools
For many refugees, a knife is the most basic tool.

Water
If you're fleeing within central Africa, you're going to need at least two litres every day. There are wells and water supplies in some villages – try to get hold of a bottle or can.

Blankets
If you're a Kurd fleeing Iraqi death squads, you're probably headed to the mountains in south-east Turkey. Night-time temperatures can drop to -20°C or lower. This is cold enough to kill a fit person in one night.

Food
You may be able to scavenge on the road but in war zones, this is highly dangerous. Do not weigh yourself down with supplies.

Shoes
Most refugees travel on foot. If you don't have adequate protection for your feet, you will have cuts and blisters. In hot climates, wounds become a breeding ground for maggots and other parasites. Old tyre tread is easily cut for replacement sandal soles.

Many people endure years of persecution before they finally leave behind everything they've ever owned. The ones who get out fast are the lucky ones.

In 1948, the Universal Declaration of Human Rights stated that anyone in fear of persecution should be able to seek a safe refuge.

It is a very basic human right. We'd like to remind every government in the world of that.

And to say that closing doors on refugees is simply sending people back to meet their fate.

© Amnesty International

Refugee children and adolescents

More than half of the world's 22.4 million refugees and other persons of concern to UNHCR are children and adolescents under the age of 18. Each day, another 5,000 children become refugees; one in every 230 persons in the world is a child or adolescent who has been forced to flee his or her home.

Given these tragic statistics, UNHCR is accelerating efforts to place refugee children and adolescents squarely at the centre of its prevention, protection and assistance efforts. Maintaining its traditional focus on primary school education, health and nutrition, the Office is also rapidly expanding its agenda on behalf of at-risk refugee children, including unaccompanied minors, adolescent girls and boys, and children subjected to violence.

Machel Study plans of action

The importance of placing children and adolescents at the heart of the international community's humanitarian agenda has become increasingly evident in recent years. One of the catalysts of this growing awareness is Ms Graca Machel, author of the United Nations Study on the *Impact of Armed Conflict on Children*.

The High Commissioner has requested that each of her offices prepares a comprehensive follow-up strategy to the Machel Study recommendations, drawing attention to five areas of immediate concern to UNHCR: adolescents, sexual exploitation, promotion of girls' education, prevention of military recruitment, and separated children. Sixty-two offices have developed plans of action covering programme, protection and advocacy measures for war-affected children and youth. Programmes now being implemented include:

- *Peace-Building*: the 'Tolerance through Arts and Culture' programme in the Ukraine promotes reintegration of formerly deported people through activities related to tolerance and cultural revitalisation.
- *Girls' Education*: in Pakistan, efforts to provide education to Afghan girls as well as boys have been expanded, including recruitment of female teachers, promotion of special schools for girls, and support to home-based schools. The total enrolment of girls increased by 17 per cent over the last year; an additional 20 per cent increase is projected for 1999.
- *Adolescents*: in Ngara, Tanzania, adolescents are involved in youth leadership groups to help the most vulnerable individuals in the community. Many country programmes include youth campaigns on issues such as drug use, AIDS and early marriage.
- *Separated Children*: in Rwanda, Burundi and the Democratic Republic of the Congo (DRC), UNHCR, in co-operation with other international agencies, has developed a highly effective mechanism for tracing the families of separated children, including photo tracing and community-mobilisation campaigns. Support to foster families is also central to these programmes.
- *Child Soldiers*: in Liberia, UNHCR and Save the Children have worked together to identify former child soldiers among the newly arrived refugees from Sierra Leone. These children are provided with psycho-social support, 'catch-up' education, vocational training and peace education.
- *Sexual Exploitation*: in Uganda, UNHCR offers regular seminars and workshops on the causes, consequences and means to prevent sexual violence. In Kenya, UNHCR runs psycho-social programmes for victims of sexual abuse, drop-in centres where victims can receive treatment and counselling, and community follow-up.

Regional Policy Officers for Children

There is always a danger that refugee boys and girls may simply be considered as part of a broad category of persons described as 'vulnerable', without a great deal of attention paid to their specific rights and needs. In an effort to begin to address this problem, UNHCR has established new posts, entitled the Regional Policy Officer for Children, in West Africa, the Horn of Africa, Central Asia, and the Commonwealth of Independent States. The work of these Officers includes developing child rights-based performance objectives, programming, training and institutional capacity.

These Officers will continue to play a key role in maintaining the focus on programmes for refugee girls and boys.

Action for the Rights of Children

The Machel Study concluded that children's needs will only be adequately met at an operational level when 'United Nations personnel and staff of humanitarian organizations view children affected by armed conflict as a distinct and priority concern'.

In response to this finding, Save the Children Sweden and UNHCR have developed the Action for the Rights of Children (ARC) training programme, with the goal of increasing the capacity of UNHCR, government and NGO staff to protect and care for refugee boys and girls during all stages of refugee situations, from emergency interventions to durable solutions. ARC offers a comprehensive set of training modules on children's issues, developed and reviewed by representatives of UNHCR, UNICEF, WHO, the International Rescue Committee and other organisations.

Training and capacity-building workshops have been completed in the Horn of Africa, Central Asia, the Commonwealth of Independent States and West Africa. ARC will be substantially expanded in 1999 and mainstreamed into UNHCR protection and emergency response training programmes.

Education for peace

The Machel Study highlighted the important role that structured activities and education play in prevention, protection and recovery of war-affected refugee children, and stressed the strategic potential of education to promote tolerance and conflict resolution. In response, UNHCR launched an initiative in Kakuma and Dadaab refugee camps in Kenya, as well as in the refugee school programme in Guinea.

Community and youth groups, as well as community leaders, have received extensive training. Refugee schools in Kenya now include weekly sessions on peace and on life skills, as well as regular in-service teacher training on these subjects. In 1999 this initiative will expand to cover the entire span of primary and post-primary schooling. UNHCR also intends to extend this programme to other major refugee school systems, with necessary adaptations, translations and training of trainers and teachers.

Operational partnerships

UNHCR-NGO partnerships are critical to providing on-the-spot protection to war-affected girls and boys. The International Save the Children Alliance and UNHCR have embarked on new capacity-building initiatives in West Africa, the Horn of Africa and Europe. In Africa, the aim is to assist NGOs in addressing the needs of war-affected children and young people; in Europe, the intent is to promote a common set of best practices for unaccompanied children and to mobilise an NGO network to work on their behalf. Collaboration with UNICEF is equally essential. In Liberia, the two agencies are jointly implementing the Liberian Children's Initiative (LCI), designed to address the particular reintegration needs of refugee and returnee children and youth in main areas of return. The LCI focuses on: reintegration education for all returnee children as well as community capacity-building programmes to support children's education in the long term; enhancement activities for girls and at-risk teenagers; family reunification and reintegration support for unaccompanied children; and promotion of child welfare reform. Protection indicators have also been established with NGOs to help a range of agencies monitor child protection concerns; and an environmental component is included to engage returnee youth in environmental activities.

UNHCR provides support to Mr Olara Otunnu, Special Representative of the Secretary-General for Children and Armed Conflict, and is a member of his advisory group. The Office continues to work closely with the United Nations High Commissioner for Human Rights and the Committee on the Rights of the Child.

© United Nations High Commission for Refugees (UNHCR)

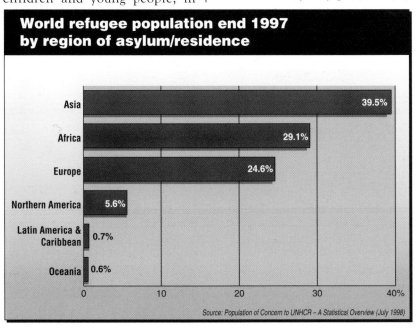

World refugee population end 1997 by region of asylum/residence

Region	%
Asia	39.5%
Africa	29.1%
Europe	24.6%
Northern America	5.6%
Latin America & Caribbean	0.7%
Oceania	0.6%

Source: Population of Concern to UNHCR – A Statistical Overview (July 1998)

Keeping children with families in emergencies

Information from Save the Children

Purpose of briefing

To explain the importance of preventing children from becoming separated from their families in emergencies, such as a refugee crisis . . . to describe what agencies and governments can do, in the light of lessons learned from the refugee crisis in and around Rwanda after the 1994 genocide . . . to say what should happen in the future

How do children get separated from families in emergencies?

This can happen accidentally, or sometimes voluntarily. It happens accidentally when people are forced to move *en masse* and in a panic, as they did from Rwanda to the former Zaire. Children can easily get left behind or lost in the crowds. Voluntary separation can happen when families leave children in a safe place (e.g. a hospital, feeding centre or children's centre, or with friends or relatives). Children may also leave their family to go in search of food, or to escape fighting. It is possible and desirable to prevent both types of separation – because children have a right to be with families. They suffer less emotional upset and are almost always better protected that way.

What can be done to prevent this?

Trained staff need, if possible, to be in place before emergencies occur. They should have a good understanding of the ways in which children become separated from their families and the importance of the family. This can help prevent separation. Raising people's awareness is very important, and simple measures help a lot.

For example, before a mass movement, parents can be given tags to attach to children with their name and village written on them. They

can be encouraged to teach children their names, village and landmarks by heart. A piece of string can be tied to children's waists, so parents can hold onto them in a crowds. Young children can be given bracelets, with basic biographical information on them. Megaphones can be used to tell people what to do if they get separated from their children.

Voluntary separation can be prevented by distributing food and other aid in an appropriate way as people are moving. If the crisis is prolonged and people face long-term food shortages and insecurity, then voluntary separation can be reduced by targeting aid at whole families rather than individuals. Helping whole families is a basic principle for organisations to follow in an emergency.

What about children who are already separated?

Save the Children documents them as quickly as possible, finds out information from them, and organises and uses this information to trace family members more easily, especially when few details are known about a child. Save the

Children holds community meetings, and uses the media – radio, newspapers or television – whatever is available – to display in public places, in the hope that their relatives will recognise them.

What changes do we want to see?

Collaboration and co-ordination between all the organisations involved in an emergency is critical. Action to prevent children being separated should include:

- Raising awareness at all levels about the causes of separation and how to prevent it.
- Agreeing and distributing guidelines on preventing separation, e.g. among aid agencies, military and peacekeeping forces, and government staff.
- Employing experienced staff, and training non-specialists who might be called on in emergencies.
- Focusing in particular on preventing the separation of under-fives and children with special needs who can't give information about their relatives.
- Ensuring that immediate tracing takes place.

Newsbites

RightAngle's quick round-up of recent events affecting young people around the world

Kosovo

During the past year existing tensions between the ethnic Albanian population of Kosovo and the Yugoslav government authorities have worsened. In parts of Kosovo whole villages have been cleared of their inhabitants, and their houses destroyed. The United Nations High Commission for Refugees estimates that the total number of ethnic Albanian refugees and displaced people could now be as high as 180,000. This includes 140,000 internally displaced people seeking refuge with residents of villages in safer areas, in villages abandoned due to previous fighting, or simply camping out in the hillsides or valleys.

Many children have been killed in the fighting. However these needs of children have begun to be recognised. Save the Children recently brokered the first multi-ethnic meeting between Serb and Albanian non-governmental organisations with an interest in children's rights. Leaders and combatants on both sides were encouraged to see children as people

---

Facts and figures

- One million children were separated from their parents by conflict between 1985 and 1995.
- 22,000 Rwandan children were separated from their families during the mass repatriation from former Zaire between November 1996 and September 1997.
- Swift action by agencies meant that 88 per cent of them were reunited with their families.

Save the Children works both to prevent separation, and reunite separated children with families in: Angola, Bosnia, Burundi, Côte d'Ivoire, Democratic Republic of Congo, Federal Republic of Yugoslavia, Guinea, Liberia, Rwanda, Sierra Leone and Sudan.

---

who should be kept out of the conflict and protected from its effects. In the process, steps have been made to create a group with the power to speak out about the plight of children in Kosovo.

Bangladesh

Annual floods are a normal part of the weather cycle in Bangladesh. They are brought on by cyclones and tornadoes during the rainy season between June and October. These floods are usually vital in helping to renew fish stocks and ground water levels. However, the recent floods were the worst in Bangladesh's recorded history. More than 75 per cent of the country has been flooded. By early October the waters started to recede. But by then the communities were facing unemployment, food scarcity, sickness and disease, shortage of safe drinking water, damaged or destroyed homes, as a result of the floods. As the rehabilitation of communities continues, Save the Children, which has been working in Bangladesh since 1970, supported emergency health-care programmes in the immediate aftermath of the floods. Working with partner organisations, Save the Children is now providing cash grants to families to help with rebuilding homes and livelihoods, and preventing them from falling into debt. Save the Children is also continuing to monitor nutrition levels of children in order to assess their future needs.

- The above is an extract from *RightAngle*, a magazine produced by Save the Children Youth Education Programme. See page 41 for address details. *© Save the Children*

Surviving conflict and disaster

Older women in emergency situations

Women and children belonging to the civilian population and finding themselves in circumstances of emergency and armed conflict in the struggle for peace, self-determination and independence, or who live in occupied territories, shall not be deprived of shelter, food, medical aid or other inalienable rights . . . '

United Nations Declaration on the Protection of Women and Children in Emergency and Armed Conflicts, Article 6

According to the UN High Commissioner for Refugees, towards the end of 1994 there were 20 million refugees and 25 million internally displaced people throughout the world, a substantial increase on the previous years. While there are no precise statistics, UNHCR believes that women and children constitute the majority of refugee populations.

In absolute terms, older women who are refugees or internally displaced constitute a relatively small group. But when war, drought or famine spark off a major population exodus, they are among those most at risk.

The agencies responding to the crisis rarely focus on the situation facing older people who have reached the refugee camps – although UNHCR has begun to address the problem.

Thus in Tanzania, workers among the refugees from Rwanda discovered that older people suffered undue hardship in the already difficult conditions of the refugee camps. Many were unable to walk to the food distribution points, or stand for two hours or more waiting for rations to be handed out. Furthermore, they could not digest the unground maize which was being allocated. Malnourishment was the result: one survey found that 20 per cent of the older women who came for health checks in one camp were malnourished.[1]

People can remain as refugees or displaced people for many years. Only a small minority will resettle in new countries, the majority waiting to return home. Once the original emergency is past, new priorities have to be addressed, some of which are not dissimilar from the general challenges of development.

Older men and women face particular problems in these conditions. In the worst cases they have lost, or become separated from, their family. They all suffer from the loss of the physical and social landmarks which previously gave security to their lives. As in development work generally, few agencies recognise the contribution they can make. One exception is the International Federation of Red Cross and Red Crescent Societies which has acknowledged the value of older people's experience and employs them within refugee camps because they are often more trusted by community leaders than younger staff.[2]

When conflict or famine drive people away from their homes, older people often stay behind. Complex factors come into play here: older people are only too well aware that they may not survive the hardships and may feel that they should not burden their family. They may also fear to leave their home for an unknown, and possibly dangerous, new environment.

In the former Yugoslavia, where there have been repeated displacements of population, often only a few older people remain in destroyed and abandoned villages. In Bagel, a village in Deriver municipality in Croatia supported by a home-visiting project, the average age of the 30 people remaining in 1994 was 65. They were still living surrounded by buildings burnt in the fighting of 1991, in houses without water, electricity or window panes.[3]

Many of the refugees who return home have grown old in exile. In the intervening years, they may have experienced the death of their spouse, and their children may have settled in the host country. Women especially often face having to rebuild their lives alone. Chirodzi Pone, a village in Tete Province in Mozambique to which refugees have been returning from Zimbabwe, is probably not unusual in that nearly half the women surveyed in 1995 were living alone, in contrast to the men, all of whom were married. Marina Cansolo, a 65-year-old widow, had one daughter in Mozambique, living a hundred kilometres away, her other four children having remained in Zimbabwe.[4]

Older people are particularly vulnerable in times of natural disasters, famines and droughts. For example, following the famine in 1974 in Sri Lanka, there was a 45 per cent increase in deaths among older people, while infant deaths in the same period rose by 20 per cent. Older women are among those who need specific help after any emergency. In Bangladesh a non-governmental organisation, Resource Integration Centre, helped many older women not only to rebuild their homes after the cyclone in 1991, but also to set up as small traders through a revolving loan scheme.[5]

In parts of the world, notably sub-Saharan Africa, droughts and famines are so frequent that the people have developed survival strategies to cope. Leaving the area is very much the last resort. As Nizela Idriss, a Chadian woman, described it: 'We have suffered four major famines during my lifetime . . . Finally, in 1985, the big famine came upon us.

'We called this "Laãtche", meaning "the year when everyone fled from the area". At other times of difficulty, the men would go and leave the women behind.'[6]

Older people are among the most traumatised by disaster and war; there are also many who contribute to rebuilding the lives of others. In pioneering schemes in the former Yugoslavia, older women are among groups of refugees trained to work as befrienders of other distressed refugees. In this way they are able both to help other survivors and to regain their own dignity and self-respect.[7]

Returned from exile – a case study from Rwanda

Elvania Nyramvumba is thought to be 75. She came from a rich family in Rwanda and married at 18. She and her husband lived comfortably and had four children, but when the war started, they fled to Burundi. This was back in 1960.

In Burundi they worked as farmers and kept cattle. Life was good until war also broke out in Burundi. Mrs Nyramvumba decided she wanted to return to Rwanda, so they sold their cattle to pay for the return journey. Mrs Nyramvumba's husband died before their return and she had to travel back with her son, his children and her widowed daughter, but none of their possessions.

She now lives with her widowed daughter and her son lives nearby. She says that she feels very weak now and is no longer able to farm.

She spends a lot of her time with her six grandchildren.

In Burundi she had cattle and a farm, back in Rwanda she has no land, cattle or house of her own and she finds life difficult. Despite this she is very happy to be back in Rwanda and she says she does not want to leave her country again.[8]

Notes
1. HelpAge International internal reports, London, 1994.
2. International Federation of Red Cross and Red Crescent Societies, *World Disasters Report 1995*, Geneva, 1995, p.15.
3. HelpAge International internal report, London, 1994.
4. HelpAge International, 'Needs assessment in Changara District, for Development of the Resettlement Programme in Tete' (unpublished), London, 1995.
5. Material provided by A.H. Khan of RIC, 1995.
6. N Cross and R Barker (eds.), *At the Desert's Edge – Oral History from the Sahel*, Panos/SOS Sahel, London, pp.156-7.
7. HelpAge International internal reports, London, 1994/95.
8. Interview conducted in Rwanda by H. Atkinson, HelpAge International, 1995.
9. Adapted from data on *Refugees by Host Countries in World Disasters Report 1995*, p.108.

• The above extract is from *Older Women in Development*, published by HelpAge International in 1995, written by Katrina Payne and edited by Anne-Marie Sharman. Available from their web site which can be found at http://www.oneworld.org/helpage/

International humanitarian law

How does humanitarian law protect refugees and displaced persons?

Refugees are people who have fled their countries, while displaced persons are those who have not left their country's territory.

Refugees enjoy first and foremost the protection afforded them by refugee law and the mandate of the Office of the United Nations High Commissioner for Refugees (UNHCR). They are also protected by international humanitarian law when they are the victims of an armed conflict, in the hands of the adverse party or affected by hostilities in the host country. The Fourth Geneva Convention and Protocol I accord special protection to refugees, particularly those in occupied territories. The Fourth Convention also refers to the principle of *non-refoulement* on which refugee law is based.

In an armed conflict, persons displaced within their own country are protected by the rules of international humanitarian law, which offers broad protection to the civilian population. Those rules are intended more especially to protect civilians from the effects of hostilities; for instance, it is forbidden to attack or terrorise them, to use famine as a method of warfare or to destroy goods essential to their survival.

In an internal conflict, displaced persons are protected by Article 3 common to the four Geneva Conventions and by Protocol II.

Humanitarian law prohibits forced displacement except in cases where displacement is essential to ensure the safety of the population itself, or for overriding military reasons. Moreover, the general protection guaranteed to civilian populations by humanitarian law should have the effect of limiting displacements. Unfortunately, these rules have all too often been broken in recent conflicts, so it is above all important to ensure greater respect for the provisions in force rather than draft new ones.

International refugees

Refugee law is based in particular on the following texts:
• the 1951 United Nations Convention on the status of refugees;
• the 1967 Protocol relating to the status of refugees;
• the 1969 Convention of the Organisation of African Unity governing aspects peculiar to refugee problems in Africa;
• the 1984 Cartagena Declaration on Refugees;
• resolutions adopted in particular by the UN General Assembly.

Definition of a refugee

According to Article 1 of the 1951 Convention, the term 'refugee' applies to any person who 'owing to well-founded fear of being persecuted for reasons of race, religion, nationality, membership of a particular social group or political opinion, is outside the country of his nationality and is unable, or owing to such fear, is unwilling to avail himself of the protection of that country; or who, not having a nationality and being outside the country of his former habitual residence as a result of such events, is unable, or owing to such fear, is unwilling to return to it'.

The OAU Convention and the Cartagena Declaration have broadened that definition to include persons fleeing events which seriously disrupt public order, such as armed conflicts and disturbances.

• The above information is from the International Red Cross Committee . Their web site can be found at http://www.icrc.org/

> *In an armed conflict, persons displaced within their own country are protected by the rules of international humanitarian law*

The endless diaspora

The history of the last half century has been a tale of exodus, mostly without the hope of return. John Vidal reports

What will happen to baby Valon Leskovica, who crossed the border of Kosovo into Macedonia yesterday in his parents' arms and began an uncertain life in Europe's most turbulent region? What will happen to Benjamin, a humanitarian shuttle-cock who has been tossed between three countries in central Africa in the past five years after the Rwandan crisis? Or Jovan Jojnovik who fled Croatia in 1995 and now lives in Montenegro?

The history of the past 50 years, and the 1990s in particular, has been the forced exodus of populations from their homes and great waves of people fleeing state-inspired terrorism, ethnic cleansing and human rights abuses. The Office of the UN High Commissioner for Refugees (UNHCR) believes there are now more than 25 million people who have been forced to leave their countries and another 25 million who are now internally displaced within their own countries but unable to return to their lands or villages.[1]

They are, says the writer William Shawcross, the 'Fourth World' living without rights, home or, most often, hope of return.

But the official figures are just the tip of the iceberg. Many millions have been displaced by the partitions of countries, massive development programmes and the tactics of rural depopulation to facilitate land grabs. Mostly, like the Palestinians, these people never register on the official statistics.[2]

And in an increasingly insecure, globalised world, where populations are burgeoning in the poorest countries, abject poverty has caused millions of economic and environmental refugees to flee the land. It is possible that more than 75 million have been forced to uproot in the past 60 years.[3] Internal displacement of populations is now as significant in humanitarian terms as the more conventional flights across state boundaries. History suggests that most of these population flows were made to happen – aggressors usually win – and that the first law of diasporas is that return is painfully slow.

The reality of the refugee crisis, which is now a world-wide pheno-menom as countries implode, is that few refugees return for good. Only 250,000 people, a fraction of the millions displaced in the Balkans in the past decade, have returned and very few of them to their previous homes.

Even before the exodus of the past few weeks, Croatia had 90,000 refugees from Bosnia Herzegovina along with 62,000 displaced Croats and Serbs; in Bosnia Herzegovina itself there were more than 383,000 Muslims and ethnic Croats expelled by the Serbs who now mix with 107,000 internally displaced people. Meanwhile in the republic of Sraska there are more than 300,000 'ethnically cleansed' Serbs. Thou-

Major refugee and internally displaced peoples

1 Mexico: Up to 100,000 Guatemalans in exile	**8 Cyprus:** 265,000 internally displaced	**15 Nepal:** 115,000 refugees from Bhutan, Tibet	**21 Sudan:** More than 400,000 refugees, mostly from Eritea and more than four million internally displaced
2 Colombia: 900,000 displaced by political violence	**9 Turkey:** Up to 2 million internally displaced Kurdas	**16 Myanmar (Burma):** Up to one million displaced or forcibly relocated	**22 Ethiopia:** Up to 400,000 refugees from Kenya, Somalia, Sudan
3 Bosnia and Herzegovina: Almost 2 million uprooted	**10 Azerbaijan:** 500,000 internally displaced	**17 Thailand:** More than 100,000 from Cambodia, Laos and Vietnam	**23 Uganda:** 285,000 refugees, mostly from southern Sudan
4 Sierra Leone: 1.6 million internally displaced	**11 Palestinians:** Over 3 million have fled since the diaspora to Jordan, Syria, Lebanon and Gaza	**18 Sri Lanka:** More than one million displaced by war	**24 Burundi:** One million displaced in camps
5 Liberia: More than 800,000 displaced	**12 Iraq:** More than one million displaced	**19 India:** More than 300,000 Sri Lankans, Tibetans, Bangladeshi Chakmas and Afghanistans	**25 Democratic Republic of Congo:** More than 320,000 displaced from surrounding countries
6 Ivory Coast: Up to 165,000 refugees have fled the Liberian civil war	**13 Iran:** About two million Afghani refugees	**20 Pakistan:** More than one million Afghanis in exile	**26 Angola:** Up to 1.2 million displaced
7 Algeria: 165,000 refugees from Western Sahara	**14 Afghanistan:** Up to 1.2 million internally displaced		

Source: 'State of the World's Refugees'. UNHCR

sands of others are now living precariously in Albania, Montenegro, and Macedonia. Few are expected ever to return.

But the figures are dwarfed by what has happened outside Europe in the past few decades. The great diasporas this century include the Jews and Armenians fleeing genocide, massive forced relocations under Stalin, millions of people fleeing communism, and more than 200 countries – including Mozambique, Cambodia, Bulgaria, Turkey, Western Sahara, Cyprus, Angola, Sri Lanka, Sudan, Iraq and Georgia, Sierra Leone, Ethiopia and Eritrea – have been torn apart by populations fleeing repression.

History also shows that despite clear warnings and increased concern by the international community, it is next to impossible to stem the tides of refugees.

But there have been some notable successes: in the 1990s, conflicts in Central America, Southern Africa and South-east Asia and Afghanistan have been largely resolved or have stabilised, and almost 10 million people have been repatriated.[4]

But 15 million from these and other wars have still not returned to their own country, let alone to their homes or lands, which have often been destroyed or occupied by others. Many millions of people remain displaced from the cold-war years, the collapse of old ideologies and formation of new states, even the Second World War. Some are only now returning.

The modern state knows that it is easier than ever to make people flee. New forms of warfare, the spread of light weapons and cheap landmines can easily panic populations. The use of mass evictions and expulsions as a weapon of war has now become common as a way for states to establish culturally or ethnically homogeneous societies, such as in the Caucasus or in the former Yugoslavia.

The UNHCR suggests that the speed at which these flights and expulsions are taking place is quickening. In recent years, the exodus of more than a million Iraqi Kurds, up to four million people in the former Yugoslavia, over a million Rwandan citizens and two million people within and from Liberia have been notable.

The people most usually affected, say the humanitarian agencies who are left to pick up the pieces, are the most marginalised. Minority groups, the already stateless, indigenous populations and others in poor or medium poor countries who have little or no representation.[5]

'The forced displacement of minorities, including de-population and re-population tactics in support of territorial claims and self-determination, has become an abominable characteristic of the contemporary world,' says Sadako Ogata, the UN High Commissioner for Refugees.

The lot of the refugee or the displaced person is increasingly hard. Globally, there is mounting rejection of refugees, and states have been quick to erect physical and administrative barriers. On top of the physical and emotional pain, asylum seekers may spend years in fear of expulsion, be denied the right to settle permanently, to work, be disqualified from welfare benefits or be kept in detention or, most often in the poorest countries, in camps.

The geography of exodus is more complex than ever. Several regions are locked into a pattern of strife and displacements that are intensely difficult, perhaps impossible to resolve. In the Caucasus six countries, Abkhazia, Armenia, Azerbaijan, Chechenia, and north and south Ossetia, are all importing and exporting refugees between them in a linked regional conflict. Similarly in central Africa, Angola, Burundi, the Central African Republic, Rwanda, Zambia and four other countries are now producing ever more uprooted people.

The history of the past 50 years, and the 1990s in particular, has been the forced exodus of populations from their homes

---

Increasingly, too, says the UNHCR, the actual movements of people are becoming more complex, with millions being constantly relocated, expelled and received for short periods. In many cases people have effectively been held as hostages and moved, according to political expediency or whim, between three or even four countries. Only a tiny minority has the means or the will to flee to the richer countries. Of these, only Australia, New Zealand, Canada, the US, Ireland and Chile have any permanent resettlement programmes. In most other countries the walls are going up.

Paradoxically, says the UNHCR, many people have found it impossible to flee. In Bosnia and Sri Lanka, government and opposition forces desperate to maintain control over civilian populations have forcibly prevented people leaving the country. The international community's proposal for safe havens has seldom worked and indeed, has often denied the human right of people to go elsewhere.

If the people now fleeing Kosovo ever return, they may find life harder than ever. The trauma of flight and exile can be matched by the return which, although often portrayed as joyful, can be harrowing as exile itself.[6]

Humanitarian agencies report that people returned forcibly can feel as insecure as when they left. Voluntary returnees may have over-optimistic ideas of what they will find and are often thrown into conflict for increasingly sparse land resources. Mostly, the social and physical infrastructure has been destroyed, there is no work and no help.

Sources
1 UNHCR *State of the World's Refugees*, 1997
2 International Institute for Strategic Studies
3 Worldwatch Institute, Washington
4 UNHCR statistics, 1999
5 Human Rights Watch, New York
6 UN Research Institute for Social Development, Geneva
© *The Guardian April, 1999*

Integrating refugees into UK society

UK Government joins UNHCR and European partners to integrate refugees into society

Genuine refugees fleeing from persecution must be helped to develop successful lives free from the fear of racism and harassment, Home Office Immigration Minister Mike O'Brien said today.

Mr O'Brien was speaking at the UK launch of a year-long campaign aimed at integrating refugees into UK society. The campaign has been funded by the European Commission and developed by the United Nations High Commissioner for Refugees to run throughout the European Union.

Focussing on genuine refugees who have been granted the right to remain and settle in the UK, Mr O'Brien said the Government was not in the business of forced integration. The 'British way of life' gave them freedom of choice which they had to be able to exercise.

Assimilation or retention of a distinctive culture were both entirely compatible with multi-cultural Britain. But if refugee communities were marginalised, allowed to suffer social isolation and high levels of unemployment, it was both wasteful of talent and undermined good community relations.

Mr O'Brien said: 'Restoring integrity to our asylum system is part of our human rights policy. That means deterring economic migrants who would abuse our system as well as helping genuine refugees fleeing for their lives.

'The Government's aims for integration in the broadest sense means refugees being included in society and obtaining the same status as other members of the community. The way this aim can be met is for genuine refugees to have access to jobs, housing, education and other services without discrimination.

'We must condemn the racism and harassment suffered by some refugees and the lurid stories that can fuel intolerance'

'Many refugees need some assistance to get started in their new lives. The Government has given just over £4 million this year to voluntary organisations who assist with reception and settlement services. We are currently working with the voluntary sector looking at the broader agenda of integration and how asylum seekers recognised as refugees can be helped to settle here successfully.

'To help refugees we also have to help the people living around them to understand why they have fled for their lives. We must reinforce – or sometimes rekindle – the values of respect, compassion and tolerance which are strong British traditions.

'We must condemn the racism and harassment suffered by some refugees and the lurid stories that can fuel intolerance.'

Mr O'Brien warned that the Government intended to remove from those seeking asylum the right to cash welfare benefits. Many would in future be accommodated outside London.

The Government would honour its international commitments to allow asylum seekers to live in dignity while pursuing their claims. But it was important to send out a strong deterrent message to those who were thinking of coming to the UK but who were not in real fear of persecution in their homeland. Many such people, duped into believing they had an asylum claim, were being persuaded to pay their life savings, endure terrible hardship on a journey to the UK, only to find their claim could not be substantiated and that they were turned back.

© Home Office
February, 1999

'... THEY'RE ALL WAITING FOR THE RIGHT MOMENT TO LEAP OUT AND SHOUT **WELCOME** ... AREN'T THEY?'

Playing the numbers game

Tubby Files is a cuddly name for a Home Office problem that condemns thousands of refugees in Britain to years of misery. Today a rising young minister will say how he intends to deal with the problem. But he will need more than brave words, as Alan Travis reveals

An ambitious and rising young Home Office minister, Mike O'Brien, will give the first real indication today of how this Labour government intends to deal with an immigration system it has already condemned as being in a complete shambles.[1] The heart of that crisis lies in the backlog of about 76,000 asylum seekers who are waiting, some for years, for a final decision in their cases. The worst are to be found amongst the foot-thick paper files in the civil service filing cabinets marked 'Tubby Files' in offices at Heathrow Airport's terminals three and four.

Nearly ten thousand of these people have been waiting since 1992 to learn their fate. It is now expected that they will be told they can stay as a one-off exceptional measure in an attempt to give the Immigration and Nationality Department some hope of getting on top of the backlog.

Ministers will resist any use of the word 'amnesty' to describe this announcement because they believe that would be seen as rewarding law-breakers and might encourage others to abuse and undermine Britain's asylum procedure.

They are already extremely nervous about how the politics of this announcement might play. Ever since the election, planted stories have appeared in papers such as the *Daily Mail* and the *Daily Telegraph* designed to demonstrate that Labour is tough on immigration. In June last year the *Daily Mail* told its readers: 'Straw set to kick out thousands of illegals'. At the same time the *Daily Telegraph* proclaimed on its front page: 'Labour to send back 50,000 migrants'. Earlier this year the *Mail on Sunday* even erroneously claimed that a blanket amnesty for a presumably different 50,000 people was being planned.

Ministers have openly started to prepare the ground by pointing out publicly that the Conservatives themselves gave 'exceptional leave to remain' to 15,232 people in 1992 alone without trumpeting the policy. Labour ministers now pointedly ask if that was 'a Tory amnesty or the pragmatic granting of ELR to cut the backlog?'[2]. In many cases the decision to grant exceptional leave to remain is taken for humanitarian reasons. The Home Office now publicly states that applicants will also be allowed to stay in Britain if there is not a decision on their case within seven years – a policy which has been in effect for more than a decade.

Some observers believe one guesstimate that about 250,000 asylum seekers have settled in London since 1990

It is against this background that the recent hard-line posture taken against Czech Roma and Kosovan asylum seekers arriving at Dover and warnings about the increasing use of detention should be seen. This newly toughened approach has been laced with some tender liberalism. The iniquitous 'primary purpose rule' which split up genuine marriages has been abolished and the confidential rule books and country reports which guide immigration decisions are to be published for the first time. Appeal rights for visitors stopped from coming to Britain for family weddings and funerals are also to be restored.

But underlying this 'firm but fair' approach to immigration politics lies a flirtation by Jack Straw with the perennial question posed by right-wing backbenchers and tabloid newspapers: 'Yes,' they ask, 'but how many illegal immigrants are there really in Britain today?'

Ever since this particular numbers game became a populist occupation around the time of Enoch Powell's Rivers of Blood speech in 1968, the Home Office has always refused to take part in the game. 'There are no official estimates of the number of people who are in breach of the immigration laws. It is not possible to determine whether a person is here without permission until they have been interviewed,'[3] is the official 'it's a Catch 22' response.

The Immigration Service says the number of illegal entrants found trying to enter Britain clandestinely was stable until the early months of this year, when they suddenly increased sharply. But the Home Office believes that this sudden surge had more to do with sniffer dogs and better detection techniques at British ports and less to do with a new influx. They say that they now pick up 50 per cent of clandestine entries at the port where before they were only catching 20 per cent.

In opposition Labour toyed with the idea of scrapping this policy of refusing to estimate the number of illegals. In an unpublished policy document, written by Jack Straw and Doug Henderson, Labour argued that headlines and theories were no substitute for well-considered action and practice. It said: 'We need to seriously address the failures of the system, rather than use it as a cheap political football, and have an informed debate about priorities. For example, it is time to put a stop to inflammatory speculation with accurate research. It is astonishing that after 17 years in government the Home Office has not sponsored any proper research into the scale of illegal immigration. Labour will commission the necessary research.'[4]

That decision has not yet been taken. Ministers now seem to regard such an exercise with some suspicion. By the nature of the problem, we do not know, and estimates may be misleading... Provisional figures for 1997 show that 14,150 people were traced and served with illegal entry papers, but many of them may have entered in previous years,' Mike O'Brien recently told the Commons.[5]

This business of how many failed asylum seekers and illegal entrants actually left the country is the really hot potato. Tory MPs point out that 250,000 people have applied for political asylum in Britain over the past ten years and official figures show that 10,700 have been granted asylum and 13,000 deported. 'Where are the other 226,300 people?' they ask.

This ignores the 76,000 people whose cases are still stuck in the backlog and that some 5,000 a year are granted exceptional leave to remain. But undoubtedly some thousands have overstayed and simply disappeared.

Mike O'Brien has promised to speed up the process of removals of failed asylum seekers and illegal entrants. He has argued that although Tory ministers doubled the number of deportation orders they signed, the numbers removed from Britain actually fell.[6]

It is impossible to know how many people actually leave the country each year because of Home Office action. The Immigration Service draws a sharp distinction in its records between removals and deportations. Illegal entrants face removal once their compassionate circumstances and appeal rights are exhausted. They may return to Britain providing they can satisfy the entry requirements.

Deportation is different. Before a minister signs a deportation order the individual is given the chance to leave the country voluntarily. If they go quietly then they will be given the chance to come back to Britain but if they refuse to leave then they are banned from returning for at least three years. The Home Office does not produce figures for all these

---

It is impossible to know how many people actually leave the country each year because of Home Office action

---

categories of failed asylum seekers and illegal immigrants who leave under these different procedures. Neither does it count how many dependants go with them. So it is impossible to know the total thrown out each year and how many stay.

Some observers believe that one guesstimate is that about 250,000 asylum seekers have settled in London since 1990 – that's about half the number Germany has been taking in each year. Most are here legally and many are banned from claiming social security benefits. Little official effort has gone into the problems they face in settling into a new country. But it is a testimony to the multicultural nature of British society that such an influx has been absorbed without any major racist explosions. Except, that is, for an explosion in London's restaurant and music scenes.

Sources
1   Reply to Chief Inspector of Prisons Report on Campsfield House, April 16, 1997
2   *Hansard* March 30, 1998 , col 881
3   Immigration and Nationality Directorate briefing May 7, 1998
4   Fairer, faster and firmer, Labour's approach to asylum and immigration, unpublished
5   *Hansard* March 30, 1998
6   Private office note, June 1997

© The Guardian
May, 1999

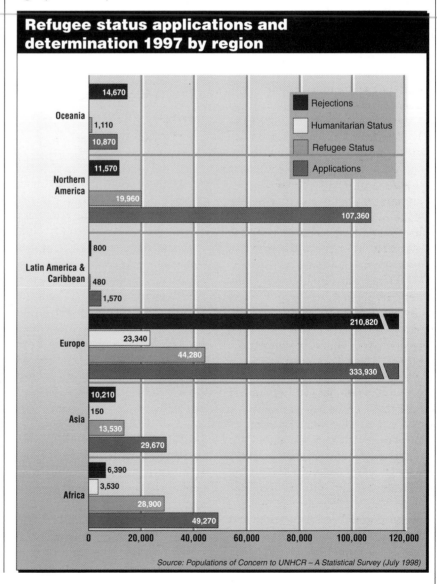

Refugee status applications and determination 1997 by region

Source: Populations of Concern to UNHCR – A Statistical Survey (July 1998)

Stateless and unregistered children

Information from UNHCR

In most countries, babies are registered with the relevant authorities soon after they are born, enabling them to receive a birth certificate.

Without such a certificate, it can be very difficult for a person to lay claim to a nationality or to exercise the rights associated with citizenship. Individuals who lack a birth certificate may, for example, find it impossible to leave or return to their own country, register as a voter or gain access to public health and education services.

The legal framework

Recognising the importance of these issues, Article 7 of the 1989 Convention on the Rights of the Child states that every child 'shall be registered immediately after birth and shall have the right from birth to a name, the right to acquire a nationality and, as far as possible, the right to know and be cared for by his or her parents'. The convention continues by stipulating that signatory states 'shall ensure the implementation of these rights in accordance with their national law and their obligations under the relevant international instruments in the field, in particular where the child would otherwise be stateless'. The Convention on the Rights of the Child has now been signed by 140 states, very few of which have entered any reservations to Article 7.

Several regional instruments have also reiterated a child's right to registration at birth and to a nationality, including Article 6 of the 1990 African Charter on the Rights and Welfare of the Child and Article 20 of the 1969 American Convention on Human Rights. Moreover, these instruments state that children should be granted the nationality of their place of birth if they do not have another nationality.

As discussed elsewhere in this article, nationality is normally granted on the basis of a person's place of birth (*jus solis*) or on the basis of their descent (*jus sanguinis*). There has been a tendency in the existing (and very sparse) literature on children and nationality to equate registration at birth with the right to a nationality. But the two are not always synonymous. Although the right of children to registration at birth is unequivocal, this does not always give them an automatic right to a particular nationality.

There are many young people throughout the world who are effectively stateless. This can arise for a variety of reasons

---

In those countries which grant citizenship on the basis of place of birth, as in much of the Americas, registration at birth gives a child automatic rights to the citizenship of that country if he or she cannot claim citizenship by descent. However, in countries which grant citizenship exclusively on the basis of *jus sanguinis*, as is the case throughout most of Asia, registration at birth does not give a child a right to citizenship in their country of birth if the parents are not nationals of that state.

Children without a nationality

Despite the clear legal guidelines which exist in relation to a child's right to a nationality, there are many young people throughout the world who are effectively stateless. This can arise for a variety of reasons, the most important of which are summarised below:

- if a child is born out of wedlock;
- if a child's birth is not registered because of the parent's failure to do so, because of flawed administrative practices or because the authorities refuse to register the birth;
- if a child is born in a refugee camp or to parents who are refugees, asylum seekers or migrant workers, and if the birth is not registered with the authorities;
- if a child is born in a country of asylum and the registration of that birth is not accepted by the authorities in the child's country of origin; and
- if a child is born during a civil or international war, or during a process of state dissolution, and the authorities are unable or unwilling to register the birth;
- if nationality is granted on the basis of *jus sanguinis* and one or both of a child's parents are stateless or their nationality is disputed.

Although cases of stateless children have come to UNHCR's attention in countries across the world, the problem is particularly prominent in those areas which grant citizenship on the basis of *jus sanguinis* and where the nationality of one or both of the child's parents is disputed.

This is the case in Bhutan, for example, where the 1985 Citizenship Act stipulates that children do not have a right to Bhutanese nationality if they are born to parents who are stateless or who are not entitled to Bhutanese citizenship themselves. Children born in Bhutan to non-Bhutanese nationals and who are unable to obtain the nationality of their parents are therefore rendered stateless. The citizenship status of those children born and registered in the Bhutanese refugee camps of Nepal is even less clear.

A somewhat similar situation has arisen in Myanmar. The Rohingyas, a Muslim minority group living in the west of the country, are generally not recognised as Myanmar nationals because of the country's very restrictive citizenship laws. The citizenship status of Rohingya children who were born in refugee camps in Bangladesh and who have returned to Myanmar is even more precarious.

The problem of stateless children is not restricted to those countries which provide citizenship on the basis of *jus sanguinis*. Unfortunately, children can also face difficulties in obtaining a nationality in countries which provide citizenship on the basis of *jus solis*. This usually occurs because the authorities of those countries are reluctant to register the births of certain children born on their territory. This has been a common problem for the children of refugees, asylum seekers and migrant workers in several countries in Central and South America, where the authorities have been reluctant to register their births for the very reason that this will give them an automatic right to citizenship.

In Honduras, for example, none of the children born in the Salvadoran refugee camps during the late 1970s and 1980s were registered with the authorities. Although the Honduran authorities were legally obliged to register all children born on their territory, in practice, the refugee camps were treated as if they had extra-territorial status.

A similar situation arose in the Guatemalan refugee camps of Mexico. Until 1993, the Mexican authorities refused to issue children born in those camps with birth certificates, despite domestic legislation obliging them to take such action. Following lengthy negotiations with UNHCR, the Mexican government finally decided in 1993 to retroactively provide birth certificates to all the children concerned – some 10,000 children in all, who, when they reach the age of 18, will be entitled to Mexican citizenship.

Asylum seekers in the Russian Federation have also been affected by this problem. According to Russian nationality laws, children born on Russian territory to non-Russian parents are considered to be Russian if the states of which their parents are nationals do not provide them with citizenship. Similarly, children born to stateless parents on Russian territory have the right to Russian citizenship.

In practice, however, non-Russian or stateless parents are unable to register the births of their children if they are not themselves legally resident in the country. As asylum seekers from countries outside the former Soviet Union find it almost impossible to regularise their status with the Russian authorities, and as many are unwilling to approach the embassy of their country of origin, their children can easily become stateless. Like stateless and un-registered children in other parts of the world, they are unable to attend school or seek medical assistance, and are more likely to be exposed to illegal adoption, trafficking and sexual exploitation.

• The above is an extract from *The State of the World's Refugees*, produced by UNHCR. Extracts are available on their web site which can be accessed at http://www.unhcr.ch
© United Nations High Commission for Refugees (UNHCR)

The 'gun' that finds refugees in a heartbeat

Brussels: A device has been developed to detect refugees who stow away on ferries. When the hand-held machine is pointed at a container, it can pick up the heartbeat of anyone hidden inside in under 30 seconds.

It has been on trial at the Belgian port of Zeebrugge since January and is credited with the discovery of 42 migrants, mostly from Kosovo. They were handed over to the police for questioning before being expelled from the country.

It is hoped the device, called the LifeGuard, will soon be used to help halt the stream of refugees pouring across the Channel into Britain.

The overwhelming majority of illegals sneak into Britain by climbing aboard the lorry trailers at lay-bys close to French and Belgian Channel ports.

Just under three feet long when fully extended and weighing less than two pounds, the machine, which looks like a science-fiction ray gun, was developed and built in the US.

At Dover, where there are 3,500 incoming trailers to check each year, only 7 per cent are controlled

---

Hedwig van Roy, whose firm DKL is importing the device, said yesterday: 'Normally it takes seven to 15 minutes to undo a truck and make a thorough search.

'This takes time and at Dover, where there are 3,500 incoming trailers to check each year, only 7 per cent are controlled. You can imagine how many thousands of migrants get in every year on lorries which have to be waved through because of lack of time to examine them. Now it should be possible to plug this gaping hole in the security screen.'

• Each LifeGuard sells for about £18,000. *© The Daily Mail March, 1999*

Asylum in the UK

Bogus refugees or bogus refusals?

Terrible abuses of human rights – torture, execution, imprisonment of the innocent – take place on a daily basis in dozens of countries around the world. Yet, people fleeing such abuse are finding it harder than ever to get asylum in the UK, even when they relate the most compelling accounts of suffering. Instead of the protection they hope for, they find themselves having to justify, to often unsympathetic officials, why they should not be sent straight back to countries where they face persecution. Hundreds are imprisoned without trial. Legislation introduced in 1996 further eroded refugees' rights and made thousands destitute.

Who is a refugee?

The 1951 UN Convention on Refugees defines a refugee as someone who has 'a well-founded fear of being persecuted for reasons of race, religion, nationality, membership of a particular social group or political opinion'. Anyone can be persecuted for these reasons. Our clients range from teachers or university students to farmers and business people.

Some people do not qualify for asylum even though they have suffered human rights abuses. This is because they have not been persecuted for one of the reasons set out in the above definition. In such circumstances people are sometimes given 'exceptional leave to remain' ('ELR') which is in effect permission to stay on humanitarian grounds. ELR does not give the same protection as refugee status but it does stop people from being sent back to danger. Whether or not someone is granted ELR is entirely at the discretion of the Home Office.

Why should we help them?

Helping those in danger is the mark of a civilised society. It would be morally reprehensible to return people to persecution, torture and death. However, refugees have more than a moral right to protection. They also have a legal right. They have the right to asylum in this country because we have signed the 1951 UN Convention on refugees and pledged to protect them from persecution.

Isn't the UK being inundated?

The UNHCR estimates that there were about 12.9 million refugees world-wide in 1997.[1] (This figure does not include people who were displaced within their own countries.) In the same year, the UK received 32,500 asylum applications' or just 0.25% of the above figure. The fact is that the vast majority of refugees flee to neighbouring countries. Few can afford to travel to the UK. It is the poorer countries which take most responsibility for the world's refugees. The major refugee populations world-wide are to be found in Africa, the Middle East, Asia and South America.

The British government also tries to discourage refugees from getting here. One of its methods is to make citizens of countries experiencing internal turmoil into 'visa nationals' i.e. people who have to get a visa from the British Embassy in their own country before travelling to Britain. Visa requirements together with The Immigration (Carriers' Liability) Act 1987 make it difficult for refugees to travel to the UK. The 1987 Act enables the government to fine airlines for each passenger they bring to the UK without the right visa. In July 1991, the fine was doubled to £2,000 per passenger. Consequently, unaccountable airline staff play the role of immigration officials and stop people from boarding planes to the UK.

In 1989 when the Turkish military stepped up its activities against Kurds in South-East Turkey, Turkish citizens were made visa

Populations of concern

UNHCR's founding mandate defines refugees as those who are outside their countries and who cannot or do not want to return because of a well-founded fear of being persecuted for reasons of their race, religion, nationality, political opinion or membership in a particular social group. Persons of concern to UNHCR at 1st January 1998, by category.

Region	Refugees	Asylum Seekers	Returnees	IDPs & others of concern	Total
Africa	3,481,700	37,700	2,171,700	1,694,000	7,385,100
Asia	4,730,300	15,000	824,100	1,889,100	7,458,500
Europe	2,940,700	267,400	459,400	2,389,000	6,056,500
Latin America	83,200	600	17,800	1,700	103,300
North America	668,500	626,400	–	–	1,2494,900
Oceania	71,100	6,900	–	–	78,000
Total	11,975,500	954,000	3,473,000	5,973,800	22,376,300

Source: UNHCR

nationals. The same restriction was imposed on citizens of most former Yugoslavian states at the height of the Balkan conflict in 1992. In other words, the worse the human rights situation gets in a particular country, the more difficult it becomes to flee to the UK.

What happens when a refugee gets to the UK?

Despite the obstacles thrown in their way, people still manage to get to the UK to claim asylum. But not without experiencing considerable anxiety and distress. Many refugees arrive in Britain traumatised. They are also terrified of being sent back. Often, they have little more than a suitcase of clothes. People who are fleeing for their lives have to make do with the bare necessities. Many would also have spent their life savings to escape.

Some refugees are detained from the moment they arrive in the UK. In this country, refugees are detained in prisons and in immigration detention centres. They are not charged or brought before a magistrate or judge. Immigration Officers at the air/sea ports where they enter the country (referred to as the 'ports of entry') can decide independently to detain a refugee. There is no limit to the length of detention. The Immigration Service argues that it only uses detention as a last resort when they think that someone will abscond. However, in the experience of legal advisers, detention is often arbitrary. Detention is also clearly used as a deterrent. For example, when quite a large number of Czech and Slovak Roma claimed asylum towards the end of 1997, the Immigration Service detained most of the men but not their families. The detentions were obviously intended to dissuade other Romanies from coming here.

Many refugees remain in detention while their asylum claims are being considered and some are held for over a year. It is difficult for them to understand why they have to be incarcerated. No other European country has, or uses, such wide-ranging powers to detain.

Does it matter when you claim asylum?

Yes it does. Following the introduction of new benefits regulations in 1996 by the Conservative Government, those who fail to claim asylum at the port when they arrive in the country are not entitled to benefits such as income support and housing benefit. In other words, they are left destitute and denied their dignity. They have to rely on their local authority for basic accommodation (often in a hostel) and cooked food or food vouchers. They may not receive cash for basic needs such as travel and clothes.

The previous government justified the regulations by arguing that genuine refugees would claim asylum the moment they arrived. Considering the state of mind many are in when they arrive, this assertion is not only untrue but is also totally insensitive to human suffering. The Home Office's own statistics not only disprove this assertion but suggest that the opposite is true. In the two years prior to the introduction of the benefits regulations, asylum seekers who applied for asylum *after* entering the country were about twice as successful as those who applied on arrival. The same was true the year the regulations were introduced.

What happens after someone has claimed asylum?

When somebody claims asylum, he or she is expected to explain to the Home Office why he or she cannot go back to his or her own country. In some cases, the applicant is given a questionnaire to fill in but in most cases, he or she will be interviewed about his or her case. Asylum is clearly a serious matter. A wrong decision could cost someone his or her life. However, unlike people accused of criminal offences, refugees do not have the automatic right to have a legal representative present when they are interviewed about their claims.

In a lot of cases, people who apply for asylum on arrival are interviewed about their claim at a later date. However, it is also common for refugees to be subjected to long interviews by Immigration Officers just hours after they arrive,

before they have had a chance to get representation. At this stage, most are afraid, disorientated and tired from the long journey. Many remain traumatised for a long time. Unsurprisingly, they sometimes leave out important information or get some facts wrong when giving their account of persecution.

Most refugees don't know what the Home Office requires of them. They are not aware that the Home Office expects them to provide evidence e.g. documents to support their asylum claims. They believe that the Home Office has the means to verify their claims and that it will do so. So, one of our clients, a Burmese man who was an opposition party candidate in the 1990 Burmese general elections did not give the Home Office a copy of his election leaflet, which proved who he was, until he approached us some years after applying and was advised to do so by us.

In addition, the majority of refugees have never been to the UK before and do not speak English. They have to rely on interpreters who do not always correctly interpret what is being said.

Surely the Home Office won't hold such errors against them?

Unfortunately, the Home Office tends to see all errors or discrepancies, however small, in the worst possible light. The simplistic assumption is that discrepancies, contradictions, forgetfulness etc. automatically mean that the account given is untrue. This is by far the most common way that the Home Office discredits (and therefore refuses) asylum claims. So, for example, one of our clients from Sudan was refused asylum primarily because he had got the date of his release from prison, where he was severely tortured, wrong by a matter of a few days.

Aren't most refugees refused because they are not 'genuine'?

No. The Home Office argues that since only about 30% of asylum applicants are successful, the majority of refugees are 'bogus'. However, this statement is misleading. Firstly, the number of successful asylum applications for each year is closer to 50%. The figure cited by the Home Office does not include those who have been granted exceptional leave to remain or those who have successfully appealed against the Home Office's refusal to grant them asylum. Secondly, a large number of refugees, including known opponents of repressive regimes and victims of torture, are unfairly refused asylum every year.

In 1995, Asylum Aid produced a report entitled *No Reason at All* which examined Home Office decisions on asylum claims. The report concluded that in making such decisions, the Home Office often relied on wrong information, ignored cogent evidence, including medical evidence supporting claims of torture, and applied a standard of proof which was well above that required by the law. As our 1998 update of this report, *Still No Reason At All* shows, very little has changed. Some of the extraordinary reasons for refusal cited in the report include:

- A West African whose beatings in detention had necessitated four month's hospital treatment was told by the Home Office that his injuries *could have occurred in another way*. At appeal however, the special adjudicator, however, agreed with the examining doctor in finding that 'the multiple injuries to his legs, resulting in scars in the same place meant that he was injured again and again in the same place which is totally consistent with the Appellant's claims that he was beaten and tortured.'
- Targeted for his political activities, one man was recently refused asylum because: 'You state that the men drove you to a place one and a half hours away and told you to run before they opened fire on you. The Secretary of State . . . considers that if the men had intended to kill you they would have done straight away rather than give you a chance to escape.

It is surely self-serving to refuse asylum applications unfairly then refer to the fact that few succeed to support an assertion that most refugees are not genuine. As if the situation wasn't bad enough, the benefits regulations introduced in 1996 deprived those who had been refused of benefits, leaving them, not only dejected but also destitute.

Another significant reason for the low success rate is the severe shortage of good representation. Many asylum seekers have their cases jeopardised or destroyed by incompetent or unscrupulous advisers who have been able to flourish due to the lack of regulation in this area. Our Burmese client who was mentioned earlier was initially refused asylum because his first representative sent the Home Office wrong information and failed to submit important evidence which supported his case. Following Asylum Aid's intervention, the Home Office has agreed to review his case.

Can't refugees appeal against unfair decisions?

Yes they can. In fact, most are forced to because the Home Office refuses the majority of people. An asylum seeker who is refused asylum can appeal to the Immigration Appellate Authority and can challenge the Home Office's decision before an Adjudicator. Hundreds of people win their appeals every year but a large number are refused.

The Home Office often points to this as support for their argument that most refugees are not genuine. However, once again, the figures are

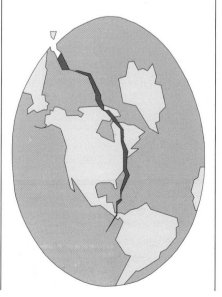

misleading as there are major problems with the asylum appeal system. Legal representatives of refugees have long been concerned about the way in which many Adjudicators approach asylum appeals. Research carried out by the Asylum Rights Campaign, helped by Asylum Aid, which studied 722 determinations of Adjudicators promulgated during the second half of 1995, found that Adjudicators differed widely in their assessment of the human rights situation in certain countries. So, in our system, somebody's life or liberty can depend on which Adjudicator they come before.

Adjudicators also consider their personal assessment of a refugee's credibility while he or she is giving evidence to be extremely important. An appeal can fail simply because the Adjudicator does not believe the refugee. This is despite the fact that many refugees are traumatised by their experiences and are nervous during appeal hearings because they are unfamiliar with legal processes.

Many refugees are also unrepresented at appeal hearings because Legal Aid is not available for asylum appeals. The complicated and fast-changing nature of asylum law makes it difficult for those without expert representation to succeed.

So, Britain's not such a great place for refugees then?

The fundamental problem with our asylum system is that it is not designed to protect those fleeing from human rights abuses. It is designed to keep people out. If the UK is truly committed to promoting human rights globally, as the government says it is, then we must get our own house in order and reform our asylum system. Until then, we will continue to abuse the human rights of those who have already suffered dreadfully.

References
1. *Populations of Concern to UNHCR – 1997 Statistical Overview.*
2. *Home Office Statistical Bulletin – Asylum Statistics UK 1997.*

© Asylum Aid

Telling the truth

Countering false reporting about asylum seekers

There has been a concerted campaign in the press – including local press – against asylum seekers. For many people, the press provides the only information that they have on the subject. Much of it is false or misleading. This can have the effect of turning local residents against asylum seekers, especially in economically troubled communities, where people may think that resources devoted to helping asylum seekers should be spent on local residents' problems. A *Guardian/ICM* poll published in February 1999 showed that 33% of people in Britain think that all refugees should be sent back, even if they can prove that they would be tortured or killed. Only 49% believe that such refugees should be allowed to stay in Britain. That is why it is important to challenge false or misleading statements on radio or in the press. The following information should help you to do that. If it does not cover the points that you need to counter, call the Refugee Council's Information Officer on 0171 820 3082.

'Asylum seekers all come to Britain because we're a soft touch'

In 1998, 46,010 people applied for asylum in the United Kingdom. That is more than in 1997, but compared to the total number of refugees in the world (over twenty million) it is small. Most refugees stay closer to home – Africa contains more refugees than Europe, with fewer resources to support them. It is also small compared to the number of asylum seekers applying in Germany and, per head of population, it is smaller than the number of applications in Holland. Asylum seekers do not all make for Britain, considering it a 'soft touch': every other European Union country receives people applying for asylum too. The removal of benefits from many asylum seekers in 1996 was intended to reduce the flow of refugees to Britain. It did not. The reason: asylum seekers come to Britain because of extremely difficult situations in their home countries, not because of the British benefits system.

'Most asylum seekers are just economic migrants; they're not really refugees'

The main nationalities of those applying for asylum in 1998 were:

Former Yugoslavia 7,980 – there was war in Kosovo and continuing ethnic tensions in Bosnia and parts of Croatia

Somalia 4,680 – there is war between different armed factions and total breakdown of civil society

Sri Lanka 3,505 – there is war between Government forces and Tamil Tiger guerrillas against a background of tension between Sinhalese and Tamil populations

Former USSR 2,915 – there is widespread breakdown of public services and powerful organised crime

Afghanistan 2,390 – there is continuing civil war and the Govern-ment enforces a very strict version of religious law

Turkey 2,010 – there is armed repression of the Kurdish minority and other human rights abuses by Government forces

Other countries producing refugees included:

Iraq, where Saddam Hussein cracks down on any form of dissent;

Algeria, where Government forces and armed fundamentalists were engaged in a bloody 'dirty war' in which most of the population is caught in the middle;

Colombia, torn apart by the violence of drug barons, Government-backed death squads and armed guerrillas;

Rwanda, still suffering from the aftermath of the civil war in which hundreds of thousands died as a result of ethnic cleansing;

Democratic Republic of the Congo, where the Government which ousted dictator Mobutu Sese Seko was repeating many of the human rights abuses for which he was overthrown;

Czech Republic and Slovakia, where the Roma minority was subject to harassment by local authorities and police and vicious racist attacks by neo-Nazi gangs with police complicity;

Nigeria, which was under military dictatorship.

In 1998, the Government made 26,720 decisions on asylum claims: 20% got refugee status, 15% got Exceptional Leave to Remain, 'ELR'. The 1951 Refugee Convention gives a rather narrow definition of persecution – someone fleeing general chaos and civil war may not count as a refugee under the Convention. Such people are often given ELR. 65% of applications were rejected, but 8% appealed successfully against this. So over 40% of applications resulted in the asylum seeker being allowed to stay on the grounds that he or she would face death or grave suffering if sent back.

'Well, anyway, we can't afford to look after them'

The 1996 Asylum and Immigration Act stopped most asylum seekers getting state benefits. They have no right to work in the UK for at least

---

Refugees bring with them many skills which would benefit British society

---

six months, after which they have to apply for permission. Those who are destitute may be supported by local authorities under the 1948 National Assistance Act. Central government subsidises local authorities to do this – up to a maximum of £165 for a single asylum seeker, more for families. The asylum seekers do not get the cash: that goes on rent, food vouchers and the local authority's administration costs. Asylum seekers are not eligible for council housing and are therefore not jumping any queues to get it. Local authorities have to house them wherever accommodation is available – which is why asylum seekers in London or

other large cities may be sent to seaside boarding house, holiday camps, hotels or even closed-down hospitals. The 1999 Immigration and Asylum Bill will make things even more difficult for asylum seekers.

Britain is a prosperous country. If the political will were there, we could easily take care of refugees without sacrificing the needs of low-income residents.

Refugees in fact bring with them many skills which would benefit British society if refugees' qualifications were accepted. Refugees have helped to create thousands of jobs in Britain and their cultural and economic contributions have enriched everyone. (For example: Marks and Spencer was founded by a refugee; many Ugandan Asian refugees from Idi Amin's dictatorship in the 1970s settled in Leicester and created 30,000 new jobs in textiles and other trades.)

© Churches Commission for Racial Justice

Cruel myths

Nick Hardwick argues that public perceptions of who refugees are and how they are treated are so often twisted by press coverage that a proper debate about them is nigh impossible

---

There's nothing new about refugees arriving in this country being greeted with a cacophony of abuse, lies and hysterical headlines. The problem with such a response from parts of the press – evident again after last week's publication of the Asylum and Immigration Bill – is that it prevents a sensible debate about asylum issues, based on facts and substance.

There are so many half-truths about refugees in the UK, but there are three big myths that must be dispelled:

Myth: Refugees only come here for the money.

Fact: After the Conservatives' reforms, we treat asylum seekers very badly, and almost all of our European partners have far more generous welfare benefits systems for asylum seekers than we do. In Britain, most asylum seekers are not entitled to

any welfare benefits and live on food vouchers and accommodation provided by local authorities. In other European countries, the cash allowance paid to asylum seekers varies from £39.29 per week in Sweden to £48 per week in Luxembourg and £63.51 per week in Ireland.

Myth: Britain is a soft touch and takes more than its fair share of refugees.

Fact: We are 11th out of 17 in the European league table. Many other European countries take far more refugees than we do per head of population, including Switzerland, the Netherlands, Norway, Sweden and Germany.

Myth: Only a tiny proportion of refugees are genuine and the rest are bogus.

Fact: In 1998 the Home Office allowed 35 per cent of asylum seekers

to stay in the UK (20 per cent received refugee status and 15 per cent exceptional leave to remain on humanitarian grounds). Successful appeals take the rate closer to 40 per cent.

Even when the myths have been exploded we need to remember that this isn't a debate about numbers, but real people. I met a middle-aged Kosovan man who came to the Refugee Council for help after finding himself destitute on the streets of London. He told me he was a geologist who had worked for the government. When war came to his country, he found himself in trouble for working for the Serb authorities and had to flee.

He is just one of a growing number of Kosovan refugees we see every week. All they are doing is asking for the chance to rebuild their lives here, where they are safe from persecution.

We aren't saying that everyone who applies for asylum has a good case. The Government has the right to remove those who have no legal or humanitarian reason to stay, provided the decision-making system is open, fair and accountable. So far, we've heard a lot about how the Government is going to make the asylum system firmer, but not enough about how it's going to make it fairer and faster.

Making fairer decisions on asylum claims is the real key to a faster, more credible system.

The biggest change the Government is proposing is its new system of support for asylum seekers.

People arriving destitute will get just one offer of food and shelter and no choice where that is. There will be no cash, even for families with children. This is a massive social engineering project which the Government is about to embark on at huge risk. There is a danger of creating ghettos where asylum seekers are trapped on some nightmare estate far from family and friends – stigmatised by having food vouchers, imprisoned by having no cash, unable to go anywhere.

They could become victims of racial harassment and attacks; schools might by unwilling to take their children; reception zones could become dumping zones, with asylum seekers foisted on unwilling communities and facing a backlash from people who've been fed the lies that

they're all scroungers come to rip us off. And they could be stuck in these ghettos for years if the Government's target of making decisions on asylum claims within six months does not become reality.

It is in no one's interest if the new support system fails. That will just mean more misery for asylum seekers; a waste of public money and a further erosion of public confidence in the asylum system.

Areas chosen as reception zones will need cash to develop infrastructure and services to meet refugees' needs: grassroots refugee community organisations, which provide most of the support to newly-arrived asylum seekers, will need help in supporting a dispersed population of asylum seekers.

The voluntary sector can play a big role here. We are talking to the Government about what needs to

happen to give the new system the best chance of working in a humanitarian and practical way. We need to learn from the mistakes in the current chaotic support arrangements and not add to the shambles.

The next few months will be crucial, with the bill being debated in Parliament. We will continue to argue for changes to the Government's proposals so we create an asylum system which is credible and has the confidence of refugees and the public alike.

As the late Rabbi Hugo Gryn, a survivor of Auschwitz, said: 'Asylum issues are an index of our spiritual and moral civilisation. How you are with the one to whom you owe nothing, that is a grave test . . . and I hope and pray that it is a test we shall not fail.'

• First published in *The Guardian*, February, 1999.   © *Nick Hardwick*

Improving the odds for child refugees

Contrary to what might be expected, children who seek asylum in industrialised countries often encounter more difficulty with immigration authorities than adults. Child Newsline looks at efforts to help children through this difficult process.

Simon Russell, Amnesty International's refugee officer in London, vividly remembers the first child asylum case he worked on in 1994.

By Mike Crawley, a Canadian journalist currently working with Gemini News Service in London

She was a 15-year-old girl from Uganda whose entire family had been shot dead. She escaped to Kenya, where she was raped, and then came to Britain.

On arrival, immigration officers

interviewed her without any adult representing her. Her asylum case was rejected because of 'variations' in her story and Britain's Home Office refused to reconsider the case. Officials said she should have claimed refugee status in Kenya. In other words, she should have asked for protection in the place where she was raped.

On appeal, the lawyer for the Home Office cross-examined her vigorously on the rape.

'It was outrageous behaviour, the process for that girl of not being believed, cross-examined in a way nobody should be cross-examined,' says Russell.

'She was such a strong case, she should have been given refugee status immediately.'

Fortunately, the judge allowed her appeal and the girl is now living a new life in Britain. But the stories of many refugee children who come to the West don't have a happy ending and the treatment they receive from officials is just as aggressive.

For this reason, international humanitarian organisations are drafting codes of practice for dealing with refugee child asylum seekers, aimed particularly at North American and European Union countries. They hope to persuade governments to adopt the guidelines and order immigration officers and other staff to put them into practice.

The need for such guidelines is pressing because children make up a growing number of the refugee claimants arriving at airports and borders of industrialised countries.

Figures from Britain's Home Office show 1,100 unaccompanied children claimed refugee status in Britain in 1997. The number rose to well over 2,000 last year. Typically, the child has no parents or close family ties. In some cases, the applicant is a former child soldier, dealing with the additional trauma of having engaged in conflict and facing the prospect of retribution at home.

International Save the Children says precise statistics are hard to come by, but it estimates more than 100,000 children in Europe are in need of international protection.

Kosovans and Afghanis make up the largest proportion of the child refugees claiming asylum at European borders. The United Nations High Commissioner for Refugees (UNHCR) says about half of the world's estimated 12 million refugees are children.

'Refugee children are children, first and foremost,' says Dennis McNamara, the UNHCR director of international protection.

'Children have always been the easiest victims of human rights abuses. Refugee children suffer double jeopardy: the most vulnerable category of a vulnerable population.'

Only one country – Canada – has in place a set of procedures for dealing with the special circumstances of child asylum seekers

---

Yet in Britain, which boasts a humanitarian foreign policy, child asylum seekers are twice as likely to be put in detention as adults.

According to Home Office figures, about three per cent of all child refugee claimants in Britain are detained.

Their asylum claims are also less likely to be accepted. In the past two years, children (aged under 18 years) were seven times less likely to be given refugee status in Britain than young adults aged from 25 to 29. In addition, only seven per cent of children were given 'exceptional leave to remain' (permission to stay on compassionate grounds) compared with a quarter of young adults.

'We do not believe a child should be detained in any circumstances,' says Terry Smith, head of the British Refugee Council's children's section. Since 1994, the organisation has worked with 154 children in detention, half of them in the last two years alone.

Refugee detention centres are little different from jails. Guards treat detainees like prisoners. Children who are detained end up in close quarters with possibly violent people. It can be a second traumatisation for a child who has fled violence and persecution.

A ban on detention would be only one element of the codes of practice that humanitarian groups want governments to adopt. Generally, activists want the best interests of the child placed at the forefront of all decision-making.

Some other proposed guidelines include the following:

- children should not be deported to conflict zones, and if they are deported anywhere, they should be accompanied and protected;
- officials who deal with child claimants should be specially trained;
- interviews should be conducted in a child-friendly way, and should take into account differences in culture;
- interpretation and legal representation must always be available, and confidentiality must be maintained;

- children must be given adequate information and services, such as education and health care, and the organisations who deliver the services must co-operate;
- decisions should be made in a timely fashion, and efforts should be made towards reuniting children with their families.

Activists are trying to ensure that children are not victimised by the growing tendency in Europe and North America towards a 'get-tough' approach to refugees. Britain, for instance, has just announced it plans to overhaul its asylum policy which includes removing cash welfare benefits for asylum seekers.

Concern about the treatment of child refugees has led several agencies to take action on the issue.

Save the Children UK, in a report released late last year, spells out in great detail how legal representatives and other professionals such as social workers and teachers can help children through the asylum process. In particular, the report – called 'Supporting un-

accompanied children in the asylum process' – says that lawyers working with children requesting asylum should have specialist knowledge of asylum laws and some skills in communicating with children.

The report also recommends that the British government not detain children and adopt a child-friendly process for asylum application. Save the Children UK also wants the government to withdraw its reservation to allow lawyers to use the Convention on the Rights of the Child to argue an asylum claim.

Meanwhile, Russell is developing Amnesty International's proposed guidelines for determining refugee status of children.

He says there is a need for a document showing how all the legal instruments – the Geneva Convention on Refugees, the Convention on the Rights of the Child – apply specifically to refugee children.

'The protection needs of children are different from those of adults and the responses to those needs are going to be different as well,' says Russell. 'Guidelines are necessary to bring all elements into an easily digestible whole.'

Only one country – Canada – has in place a set of procedures for dealing with the special circumstances of child asylum seekers.

Once the guidelines have been drawn up, humanitarian organisations will have to embark on the more difficult part of the task — persuading the world's governments to follow them.

• The above is an extract from the Child Newsline web site which can be accessed at http://www.gn.apc.org/childnewsline

© Child Newsline

Ministers try to turn the human tide

By Philip Johnston

In the Queen's Speech tomorrow, the Government will begin yet another attempt to reform Britain's asylum laws. Ministers – safe in the knowledge that they had nothing to do with the development of the system – have described it as a 'shambles'.

But will the proposed Asylum and Immigration Bill make any difference, or will the new ministers in the Home Office be forced to concede that they, like their predecessors, can only watch the advance of the tide?

Fortress Europe is a joke among British immigration officials. They watch bemused as illegal immigrants enter the EU and then use the open borders policy known as the Schengen agreement to cross the continent to the shores of Britain.

Italy is Europe's soft underbelly. It is largely through its southern ports, such as Bari, that thousands of illegal migrants are marshalled by gangs for whom the trade in people has become even more profitable than smuggling drugs.

Austria has also become an important transit point since border controls with eastern Europe were relaxed.

The fragmentation of Yugoslavia and the consequent political turmoil in the Balkans has made Albania and Kosovo the principal source of refugees, many of whom are escaping economic privation rather than political persecution.

Since the upheaval in Albania caused by the collapse two years ago of the pyramid investment schemes that devoured the nation's personal savings, thousands have fled the country. The turmoil also fuelled the gang culture in Albania, not least through the looting of army weapons stores.

Tribe-like families have emerged with close links to the Italian Mafia, for whom Albanians often work as couriers, driving stolen cars packed with drugs into Slovenia, from where they fan out across Europe.

The conflict in Kosovo has also provided the Albanian gangs with the opportunity to move into illegal immigration. While Britain looks sympathetically upon refugees from Kosovo, most of those claiming to be so are actually from Albania.

Even some of the genuine Kosovans are said by immigration officials to be economic migrants since they can afford the high fees charged by the gangs to provide false documents and transport across Europe.

There is growing concern among the police at the potential for Kosovan involvement in serious crimes, given their links with drug trafficking elsewhere in Europe. Pascal Auchlin, a Swiss criminologist, said: 'In half-a-dozen Western countries, there is now an ant's trail of individual drugs traffickers; a trail that leads right to Kosovo.'

Since the collapse of the Soviet bloc, illegal immigration into Europe has become big business. Criminal gangs have been attracted to the profits that can be made.

The most noticeable development in the flow of asylum seekers to the UK in recent years has been the involvement of gangs, where in the past individual agents would have performed the task on a much lesser scale.

They offer packages, often costing thousands of pounds, that can include false papers, transport – including access to lorries travelling to Britain – legal advice and contacts at the other end. Many, however, are just dumped once they are in the country.

While Albanians and Kosovans are by no means the only nationalities seeking entry to Britain – the number of Chinese and Sri Lankans is also high – they pose the most immediate burden on the system.

The organisation behind their migration is also a sign of how the problem might worsen if instability in the Balkans continues. Once they have entered Italy by sea, they can then travel to France or Belgium without showing any documentation. Many, however, have forged papers to ease the most difficult leg of the journey to the UK.

It is not the continued existence of border controls in the UK that they are worried about. It is the knowledge that the ferry companies, the airlines and, now, Eurostar from Brussels may turn them away if they do not have documents. The British Government fines carriers heavily for each passenger arriving without proper papers.

Tighter controls at the Channel ports have led to more and more refugees using clandestine means to enter Britain, often in lorries. Some illegals travel all the way from eastern Europe, sometimes with their families, on board trailers bound for the UK.

Albanians and Kosovans are by no means the only nationalities seeking entry to Britain – the number of Chinese and Sri Lankans is also high

---

Others hide on lorries parked at French and Belgian ports. The gangs and agents often look for vehicles going to the smaller British ports. Among the favourite destinations are Purfleet, Felixstowe, Ramsgate, Hull and the unmanned ports of Dagenham and Dartford.

Often, drivers have no idea the stowaways are on board until they make themselves known on arrival in Britain.

If they are intercepted at the port by British immigration officials, the clandestines need only claim asylum to be allowed to stay and then enter the system.

They cannot be returned as illegal entrants immediately, and a European agreement known as the Dublin Convention that was meant to share the burden of illegal immigration has proved a failure.

If they get into the country without being discovered, they either disappear or make themselves known to police. In the past, they would be taken to a police station and then be visited by immigration officials.

But the system is now under such pressure that the police, especially in the South-East, are advised to give the refugees a leaflet – now printed in Albanian – with details of how to reach the immigration reception centre at Croydon.

Many do so, as they need to get into the system in order to claim benefit or local authority assistance. But there is no way of knowing how many others just disappear.

© *Telegraph Group Limited, London 1998*

International comparisons

Asylum applications by country January to December 1998

Country	Applications
Austria	13,805
Belgium***	21,965
Denmark	5,699
Finland	1,272
France*	22,375
Germany****	98,644
Ireland	4,626
Italy	6,939
Netherlands	45, 217
Norway	8,277
Spain	6,639
Sweden	12,844
Switzerland	41,302
UK**	58,000
Total EU	**347,604**
Australia	7,992
Canada	24,937
USA	52,081

*   Data does not include accompanied inors dependants
**   Monthly/quarterly data on asylum applications does not include dependants. Yearly estimated include dependants
***   Data on asylum applications does not include dependants
**** Dependants are only counted if an applications is filed separately

Source: IGC Secretariat, Geneva

Give me shelter

Incompetent and corrupt advisers are letting refugees down – and new legislation could make matters worse. Danny Lee reports

When Ne Wong arrived in Britain after escaping from political persecution in Burma, he immediately sought advice on how to apply for asylum. Undaunted by Wong's weak grasp of English, a solicitor conducted a full interview with him – without an interpreter – and failed to note down even the most basic facts that would have proved his client's claim. If another advice agency hadn't intervened, Wong's case would have been refused, leaving him to be deported into the hands of his persecutors.

Wong's case would still be shocking if it was a rare example of refugees receiving poor advice, but shoddy and even fraudulent assistance is often all that vulnerable newcomers get to help them through the labyrinthine immigration laws. Immigration minister Mike O'Brien – a lawyer himself – angered the Law Society last week with a blistering attack on the profession for failing to root out 'seamy', 'incompetent' and 'corrupt' immigration lawyers.

'A minority get good advice,' says Alasdair Mackenzie of Asylum Aid. 'The rest get bad or indifferent advice. There aren't enough good advisers and neither the OSS [Office for the Supervision of Solicitors] nor the Government is doing enough to help.'

As well as poor advice, many asylum seekers find themselves on the wrong end of legal aid scams. Mackenzie explains: 'Unscrupulous solicitors frequently ring up refugee detention centres, get a person's name, phone the Home Office to say they are representing the detainee and then claim legal aid. They then do no work but still claim payment.'

Last month, two London law firms were closed down as a result of information the Legal Aid Board gave the OSS, which has been widely criticised in the past for not being tough enough on wayward solicitors.

Another 40 firms are under investigation.

Immigration solicitor Jane Coker sees the trail of havoc wreaked by shoddy advisers: 'If a client comes to us from one of a number of firms, we will automatically take the case on. There are others where we know the advice is good, so we would not take the client on. There is no point in changing solicitor for no good reason.'

Coker also points to a wider crisis: 'There aren't enough people who give advice on this type of law, and those who do are very overworked.'

She is talking at her office at a not untypical 7.30pm, with a mound of work still demanding her attention.

> **'There aren't enough people who give advice on this type of law, and those who do are very overworked'**

Practitioners are warning that the situation could get worse when the new Asylum and Immigration Act comes into effect, and immigration centres are scattered throughout the country to areas which may have no or few advisers.

Dealing with an immigration case is no simple task. Laws and appeal processes are notoriously complex and, says Coker, 'these are often life-and-death decisions'. European human rights laws, children, international treaties and distressed, non-English-speaking clients are just a few of the issues that need to be addressed.

These complexities are being taken into account, argues the Law Society, in its launch of a new panel of specialist immigration solicitors next June. And the Legal Aid Board (soon to become the Legal Services Commission) aims in future to award exclusive block contracts for such work only to firms who meet quality standards.

The OSS defends itself against accusations of inaction by pointing out that it has no power to investigate firms making fraudulent legal aid applications. 'We would like powers similar to the Legal Aid Board's, to enable us to demand files from suspect solicitors,' said a spokesman.

OSS director Peter Ross criticises the Home Office for failing to help it crack down. His office claims the Home Office has given it a list of about 40 practitioners and firms with no details of their suspected offences.

Much of the bad advice comes from immigration advisers who are not solicitors, says Jawaid Luqmani of the Immigration Law Practitioners' Association. 'There is a lot of poor advice from people outside the control of solicitors' organisations. It would be a good idea to have compulsory regulation by an outside body where people are giving advice for reward.'

In a speech last year, former Law Society immigration law sub-committee secretary Richard Dunstan claimed: 'The majority of lawyers and non-lawyers in the asylum field are either insufficiently competent, dishonest or both.'

Future improvements will be little comfort for asylum seekers like Wong. Without the intervention of a reputable advice agency, he might have lost any chance of remaining in this country. Others may not be so lucky, finding themselves unjustly turned away from the country that has prided itself on offering a safe haven from persecution.

Ne Wong is a pseudonym

• First published in *The Guardian*, March, 1999. © *Danny Lee*

Children of the storm

Support for young refugees in Britain

Young refugees in Britain

It is estimated that every year about 6,000 refugees under the age of 17 claim asylum in the UK; over 900 of them are not accompanied by any family members. Most are innocent victims of political turmoil and civil strife in different parts of the world who have come to Britain because their lives were threatened at home. Unfortunately, young refugees, of which there are over 40,000 in the UK, quickly find that life in the UK can be very difficult. Complicated legislation, racial stereotyping and lack of English language are just three obstacles hindering their social development and educational progress.

Under international law, a refugee is someone who 'owing to a well-founded fear of being persecuted for reasons of race, religion, nationality, membership of a particular social group or political opinion' has fled their country of origin to seek asylum elsewhere. Refugees are legally entitled to protection under the 1951 UN Convention Relating to the Status of Refugees; this protection includes access to social service benefits and education in the country in which they have chosen to take asylum. There are over 27 million refugees world-wide, only 0.5% of them claiming asylum in the UK (1997).

Although for the purposes of this article we use the term refugee to cover all young asylum seekers regardless of their status, in Britain someone is only classed as a refugee after their claim for asylum has been approved by the Home Office – only 13% of applications for refugee status in 1997 were granted.

While the need for support mechanisms for young refugees is growing, government legislation has cut services and benefits available to refugees. The Asylum and Immigration Act of 1996 took away the entitlement to benefits for large numbers of asylum seekers. As a result, in April 1997, over 2,300 families and 525 unaccompanied children were without access to benefits. Responsibility for provision of their welfare fell to local councils, charities and community groups. Faced with the inadequacy of state benefits, it is becoming increasingly incumbent on the non-governmental sector to fill in the gaps in support that asylum seekers need.

The constant changes to the law surrounding the rights of asylum seekers to social services do little to foster a young person's sense of security. Moreover, the state takes little account of the fact that an unaccompanied 16-year-old may not have the emotional maturity to cope with living alone. Eligibility for benefits depends largely on an individual's circumstances, but provision is rarely sufficient; when a refugee reaches the age of 18 for example, he/she is entitled to only £24 a week in food vouchers, and accommodation at a B&B.

Key issues facing young refugees in Britain

For most young refugees, continuing their education is their greatest wish. However, many find it very difficult to adapt to the British education system. This is partly caused by the differences between the British system and that found in their native country. In the former Yugoslavia, for example, exams are done on a continuous basis, with presentations given before the class and weekly grades averaged to give a final mark. In Somalia there is a strong oral tradition in education, much of it having its base in Islam. As such, schooling in Britain may appear not only hostile but irrelevant to their needs. Language and cultural differences make integration with their cohorts even more difficult.

While integration into British society is useful for making friends etc., it is vital that young refugees, especially those that are unaccompanied, are kept in touch with their home communities. If they are ever to go back to their homeland or be reunited with their families it is essential that they have knowledge of their native language, culture and religion. Schools will not always be able to help provide the cultural and religious education that is required, therefore it is important to put unaccompanied refugee children in touch with other people who have come to Britain from their country.

Malnutrition and post-traumatic

stress disorder are just two conditions which refugees may be suffering from on entry to the UK so comprehensive health checks on arrival are necessary. In reality often these checks do not take place, either because the children are too frightened to see a doctor, or because they do not understand what medical treatment they are entitled to or how to access it.

Being separated from their families for the first time, young unaccompanied refugees may not have the knowledge necessary to keep themselves healthy. Respons- ible attitudes towards health and lifestyles are traditionally built within the family environment so without an adult to advise them, un- accompanied youngsters are more likely to fall prey to illness.

For refugees aged 16-21, finding suitable accommodation can present a big problem. Many landlords will not accept tenants who are dependent on benefits, and most refugees – as they are not entitled to work – are dependent on the small amount which the social services are prepared to pay. In these circum- stances, finding housing can be a long and tedious process.

Background and aims
Children of the Storm (COTS) was established in 1989 to cater for the emotional and material needs of the increasing number of young asylum seekers entering Britain. The charity is founded on the belief that asylum seekers deserve to be treated with humanity and respect. We believe that we have a social responsibility to extend hospitality to those who have sought refuge in our country, especially children who are often the innocent victims of war and the least able to fend for themselves.

Children of the Storm supports refugees under the age of 21, directly and indirectly, through projects which aim to:

Raise awareness
COTS raises awareness of refugee issues in the community at large through producing information material, lobbying parliament and holding publicity events. We advo- cate change in the way benefits are issued and the way in which refugee care in schools is evaluated by the government.

Provide financial assistance
COTS runs a small grants scheme to provide emergency financial support to refugee children. Examples of items we have funded include cold weather clothes, educational mater- ials, and temporary accommodation costs.

Build schools' capacity
COTS, through the 'Schools Link' project, promotes peer support groups, and gives presentations and advice to schools and community groups on how to increase their capacity to integrate refugees and give them support.

Create opportunities
COTS runs study support schemes which assist refugee youngsters with learning English and doing home- work. Through partnership pro- grammes we give opportunities for youngsters from refugee and non- refugee communities to work and play together so as to improve mutual understanding and develop independence.

Case study
Ruba escaped from Sarajevo in an ambulance with the help of an aid agency who agreed to get her out of the war zone and pay for her studies. Her father, a doctor, was in prison, her brother in the army and her mother in Croatia.

When COTS met Ruba her relationship with the aid agency had fallen apart and she was left with nowhere to live and no support to find a suitable school. COTS got her a place in school where she immediately started studying for 'A' levels. However, Ruba's attendance at school soon dropped and during one six-month period she never went to one lesson. The main reason for this was that she was terrified to be put in an environment where she would have to make friends who she knew she would later leave.

With counselling at a local clinic, support in her school work at a study support club, and financial assistance for accommodation and educational materials, Ruba gradually regained confidence in herself and began to make friends. Good news also started arriving from home – a cease-fire was put in place, her father was released from prison and her mother had managed to join her brothers in Sarajevo. Ruba returned to Sarajevo in the summer of 1997.

The poem below was written by Ruba before she left London.

London Prose
I fear to say I love you,
    it might be the last time I see you, just like many others before you.
    So I'll pretend to be a stranger, with no feelings and no expectations.
    We could have been friends if only I came with different luggage.
    So I'll walk the streets pretend- ing not to notice the wind carrying a piece of me in it,
    or rain crying for all those left without tears.
    You can never be like the one that gave me this life and all that comes with it,
    but that wouldn't stop us from liking each other.
    Maybe I could even enjoy you, maybe it doesn't matter how long it's going to last;
    I know you are a temporary stop on a long journey, but I still know you like me.
    But it is never us who decide.
    They'll never understand that it's not about giving or taking but about sharing
    these few precious moments of my life.
    I'll remember you with sadness, love and fear.
    That way it's the best;
    you'll stay just another country where I never belonged, but found myself.
    You'll stay theirs, and yet the back piece of my brain will know the truth.
                                    E.B. 1995

Children of the Storm Services
The following projects are run by Children of the Storm:

'Schools Link' project
COTS run presentations in schools and youth clubs to highlight

problems facing young refugees in Britain and give ideas on how they can be supported within the organisation's environment. This service is free and presentations can be tailored to suit youngsters or adults.

Study support and English language training

COTS manage study support programmes to assist refugee children who are experiencing difficulties with school work and English. The programmes are run at different venues in London.

Small grants scheme

The small grants scheme provides a source of funds for young refugees in particular need. Grants are agreed by the board of trustees and are given on a one-off basis. Grant application forms are available from the COTS office.

Resources

COTS produce *Square Fish* – a video made by young refugees about their experiences in the UK – and *Invisible Students*, a book giving advice on practical ways of integrating refugees into schools. To receive these resources please send a self-addressed envelope to the address on page 41.

Partnership scheme

As a way of building individual confidence and promoting mutual understanding, COTS run a partnership scheme linking unaccompanied young refugees with local families.

• The above information is from Children of the Storm (COTS). See page 41 for address details.

© *Children of the Storm*

Young refugees in the late 1990s

Information from Children of the Storm

Since the end of the Cold War the nature of armed conflict around the globe has changed considerably. Weapons are more destructive and more easily available than ever before, and rapid shifts in the global interests of the superpowers have quickened the collapse of precarious regimes. Nationalism and ethnic rivalry have been quick to take root in the vacuum left by the collapse of the Communist ideology in the Soviet bloc, and in Africa wars are more often fought along tribal lines within countries rather than internationally.

The decades following the Second World War saw a proliferation of internal or civil wars across the globe. The 'internal' nature of these conflicts means that the traditional international peacekeeper, the United Nations, whose mandate forbids it to infringe upon a nation's sovereignty, is powerless to act in a meaningful way. Moreover, with the collapse of the Soviet bloc as a military threat, many of these war-torn countries are no longer of any strategic importance to the West, thus are not deemed worthy of external intervention.

In civil conflicts, where society splits along ethnic or religious lines, making every civilian either a friend or an enemy, the implications for children are far greater than they would be in a 'conventional' international war. In the 1990s civilians account for about 90% of war casualties and there are currently about 57 million people displaced by war world-wide, at least half of which

are children (UNICEF, 1997). In this changing context of war, children are often perversely made legitimate targets or are conscripted into the army – sometimes to fight their own people. In Bosnia and Herzegovina, for example, the rape of girls and women was used as a tool of war, and in Rwanda thousands of children were massacred, often by people who were their neighbours, when internecine violence exploded in 1994. As the arena in which battles are fought shifts from national frontiers to the areas in which families live, children are exposed to horror which can result in severe physical and mental trauma.

For parents facing these threats, their obvious and natural reaction is to remove their children from the war zone, and with modern methods of transport this is far easier than in the past. In a large number of cases movement will be to an area of the country less affected by the conflict (technically becoming an Internally Displaced Person), but the search for safety can also mean leaving the country altogether, thus meeting the United Nations' definition of a refugee. Of course, war is not the only reason that people seek refuge in other countries. Famines, natural disasters and economic factors can

also precipitate the movement of people over international boundaries for the purposes of survival.

The rights of people who have fled their home country because of an abuse of their human rights are protected by a number of internationally recognised laws and declarations. The main one is the 'UN Geneva Convention Relating to the Status of Refugees' of 1951 which states that an individual has to be granted refugee status by a host country if they can prove they have a 'well-founded fear of being persecuted for reasons of race, religion, nationality, membership of a particular social group or political opinion'. Entrants to Britain will be granted asylum if they can prove that they will be persecuted in their country of origin for one of the above 'Convention reasons'.

Most of the millions of refugees in the world are women and children and, contrary to what the press sometimes allude to, only 0.5% of them seek asylum in the UK at any one time. The bulk of refugees move to the countries bordering their country of origin – Germany in the case of former Yugoslavia, and Kenya in the case of Somalia, for example. Britain receives around 30,000 asylum applications a year; the countries of origin include: Afghanistan, Algeria, Angola, Bosnia, Colombia, Congo Kinshasa, Czech Republic, Ethiopia, India, Iran, Iraq, Kenya, Nigeria, Pakistan, Poland, Serbia, (Kosovo), Sierra Leone, Somalia, Sri Lanka, Sudan, Tanzania, Turkey, and Uganda (Refugee Council, 1997). Analysts agree that numbers of asylum seekers are likely to rise over the coming years.

71% of asylum seekers arrive in the UK at Gatwick or Heathrow airports (Immigration Research and Statistics service, May 1998). That they can afford to buy air tickets is an indication that the majority of refugees in the UK are from the upper socio-economic strata in their country of origin. Reasons for choosing Britain as a place of refuge include the presence of friends and relatives here, common language or the perception that Britain is a country which upholds human rights and will, therefore, treat asylum seekers fairly.

It is estimated that in the UK 20% of asylum seekers are children and 564 unaccompanied refugee children sought asylum in Britain in 1997 (Refugee Council, 1998). Those entering the country join the growing child refugee population mainly located in schools in London, although, for financial reasons, the Government is beginning to house new arrivals in cities like Liverpool. There are over 40,000 refugee children in schools in the UK at present.

© *Children of the Storm* (COTS)

Straw backs fingerprint bank to fight asylum fraud

Jack Straw last night welcomed an agreement in Brussels which could cut the number of bogus asylum seekers and illegal immigrants entering Britain.

EU Home Affairs Ministers decided to set up a Europe-wide computer database to store their fingerprints.

All asylum seekers and illegal immigrants entering other EU countries will now be fingerprinted, as they are already by Britain.

The data will be available to all 15 EU states, so that applicants refused entry to one country, or expelled, cannot change their papers and try to enter a neighbouring country.

The Home Secretary, who attended the Brussels meeting, said: 'This is an important decision. There is real abuse by criminal gangs and economic migrants, and it must end. This database will greatly improve the enforcement of the rules.'

By John Fraser in Brussels

He said that illegal immigrants and bogus asylum seekers were placing 'huge pressure' on councils in many inner London boroughs and in Kent.

Last week, Home Office figures showed that a record number applied for asylum in Britain in October. The figure of 5,010 was a 67 per cent rise on the same month last year. It is feared more than 44,000 will seek asylum this year – another record.

All asylum seekers and illegal immigrants entering other EU countries will now be fingerprinted, as they are already by Britain

Yesterday's meeting of Ministers also agreed other moves to curb the rising tide of asylum seekers.

They decided to set up a European task force to reduce the flow at source by tackling the economic, social and safety problems that cause asylum seekers to flee their own countries and head for the EU.

The Dutch are planning to install cameras at frontier crossing points to stem the tide of illegal immigrants and criminals entering Holland.

They come and go as they please since Holland dropped border checks on EU travellers under the Schengen Agreement.

The laser cameras have been developed by Neurodynamics of Cambridge. Within three seconds, the photos they take can be compared with pictures of known criminals stored on a database.

© *The Daily Mail* December, 1998

Fortress Europe's four circles of purgatory

This week President Vaclev Havel of the Czech Republic is in London pressing his country's case for crossing the moat and joining the countries behind the battlements. Soon there could be an extra admission charge, says Alan Travis – signing up to a highly restrictive policy on asylum seekers and tighter controls on the movement of potential immigrants.

Britain's procedures for coping with refugees and asylum seekers are breaking down. The treatment accorded Slovak gypsies at Dover claiming abuse of their civil rights at home and people fleeing the conflict in Kosovo has recently shown the holes. When more than 250 Kosovar asylum seekers arrived at Heathrow in one week this summer the system of support for would-be refugees was shown to be a patchwork. One London local authority, Ealing, even went as far as to refuse to help any more in spite of its legal obligations and instead challenged the refugee welfare organisations to sort out the mess.

Ealing's refusal to help triggered yet another Whitehall mini-crisis in asylum policy – the latest in a long line of high court battles and high profile government crackdowns. It is a story familiar to the authorities in nearly all the capitals of Europe. It's a product of the piecemeal way in which the European Union has built its 'Fortress Europe' approach to migration in the past four years.

But now the Austrians, traditionally tight in control of their borders, at least to their east, hold the presidency of the EU and have put forward a plan which is gathering widespread support. It envisages a uniform EU immigration and asylum policy which would effectively tear up the traditional legal right of individuals to claim asylum which is enshrined in the Geneva Convention. Instead of a right to settle in the country to which asylum seekers have come seeking succour,

the Austrian paper proposes a new system of temporary protection, perhaps even involving putting asylum seekers in camps.

Essentially the presidency strategy now doing the rounds in Brussels argues that the 1951 convention is out of date. The argument runs that this was a document of its times; it was framed by, amongst others, British civil servants to cope with refugees fleeing the authoritarian cold-war regimes of the communist world. It could not have been intended to cope with emergency influxes by those displaced by inter-ethnic conflicts or to deal with sustained mass emigration from crisis regions particularly in Africa and other parts of the Third World.

So, instead of guaranteeing a legal right to asylum the Austrians are suggesting that the Geneva Convention should be 'supplemented', amended or replaced'. In its place EU countries would make only a 'political offer' to those on the move if they chose. This would mean that in future asylum would cease to be a legal status based on right;

'Immigration continues to exceed 1.5 million immigrants per annum, and the proportion of illegal immigrants in this total has clearly increased'

---

protection would only be temporarily offered. Indeed the EU paper actually criticises the Geneva Convention for encouraging refugees to settle permanently in the host country.

This confidential set of proposals was tabled in the EU's secret K4 committee the day after the British government stepped down from the presidency. The disclosure of its existence by the Austrian paper *Die Presse* has caused alarm amongst human rights campaigners across Europe. They have already attacked it as 'dangerously Euro-centric'. It is due to be discussed in the Justice and Home Affairs Council of Ministers meeting in December.

Are the criticisms just when, surely, something has to be done? The Austrians' underlying approach is made clear by the paper's explicit assumption that 'no European country today would consider going it alone in opening up the right to asylum'. Its theme is not how the EU needs to give asylum to genuine refugees but how to deter future waves of illegal immigration.

The analysis upon which it is proposed to sweep away this basic human right – to find assistance and a place to stay outside one's home country when it becomes oppressive – starts with the idea that the EU's 'Fortress Europe' policy has failed to halt the 'incessant influx of illegal migrants' in the last five years. More than 70 immigration and asylum measures have been adopted by the Council of Ministers in the past five years but migration flows to Europe show no signs of abating.

Asylum *was* the issue of the early 1990s, the paper says, when the war in the Balkans and the collapse of Eastern Europe led to the largest mass movement of people in Europe since the Second World War. Some 10 million people left their homes over five years and 4 million of them came to Western Europe. The

number of asylum seekers heading for the EU has 'stabilised and is even following a constant downward trend' but the paper says this has happened without a similar drop in the number of illegal immigrants; 'Asylum reforms enacted in many EU countries have made it less attractive for illegal immigrants to seek asylum so that many of them now refrain from taking this step.'

But the paper says the EU has failed to achieve 'the really crucial breakthrough' of reducing the number of manifestly unfounded applications for asylum. It suggests that the question of what it calls the abuse of the 'asylum business' and how to combat and expel the rising number of illegal migrants and the traffickers behind them is where political interest now lies. 'Only once in the last four years has the EU been able to prevent a mass exodus through a successful package of measures and that was in Albania in 1997. However experiences in connection with the influx of Kurds and with Kosovo tend to give rise to scepticism,' it says.

But such failures by the EU are not the only reasons the Austrian Ministry of the Interior cites as to why it is necessary to develop an entirely new Europe-wide asylum and immigration strategy. 'The situation in Africa is now much worse than a decade ago,' it states bluntly. 'Each year 80 million young people reach working age there and 100 million in this part of the world migrate to the large metropolitan centres, without really having any chance of an occupation offering a secure livelihood.

'For migration towards the rich, especially western European, states, this means that total immigration continues to exceed 1.5 million immigrants per annum, and the proportion of illegal immigrants in this total has clearly increased. It must now be assumed that every other immigrant in the First World is there illegally.'

To deal with this situation it proposes to replace the current Fortress Europe strategy with one based on 'concentric circles'. Inside the fortress are the target countries, which need high levels of border

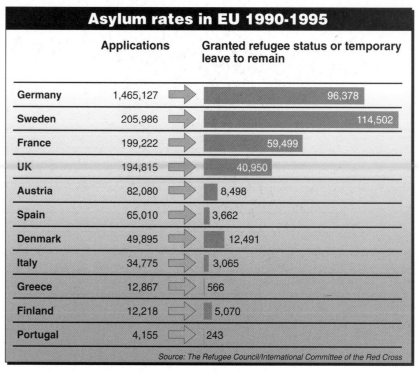

Asylum rates in EU 1990-1995

	Applications	Granted refugee status or temporary leave to remain
Germany	1,465,127	96,378
Sweden	205,986	114,502
France	199,222	59,499
UK	194,815	40,950
Austria	82,080	8,498
Spain	65,010	3,662
Denmark	49,895	12,491
Italy	34,775	3,065
Greece	12,867	566
Finland	12,218	5,070
Portugal	4,155	243

Source: The Refugee Council/International Committee of the Red Cross

'It must now be assumed that every other immigrant in the First World is there illegally'

controls, stiff visa policies, guarantees for genuine refugees and a common policy of returning all those who cross borders illegally. Then there are the other members of the European Union, Britain especially, which have not signed the Schengen accord for harmonising border controls and policing of migration. Countries aspiring to join the EU would be expected to assume all the obligations though the Austrians intriguingly say 'linking financial benefits and the granting of privileges to specific objectives in the migration field is clearly prohibited'. Should it be?

At the moment some of these countries (in the east of Europe for example) are 'transit countries', which no longer produce people wanting to move into the EU but which do not control the movement of people very effectively. Visa restrictions will need to apply.

The fourth 'outer' circle would be main migrant producing countries of the Middle East, China, and black Africa. In these countries, the paper argues, the whole range of EU

migration policies needs to be effective. As well as an increased aid programme to prevent mass exoduses it talks of a 'penal and police policy of zero tolerance of those who facilitate illegal immigration' from these parts of the globe. Progress in stopping outflow of people would serve as an important criterion when decisions about aid are taken.

It is an alarming paper. So far the British Government Office has not yet taken a position. However, the signs so far from Brussels are that it could well prove a runner and British ministers will have to decide whether they too want to build the fortress walls thicker and higher.

Yet if Britain does decide to oppose this radical rewriting of the Geneva Convention one aspect is worth keeping. For the first time policy would draw a link between the EU's policy on overseas aid and asylum. Before the election Labour promised to tackle the root causes of illegal immigration. 'Poverty, instability and conflict in the developing world push people out and set up migration streams,' said Jack Straw in a policy document. 'In government we would promote human rights and democracy and start to shift resources towards programmes that helped the poorest people in the poorest countries.'

© The Guardian October, 1998

Brussels is dumping refugees in London

By Philip Johnston, Home Affairs Editor

Hundreds of bogus asylum seekers are travelling to Britain from Belgium on Eurostar trains after being ordered to leave Europe's 'open-borders' Schengen area.

They have been arriving in London bearing a seven-day 'notice to quit' from Belgium. The document also stipulates that they should leave the territory of the other Schengen signatories – Germany, Austria, Spain, France, Greece, Italy, Luxembourg, Holland and Portugal. This effectively leaves Britain as the only option.

In the past four weeks 140 Kenyan asylum seekers and more than 250 from the former Yugoslavia have arrived from Belgium without proper documents. Immigration officers want ministers to lodge a formal complaint with Belgium over a practice that highlights the growing shambles of European asylum policy.

The Home Office said last night: 'We are aware this is an increasing problem and are in discussions at an operational level with our opposite numbers in Belgium to try to resolve it. Consideration will be given to taking the matter up at a higher level if we don't find ourselves coming to sensible solutions.'

The latest development has alarmed officials who have had to cope in recent months with an influx of Somalis arriving on the Eurostar from Paris and coach loads of Slovak gypsies at Dover. But while they appear to have first declared their status on arriving in Britain – despite travelling through other European Union countries – the latest group has clearly had contact with Belgian police.

The responsibility for dealing with asylum seekers entering the EU has been complicated by controversy over the Dublin Convention, an agreement that came into force last September.

Until then, the EU state in which applicants first arrived was obliged to deal with them and if they came to Britain, they could be returned. Since September, however, the safe country is deemed to be not the first Union state they reach – but the country where they seek asylum.

It is not clear whether the latest refugees have applied for asylum in Belgium – which should in any case be recorded on a central database. Most have indicated that they have not applied for asylum before arriving at Waterloo station.

'They appear to have been bundled on a train bound for London,' one source said.

According to immigration sources, some of the asylum seekers have already been to other parts of the EU, particularly Germany and Holland. 'What the Belgians are doing is completely unethical,' said a source.

The Eurostar is also being used because there are no immigration checks at Brussels and the service is not subject to so-called carriers' liability, which affects airlines and ferry companies.

They face a £2,000-a-head fine if they bring in bogus refugees whose papers are not in order and are required to pay for their repatriation.

Last summer, after an influx of Somalis from France, the Home Office threatened Eurostar with similar penalties but it is thought John Prescott, the Deputy Prime Minister, is opposing the move because of the financial problems affecting the company.

Tighter controls have been introduced at the Gare du Nord terminal in Paris and Whitehall sources said that while the Paris problem has declined it might merely have been pushed on to Brussels.

Figures published by the EU this week showed that the influx of asylum seekers to Britain dropped sharply in 1996 as a result of stopping the payment of benefits and a decline in applicants from the former Yugoslavia.

But Britain still has one of the highest levels of applications in Europe, with almost 30,000 in 1996. Only Germany – 117,333 – dealt with more. France received 17,153, Spain 4,730 and Italy 681. Applications for asylum in the EU as a whole fell by 16 per cent from 274, 000 in 1995 to 226,000 in 1996.

© Telegraph Group Limited, London 1998

Refugees and asylum seekers world-wide

Beginning in 1989, these figures include the number of new asylum applications during the year in countries with asylum adjudication procedures, primarily in Europe and North America. Figures given represent the number of refugees and asylum seekers at year's end.

Year	Number
1989	15,100,000
1990	16,700,000
1991	16,600,000
1992	17,600,000
1993	16,300,000
1994	16,300,000
1995	15,300,000
1996	14,500,000
1997	13,600,000

Source: U.S. Committee for Refugees (USCR)

Ministers may tag refugees

By Lucy Ward and Vikram Dodd

Refugee groups last night reacted with anger after the Government revealed it was considering electronically tagging asylum seekers.

Ministers disclosed that the move followed concern at the numbers who vanish from the sight of the Immigration Service while awaiting the outcome of their cases.

The Home Office is studying trials of tagging of criminals on parole to gauge whether that approach could be used for asylum seekers as an alternative to detention.

Home Office minister Lord Williams of Mostyn told Liberal Democrat Lord Avebury in a Lords written reply last night: 'We are following with interest the pilot schemes for the use of electronic tagging within the criminal justice system and will, in due course, consider whether a similar system would be beneficial to the Immigration Service.'

Amnesty International last night condemned the proposal. Spokeswoman Androulla Kyrilloy said: 'This is another example of the Government treating asylum seekers as if they are criminals.'

Nick Hardwick, director of the Refugee Council, condemned the proposal as a 'big brother control'. He said: 'This will send a shiver down everybody's spine.'

Saying he feared large numbers of people seeking refuge here would be tagged, he added: 'We are talking about people who have not been accused of any criminal offence. It's not clear if there would be any safeguards. The danger is this would be used indiscriminately without any reference to the courts.

> **'Under the current system it is simply up to an immigration officer to detain someone without reference to the courts. Presumably tagging would work the same way'**

'It is fundamentally wrong to restrict someone's liberty and exercise big brother control without a specific reason to do so. Where does it stop?

'Under the current system it is simply up to an immigration officer to detain someone without reference to the courts. Presumably tagging would work the same way'.

He added that tagging asylum seekers could only be justified for 'specific reasons relating to the individual'.

Last night the Home Office sought to play down the proposal. A spokeswoman said: 'Ministers will not even look at the issue until the pilots (of tagging of criminals) are completed. It is possible it may prove impractical.'

Home Office statistics show that around 1.5 per cent of all asylum seekers are detained. In 1997, there were 32,500 applications for asylum. According to Government figures, the backlog of cases still to be fully processed was 76,000 in July.

In dealing with asylum seekers, the Government has attempted to combine tough proposals aimed at curbing fraud with an effective amnesty for some 30,000 long-term applicants and their families.

An asylum bill expected in next month's Queen's Speech will pave the way for the amnesty – together with a plan to disperse the remaining asylum seekers whose cases are unresolved to hostels and B & B accommodation in order to ease the burden of provision for local authorities in London.

Applicants will no longer receive welfare benefits while their cases are being processed, but will receive 'in kind' vouchers to exchange for food and other essentials, with cash payments kept to a minimum.

© *The Guardian*
October, 1998

35

Detention more likely for refugees

By Alan Travis,
Home Affairs Editor

A large-scale expansion in the detention of asylum seekers in special centres is being considered by ministers in an overhaul of Britain's refugee and immigration system.

A sharp increase in the 800 asylum seekers now detained without charge is expected to provoke a row among Labour MPs.

Later this week, two damning inquiries into conditions at the country's biggest detention centre, Campsfield House, Oxfordshire, will be published. David Ramsbotham, the Chief Inspector of Prisons, is expected to be critical of the way the centre is run by Group 4, as well as scathing in his judgement about asylum policy.

Whitehall officials, grappling with how to improve a system that has a backlog of 76,000 cases, some dating back more than five years, believe extending detention will tighten asylum policy and ensure it is not seen as 'a soft touch' for economic migrants.

Ministers are believed to want to see a sharp increase in the number of detentions for those who have appealed against being refused asylum or who are awaiting deportation. A proposal to introduce some form of judicial scrutiny of the decision by immigration officers to detain individuals by the courts, is believed to have been rejected.

The alternative to an extension of detention is to start 'chartering planes' to increase deportations from Britain of failed asylum seekers. Only a small proportion of rejected asylum seekers are removed from the country.

Whichever option is adopted, ministers will insist asylum applicants report weekly to a police station so that they cannot 'disappear'.

But these tougher moves are expected to be accompanied by limited restoration of welfare benefits for most asylum applicants, a quicker and fairer appeals system, and the permission to stay for about 10,000 people who have been awaiting a decision for more than five years.

The package, to be announced in July, is emerging from Whitehall reviews of the asylum and immigration system. Civil servants have told Home Office ministers that the entire system is now 'a complete shambles' and costs £500 million a year to run. They warn that if nothing is done the bill will rise to £800 million annually by 2002.

The 10,000 applicants who have been waiting since 1992 for their cases to be resolved, may soon be allowed to stay – although talk of an 'amnesty' will be strongly resisted for political reasons. Those who cannot return, or whose cases are too difficult to resolve, could get 'exceptional leave to remain', a classification just short of full refugee status. Many of these people have now put down roots in Britain.

The initial interviews of asylum seekers will also be improved, through a training programme and a shorter but fairer system of appeals. Appeal tribunals will be chaired by a High Court judge, and only one hearing will be allowed, but humanitarian grounds will be admissible for the first time. Rulings in one case will set a precedent for others.

The Home Office has already announced that it will publish the secret rule books guiding immigration decisions, and the 'country assessments' that determine asylum applications.

Ministers are also considering ways of restoring welfare benefits through 'an asylum seekers' allowance', which would fall short of full Income Support but be higher than the legal basic rate for food and accommodation provided by local authorities.

A draconian option of all asylum seekers staying for a month in a very basic reception centre before being able to claim welfare benefits, has been rejected. Officials fear that such sparse conditions – as a deterrent to late asylum applications from, say, east European au pairs – could cause riots.

Instead, a proposal is to ban 'under serving' applicants from the allowance. These would be allowed a 'food, warmth and shelter' safety net, but it would be administered by the Government rather than local authorities.

Nearly 250,000 asylum seekers are thought to have settled in London since 1990 and been absorbed without much conflict. But so far little has been done to address their problems.

© The Guardian
April, 1998

... YOU WANT TO SEEK ASYLUM FROM THE GOVERNMENT YOU'RE ALREADY SEEKING ASYLUM WITH?! — I ESCAPE DEATH FOR DETENTION.

One in three asylum seekers told to stay

Revealed, how campaign to stem migrant flood is faltering

By Sonia Purnell, Whitehall Editor

Jack Straw faced embarrassment last night as it emerged that almost one-third of new asylum seekers have been allowed to remain in Britain.

Despite a campaign to tighten the system, nearly one in three of the 42,925 who applied in the past 12 months have already been granted permission to stay.

That represents a 50 per cent increase in successful applications since Mr Straw became Home Secretary.

Last year, 20 per cent of asylum seekers were successful, but now the figure is 30 per cent.

Of these, 17 per cent were granted full asylum and another 13 per cent granted exceptional leave to stay in the country, which immigration officials consider to be a virtually indistinguishable status.

The figures, published by the Home Office, represent a serious blow for the Government's stated attempts to stem the flood of immigrants. They also show that the number of asylum seekers rose by 55 per cent in September compared with a year ago. By the end of this year, the total number of people seeking asylum is bound to exceed the previous record for a year.

That was in 1991, when 44,840 migrants sought refuge in Britain.

By Christmas, on present trends, about 15,000 asylum seekers from across the globe will have been granted leave to stay during 1998.

The figures, released on a dedicated computer website yesterday, will spark charges that the Government has 'gone soft' on winning the war against bogus asylum seekers. Immigration officials fear the high approval rate will simply spur yet more migrants to try their luck here – raising the prospect of some of London's parks being turned into 'tent cities' to accommodate them.

September's 4,455 applicants is believed to be the highest number ever, followed closely by the numbers recorded in August and July.

Britain is now the second most popular country in Europe behind Germany among asylum seekers, having recently overtaken the Netherlands.

A benefits crackdown under the last government reduced applications for a while, but the decline was reversed last year.

Migrants from the former

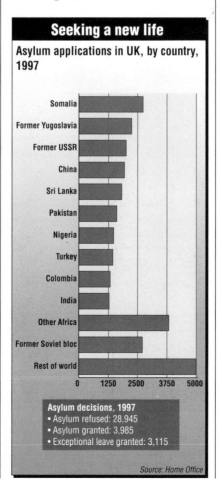

Seeking a new life

Asylum applications in UK, by country, 1997

(bar chart, countries top to bottom: Somalia, Former Yugoslavia, Former USSR, China, Sri Lanka, Pakistan, Nigeria, Turkey, Colombia, India, Other Africa, Former Soviet bloc, Rest of world; x-axis 0, 1250, 2500, 3750, 5000)

Asylum decisions, 1997
- Asylum refused: 28,945
- Asylum granted: 3,985
- Exceptional leave granted: 3,115

Source: Home Office

Yugoslavia continue to be the largest single group of asylum seekers.

They made up a total of 3,300 applications during the four months up to September as the unrest in the ethnic Albanian province of Kosovo continued.

Applications from Czech and Slovak gypsies claiming persecution at home also soared from 70 a year ago to 340 in September.

Otherwise Somalis, Sri Lankans, Turks and Afganistanis were the most frequent nationals to seek asylum. While a number of refugees are genuine victims of persecution, the cost of supporting the colossal official system which processes asylum seekers could reach £3 billion this year, the equivalent of 1.5p on income tax.

Applicants are provided with health care, housing, education and, until now, benefits – although these are expected to be replaced soon with payments in kind consisting of food, clothes and toiletries.

In the last ten years, the cost of dealing with asylum seekers is believed to have been £12 billion, equal to the Government's annual housing and transport budgets combined.

London councils alone say it costs them £2 million a week to house 20,000 refugees.

It is thought that some 60,000 illegal immigrants are 'missing' in the system, thousands of whom will now be granted an amnesty allowing them to stay as part of a desperate bid to clear huge backlogs of applications and appeals stretching over the past decade.

The overload has led to threats of industrial action by immigration officers at Dover and Heathrow, where the brunt of the crisis is borne.

Overhaul of 'shambolic' asylum laws

By Philip Johnston,
Home Affairs Editor

Nearly 60,000 asylum seekers who have entered Britain since 1989 are unaccounted for, according to an analysis of official figures published as the Government begins a fresh attempt to reform the 'shambles' of the current legal framework. Legislation to be announced in the Queen's Speech tomorrow will include proposals to remove cash benefits for refugees and dictate where they should live.

Ministers also want to speed up the appeals system for deciding whether asylum seekers are genuinely fleeing persecution in their homelands or can be classed as 'economic migrants'. However, disagreements continue in Whitehall over whether senior judges should – or would even wish to – preside over a single-tier appeals system.

The Government has also been unable to find a way of stopping unsuccessful applicants making a final appeal by means of judicial review – a rapidly-expanding last resort for many refugees that causes further backlogs in the system.

The Home Office has condemned the current legal framework as a 'shambles' and ministers believe it is being used as a back-door method of immigration to Britain. Even though fewer than one-quarter of asylum seekers are given refugee status or exceptional leave to remain, fewer than 10 per cent are removed.

Of the 268,595 who have come to Britain in the past 10 years, 14,685 have been granted asylum. Yet only 20,000 are known to have been removed or have voluntarily departed the country.

Figures prepared by the Immigration Service Union (ISU) also show that 59,198 – or 22 per cent of the total – are unaccounted for when the numbers still in the appeals system are taken into consideration. It means that more than 180,000 asylum seekers remain in Britain without permission, not counting their dependants.

John Tincey, research director at the ISU, who has compiled the figures, said the annual cost of asylum – including welfare, housing, education and health provision – is £2 billion and the cumulative cost over the last decade £12 billion.

This is disputed by the Government, which says it is closer to £500 million per annum. However, an internal Treasury estimate assumed that £20,000 a year for each principal applicant – not including dependants – was a 'reasonable figure'.

Mr Tincey said: 'Is the public willing to go on supporting these, and ever-increasing, costs? Is allowing any individual to come to Britain to make an asylum application, rather than seeking out refugees where they are suffering, a viable response to modern refugee problems?'

Legislation to be announced tomorrow will endeavour to make good the Government's pledge of a 'firmer, faster, fairer' asylum system. Its twin aims are to make Britain a less attractive proposition to economic migrants by tightening controls over benefit payments and speeding up the appeals procedure.

In future, support for asylum seekers would be separate from existing welfare arrangements. There

> **Even though fewer than one-quarter of asylum seekers are given refugee status or exceptional leave to remain, fewer than 10 per cent are removed**

would be no cash available for accommodation and this would be offered on a 'no choice' basis. Other needs under a new national support system administered by the Home Office would be met by providing vouchers for food and clothing.

Local authorities will no longer be obliged to carry the burden of looking after asylum seekers, though they would be expected to assist where possible – including making housing available on a contractual basis.

Ministers are also determined that asylum seekers should be required to pursue appeals in jurisdictions where there is little or no backlog. Some London tribunals can take two years or more to hear a case, while courts in the provinces have a waiting list of only a few weeks.

One minister said: 'There is no reason why they should not go to Leeds or Liverpool for a case to be heard and if they don't turn up they will be deemed to have lost.'

The Bill will coincide with renewed efforts in Europe to deal with economic migration. An Austrian presidency paper to be discussed by interior ministers next month says the fight against illegal immigration is 'not proving successful'.

It adds: 'Asylum applicants make up a major proportion of immigrants. An asylum application is, after the visa, the most frequent entry ticket to Europe for people who are not refugees.'

However, the European Council of Refugees and Exiles said: 'This stigmatises all asylum seekers as potential immigrants in disguise and with fraudulent intent.

'It is up to host states to ensure that asylum seekers whose applications are properly rejected are not allowed to stay as *de facto* immigrants. It is a problem of exit, not entry.'

Somalis swell the queue for asylum

A record number of asylum seekers entered Britain last month, according to latest figures.

But only one in seven of the 5,060 refugees came from war-torn Kosovo or Serbia, despite widescale ethnic cleansing by Slobodan Milosevic's army.

The largest number came from Somalia and, at 760, was more than double the number of Kosovar Albanians airlifted to Britain since the start of the Balkans conflict. March's figure, the highest ever monthly level, also included hundreds of people from countries like Romania, Croatia, India, Sri Lanka, Pakistan and the former Soviet Union, where no new crises have broken out in recent months.

Yesterday critics of the asylum system claimed that the new figures are a dramatic illustration of the way economic migrants are exploiting the rules at the expense of the truly needy.

Martin Slade, general secretary of the Immigration Service Union, said: 'A lot of those refugees who can get here do not appear to come from places which are particularly troubled.'

The March figures show 755 asylum seekers came from the Federal Republic of Yugoslavia, which includes Kosovo, Serbia and Montenegro, after making their own way to the UK. Mr Slade added: 'Kosovar Albanian refugees who are in dire need of help have no way of getting to Britain.

'Those that have arrived are, we believe, middle-class Albanians, people who have enough money to pay for transport. The real refugees have nothing.'

Nato bombing of Serbia began on March 24 and refugees began pouring into Macedonia and Albania within two days. But Nato and the Government say many Kosovar Albanians were being driven from their homes in the preceding weeks.

By Steve Doughty, Social Affairs Correspondent

By contrast, large-scale fighting in Somalia ended in 1996.

The 5,000 asylum seekers a month level has been topped twice in the last six months – 5,010 refugees came in during October – as against figures of just over 3,000 early last year.

> **The largest number came from Somalia and, at 760, was more than double the number of Kosovar Albanians airlifted to Britain since the start of the Balkans conflict**

The statistics also show that 54,455 asylum seekers entered the country in the year up to March, compared with just over 46,000 in the year to December.

The numbers are rising despite the Government's 'Fairer, Faster and Firmer' policy designed to discourage economic asylum seekers, which includes new legislation to limit where refugees can live and cut back on cash handouts. The figures also show that changes to the way cases are handled have cut the number of decisions made on whether or not claimants are genuine.

In March, 1,855 asylum decisions were made, two-thirds of the number made in November. Mr Slade said: 'Enforcement officers have nothing to do because no decisions are coming from management. Bogus asylum seekers are not being deported.

'The Government seems to spend its time blaming the previous government.'

The number of Slovakian asylum seekers, who arrived in large numbers last year, has slumped after new visa rules fining airlines for carrying travellers without proper papers.

© The Daily Mail May, 1999

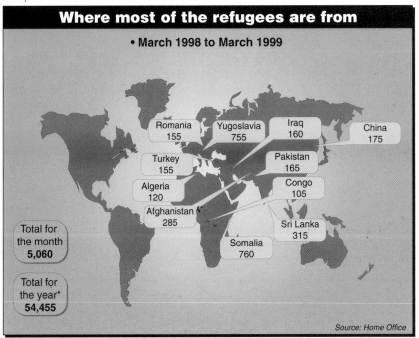

Where most of the refugees are from
• March 1998 to March 1999

Romania 155 · Yugoslavia 755 · Iraq 160 · China 175 · Turkey 155 · Pakistan 165 · Algeria 120 · Congo 105 · Afghanistan 285 · Sri Lanka 315 · Somalia 760

Total for the month **5,060**

Total for the year* **54,455**

Source: Home Office

More cash for asylum seekers

*By Alan Travis,
Home Affairs Editor*

Home office ministers are to increase the daily cash allowance for asylum seekers to £1 for adults and 50p for each child following protests over the new asylum bill.

But any increase will be accompanied by a cut in the value of the proposed food and accommodation vouchers that asylum seekers will have to rely on once Labour's legislation becomes law.

This is because the overall value of the support package at £90.80 a week for two adults and two children will remain unchanged at 70% of income support levels.

The daily cash rates are at the centre of protests over the bill, which will be heard again when MPs reconvene to discuss its committee stage tomorrow. They come as Home Office ministers have renewed an instruction that no Kosovans should be held in detention centres or prisons for immigration or asylum reasons.

The immigration minister, Mike O'Brien, has told MPs: 'We have agreed to consult further on the amount of cash that will be provided, but our view is that it is necessary to have a system involving some form of alternative support, which may take the form of vouchers, direct provision, or a number of other options.'

The support package for asylum seekers will provide furnished accommodation, including utensils, linen and other provisions, and will cover council tax, gas and electricity bills. For a family of four it amounts to £90.80 a week, of which £21 will be paid in cash.

Thousands supermarket checkout staff will have to be told how to operate the voucher system. At present asylum vouchers can only be used in one designated supermarket in each area but ministers are to hold talks with the supermarket chains to ensure there is wider choice.

Although the voucher system is to be introduced to deter those who abuse the asylum system, Mr O'Brien has conceded that the Home Office will need to find ways to ensure a black market does not develop in 'asylos', as the vouchers have been dubbed.

Ministers have also made clear that those asylum seekers who have savings or significant capital tied up in gold or jewellery will not get even the minimum levels of support. The social security system 'disregard' of the first £3,000 of savings will not apply. Instead an asylum seeker with say £2,900 in personal valuables such as gold jewellery will not be regarded as destitute and will be expected to sell them before receiving assistance.

Detailed regulations accompanying the bill also make clear that an asylum seeker who causes criminal damage to accommodation will lose the right to claim the support package and will be evicted.

Mr O'Brien yesterday dismissed a report that the immigration and asylum system was on the point of collapse, saying claims of telephone calls going unanswered and sacks of letters left unopened at the immigration service's Croydon headquarters were out of date.

'The control is not about to collapse. The Home Secretary has set up a task force to sort out the problem and a recovery programme has been in place for some time,' said Mr O'Brien. 'Staff recruitment is up and the immigration and nationality directorate has been given priority to receive newly promoted staff from the Home Office.'

*© The Guardian
May, 1999*

ADDITIONAL RESOURCES

You might like to contact the following organisations for further information. Due to the increasing cost of postage, many organisations cannot respond to enquiries unless they receive a stamped, addressed envelope.

ActionAid
Hamlyn House
MacDonald Road
London, N19 5PG
Tel: 0171 281 4101
Fax: 0171 281 5146
Web site: www.actionaid.org
A charity working with children, families and communities to improve the quality of life in some of the poorest parts of the world. Ask for their publications list.

Amnesty International UK
Youth Action Network
99-119 Roseberry Avenue
London, EC1R 4RE
Tel: 0171 814 6200
Fax: 0171 833 1510
Youth Action is the youth movement of Amnesty International, made up of around 10,000 young people. The majority are involved in one of Amnesty's Youth Action Groups. They produce action magazines and newsletters and are involved in campaign activities. Contact them at the above address or e-mail them on student@amnesty.org.uk

Asylum Aid
244a Upper Street
London, N1 1RU
Tel: 0171 359 4026
Fax: 0171 354 9187
E-mail: asylumaid@geo2.poptel.org.uk
Web site: www.asylumaid.org.uk
Provides advice and representation to refugees and asylum seekers in the UK.

Children of the Storm (COTS)
61 Oak Grove, Cricklewood
London, NW2 3LS
Tel: 0181 450 0223
COTS was established in 1989 to cater for the emotional and material needs of the increasing number of young asylum seekers entering Britain. The charity was founded on the belief that asylum seekers deserve to be treated with humanity and respect.

HelpAge International (HAI)
3rd Floor, 67-74 Saffron Hill
London, EC1N 8QX
Tel: 0171 404 7201
Fax: 0171 404 7203
E-mail: hai@helpage.org
Web site: www.oneworld.org/helpage
HelpAge International is a global network of not-for-profit organisations working with and for disadvantaged older people world-wide to achieve a lasting improvement in the quality of their lives. There are over 50 member organisations throughout the world.

International Committee of the Red Cross (ICRC)
Public Information Centre
19 avenue de la Paix
CH 1202 Geneve
Switzerland
Tel: + 41 22 734 6001
Fax: + 41 22 733 2057
E-mail: webmaster.gva@icrc.org
Web site: www.icrc.org
The ICRC is an impartial, neutral and independent organisation whose exclusive humanitarian mission is to protect the lives and dignity of victims of war and internal violence and to provide them with assistance. Produces reports and weekly ICRC News.

Oxfam
274 Banbury Road
Oxford, OX2 7DZ
Tel: 01865 311311
Fax: 01865 312600
E-mail: oxfam@oxfam.org.uk
Web site: www.oxfam.org.uk
Produces a wide range of publications including 'Information from Oxfam' factsheets, *Life as a refugee* and *Refugees and displaced people*. They also produce the Oxfam Education and Resources for Schools catalogue which outlines publications by Oxfam and other organisations.

Refugee Council
Bondway House, 3-9 Bondway
London, SW8 1SJ
Tel: 0171 820 3000
Fax: 0171 582 9929
E-mail: refcounciluk@gn.apc.org
Provides a forum in which the Council's members can meet to discuss refugee situations and formulate policy on refugee issues.

Save the Children
17 Grove Lane
London, SE5 8RD
Tel: 0171 703 5400
Fax: 0171 703 2278
Produces a wide range of materials. Ask for their catalogue.

UNICEF
55 Lincoln's Inn Fields
London, WC2A 3NB
Tel: 0171 405 5592
Fax: 0171 405 2332
E-mail: info@unicef.org.uk
UNICEF is committed to ensuring special protection for the most disadvantaged children – victims of war, extreme poverty, and all forms of violence and exploitation.

United Nations High Commission for Refugees (UNHCR)
21st Floor, Millbank Tower
21-24 Millbank
London, SW1P 4QP
Tel: 0171 222 3065
Fax: 0171 222 4813
UNHCR promotes public awareness of refugee issues. Provides the latest statistics on refugees and displaced persons. Publishes a magazine called *Refugee*.

World Vision UK
599 Avebury Boulevard
Milton Keynes, MK9 3PG
Tel: 01908 841000
Fax: 01908 841021
E-mail: info@worldvision.org.uk
Web site: www.worldvision.org.uk
Works to aid the hungry, the homeless, the poor and the sick in over 90 developing countries.

INDEX

The Internet has been likened to shopping in a supermarket without aisles. The press of a button on a Web browser can bring up thousands of sites but working your way through them to find what you want can involve long and frustrating on-line searches.

And unfortunately many sites contain inaccurate, misleading or heavily biased information. Our researchers have therefore undertaken an extensive analysis to bring you a selection of quality Web site addresses.

* * * * *

Amnesty International – British Section

www.amnesty.org.uk
Type the word Refugees in the search field and you will gain access to a vast collection of refugee-related press releases from Amnesty.

United Nations High Commission for Refugees (UNHCR)

www.unhcr.ch
This site is a must for anyone researching issues relating to refugees and asylum seekers. The site includes the following: press releases and other timely information about refugee situations world-wide; the UNHCR Newswire Service; Country Updates and Refugees Daily, a daily digest of the latest refugee news, as reported by the world's media.

BBC News

http://news.bbc.co.uk
Click on News, under the Main BBC Sites heading, enter Refugees in the search field and hundreds of refugee-related news items appear. Well worth a visit.

European Council on Refugees and Exiles (ECRE)

www.ecre.org
The European Council on Refugees and Exiles (ECRE) is an umbrella organisation established in 1974 for cooperation between non-governmental organisations in Europe concerned with refugees. ECRE currently has more than 60 member agencies in 23 countries.

Immigration Advisory Service (IAS)

www.vois.org.uk/ias
IAS is the largest, most experienced charity giving free advice and representation in immigration and asylum matters. Their Solicitors Unit deals with judicial review and appeals to the higher courts. Click on Enter then click Immigration Info for a series of factsheets.

Refugee Council

www.gn.apc.org/brcslproject
The Refugee Council gives practical help to asylum seekers and refugees and advances their rights both in the UK and abroad. This site is still under construction but it may be worth checking.

ACKNOWLEDGEMENTS

The publisher is grateful for permission to reproduce the following material.

While every care has been taken to trace and acknowledge copyright, the publisher tenders its apology for any accidental infringement or where copyright has proved untraceable. The publisher would be pleased to come to a suitable arrangement in any such case with the rightful owner.

Chapter One: Refugees

The invisible generation, © United Nations High Commission for Refugees (UNHCR), *10 facts you should know about refugees*, © United Nations High Commission for Refugees (UNHCR), *Governments callous about fate of refugees*, © Amnesty International, *Refugees and Asylum Seekers world-wide*, © U.S. Committee for Refugees, *You've got 10 minutes to get out*, © Amnesty International, *Refugee children and adolescents*, © United Nations High Commission for Refugees (UNHCR), *World refugee population end 1997 by region of asylum/residence*, © United Nations High Commission for Refugees (UNHCR), *Keeping children with families in emergencies*, © Save the Children, *Surviving conflict and disaster*, © HelpAge International, *International humanitarian law*, © International Red Cross Committee (ICRC), *The endless diaspora*, © The Guardian, April 1999, *Major refugee and internally displaced peoples*, © United Nations High Commission for Refugees (UNHCR), *Integrating refugees into UK society*, © 1998-99 Crown Copyright, *Playing the numbers game*, © The Guardian, May 1998, *Refugee Status applications and determination 1997 by region*, © United Nations High Commission for Refugees (UNHCR), *Stateless and unregistered children*, © United Nations High Commission for Refugees (UNHCR), *The 'gun' that finds refugees in a heartbeat*, © The Daily Mail, March 1999.

Chapter Two: Asylum Seekers

Asylum in the UK, © Asylum Aid, *Populations of concern*, © United Nations High Commission for Refugees (UNHCR), *Telling the truth*, © Churches Commission for Racial Justice, *Cruel myths*, © Nick Hardwick, February 1999, *Improving the odds for child refugees*, © Child Newsline, *Ministers try to turn the human tide*, © Telegraph Group Limited, London 1998, *Give me shelter*, © Danny Lee, March 1999, *Children of the storm*, © Children of the Storm (COTS), *Young refugees in the late 1990s*, © Children of the Storm (COTS), *Straw backs fingerprint bank to fight asylum fraud*, © The Daily Mail, December 1998, *Fortress Europe's four circles of purgatory*, © The Guardian, October 1998, *Asylum rates in EU 1990-1995*, © The Refugee Council/International Committee of the Red Cross, *Brussels dumping refugees in London*, © Telegraph Group Limited, London 1998, *Refugees and asylum seekers world-wide*, © U.S. Committee for Refugees (USCR), *Ministers may tag refugees*, © The Guardian, October 1998, *Detention more likely for refugees*, © The Guardian, April 1998, *One in three asylum seekers told to stay*, © The Daily Mail, November 1998, *Seeking a new life*, © 1998-99 Crown Copyright, *Overhaul of 'shambolic' asylum laws*, © Telegraph Group Limited, London 1998, *Somalis swell the queue for asylum*, © The Daily Mail, May 1999, *Where most of the refugees are from*, © 1998-99 Crown Copyright, *More cash for asylum seekers*, © The Guardian, May 1999.

Photographs and illustrations:

Pages 1, 7, 23, 28, 40: Pumpkin House, pages 5, 9, 13, 21, 24, 30, 35, 36: Simon Kneebone.

Craig Donnellan
Cambridge
September, 1999

API Flags

Appendix B contains a complete list of WinInet API flags that may be used with certain WinInet functions. These flags give you ultimate control over the behavior of a WinInet function. In particular, the WinInet flags allow you to control functionality in areas like asynchronous calls, caching, SSL, certificate validation, authentication, and many other areas.

Not all WinInet functions accept WinInet flags. Furthermore, if a function does accept a flag parameter, only some of the WinInet flags are meaningful to the given function. Throughout this chapter and the rest of the book I'll cover the WinInet flags as they apply to the WinInet functions at hand. For example, as I cover InternetOpen, I'll discuss the flags that can be used to control InternetOpen's behavior. Nevertheless, I recommend a quick review of the entire set of WinInet flags before continuing. To do so, once again refer to Appendix B.

HINTERNET Handles

WinInet is a set of Win32 Internet functions. Like all Win32 functions, you have to understand how they all work together. There are often dependencies between distinct functions. For example, in the Win32 API, you have to call OpenFile and produce a valid handle to the opened file before calling ReadFile. ReadFile takes an HFILE (a handle to a file) as its first parameter. If you don't pass it a valid HFILE, the function generates an error.

WinInet relies on handles in the same way as the Win32 API. The type of handle produced by the WinInet functions is called HINTERNET. The HINTERNET handle is either used or produced by almost all WinInet functions. These handles are unique for the Win32 Internet functions and cannot be used interchangeably with the base Win32 handles. For example, you cannot pass an HINTERNET to ReadFile. Conversely, you cannot use the base Win32 handles with the WinInet functions. In other words, you can't pass an HFILE to InternetReadFile.

WinInet General Functions

There are four main WinInet general functions that you'll use in almost every WinInet application: InternetOpen, InternetConnect, InternetSetStatusCallback, and InternetCloseHandle. These functions are used to establish the Internet session, connect to an Internet server, monitor the session status, and terminate the Internet session (see Table 2-1).

2
Chapter

WinInet General Functions

WinInet can be broken down into the following five categories:

1. General Internet functions
2. URL functions
3. HTTP functions
4. FTP functions
5. Gopher functions

To use the latter four categories effectively, you must understand completely how to use the functions that make up the first category. In fact, if you ever use WinInet in your applications, I can guarantee that you'll have to use at least some of the functions that are part of the general category (unless you're using the WinInet MFC classes, which take care of most WinInet general functions behind the scenes).

In this chapter I'll cover the WinInet general functions. In particular, I'll cover functions like InternetOpen, InternetCloseHandle, InternetConnect, InternetReadFile, and InternetWriteFile to name a few. Plus, I'll cover all of the general helper functions that will make your WinInet life much easier.

This chapter presents the building blocks that are required to start building WinInet-based applications. By the time you're done reading this chapter, you'll be ready to start writing simple WinInet programs and to explore the URL and protocol-specific functions in the succeeding chapters.

At this point you should not only know how to obtain the WinInet development files and associated reference materials, but also how you can take advantage of WinInet in various real-world scenarios. Throughout the rest of this book you'll learn how to master WinInet while adding a new level of functionality to your Windows applications.

```
            CHAR lpszBuffer[BUFFLEN];
            DWORD dwRead;

            //read until dwRead == 0
            while (InternetReadFile(hFile, lpszBuffer, BUFFLEN-1, &dwRead))
            {
                if (dwRead == 0)
                    break;
                lpszBuffer[dwRead]=0;        //null terminate temp buffer
                m_strResult += lpszBuffer;   //add to end of complete result
            }
            //close the file handle created by InternetOpenUrl
            InternetCloseHandle(hFile);
        }
        //close the session handle created by InternetOpen
        InternetCloseHandle(hSession);
    }
    //update dialog controls
    UpdateData(FALSE);
}
```

This example is indicative of how straightforward the WinInet API really is. WinInet simplifies the code by hiding all of the protocol details. As you can see, the code doesn't even reference the HTTP protocol. Instead it uses generic functions like InternetOpen and InternetOpenUrl, which implement the protocol behavior for us. Don't worry if you're feeling uncomfortable with this code at this point. In Chapters 2 and 3 I'll cover all the WinInet functions used in this sample. Then, at the end of Chapter 3, I'll look at this sample program once again.

Conclusion

By now you should feel comfortable with where this book is going. I've introduced to you the concept of developing Windows Internet applications, and presented the advantages and disadvantages of the Microsoft Internet client interfaces: Winsock and WinInet. As you've learned, WinInet is a powerful tool for Internet application development that offers many advantages over the traditional Winsock layer.

Table 2-1 **General Internet functions**

General Internet Function	Description
InternetOpen	Initializes an application's use of the Win32 Internet functions.
InternetConnect	Opens an FTP, Gopher, or HTTP session for a given site.
InternetSetStatusCallback	Sets up a callback function that Win32 Internet functions can call as progress is made during an operation.
InternetCloseHandle	Closes a single Internet handle or a subtree of Internet handles.

You'll use these functions either directly or indirectly (in the case of MFC) in every WinInet application. Therefore, it's crucial that you understand every aspect of these functions before moving on.

Handle Hierarchy

InternetOpen is at the top of WinInet HINTERNET handle hierarchy. This means that InternetOpen must be called before calling any other WinInet function. In this sense, InternetOpen is the mother of all WinInet functions. If InternetOpen hasn't created an HINTERNET, attempting to create another HINTERNET (by calling another WinInet function like InternetConnect) fails.

Figure 2-1 illustrates the HINTERNET handle hierarchy for the main WinInet general functions. If a function is depicted as a child of another function, the child function requires an HINTERNET handle created by the parent function. As you can see, this hierarchy is very simple. Every WinInet general function discussed in this section requires a handle created by InternetOpen (except InternetOpen, of course).

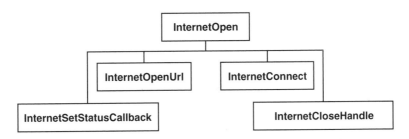

Figure 2-1 General Internet functions handle hierarchy

These aren't the only functions that require a handle created by InternetOpen. Many other WinInet functions are dependent on InternetOpen. However, to keep things simple, I want to focus on the functions at hand.

 WinInet has its own Windows handle type called HINTERNET.

InternetOpen

InternetOpen is to WinInet what CoInitialize is to COM. If you're familiar with COM, you know very well that you cannot use any COM-related function until after you call CoInitialize. CoInitialize, as its name suggests, initializes the COM library in preparation for other COM function calls. Like CoInitialize, InternetOpen initializes the WinInet environment in preparation for other WinInet function calls.

Specifically, InternetOpen tells the WinInet DLL to initialize its internal data structures and to wait for future WinInet calls on the newly created handle. After you're done using the WinInet functions, you must call InternetCloseHandle to free the HINTERNET handle and the internal resources allocated by InternetOpen. I'll cover InternetCloseHandle in more detail shortly. Now let's take a look at InternetOpen's function declaration:

```
HINTERNET InternetOpen(
    IN LPCSTR lpszAgent,
    IN DWORD dwAccessType,
    IN LPCSTR lpszProxyName,
    IN LPCSTR lpszProxyBypass,
    IN DWORD dwFlags
);
```

The first parameter, lpszAgent, is the address of a string containing the name of the application or entity calling the function. For example, if your application's name were MyApp, you would probably want to use MyApp/1.0 in this parameter. WinInet uses the string pointed to by lpszAgent in the User-Agent header for all future HTTP requests made on the handle returned from InternetOpen (or one of its child handles).

If you're also developing the server-side components (CGI scripts, ISAPI DLLs, ASP pages, and so forth), with which your WinInet client will be communicating, the User-Agent HTTP header can come in handy. A server-side component can look at the User-Agent header each time it gets a request and behave accordingly. Using this strategy, you can develop one set of server-side components that handles both requests made from an Internet browser and requests made from your WinInet application. For example, the server-side component could return HTML in response to browser requests and an application-defined format in response to WinInet application requests.

The second parameter, dwAccessType, specifies how this Internet session should attempt to access the Internet. The possible values for this parameter are described in Table 2-2.

If you use the value INTERNET_OPEN_TYPE_DIRECT, WinInet won't attempt to use any proxy information. It assumes that you're not connected through a proxy. If you use INTERNET_OPEN_TYPE_PRECONFIG or INTERNET_OPEN_TYPE_PRECONFIG_WITH_NO_AUTOPROXY, WinInet retrieves the connection information from the registry.

To access this information on your computer, right click on the Microsoft Internet Explorer icon found on your desktop and select Properties. All connection information, including proxy information, is found on the Connection tab (see Figure 2-2). WinInet uses the settings configured in the Connection tab automatically if either of the PRECONFIG values is supplied.

Table 2-2   InternetOpen access types

Access Type	Description
INTERNET_OPEN_TYPE_DIRECT	Resolves all host names locally.
INTERNET_OPEN_TYPE_PRECONFIG	Retrieves the proxy or direct configuration from the registry.
INTERNET_OPEN_TYPE_PRECONFIG_WITH_NO_AUTOPROXY	Retrieves the proxy or direct configuration from the registry and prevents the use of a start-up JScript or Internet Setup file.
INTERNET_OPEN_TYPE_PROXY	Passes requests to the proxy unless a proxy bypass list is supplied and the name to be resolved bypasses the proxy. In this case, the function uses INTERNET_OPEN_TYPE_DIRECT.

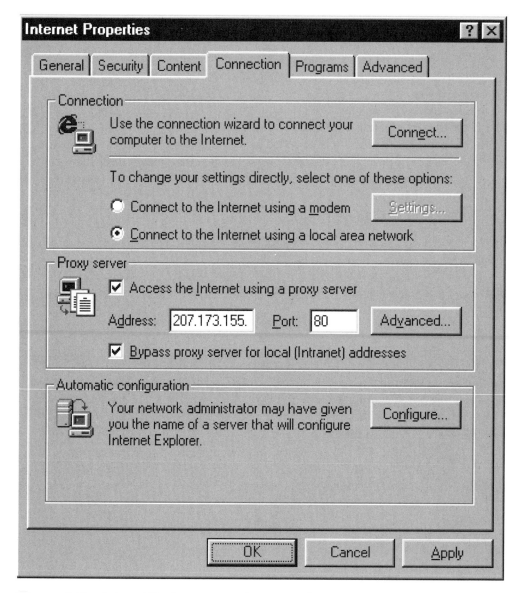

Figure 2-2 Internet Explorer connection properties

 You can access your machine's proxy configuration by right clicking on the Microsoft Internet Explorer desktop icon and selecting Properties. All connection information, including proxy information, is found on the Connection tab.

If you specify INTERNET_OPEN_TYPE_PROXY, WinInet expects you to provide proxy information manually in the lpszProxyName and lpszProxyBypass parameters. lpszProxyName is the name of the proxy server that this session uses, and lpszProxyBypass is a list of proxy servers that don't require a proxy and are safe to bypass altogether These two parameters are often misunderstood.

By default, InternetOpen assumes that the proxy specified by lpszProxyName is a CERN proxy. For example, if you specified a value of MyProxy for lpszProxyName, WinInet assumes it's a CERN proxy called MyProxy that listens on port 80 (decimal). One thing that most developers don't realize is that you can specify more than one proxy in lpszProxyName. You can even specify different proxies for the different WinInet-supported protocols. For example, lpszProxyName could be the following:

```
"http=http://http-proxy.com ftp=ftp://ftp-proxy:22 cern-proxy"
```

In this case, all HTTP requests are made through http-proxy.com on the default HTTP port (decimal 80), all FTP requests are made through ftp-proxy on port 22, and all other requests (for example Gopher requests) are made through a CERN proxy called cern-proxy. If your application is only going to be using the HTTP protocol with the handle returned from InternetOpen, you only need to specify a protocol. For example, in this case, lpszProxyName could simply contain the following:

```
"http-proxy.com"
```

You only need to specify the protocol names if you use more than one protocol with the handle returned by InternetOpen. Otherwise, WinInet assumes the protocol being used.

The lpszProxyBypass parameter allows you to specify the addresses that can bypass the proxy server. These addresses can be configured in the Advanced Proxy Settings dialog (see Figure 2-3), which can be accessed from the Internet Explorer Properties dialog.

In the Exceptions area you can specify a list of host names or IP addresses that are safe to bypass (use semicolons to separate the entries). You can even use wildcards. For example, specifying aarons* bypasses any host name that begins with aarons such as aarons.axtech.com or aarons1.axtech.com. Specifying *aarons* bypasses any host name that contains the substring aarons, such as axiom.aarons.com or coolserveraarons.com. Finally, specifying 157.55.* bypasses any IP address that begins with 157.55., such as 157.55.1.1 or 157.55.255.255.

 You can use the wildcard symbol * when specifying proxy bypass addresses.

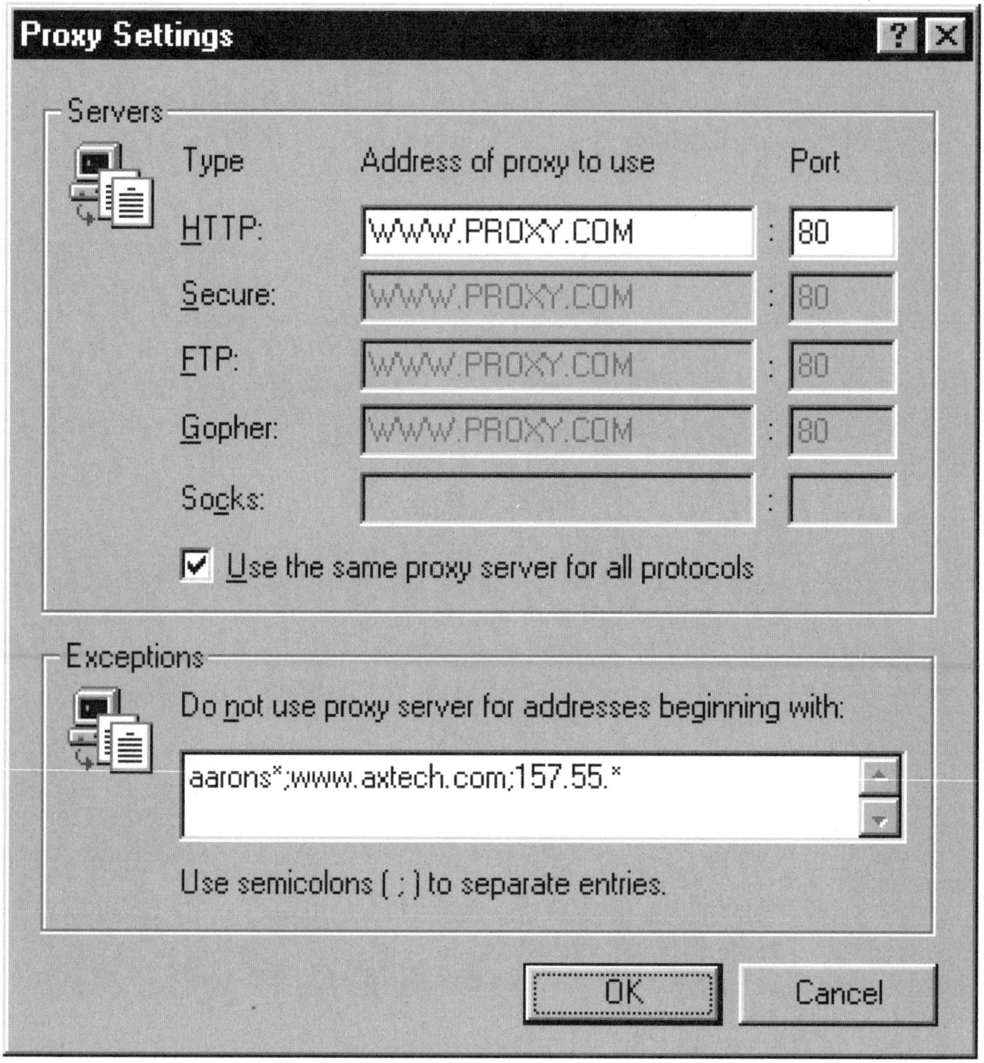

Figure 2-3 Advanced proxy settings dialog

InternetOpen expects the lpszProxyBypass parameter to be formatted as described. For example, if I pass the following string in lpszProxyBypass to InternetOpen,

```
"aarons*;www.axtech.com;157.55.*"
```

the result would be the same as using INTERNET_OPEN_TYPE_PRECONFIG with the proxy configuration specified in Figure 2-3. In fact, using the access type

INTERNET_OPEN_TYPE_PRECONFIG causes WinInet to use the proxy settings configured in the Advanced Proxy Settings dialog (see Figure 2-3).

You can also use the "local" macro to tell WinInet to bypass all local addresses in the following manner:

```
"<local>"
```

This tells WinInet to bypass all addresses that don't contain a period. For example, the address *www.microsoft.com* would be routed to the proxy, whereas the address *aarons* would not.

 You can tell WinInet to bypass all local addresses by using `"<local>"` in the bypass list.

The final InternetOpen parameter, dwFlags, allows you to control a few aspects of the Internet session behavior. There are only two WinInet flags that may be used in conjunction with InternetOpen: INTERNET_FLAG_OFFLINE and INTERNET_FLAG_ASYNC. These flags are described in Table 2-3.

The first flag, INTERNET_FLAG_OFFLINE, puts the Internet session in offline mode. This has the same effect as going to the File menu in IE and pressing Work Offline. All future requests made on the HINTERNET handle returned by InternetOpen (or any handle descendants) are satisfied through the persistent cache. If the request cannot be satisfied, WinInet returns the appropriate error code.

The second and last flag, INTERNET_FLAG_ASYNC, forces future operations made on this or descendant handles to behave asynchronously. In order for

Table 2-3   InternetOpen flags

InternetOpen Flag	Description
INTERNET_FLAG_OFFLINE	Satisfies download operations on this handle through the persistent cache only. If the item does not exist in the cache, the function returns an appropriate error code.
INTERNET_FLAG_ASYNC	Future operations on this handle may fail with ERROR_IO_PENDING. A status callback is made with INTERNET_STATUS_REQUEST_COMPLETE. This callback is on a thread other than the one for the original request. A status callback routine must be registered or the functions behave synchronously.

asynchronous behavior to succeed, you must also specify a status callback routine through InternetSetStatusCallback, which I cover later in this chapter, along with a context value for the given operation.

Asynchronous WinInet is a fairly complicated and often frustrating topic. Instead of trying to do it justice in one small section, I decided to devote an entire chapter to the topic. For a detailed study of asynchronous WinInet along with an in-depth asynchronous sample program, see Chapter 9.

Although you can make as many calls to InternetOpen as you like, usually calling InternetOpen once is sufficient. Normally you call InternetOpen in your application's initialization routine and share the HINTERNET handle throughout your code. Calling InternetOpen only once reduces overhead and simplifies your application design.

The only time you would need to call InternetOpen more than once is if you require different behavior on different InternetOpen handles. For example, you may want to specify a certain proxy server while doing certain requests, and another (default) proxy server for all other requests. The only way to accomplish this is by calling InternetOpen twice with the appropriate proxy information.

Now that you understand the ins and outs of InternetOpen, let's take a look at a simple example. The following code illustrates how to set up an asynchronous Internet session that uses custom proxy information and a list of proxy bypass addresses:

```
HINTERNET hSession = InternetOpen("MyApp/1.0", INTERNET_OPEN_TYPE_PROXY,
        "proxy.server.com", "aarons*;www.axtech*;157.55.*",
        INTERNET_FLAG_ASYNC);
```

InternetOpen is step one of every WinInet application. No matter what you're trying to do, you must call InternetOpen before calling any other WinInet function. Even if you're using the MFC classes, InternetOpen is the first WinInet function to be called by the WinInet class wrappers. By now you should understand InternetOpen enough to control the general behavior of your application's Internet session.

 InternetOpen must be called before any other WinInet function. Although calling InternetOpen once (in your application initialization routine) is usually sufficient, you may need to establish more than one Internet session if each session requires different behavior (such as different proxy configurations or asynchronous support and so on).

The Next Step

After calling InternetOpen, there are two possible paths you can take for your Internet session. The first path consists of calling InternetConnect followed by the protocol-specific functions with which you're dealing. The second path consists of simply calling InternetOpenUrl.

The second path, InternetOpenUrl, is much simpler than the first. If you're only interested in retrieving the data associated with a particular URL and don't need to access protocol specifics, InternetOpenUrl is the right choice. You can use InternetOpenUrl with any of the three protocols. The nice thing is, you don't have to know anything about the protocol being used. You simply provide a URL and InternetOpenUrl takes care of the rest.

The first path—using InternetConnect—is much more flexible than the second. This path gives you more control over the protocol being used. For example, if you're using HTTP, you may want to take advantage of different HTTP methods, specify additional Multipurpose Internet Mail Extension (MIME) accept types, or look at the HTTP response headers. You cannot accomplish any of these tasks using InternetOpenUrl. You must use InternetConnect.

Determining which path to take usually depends on your application requirements. Before deciding, you need to answer the following question: *Is there a possibility that I'll need to deal with the protocol directly?*

If the answer to this question is yes (or even a maybe), you'll want to use InternetConnect and the protocol-specific functions. If the answer to this question is a definite no, you'll save yourself a great deal of time using InternetOpenUrl.

After calling InternetOpen, there are two possible paths. Either you can use InternetOpenUrl to specify a URL resource or you can use InternetConnect to prepare to use the protocol-specific functions. Here are some tips on when you might want to use each of the two paths:

Typical InternetOpenUrl Tasks
- Download a Web page
- Download an image via HTTP
- Download a file via an FTP site
- Download a file via Gopher

Typical Protocol-Specific Tasks
- Check the HTTP response headers for a given request
- Use the HTTP POST method to send data
- Create directories and delete, rename, and upload files to an FTP server
- Use sophisticated Gopher locators

I'll cover both of these paths in detail. Let's start by covering the InternetConnect function in the next section. After calling InternetConnect, you're ready to start calling the protocol-specific functions directly. The protocol-specific functions are covered in future chapters. In the next chapter I'll cover how to use InternetOpenUrl along with the some of the URL-specific helper functions.

InternetConnect

InternetConnect is one of the first functions that you call after establishing your global Internet session through InternetOpen. InternetConnect is responsible for establishing an HTTP-, FTP-, or Gopher-specific connection handle for a given server. As you'll learn shortly, unless you decide to use InternetOpenUrl you must use InternetConnect in conjunction with all HTTP, FTP, and Gopher functions (refer to Chapters 4 through 6 for more information on the sequence of calls). In other words, you must use the HINTERNET handle returned by InternetConnect with most protocol-specific functions.

Because InternetOpen is usually only called once per application, it only requests information that is global to all WinInet operations, such as the User-Agent, proxy information, and general session behavior. InternetConnect, on the other hand, can be called many times throughout an application. Hence, InternetConnect needs the information required to establish a connection with an Internet (HTTP, FTP, or Gopher) server.

Let's take a look at InternetConnect's function declaration:

```
HINTERNET InternetConnect(
    IN HINTERNET hInternetSession,
    IN LPCSTR lpszServerName,
    IN INTERNET_PORT nServerPort,
    IN LPCSTR lpszUsername,
    IN LPCSTR lpszPassword,
    IN DWORD dwService,
    IN DWORD dwFlags,
    IN DWORD dwContext
);
```

As you've learned, InternetOpen must be called before any other WinInet function, and InternetConnect is no exception. The first parameter, hInternetSession, takes the session handle returned by InternetOpen. Once again, InternetConnect's dependency on InternetOpen is what I described in the HINTERNET handle hierarchy at the beginning of this section.

The second parameter, lpszServerName, takes the name of the server to which you wish to connect. This parameter can be in the form of a host name such as *www.microsoft.com* or an IP address such as 155.57.0.1.

Besides specifying the server name, you must also specify the TCP/IP port to use with this connection. The next parameter, nServerPort, allows you to specify the TCP/IP port number you wish to use. You can go ahead and manually specify a port number if you're planning on using something out of the ordinary. However, WinInet provides a set of default port values that will most likely fit your needs. Table 2-4 describes these values in more detail.

Using INTERNET_INVALID_PORT_NUMBER tells InternetConnect always to use the default port for the service specified in dwService. Hence, if you're always planning on using the default port values, this value allows you to let InternetConnect worry about using the right port number.

 You can use INTERNET_INVALID_PORT_NUMBER to have WinInet determine the default port for the service being used.

The dwService parameter tells InternetConnect which Internet protocol service you're going to use. Table 2-5 describes the possible dwService values.

The lpszUsername and lpszPassword parameters allow you to specify user account authentication information for the particular server. This information is used when trying to connect to a server that requires a user logon.

Table 2-4   nServerPort values

nServerPort Value	Description
INTERNET_DEFAULT_FTP_PORT	Uses the default port for FTP servers (port 21).
INTERNET_DEFAULT_GOPHER_PORT	Uses the default port for Gopher servers (port 70).
INTERNET_DEFAULT_HTTP_PORT	Uses the default port for HTTP servers (port 80).
INTERNET_DEFAULT_HTTPS_PORT	Uses the default port for secure HTTP servers—or HTTPS (port 443).
INTERNET_DEFAULT_SOCKS_PORT	Uses the default port for SOCKS firewall servers (port 1080).
INTERNET_INVALID_PORT_NUMBER	Uses the default port for the service specified by dwService.

Table 2-5   dwService values

dwService Value	Description
INTERNET_SERVICE_FTP	FTP service
INTERNET_SERVICE_GOPHER	Gopher service
INTERNET_SERVICE_HTTP	HTTP service

For example, if I open IE and navigate to my online broker (which happens to require user authentication), the dialog shown in Figure 2-4 appears, prompting me to enter my authentication information. After entering my information in this dialog and pressing OK, IE stores my user name and password in the connection handle and tries the request again.

Most Web sites don't require user authentication. Nevertheless, if you ever connect to one that does, you may need to use the lpszUsername and lpszPassword parameters in InternetConnect. Although this Web browser example is certainly applicable to HTTP sessions, the lpszUsername and lpszPassword parameters are equally important to FTP and Gopher sessions. In fact, with FTP servers a user name and password are usually always required (even though the FTP server usually accepts anonymous for the user name).

InternetConnect does some extra work for you when the type of service is INTERNET_SERVICE_FTP. As shown in Table 2-6, depending on what you pass to

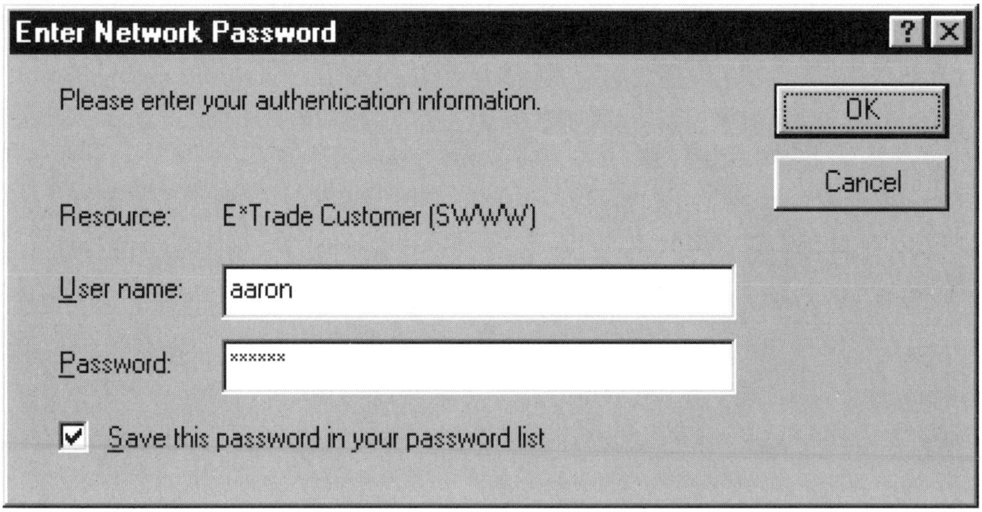

Figure 2-4   Enter Network Password dialog

lpszUsername and lpszPassword, InternetConnect passes different values to the FTP server. For example, if you pass NULL to both lpszUsername and lpszPassword, the value anonymous is sent to the FTP server for the user name, and the user's e-mail address is sent to the FTP server for the password. If you actually want to send a blank password to the FTP server, you must specify a user name in lpszUsername and leave lpszPassword blank.

I'll cover user authentication in more detail in future chapters. In Chapter 4, I show you an example of HTTP user authentication. As you'll see shortly, you can also use InternetSetOption to modify the user name and password after calling InternetConnect.

The last two InternetConnect parameters are dwFlags and dwContext. Currently there is only one flag that can be used with InternetConnect: INTERNET_FLAG_PASSIVE. This flag is only valid when dwService is INTERNET_SERVICE_FTP, in which case it causes the application to use passive FTP semantics.

dwContext is an application-defined value used to identify the application context for the returned handle. This context value is passed to the status callback function when it is called for the handle returned from InternetConnect. Context values are crucial to asynchronous WinInet. We'll look at the Internet status callback function next; however, for a complete study of asynchronous WinInet and the use of context values see Chapter 9.

Now that you're familiar with InternetConnect's parameters, let's look at a quick example of how to use it. The following code segment shows how to connect to the HTTP server on *aarons.axtech.com:*

```
#define AARONS_CONNECT_VALUE 1
HINTERNET hSession = InternetOpen("MyApp/1.0", INTERNET_OPEN_TYPE_PROXY,
        "proxy.server.com", "aarons*;www.axtech*;157.55.*",
        INTERNET_FLAG_ASYNC);
```

Table 2-6 FTP User name and password combinations

lpszUsername	lpszPassword	User Name Sent to FTP Server	Password Sent to FTP Server
NULL	NULL	anonymous	User's e-mail
Non-NULL string	NULL	lpszUsername	<empty>
NULL	Non-NULL string	ERROR	ERROR
Non-NULL string	Non-NULL string	lpszUsername	lpszPassword

```
if (hSession)
{
    HINTERNET hConnection = InternetConnect(hSession, "aarons.axtech.com",
            INTERNET_DEFAULT_HTTP_PORT, "aaron", "password",
            INTERNET_SERVICE_HTTP, 0, AARONS_CONNECT_VALUE);
}
```

As you can see from this example, setting up a connection handle is quite simple. After creating a protocol-specific connection handle with InternetConnect, you're ready to start using the protocol-specific functions, which I cover in Chapters 4, 5, and 6.

InternetSetStatusCallback

WinInet provides a mechanism for associating a callback routine with an HINTERNET handle. WinInet calls the associated routine throughout the lifetime of the handle as the status of the handle changes. For example, if you were to establish a callback routine on the handle returned from InternetOpen, a call to InternetConnect would cause the status callback function to be called when the host name was resolved, when the host name was found, when the port was opened, when the connection was established, and so on.

A callback mechanism is very useful for providing the user with valuable status information. With a status callback, you're able to show the user what WinInet is doing behind the scenes. Without a status callback, you would have no way of determining the status of a given request. If you're familiar with Windows programming, the idea of a status callback should be no surprise. The Win32 API takes advantage of them all over the place.

Although the WinInet status callback mechanism allows you to design a friendlier UI, it's also used to drive WinInet's built-in asynchronous support. In the section on InternetOpen, we looked at how to use the INTERNET_FLAG_ASYNC flag to create an asynchronous Internet session. When INTERNET_FLAG_ASYNC is specified, you must establish a status callback function with the HINTERNET handle returned from InternetOpen. If you were to call InternetConnect on an asynchronous session handle, it would return immediately with the error code ERROR_IO_PENDING, which tells you that InternetConnect will be executed asynchronously.

At this point you rely on the status callback function to notify you of the completion of InternetConnect. For a more detailed look at using status callback functions in asynchronous WinInet sessions, refer to Chapter 9, which demonstrates how to write a full-featured asynchronous Windows FTP client.

As you can see, the WinInet status callback mechanism is a key part of the overall WinInet design. You should never write a WinInet application without taking advantage of this key feature. Even if you're not using WinInet asynchronously, a status callback helps you to design a better application. Now that I'm done with my status callback sales pitch, let's look at how to set up a status callback function.

Registering a status callback with WinInet is as simple as calling InternetSetStatusCallback. Take a quick look at InternetSetStatusCallback's function declaration:

```
INTERNET_STATUS_CALLBACK InternetSetStatusCallback(
    IN HINTERNET hInternet,
    IN INTERNET_STATUS_CALLBACK lpfnInternetCallback
);
```

The first parameter is the HINTERNET handle for which the status callback function should be called. This is typically the handle returned by InternetOpen. The second parameter is the pointer to your application-defined status callback function. The only tricky part is defining your status callback function properly. As you'll notice from the definition, your status callback function should match the signature defined by INTERNET_STATUS_CALLBACK.

INTERNET_STATUS_CALLBACK is defined as the following:

```
VOID (CALLBACK * INTERNET_STATUS_CALLBACK)(
    IN HINTERNET hInternet,
    IN DWORD dwContext,
    IN DWORD dwInternetStatus,
    IN LPVOID lpvStatusInformation,
    IN DWORD dwStatusInformationLength
);
```

Thus, I could define my application status callback function—MyStatusCallback—as the following:

```
VOID CALLBACK MyStatusCallback(
    HINTERNET hInternet,
    DWORD dwContext,
    DWORD dwInternetStatus,
    LPVOID lpvStatusInformation,
    DWORD dwStatusInformationLength
);
```

Although I'll look at INTERNET_STATUS_CALLBACK in more detail in Chapter 9, let me briefly cover a few of the parameters. First, hInternet is the handle with which the callback function is associated; this is the same HINTERNET handle that is passed to InternetSetStatusCallback. This is useful if you associate a callback function with more than one HINTERNET handle.

Next, the dwInternetStatus parameter specifies the current status of the HINTERNET handle. Table 2-7 describes all of the possible dwInternetStatus values. A common thing to do in Internet applications is to display the operation status somewhere in the UI, such as the status bar. You can accomplish this using your status callback function by simply switching on the dwInternetStatus value and displaying the appropriate status string to the user.

Table 2-7   dwInternetStatus values

dwInternetStatus Value	Description
INTERNET_STATUS_CLOSING_CONNECTION	Closing the connection to the server.
INTERNET_STATUS_CONNECTED_TO_SERVER	Connected to the socket successfully.
INTERNET_STATUS_CONNECTING_TO_SERVER	Connecting to the socket address.
INTERNET_STATUS_CONNECTION_CLOSED	Closed the connection successfully.
INTERNET_STATUS_HANDLE_CLOSING	This handle value is now terminated.
INTERNET_STATUS_HANDLE_CREATED	Created the new handle.
INTERNET_STATUS_INTERMEDIATE_RESPONSE	Received an intermediate status code.
INTERNET_STATUS_NAME_RESOLVED	Found the IP address successfully.
INTERNET_STATUS_RECEIVING_RESPONSE	Waiting for the server to respond.
INTERNET_STATUS_REDIRECT	About to redirect the request automatically.
INTERNET_STATUS_REQUEST_COMPLETE	An asynchronous operation has been completed.
INTERNET_STATUS_REQUEST_SENT	Sent the information request to the server successfully.
INTERNET_STATUS_RESOLVING_NAME	Looking up the IP address of the name contained in lpvStatusInformation.
INTERNET_STATUS_RESPONSE_RECEIVED	Received a response successfully.
INTERNET_STATUS_SENDING_REQUEST	Sending the information request.
INTERNET_STATUS_STATE_CHANGE	Indicates a change beween online/offline state.

A typical status callback function would look like Listing 2-1:

Listing 2-1 MyStatusCallback

```
VOID CALLBACK MyStatusCallback(
    HINTERNET hInternet,
    DWORD dwContext,
    DWORD dwInternetStatus,
    LPVOID lpvStatusInformation,
    DWORD dwStatusInformationLength
)
{

    switch(dwInternetStatus)
    {
    case INTERNET_STATUS_RESOLVING_NAME:
        strStatus="Resolving name...";
        break;
    case INTERNET_STATUS_NAME_RESOLVED:
        strStatus="Resolved name!";
        break;
    case INTERNET_STATUS_CONNECTING_TO_SERVER:
        strStatus="Connecting to server...";
        break;
    case INTERNET_STATUS_CONNECTED_TO_SERVER:
        strStatus="Connected to server!";
        break;
    case INTERNET_STATUS_SENDING_REQUEST:
        strStatus="Sending request...";
        break;
    .

    .

    .

    default:
        strStatus="Unknown status";
    }
    GetMyMainWnd()->UpdateStatusBar(strStatus);
}
```

A status callback function is a vital part of making your WinInet application more user friendly. Without a status callback function, users have no visual representation of the status of the current WinInet request. This most often results in confused users and support calls.

dwContext is a value that you can use to determine why the status callback function is being called. Potentially you can have various WinInet functions executing asynchronously at the same time. In this scenario, calls to the status callback function on behalf of the various executing functions will be interspersed. Hence, you must use dwContext to determine the reason behind the call.

 Because only one status callback function can be associated with a given WinInet session (a session is created by calling InternetOpen), the status callback function needs a way to determine what caused the status callback function to be called. dwContext is an application-defined value that you can use to determine what part of your application caused your status callback function to be called. First you pass a dwContext value to all asynchronous function calls. Then you check the dwContext value within your status callback function.

The other two parameters—lpvStatusInformation and dwStatusInformationLength—provide information regarding the status. For example, if you call InternetConnect on an asynchronous session handle, you would look for the HINTERNET value in lpvStatusInformation when you receive the INTERNET_STATUS_REQUEST_ COMPLETE status code. I've devoted an entire chapter to the topic of asynchronous WinInet. For more information (and a complete sample application) on dwContext, lpvStatusInformation, and dwStatusInformationLength, refer to Chapter 9.

Before moving on, let's quickly look at how to use InternetSetStatusCallback in your application. Listing 2-2 shows how to incorporate the call to InternetSetStatusCallback with the InternetOpen example.

Listing 2-2   InternetStatusCallback

```
HINTERNET hSession = InternetOpen("MyApp/1.0", INTERNET_OPEN_TYPE_PROXY,
        "proxy.server.com","aarons*;www.axtech*;157.55.*",
        INTERNET_FLAG_ASYNC);
if (g_hSession)
```

```
{
    INTERNET_STATUS_CALLBACK dwStatusCallback;
    dwStatusCallback = InternetSetStatusCallback(g_hSession, MyStatusCallback);
    if (INTERNET_INVALID_STATUS_CALLBACK == dwStatusCallback)
        AfxMessageBox("Error setting status callback");
}
```

InternetSetStatusCallback returns the previously defined status callback function if successful, NULL if there was no previously defined callback function, and INTERNET_INVALID_STATUS_CALLBACK if the supplied callback function is invalid. If you're using asynchronous WinInet capabilities, you'll want to make sure that the callback registration succeeds before attempting any asynchronous calls. If the status callback function fails to be registered, all future requests behave synchronously.

InternetCloseHandle

Unlike some of the previous functions, InternetCloseHandle is sweet and simple. Take a look at the function declaration:

```
BOOL InternetCloseHandle(
    IN HINTERNET hInet
);
```

What could be simpler? Just pass the HINTERNET handle you want to close in hInet. This closes the handle and frees all resources associated with it. If you call InternetCloseHandle on a handle that has child handles, it closes the specified handle along with all child handles. Hence, you can use InternetCloseHandle to close either a single handle or a tree of handles.

InternetCloseHandle also terminates any pending requests on the specified handle and discards any outstanding data. This is very useful if you're using WinInet synchronously. For example, if you make a blocking function call from within one thread, you can cancel the blocking call effectively by calling InternetCloseHandle on the blocked handle from another thread. In this scenario, a call to InternetCloseHandle should cause the blocking function to return an error and, subsequently, allow the thread to exit.

InternetCloseHandle terminates any pending requests on the specified handle. However, if you're using WinInet asynchronously and attempt to close a handle with outstanding asynchronous requests, InternetCloseHandle invalidates the handle and waits for the asynchronous functions to complete. Any future calls on the invalidated handle return ERROR_INVALID_HANDLE.

If you're using WinInet asynchronously and attempt to close a handle with outstanding asynchronous requests, InternetCloseHandle cannot close the handle immediately. Instead, InternetCloseHandle invalidates the handle and waits for the asynchronous functions to complete. Any future calls on the invalidated handle return the error ERROR_INVALID_HANDLE.

Refer back to Table 2-7 and look up INTERNET_STATUS_HANDLE_CLOSING. This is the last status message received by the status callback function before closing a handle. Especially if you're using WinInet asynchronously, you cannot be sure that a handle is really closed until after receiving this callback status.

To summarize, you must use InternetCloseHandle to free all WinInet resources and to cancel outstanding requests. You can handle this WinInet cleanup normally in your application's exit routine.

General Internet Function Summary

I covered the four general Internet functions that you'll use in almost every WinInet application: InternetOpen, InternetConnect, InternetSetStatusCallback, and InternetCloseHandle. At this point you should feel comfortable enough with these functions to start using them on your own. However, I've still only covered how to begin an Internet session, connect with a server, establish a callback, and close the session. We still need to fill in everything in between.

Internet File Functions

WinInet offers a set of functions for dealing with Internet files. These functions are described in Table 2-8 and look a lot like the Win32 file functions ReadFile, ReadFileEx, WriteFile, SetFilePointer, LockFile, and FindNextFile. In fact, most of the WinInet functions are named the same as the Win32 functions except they start with the word Internet. For example, InternetReadFile corresponds to the Win32 function ReadFile,

Table 2-8   General Internet file functions

Function	Description
InternetReadFile	Reads data from a handle opened by the InternetOpenUrl, FtpOpenFile, GopherOpenFile, or HttpOpenRequest functions.
InternetWriteFile	Writes data to an open Internet file.
InternetSetFilePointer	Sets a file position for InternetReadFile. This is a synchronous call; however, subsequent calls to InternetReadFile may block or return pending if the data is not available from the cache and the server does not support random access.
InternetQueryDataAvailable	Queries the amount of data available.
InternetLockRequestFile	Allows the user to place a lock on the file that is being used.
InternetUnlockRequestFile	Unlocks a file that was locked using InternetLockRequestFile.
InternetFindNextFile	Continues a file search started as a result of a previous call to FtpFindFirstFile or GopherFindFirstFile.

InternetWriteFile corresponds to WriteFile, InternetLockRequestFile corresponds to LockFile, and so on.

The WinInet file functions were designed purposely to be like the familiar Win32 file functions. If you've used the Win32 file functions you shouldn't have a problem using the WinInet file functions. The functionality is virtually identical between the two sets of functions. The only difference is that the WinInet file functions deal with remote files whereas the Win32 file functions deal with local files. The good news is you don't have to worry about this. WinInet takes care of it for you.

Now, just because the functions are similar doesn't mean that we can use them interchangeably. Trying to use the Win32 file functions in place of the WinInet file functions produces nothing but headaches. All remote file manipulations should be approached using the WinInet file functions.

InternetReadFile

InternetReadFile is probably the most widely used WinInet file function. This function reads data from a handle opened by the InternetOpenUrl, FtpOpenFile, GopherOpenFile, or HttpOpenRequest functions. Once you've opened a remote file successfully through one of these WinInet functions, you can read the data just like you would with the Win32 ReadFile function.

Table 2-9 illustrates the similarities between the InternetReadFile (WinInet) and ReadFile (Win32) function declarations. The only difference between these two functions is ReadFile accepts an extra parameter, lpOverlapped, which doesn't apply to InternetReadFile. Most of the Internet file functions covered in this section have a corresponding Win32 file function that is almost identical in both definition and functionality.

Like ReadFile, if InternetReadFile returns TRUE and the number of bytes read is zero, the transfer is complete and there are no more bytes to read on the handle. One common mistake is to test the return value only. For example, look at the following code segment, which illustrates my point:

```
while (InternetReadFile(hFile, lpszBuffer, BUFFLEN-1, &dwRead))
{
    //save the buffer and continue
}
```

Common sense tells you that this should work. When I first used InternetReadFile, I also assumed incorrectly that it would return FALSE when it reached the end of the file. This is not the case. In fact, if you try using this logic, your application hangs in an infinite loop. Remember that InternetReadFile returns TRUE even when it reaches the end of the file. With that in mind, the correct logic is as follows:

```
while (InternetReadFile(hFile, lpszBuffer, BUFFLEN-1, &dwRead))
{
    if (dwRead == 0)      //if the return value is TRUE and dwRead is zero,
        break;            //we reached the end of the file
    //save the buffer and continue
}
```

Table 2-9   WinInet/Win32 comparison of InternetReadFile

InternetReadFile (WinInet)	ReadFile (Win32)
BOOL InternetReadFile(	BOOL ReadFile(
IN HINTERNET hFile,	HANDLE hFile,
IN LPVOID lpBuffer,	LPVOID lpBuffer,
IN DWORD dwNumberOfBytesToRead,	DWORD nNumberOfBytesToRead,
OUT LPDWORD lpNumberOfBytesRead	LPDWORD lpNumberOfBytesRead,
);	LPOVERLAPPED lpOverlapped
	);

So now you know how to avoid one of the most common problems encountered while using InternetReadFile. You must check both the return value and the number of bytes read to be sure of anything. If you try some other combination, you'll definitely get unexpected results.

 The Boolean value returned by InternetReadFile doesn't indicate that you've reached the end of the file. You must check both the return value and the number of bytes read. If the return value is TRUE and the number of bytes read is zero, you've reached the end of the file.

InternetWriteFile

Like InternetReadFile, InternetWriteFile is also very similar to its Win32 counterpart WriteFile. Once again, the only difference is that InternetWriteFile deals with remote files whereas WriteFile deals with local files.

It's not too obvious how you might want to use InternetWriteFile. When would you want to write directly to a remote file? The only place it makes sense to use InternetWriteFile is in combination with FtpOpenFile.

InternetFindNextFile

InternetFindNextFile continues a file search initiated by either FtpFindFirstFile or GopherFindFirstFile. You use this function to enumerate remote FTP and Gopher directories. I'll look at examples of how to use this function in both the FTP and Gopher chapters.

InternetSetFilePointer

InternetSetFilePointer sets the file position used by InternetReadFile. InternetSetFilePointer can be used on files created by InternetOpenUrl that refer to either an HTTP or an HTTPS URL resource. You can also use this function after calling HttpOpenRequest if you're using either the GET or HEAD methods. However, if you're using HttpOpenRequest and HttpSendRequestEx, you must call HttpEndRequest before calling InternetSetFilePointer.

Another issue that might throw you for a loop has to do with the WinInet flags. If the HINTERNET handle was created with either INTERNET_FLAG_DONT_CACHE or INTERNET_FLAG_NO_CACHE_WRITE, InternetSetFilePointer always fails.

Finally, if the HTTP response doesn't contain the Content-Length header, InternetSetFilePointer cannot be used safely. The WinInet implementation depends on this header to calculate total file size. For example, if you try to move to the end of the file and WinInet doesn't know the total file length (via the Content-Length header), InternetSetFilePointer fails.

Beware of this issue; it caused me terrible grief. If all Web servers used the Content-Length header, this wouldn't be such a problem. Unfortunately, most Web servers don't standardize using this header consistently. Hence, if you aren't in control of the Content-Type header, you'll want to use an alternative to InternetSetFilePointer.

 InternetSetFilePointer only works under the following two conditions: (1) neither INTERNET_FLAG_DON'T_CACHE or INTERNET_FLAG_NO_CACHE_WRITE is used to create the handle, and (2) the HTTP Content-Length header is used by the HTTP server. If either one of these conditions isn't satisfied, InternetSetFilePointer always fails.

Reading Files without the Content-Length Header

After experiencing the problems that arise while using InternetSetFilePointer with the Content-Length header, I came to the conclusion that I should use file reading logic that doesn't rely on either of these two functions. In most of my applications I use the following type of `while` loop:

```
while (InternetReadFile(hFile, lpszBuffer, BUFFLEN-1, &dwRead))
{
    if (dwRead == 0)      //if the return value is TRUE and dwRead is zero,
        break;            //we reached the end of the file
    //save the buffer and continue
}
```

This code doesn't require the Content-Length header to function properly. It simply reads from the file until it can't read any more.

Locking File Resources

You can lock a file resource associated with an HINTERNET handle by calling InternetLockRequestFile. This function places a lock on the local cached resource associated with the HINTERNET handle. While the file is locked, the resource cannot be removed from the cache. If some other activity attempts to remove the file from the cache or to overwrite its contents, it will only be marked for deletion. To unlock the file, call InternetUnlockRequestFile; effectively this gives the cache permission to delete the file.

If you put restrictions on the handle's caching behavior through the INTERNET_FLAG_DONT_CACHE or the INTERNET_FLAG_NO_CACHE_WRITE flags, a call to InternetLockRequestFile creates a temporary file with a .tmp extension separate from the cache. In this situation, however, you cannot lock HTTPS resources.

 You cannot lock an HTTPS resource that was created with either the INTERNET_FLAG_DONT_CACHE or the INTERNET_FLAG_NO_CACHE_WRITE flags.

Internet Option Functions

There are two very handy WinInet general functions that are used to query and to set the various options associated with an Internet session. Table 2-10 describes these two functions briefly.

Table 2-10   Internet option functions

Function	Description	Declaration

InternetQueryOption	Queries the setting of an Internet option.	`BOOL InternetQueryOption(`
		
		`    IN HINTERNET hInternet,`
		`    IN DWORD dwOption,`
		`    OUT LPVOID lpBuffer,`
		`    IN OUT LPDWORD`
		`        lpdwBufferLength`
		`);`

InternetSetOption	Sets an Internet option.	`BOOL InternetSetOption(`
		`    IN HINTERNET hInternet,`
		`    IN DWORD dwOption,`
		`    IN LPVOID lpBuffer,`
		`    IN DWORD dwBufferLength`
		`);`

Table 2-11   Internet option usage

Internet Option	Query	Set
INTERNET_OPTION_CALLBACK	Yes	Yes
INTERNET_OPTION_CONNECT_RETRIES	Yes	Yes
INTERNET_OPTION_CONNECT_TIMEOUT	Yes	Yes
INTERNET_OPTION_CONNECT_STATE	Yes	Yes
INTERNET_OPTION_CONTEXT_VALUE	Yes	Yes
INTERNET_OPTION_CONTROL_RECEIVE_TIMEOUT	Yes	Yes
INTERNET_OPTION_CONTROL_SEND_TIMEOUT	Yes	Yes
INTERNET_OPTION_DATA_RECEIVE_TIMEOUT	Yes	Yes
INTERNET_OPTION_DATA_SEND_TIMEOUT	Yes	Yes
INTERNET_OPTION_DATAFILE_NAME	Yes	Yes
INTERNET_OPTION_END_BROWSER_SESSION	No	Yes
INTERNET_OPTION_EXTENDED_ERROR	Yes	No
INTERNET_OPTION_HANDLE_TYPE	Yes	No
INTERNET_OPTION_HTTP_VERSION	Yes	Yes
INTERNET_OPTION_PARENT_HANDLE	Yes	No
INTERNET_OPTION_PASSWORD	Yes	Yes
INTERNET_OPTION_PROXY	Yes	Yes
INTERNET_OPTION_PROXY_PASSWORD	Yes	Yes
INTERNET_OPTION_PROXY_USERNAME	Yes	Yes
INTERNET_OPTION_READ_BUFFER_SIZE	Yes	Yes
INTERNET_OPTION_RECEIVE_TIMEOUT	Yes	Yes
INTERNET_OPTION_REFRESH	Yes	Yes
INTERNET_OPTION_REQUEST_FLAGS	Yes	No
INTERNET_OPTION_REQUEST_PRIORITY	Yes	Yes
INTERNET_OPTION_SECONDARY_CACHE_KEY	Yes	Yes
INTERNET_OPTION_SECURITY_CERTIFICATE	Yes	No
INTERNET_OPTION_SECURITY_CERTIFICATE_STRUCT	Yes	No
INTERNET_OPTION_SECURITY_FLAGS	Yes	No
INTERNET_OPTION_SECURITY_KEY_BITNESS	Yes	No
INTERNET_OPTION_SECURITY_SELECT_CLIENT_CERT	No	Yes
INTERNET_OPTION_SEND_TIMEOUT	Yes	Yes
INTERNET_OPTION_SETTINGS_CHANGED	No	Yes
INTERNET_OPTION_URL	Yes	No
INTERNET_OPTION_USER_AGENT	Yes	Yes
INTERNET_OPTION_USERNAME	Yes	Yes
INTERNET_OPTION_VERSION	Yes	No
INTERNET_OPTION_WRITE_BUFFER_SIZE	Yes	Yes

You may start wondering what the difference is between Internet options and the WinInet flags. WinInet flags control the behavior of WinInet functions. An Internet option, on the other hand, is a specific property of the Internet handle.

These functions are almost identical. With InternetQueryOption, you're retrieving one of the option settings, whereas with InternetSetOption you're modifying an option setting. Some Internet options apply only to InternetQueryOption and some apply only to InternetSetOption. Table 2-11 clarifies which options can be queried and which options can be set. There are enough Internet options to keep you busy for quite a while.

As you can see, these options allow you to control various Internet session properties like timeout values, connection retries, context values, security settings, buffer sizes, and authentication information. Throughout the rest of the book, some of these options pop up in the sample code. Instead of boring you with the details of each option, I've provided a detailed reference of all Internet options in Appendix C.

 Internet options control the behavior of a given HINTERNET handle.

Internet Time Functions

WinInet offers a set of functions for converting time values between the Windows SYSTEMTIME structure and the RFC format (specified by the official HTTP/1.0 RFC specification). InternetTimeFromSystemTime converts a SYSTEMTIME structure into a string time description that adheres to the RFC time format. InternetTimeToSystemTime converts a string time description into a Windows SYSTEMTIME structure.

Other Internet Helper Functions

There are three miscellaneous WinInet general functions that I want to cover before leaving this subject. They are described briefly in Table 2-12.

InternetConfirmZoneCrossing

InternetConfirmZoneCrossing is a very useful function that checks for changes between nonsecure and secure URLs. Depending on how you have IE configured, you

Table 2-12   Other Internet helper functions

Function	Description
InternetConfirmZoneCrossing	Checks for changes between secure and nonsecure URLs. When a change occurs in security between two URLs, an application should allow the user to acknowledge this change, typically by displaying a dialog.
InternetErrorDlg	Displays a dialog for the error that is passed to InternetErrorDlg if an appropriate dialog exists. If the FLAGS_ERROR_UI_FILTER_FOR_ERRORS flag is used, the function also checks the headers for any hidden errors and displays a dialog if needed.
InternetGetLastResponseInfo	Retrieves the last Win32 Internet function error description or server response on the thread calling this function.

may already be familiar with this concept. When an application is about to go from a nonsecure URL to a secure URL (or vice versa), the application should allow the user to acknowledge the change in security before continuing.

InternetConfirmZoneCrossing helps make this security zone crossing a no-brainer. You simply pass the previous URL along with the new URL and let InternetConfirmZoneCrossing take care of the rest. Check out the following function declaration:

```
DWORD InternetConfirmZoneCrossing(
     IN HWND hWnd,
     IN LPSTR szUrlPrev,
     IN LPSTR szUrlNew,
     IN BOOL bPost
);
```

Unless you have this feature turned off, you see the dialog in Figure 2-5 when going from a nonsecure URL to a secure URL. Notice the check box that allows you to disable this warning.

When going from a secure URL to a nonsecure URL, InternetConfirmZone-Crossing displays the dialog in Figure 2-6.

If you check the box, indicating that you don't wish to see these warnings in the future, InternetConfirmZoneCrossing will never display a warning. To make this function work (and actually display something), you need to make sure that you don't

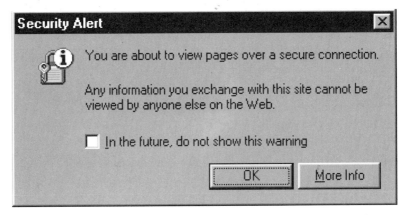

Figure 2-5   InternetConfirmZoneCrossing dialog (going from a
nonsecure URL to a secure URL)

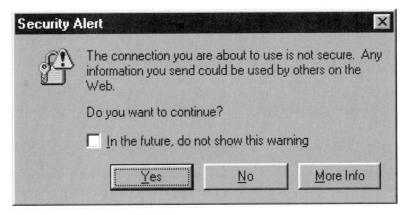

Figure 2-6   InternetConfirmZoneCrossing dialog (going from a
secure URL to a nonsecure URL)

already have the warnings disabled through IE. To check, you can look in your registry in the following location:

```
HKEY_LOCAL_MACHINE\SOFTWARE\Microsoft\Internet
Explorer\AdvancedOptions\CRYPTO\SECURE
```

You can also go to the IE Internet Options dialog and go to the Advanced tab.
Scroll down to the section on security and see if the following option is checked (see
Figure 2-7): *Warn if changing between secure and not secure mode.*

This option controls the registry setting shown here. If this option is checked,
InternetConfirmZoneCrossing will display warnings when crossing security zones.

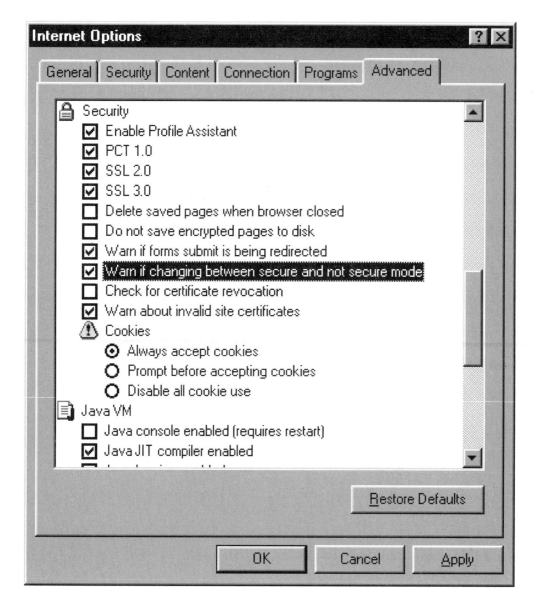

Figure 2-7 Internet Explorer Internet Options dialog

Otherwise, InternetConfirmZoneCrossing will always succeed without displaying anything.

This is an example of how WinInet is coupled tightly with IE. If the user has IE configured a specific way, the same settings will also be used by your WinInet application. Although logically this seems like what most users would desire, often you may want to impose your own application-specific settings.

InternetErrorDlg

InternetErrorDlg is another very useful API packed full of functionality. Specifically, this function displays a dialog for the error that is passed in dwError. However, if you specify FLAGS_ERROR_UI_FILTER_FOR_ERROR, InternetErrorDlg will search through the headers for any hidden errors and display a dialog if necessary. At this point this function is only used with HTTP requests.

Take a look at InternetErrorDlg's function declaration:

```
DWORD InternetErrorDlg(
    IN HWND hWnd,
    IN OUT HINTERNET hInternet,
    IN DWORD dwError,
    IN DWORD dwFlags,
    IN OUT LPVOID *lppvData
);
```

The first parameter is the handle to the parent window for the dialog. The second parameter is the handle to the Internet connection used in the call to HttpSendRequest. The next two parameters are used to control the behavior of InternetErrorDlg. dwError can be any of the following values described in Table 2-13.

dwFlags can be a combination of any of the values shown in Table 2-14.

As you can see, InternetErrorDlg is a powerful function. It reduces the amount of work you have to do while processing HTTP Internet errors. Instead of having to parse through the HTTP headers to discover the problem, InternetErrorDlg does it for you. Because, currently, InternetErrorDlg can only be used with HTTP requests, I'll look at some examples of how to use it in Chapter 4.

InternetGetLastResponseInfo

InternetGetLastResponseInfo is the last miscellaneous helper function that I'll cover in this section. This function retrieves the extended error information associated with a request. The WinInet protocols can return additional error information (in the form of a string) that describes what went wrong with the request.

Table 2-13 InternetErrorDlg dwError values

dwError Value	Description
ERROR_INTERNET_HTTP_ TO_HTTPS_ON_REDIR	Notifies the user of the zone crossing to and from a secure site.
ERROR_INTERNET_INCORRECT_ PASSWORD	Displays a dialog for obtaining the user's name and password. (With Microsoft Windows 95, the function first attempts to use any cached authentication information for the server being accessed before displaying a dialog.)
ERROR_INTERNET_INVALID_CA	Notifies the user that the Win32 Internet function does not recognize the certificate authority that generated the certificate for this SSL site.
ERROR_INTERNET_POST_IS_ NON_SECURE	Displays a warning about posting data to the server through a nonsecure connection.
ERROR_INTERNET_SEC_CERT_ CN_INVALID	Indicates that the SSL certificate Common Name (host name field) is incorrect. Displays the Invalid SSL Common Name dialog and lets the user view the incorrect certificate. Also allows the user to select a certificate in response to a server request.
ERROR_INTERNET_SEC_CERT_ DATE_INVALID	Tells the user that the SSL certificate has expired.

If a WinInet request fails, first you want to call the Win32 function GetLastError. If GetLastError returns ERROR_INTERNET_EXTENDED_ERROR, you should immediately call InternetGetLastResponseInfo. Calling InternetGetLastResponseInfo retrieves the protocol-specific error string. Here is InternetGetLastResponseInfo's function declaration:

```
BOOL InternetGetLastResponseInfo(
    OUT LPDWORD lpdwError,
    OUT LPSTR lpszBuffer,
    IN OUT LPDWORD lpdwBufferLength
);
```

You can call InternetGetLastResponseInfo multiple times for a given error. However, once you call another WinInet function, the buffer containing the last response

Table 2-14   InternetErrorDlg flags

DwError Value	Description
FLAGS_ERROR_UI_FILTER_FOR_ERRORS	Scans the returned headers for errors. Call after using HttpOpenRequest. This option detects any hidden errors, such as an authentication error.
FLAGS_ERROR_UI_FLAGS_CHANGE_OPTIONS	Stores the results of the dialog box in the Internet handle if the function succeeds.
FLAGS_ERROR_UI_FLAGS_GENERATE_DATA	Queries the Internet handle for needed information. The function constructs the appropriate data structure for the error.
FLAGS_ERROR_UI_SERIALIZE_DIALOGS	Serializes authentication dialogs for concurrent requests on a password cache entry. The lppvData parameter should contain the address of a pointer to an INTERNET_AUTHNOTIFY_DATA structure, and the client should implement a thread-safe, nonblocking callback function.

error is cleared. Hence, you must call InternetGetLastResponseInfo before any other WinInet function is called.

 The buffer containing the last response error is cleared before each new WinInet request. Hence, if you encounter an error, you must call InternetGetLastResponseInfo before calling any other WinInet function.

Conclusion

The four main WinInet general functions presented in this chapter—InternetOpen, InternetConnect, InternetSetStatusCallback, and InternetCloseHandle—are the cornerstones of a WinInet application. Every WinInet application must use at least two of these functions, specifically InternetOpen and InternetCloseHandle. However, if you want your application to be user friendly, you must also use InternetSetStatusCallback.

Although most applications end up using InternetConnect as well, a very acceptable and timesaving alternative is to use InternetOpenUrl. I'll cover InternetOpenUrl in the next chapter. Nevertheless, for ultimate control over your HTTP, FTP, or Gopher connection, InternetConnect is the best choice.

The rest of the WinInet Internet general functions presented in this chapter were designed to make your WinInet development easier. Although I presented the rest of these functions in an alphabet-soup format, you should at least be aware of their existence and be able to use them if necessary.

3
Chapter

Handling URLs

Now it's time to explore the alternative to Internet Connect—InternetOpenUrl—which is a much easier solution to downloading data. Once again, if all you care about is downloading the data associated with a URL and you don't need to deal with the individual WinInet protocols, InternetOpenUrl is definitely the way to go. InternetOpenUrl will save you time and energy.

InternetOpenUrl does just what its name suggests—it opens the specified URL and returns an HINTERNET handle that can be used with InternetReadFile. InternetOpenUrl knows how to deal with URLs containing any of the three WinInet protocols. Thus, you can use InternetOpenUrl effectively to achieve simple HTTP, FTP, and Gopher downloads. Although InternetOpenUrl is much simpler than taking the InternetConnect route, as you'll see it's also much more limited.

In this chapter, I'll cover some URL basics and show you where to find more official URL information. Then I'll cover InternetOpenUrl and show you some URL helper functions that will simplify the process of working with URLs. Finally, to help solidify the concepts covered in this chapter, I'll present a simple example that shows you how to use InternetOpenUrl to download files using any of the WinInet-supported protocols (HTTP, FTP, and Gopher).

URL Basics

According to the Microsoft Internet Client SDK, a URL is

> . . . a compact representation of the location and access method for a resource located on the Internet. Each URL consists of a scheme (HTTP, HTTPS, FTP, or Gopher—otherwise known as the protocol) and a scheme-specific string. This string can also include a combination of a directory path, search string, or name of the resource.

For more information on URLs, see RFC 1738, *Uniform Resource Locators (URL)*. This document can be found at *http://info.internet.isi.edu/in-notes/rfc/files/ rfc1738.txt.*

Let's take a look at the general URL syntax (as described in RFC 1738):

```
<scheme>://<user>:<password>@<host>:<port>/<url-path>/<extra-info>
```

Every URL that you run across on the Internet will conform to the following syntax:

```
<scheme>://<user>:<password>@<host>:<port>/<url-path>/<extra-info>
```

Keep in mind, however, that some or all of the following components may be excluded from a particular URL:

```
<user>:<password>@
:<password>
:<port>
/<url-path>
/<extra-info>
```

Now let's take a look at a sample URL and break it down into components. Here is a sample URL:

```
http://aarons.axtech.com:80/path/object.cgi?param1=value1
```

Table 3-1 describes the various components that make up the given URL. As we'll see shortly, there are a handful of helper functions that assist in creating and breaking apart URLs. These helper functions deal with the same components described in Table 3-1.

Notice that the data contained in a URL is very similar to the data required by InternetConnect. In fact, the only two URL components for which InternetConnect doesn't ask are path and extra-info. (If you're using InternetConnect, the path and extra-info components are filled in by the protocol-specific functions.) Essentially, a URL contains all the information required to download a resource from the Internet. This browserlike encapsulation of downloading Internet resources makes InternetOpenUrl very nice to work with.

You can use InternetOpenUrl with any of the three WinInet-supported protocols (HTTP/HTTPS, FTP, and Gopher). Let's take a look at the following URL examples for each of the supported WinInet protocols:

```
http://aarons.axtech.com/path/object.cgi?param1=value1
https://aarons.axtech.com:443/path/object.cgi?param1=value1
ftp://ftp.microsoft.com/developr/msdn
gopher://acs2.byu.edu/11
```

InternetOpenUrl handles these URLs just like IE. If you've never tried pointing IE to FTP or Gopher URLs, try typing the FTP and Gopher samples presented here and investigate a little. InternetOpenUrl is going to return the same data received by IE. As you can see, InternetOpenUrl allows you to use transparently any of the WinInet protocols.

Table 3-1   URL components example

URL Component	Example
Scheme	http
Host	aarons.axtech.com
Port	80
Path	/path/object.cgi
Extra-info	?param1=value1
User name	<empty>
Password	<empty>

A URL contains all the information required to download a resource found on the Internet.

At this point you may be wondering what the difference is between HTTP and HTTPS. Obviously both use the HTTP protocol. HTTPS, however, uses SSL. Specifying `https` for the scheme without specifying a port causes InternetOpenUrl to use the default SSL port 443. I'll cover this in more detail shortly.

The last thing I want to mention about URLs is the importance of proper URL encoding. Before passing a URL string to InternetOpenUrl, you must make sure that all unsafe characters have been encoded properly. For a complete list of characters that require encoding, see Table 3-2.

The way URL encoding works is quite simple. If a URL contains any of the characters listed in Table 3-2, you need to replace the character with its corresponding hexadecimal value in the following format: '%XX' except for blank spaces, which are replaced by the + character. For example, suppose you have the following URL with a few embedded blank spaces and parentheses:

```
http://www.server.com/object.cgi?param1=This is the value with (blanks)
```

After encoding this example, the URL looks like this:

```
http://www.server.com/object.cgi?param1=This+is+the+value+with+%28blanks%29
```

To get a better feel for how this works, go to Yahoo!'s Web site and play with their search engine. Any value that you type in the search field will be URL encoded. After

Table 3-2   Characters that require encoding

Description	Character Values
Any character that doesn't have a corresponding graphic character in the US-ASCII-coded character set	Hexadecimal 80-FF, 00-1F, and 7F
Blank spaces	' ' (Hexadecimal 20)
Encoding character	'%' (Hexadecimal 25)
Unsafe characters	<, >, ", #, {, }, |, \, ^, ~, [,], and '

you press Search, the encoded value (for what you typed) shows up in your browser's address/location field. For example, take a look at Figure 3-1, which contains the URL from the previous example.

After pressing Search, Figure 3-2 shows the URL-encoded data in IE's Address field.

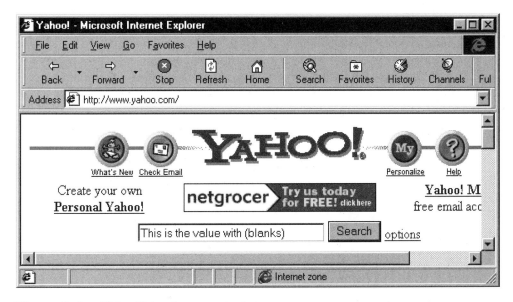

Figure 3-1   Using Yahoo! to encode data

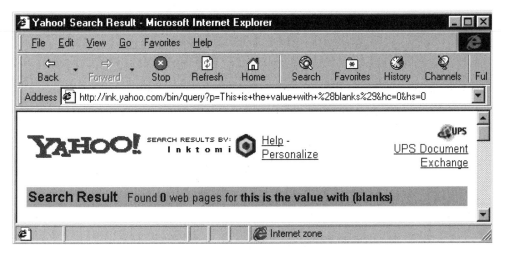

Figure 3-2   Yahoo!'s encoded search string

Fortunately, WinInet offers a handful of URL helper functions that take care of URL encoding and decoding. These functions include InternetCanonicalizeUrl, InternetCombineUrl, InternetCrackUrl, and InternetCreateUrl, which I'll talk about shortly. You can read more about URL encoding details in RFC 1738.

InternetOpenUrl

Now it's time to look at some of the InternetOpenUrl details. Remember that when you call InternetOpenUrl you're basically opening the remote resource specified by the URL. If the specified URL is complete and specifies a valid location, InternetOpenUrl should return a valid HINTERNET handle, which can then be used by InternetReadFile.

There are generally only three functions that you may want to call after using InternetOpenUrl (see Figure 3-3)—InternetQueryDataAvailable, InternetReadFile, and InternetSetFilePointer. InternetSetFilePointer, however, can only be used if InternetOpenUrl was called using HTTP or HTTPS. You can use any of these three functions in combination with InternetOpenUrl, but I tend only to use InternetReadFile.

Let's take a look at InternetOpenUrl's function declaration:

```
HINTERNET InternetOpenUrl(
    IN HINTERNET hInternetSession,
```

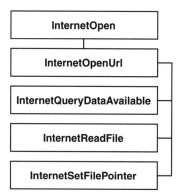

Figure 3-3   InternetOpenUrl handle hierarchy

```
    IN LPCSTR lpszUrl,
    IN LPCSTR lpszHeaders,
    IN DWORD dwHeadersLength,
    IN DWORD dwFlags,
    IN DWORD dwContext
);
```

When you understand URLs, you've got the most important InternetOpenUrl parameters conquered: hInternetSession and lpszUrl. hInternetSession expects a handle returned by InternetOpen, and lpszUrl expects a URL string that conforms to the URL format described earlier. Ninety percent of the time you'll probably only use these first two parameters (and maybe some flags).

The two header parameters, lpszHeaders and dwHeadersLength, are only applicable when using the HTTP protocol. For more information on HTTP headers and the format of lpszHeaders, see Chapter 4.

The final parameter, dwFlags, gives you a chance to specify certain WinInet flags that control certain aspects of InternetOpenUrl's behavior. Table 3-3 describes the WinInet flags that can be used with InternetOpenUrl.

Most of these flags are described sufficiently in Table 3-3. However, to understand fully how these flags work, you should play around with them in some sample code. Nevertheless, before continuing I want to make a few observations that aren't so obvious.

The first observation has to do with INTERNET_FLAG_RAW_DATA. If you point Internet Explorer to *ftp://ftp.microsoft.com* and then go to View | Source, you'll notice there is HTML in the returned document. If the INTERNET_FLAG_RAW_DATA flag is not specified or if the call is made through a CERN proxy, an HTML version of the FTP or Gopher directory is returned—this is what happens by default in IE. If you specify the INTERNET_FLAG_RAW_DATA flag, InternetOpenUrl returns the data as either a GOPHER_FIND_DATA (Gopher) structure or a WIN32_FIND_DATA (FTP) structure, depending on which protocol is used.

If you want to avoid parsing the HTML data in the returned document and you know that you won't be calling InternetOpenUrl through a CERN proxy, using INTERNET_FLAG_RAW_DATA is a good approach.

Table 3-3   **InternetOpenUrl flags**

InternetOpenUrl Flag	Description
INTERNET_FLAG_DON'T_CACHE	Does not cache the data, either locally or in any gateways. Identical to the preferred value, INTERNET_FLAG_NO_CACHE_WRITE
INTERNET_FLAG_EXISTING_CONNECT	If possible, reuses the existing connections to the server for new requests generated by InternetOpenUrl instead of creating a new session for each request. This flag is useful only for FTP connections because FTP is the only protocol that typically performs multiple operations during the same session.
INTERNET_FLAG_HYPERLINK	Forces a reload if there was no Expires time and no Last-Modified time returned from the server when determining whether to reload the item from the network.
INTERNET_FLAG_IGNORE_CERT_ CN_INVALID	Disables Win32 Internet function checking of SSL/Private Communications Technology (PCT)-based certificates that are returned from the server against the host name given in the request.
INTERNET_FLAG_IGNORE_CERT_ DATE_INVALID	Disables Win32 Internet function checking of SSL/PCT-based certificates for proper validity dates for HTTP requests.
INTERNET_FLAG_IGNORE_REDIRECT_ TO_HTTP	Disables the ability of the Win32 Internet functions to detect this special type of redirect. When this flag is used, Win32 Internet functions allow redirects transparently from HTTPS to HTTP URLs.
INTERNET_FLAG_IGNORE_REDIRECT_ TO_HTTPS	Disables the ability of the Win32 Internet functions to detect this special type of redirect. When this flag is used, Win32 Internet functions allow redirects transparently from HTTP to HTTPS URLs.
INTERNET_FLAG_KEEP_CONNECTION	Uses keep-alive semantics, if available, for the connection for HTTP requests. This flag is required for Microsoft Network (MSN), NT LAN Manager (NTLM), and other types of authentication.

InternetOpenUrl Flag	Description
INTERNET_FLAG_MUST_CACHE_ REQUEST	Causes a temporary file to be created if the file cannot be cached. Identical to the preferred value, INTERNET_FLAG_NEED_FILE.
INTERNET_FLAG_NEED_FILE	Causes a temporary file to be created if the file cannot be cached.
INTERNET_FLAG_NO_AUTH	Does not attempt authentication automatically for HTTP requests.
INTERNET_FLAG_NO_AUTO_ REDIRECT	Does not handle redirection automatically for HTTP requests only.
INTERNET_FLAG_NO_CACHE_WRITE	Does not cache the data, either locally or in any gateways.
INTERNET_FLAG_NO_COOKIES	Does not automatically add cookie headers to requests and does not automatically add returned cookies to the cookie database for HTTP requests.
INTERNET_FLAG_NO_UI	Disables the cookie dialog.
INTERNET_FLAG_PASSIVE	Uses passive FTP semantics for FTP files and directories.
INTERNET_FLAG_RAW_DATA	Returns the data as a GOPHER_FIND_DATA structure when retrieving Gopher directory information, or as a WIN32_FIND_DATA structure when retrieving FTP directory information. If this flag is not specified or if the call was made through a CERN proxy, InternetOpenUrl returns an HTML version of the directory.
INTERNET_FLAG_PRAGMA_NOCACHE	Forces the request to be resolved by the originating server, even if a cached copy exists on the proxy.
INTERNET_FLAG_RELOAD	Gets the data from the wire even if it is cached locally.
INTERNET_FLAG_RESYNCHRONIZE	Reloads HTTP resources if the resource has been modified since the last time it was downloaded. All FTP and Gopher resources are reloaded.
INTERNET_FLAG_SECURE	Requests secure transactions on the wire with SSL or PCT. This flag applies to HTTP requests only.

Using SSL with InternetOpenUrl

The second and last observation deals with the INTERNET_FLAG_SECURE flag. Although this flag only applies to HTTP requests, you should definitely be aware of its existence. Specifying INTERNET_FLAG_SECURE causes InternetOpenUrl to use the default HTTPS port (443) and SSL. SSL requires that all data be encrypted. By simply supplying INTERNET_FLAG_SECURE, all data sent by InternetOpenUrl and all data downloaded by InternetReadFile are encrypted behind the scenes by WinInet.

The nice thing about WinInet SSL support is that you never have to deal with the encrypted data directly. This means that you can call InternetReadFile just like you would if you weren't using INTERNET_FLAG_SECURE. In other words, the data read by InternetReadFile is not encrypted. If you've ever tried to implement secure sockets on top of Winsock, you'll really appreciate this powerful WinInet feature.

Because SSL is really a feature of HTTP, I'll discuss the topic in much more detail in Chapter 4. However, the not-so-obvious issue of using SSL with InternetOpenUrl has to do with being able to specify the HTTPS scheme (`https://`). If the URL in lpszUrl uses the HTTPS scheme, the flag INTERNET_FLAG_SECURE is redundant. In other words, if a URL begins with `https://`, you don't have to specify the secure flag—WinInet uses SSL semantics automatically. However, if you specify a URL beginning with `http://` and you want to use SSL, you must supply the secure flag.

InternetOpenUrl uses SSL if either of the following is true:

- You specify the INTERNET_FLAG_SECURE flag
- The specified URL contains the HTTPS scheme, `https://`

I'll let you study the rest of the InternetOpenUrl flags on your own. As you can see, there are plenty from which to choose. These flags give you much more control over the exact behavior of InternetOpenUrl; becoming familiar with these flags will open new doors in terms of flexibility.

The last major section of this chapter walks you through an example of using InternetOpenUrl in combination with the helper function InternetCanonicalizeUrl. However, before diving into the sample code, let's cover briefly the URL helper functions offered by WinInet.

Helper Functions

There are four URL helper functions designed to assist in working directly with
URLs: InternetCanonicalizeUrl, InternetCombineUrl, InternetCrackUrl, and
InternetCreateUrl. Each of these functions fulfills a specific need and greatly
simplifies the process of manipulating URL strings.

InternetCanonicalizeUrl

First let's take a look at InternetCanonicalizeUrl. This handy function performs one
simple task—canonicalization of the URL string. Canonicalizing is the process of
converting a URL that may contain unsafe characters into an accepted format.

To use this function you simply supply the suspect URL string along with a
buffer that contains the new encoded URL string. Take a look at the declaration of
InternetCanonicalizeUrl:

```
BOOL InternetCanonicalizeUrl(
    IN LPCSTR lpszUrl,
    OUT LPSTR lpszBuffer,
    IN OUT LPDWORD lpdwBufferLength,
    IN DWORD dwFlags
);
```

You can also supply a set of flags that determine exactly what
InternetCanonicalizeUrl should do (see Table 3-4). InternetCanonicalizeUrl
can be used to encode a URL string, and it can also be used to decode a URL
string. It can even be used simply to encode spaces and nothing else. If no flags
are specified, the function converts all unsafe characters and meta sequences (such
as \., \.., and \...) to escape sequences.

 One thing to keep in mind while using the URL helper functions is that
you are responsible for keeping track of the URL encoded state. For
example, if you encode a URL, your application should remember that
the URL has already been encoded. If you attempt to encode the same
URL again (by calling InternetCanonicalizeUrl), the escape sequences in
the encoded URL are encoded again.

Table 3-4   InternetCanonicalizeUrl flags

Flag	Description
ICU_BROWSER_MODE	Does not encode or decode characters after "#" or "?", and does not remove trailing white space after "?". If this value is not specified, the entire URL is encoded, and trailing white space is removed.
ICU_DECODE	Converts all %XX sequences to characters, including escape sequences, before the URL is parsed.
ICU_ENCODE_SPACES_ONLY	Encodes spaces only.
ICU_NO_ENCODE	Does not convert unsafe characters to escape sequences.
ICU_NO_META	Does not remove meta-sequences (such as "." and "..") from the URL.

Consider the following raw URL:

```
http://www.server.com/script.cgi?param1=this has spaces
```

After calling InternetCanonicalizeUrl once, the new URL looks like this:

```
http://www.server.com/script.cgi?param1=this%20has%20spaces
```

Then, if you call InternetCanonicalizeUrl on this URL string that has already been encoded, the % characters are encoded again. Hence doing so would cause the URL to look like this:

```
http://www.server.com/script.cgi?param1=this%2520has%2520spaces
```

This is obviously incorrect and will cause your program to do strange things. Your application needs to contain the intelligence required to determine when a URL string should be encoded and also when it should be decoded.

Also, another potential problem arises when using InternetCanonicalizeUrl with ICU_DECODE on URL strings that aren't completely canonicalized. For example, if you use ICU_DECODE on a URL string that contains a % character, it will attempt to decode that character even though it isn't truly an escape sequence. To avoid this type of problem, only use the ICU_DECODE flag on URL strings that have been canonicalized using InternetCanonicalizeUrl.

InternetCombineUrl

InternetCombineUrl allows you to combine base and relative URLs. InternetCombineUrl is really an extension of InternetCanonicalizeUrl because it can also canonicalize the URL string. In fact, all the flags used with InternetCanonicalizeUrl (see Table 3-4) can also be used with InternetCombineUrl.

This helper function is very useful if you're developing a browserlike application that deals constantly with relative URLs. The function declaration is simple:

```
BOOL InternetCombineUrl(
    IN LPCSTR lpszBaseUrl,
    IN LPCSTR lpszRelativeUrl,
    OUT LPSTR lpszBuffer,
    IN OUT LPDWORD lpdwBufferLength,
    IN DWORD dwFlags
);
```

Suppose you download the HTML page associated with the following base URL:

```
http://www.server.com/dir1/dir2/sample.html
```

Now suppose that sample.html contains the following relative link:

```
../../index.html
```

Calling InternetCombineUrl with those two values produces the following string:

```
http://www.server.com/index.html
```

Don't forget that InternetCombineUrl can also canonicalize the resulting URL string.

InternetCrackUrl

InternetCrackUrl is useful for breaking a URL into its various components. Take a look at the function declaration:

```
BOOL InternetCrackUrl(
    IN LPCSTR lpszUrl,
    IN DWORD dwUrlLength,
    IN DWORD dwFlags,
    IN OUT LPURL_COMPONENTS lpUrlComponents
);
```

The first two parameters, lpszUrl and dwUrlLength, refer to the URL you're passing in to break up. The dwFlags parameter allows you to specify if you also want to decode the URL in the process. The only two valid flag values for InternetCrackUrl are described in Table 3-5.

The final parameter, lpUrlComponents, is a pointer to a URL_COMPONENTS structure that contains the various URL components. Let's take a closer look at the URL_COMPONENTS structure:

```
typedef struct {
    DWORD dwStructSize;
    LPSTR lpszScheme;
    DWORD dwSchemeLength;
    INTERNET_SCHEME nScheme;
    LPSTR lpszHostName;
    DWORD dwHostNameLength;
    INTERNET_PORT nPort;
    LPSTR lpszUserName;
    DWORD dwUserNameLength;
    LPSTR lpszPassword;
    DWORD dwPasswordLength;
    LPSTR lpszUrlPath;
    DWORD dwUrlPathLength;
    LPSTR lpszExtraInfo;
    DWORD dwExtraInfoLength;
} URL_COMPONENTS;
```

Table 3-5 InternetCrackUrl flags

Flag	Description
ICU_DECODE	Converts encoded characters back to their normal form. This can be used only if the user provides buffers in the URL_COMPONENTS structure into which to copy the components.
ICU_ESCAPE	Converts all escape sequences (%XX) to their corresponding characters. This can be used only if the user provides buffers in the URL_COMPONENTS structure into which to copy the components.

Most of these fields are self-explanatory. Let me point out that dwStructSize must be set to the size of the URL_COMPONENTS structure before passing the structure to any of the URL functions.

Also, lpszScheme and nScheme refer to the type of service used in the URL such as HTTP, FTP, or Gopher. lpszScheme contains the appropriate scheme string representation whereas nScheme contains the appropriate INTERNET_SCHEME enumeration value (INTERNET_SCHEME_HTTP, INTERNET_SCHEME_FTP, and so on).

Each URL component (except for the port number) is represented by buffer (LPSTR) and buffer length variables. For example, the lpszUserName and dwUserNameLength fields of the structure represent the user name component. If the structure contains zero for both values of a given component, InternetCrackUrl won't return the given component value. If the buffer pointer is zero, but the buffer length field is nonzero, InternetCrackUrl returns a pointer to the component in the original URL string (and won't copy the value). Finally, if the structure contains nonzero values for both the buffer pointer and buffer length fields, InternetCrackUrl copies the component into the supplied buffer.

Because this is such a confusing point for most developers, I've provided Table 3-6 to summarize the behavior:

Table 3-6 URL_COMPONENT behavior

Buffer (LPSTR)	Length (DWORD)	Behavior
NULL	0	The component is not returned.
NULL	Nonzero	The pointer to the component in the original URL string is returned.
Nonzero	Nonzero	The URL component string is copied to the supplied buffer in the URL_COMPONENT structure.

For more information on the URL components, refer back to the example in Table 3-1 and the section on URL basics.

InternetCreateUrl

InternetCreateUrl does exactly the opposite of InternetCrackUrl. Whereas InternetCrackUrl breaks a URL into its various components, InternetCreateUrl

Table 3-7   InternetCreateUrl flags

Flag	Description
ICU_ESCAPE	Converts all escape sequences (%XX) to their corresponding characters.
ICU_USERNAME	When adding the user name, uses the name that was specified at logon.

constructs a URL from the various URL components contained in the URL_COMPO-NENTS structure. Here is the InternetCreateUrl function declaration:

```
BOOL InternetCreateUrl(
    IN LPURL_COMPONENTS lpUrlComponents,
    IN DWORD dwFlags,
    OUT LPSTR lpszUrl,
    IN OUT LPDWORD lpdwUrlLength
);
```

As you can see, the parameters are exactly the same as those used by InternetCrackUrl except in a different order. There are, however, a few differences with respect to the flags accepted by InternetCreateUrl. Table 3-7 describes the flags used by InternetCreateUrl. Notice the ICU_USERNAME flag, which tells InternetCreateUrl to use the user name specified at Windows logon.

The URL_COMPONENTS structure is used in the same manner described earlier in InternetCrackUrl. If you don't want to use a specific URL component, be sure to set the buffer pointer to NULL. Also, if you set the buffer length members to zero, InternetCreateUrl assumes that the strings are NULL terminated.

This function is very handy if you have all the URL components and need to construct a complete URL.

InternetOpenUrl Sample Program (InetURL)

Lastly, it's time to look at an example. In this section I'll readdress the sample program that I presented briefly in Chapter 1. This time, however, you should feel completely comfortable with the sample code. If you're still having problems grasping the sample code after finishing this section, go back and review the first few chapters before continuing.

InetURL allows you to download the text associated with any URL on the Internet. That's right. You can use HTTP, FTP, or Gopher URLs and see exactly what InternetOpenUrl accomplishes for you.

The screen shot in Figure 3-4 illustrates what InetURL looks like after downloading the text associated with *http://www.microsoft.com.*

If you browse to *http://www.microsoft.com* using IE and select View | Source, you'll notice that the source is exactly the same as what you see here. Essentially, InternetOpenUrl returns the same HTML source returned by IE for a given URL. So if you ever want to make sure your InternetOpenUrl code is working properly, you have a nice test utility—IE.

As you can see, this sample application is quite simple. The application main window is a simple dialog with a few controls. To use the sample, you simply type in the URL you wish to download in the URL edit box and press the Fetch button. After the download is complete, the returned text shows up in the read-only edit box. I intentionally kept the UI simple to focus more appropriately on InternetOpenUrl functionality.

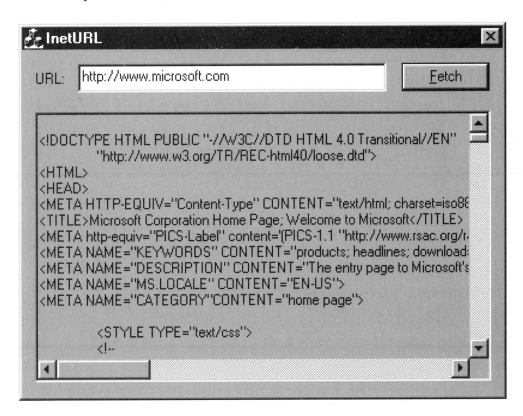

Figure 3-4   INetURL sample screen shot

Once again, you can get the code for all sample programs from the *Essential WinInet* Web site. The sample was written with Visual C++ 5.0 along with the IE 4.0 version of WinInet.

Processing OnFetch

For the purpose of this example, I encapsulated all of the WinInet code within a single function, CInetURLDlg::OnFetch. This function is called whenever the user presses the Fetch button. Listing 3-1 contains the sample code for this function, and there are comments throughout the function explaining each step.

Listing 3-1   CInetURLDlg::OnFetch

```
void CInetURLDlg::OnFetch()
{
    UpdateData(TRUE);

    //make sure that the user typed something in
    m_strResult.Empty();
    if (m_strURL.IsEmpty())
        return;
    //initialize WinInet by calling InternetOpen
    HINTERNET hSession = InternetOpen("InetURL/1.0",
            INTERNET_OPEN_TYPE_PRECONFIG, NULL, NULL, 0);
    if (hSession)
    {
        //call InternetOpenUrl with the user's URL
        HINTERNET hFile = InternetOpenUrl(hSession, m_strURL, NULL, 0, 0, 0);
        if (hFile)
        {
            CHAR lpszBuffer[BUFFLEN];
            DWORD dwRead;

            //read until dwRead == 0
            while (InternetReadFile(hFile, lpszBuffer, BUFFLEN-1, &dwRead))
            {
                if (dwRead == 0)
                    break;
                lpszBuffer[dwRead]=0;        //null terminate temp buffer
                m_strResult += lpszBuffer;   //add to end of complete result
            }
```

```
        //close the file handle created by InternetOpenUrl
        InternetCloseHandle(hFile);
    }
    //close the session handle created by InternetOpen
    InternetCloseHandle(hSession);
}
//update dialog controls
UpdateData(FALSE);
}
```

Because this code is so self-explanatory, I won't bore you by dissecting it line by line. The only tricky part that might throw you for a loop in your own code is the InternetReadFile loop. Remember that InternetReadFile must return TRUE and dwRead must equal zero before you know for sure that you're done reading.

Notice how simple this function really is. With a few lines of code, we've implemented an application that is capable of communicating via HTTP, FTP, and Gopher. Let's take a look at a few example URLs and see what InetURL returns for each of them.

HTTPS Example

We already saw an example of an HTTP URL (*http://www.microsoft.com*) in Figure 3-4. What about an example of using SSL or, in other words, a URL that begins with `https://`? Take a look at the following URL, which points to an online stock brokerage service called Datek Online:

```
https://orders.datek.com
```

If you try this URL with InetURL, you get the result illustrated in Figure 3-5.

Although at first it appears to work the same as a regular HTTP URL, there is really a lot going on behind the scenes. When you press Fetch, WinInet is going to request an encryption key from the secure Web server, encrypt all the data sent by InternetOpenUrl (including the headers), and decrypt the response read by InternetReadFile.

If you inspect the code, however, you'll notice that we didn't have to do anything to make this happen. We didn't even have to specify INTERNET_FLAG_SECURE (remember that specifying INTERNET_FLAG_SECURE with an HTTPS URL is redundant). WinInet kindly takes care of all SSL functionality for us transparently.

If you debug through this example using an HTTPS URL, you'll notice that the debugger loads quite a few more DLLs than with the HTTP URL example. For instance, the debugger loads crypt32.dll, schannel.dll, and wintrust.dll along with

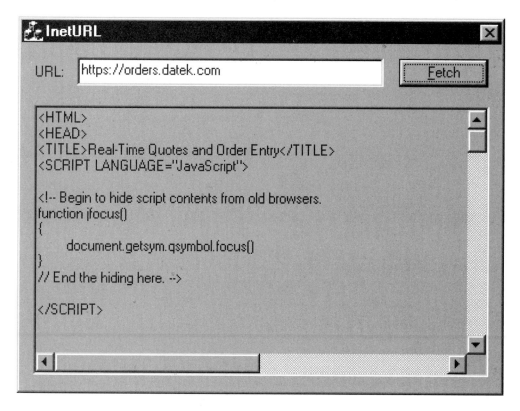

Figure 3-5   InetURL HTTPS example

others required by SSL. SSL support is one of the most powerful and valuable features offered by WinInet.

FTP Example

Now let's take a look at a simple FTP URL:

```
ftp://ftp.relia.net
```

Using this URL with InetURL produces the results shown in Figure 3-6. If you scroll down in the read-only edit box, you'll see the directory listing for the anonymous FTP site at relia.net.

If you want to change directories, you would simply supply a new URL that specifies the desired location. For example, to change to the "pub" subdirectory, you would specify the following URL and press Fetch:

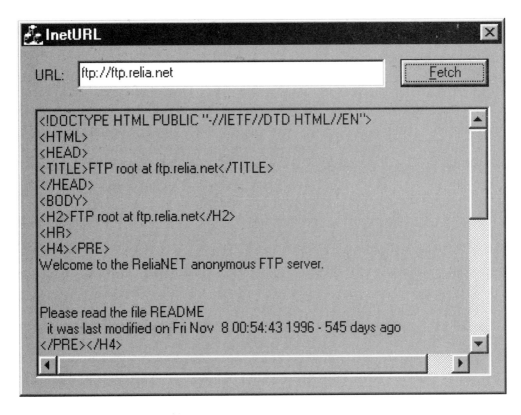

Figure 3-6 InetURL FTP example

```
ftp://ftp.relia.net/pub
```

If you wanted to go up a directory from "pub" you could either specify the absolute path like this

```
ftp://ftp.relia.net
```

or you could simply specify the parent directory command on the end of the current URL like this

```
ftp://ftp.relia.net/pub/..
```

Either way, you'll end up back at the root anonymous FTP directory. Playing around with FTP commands using this sample application is a good way to become familiar with the FTP protocol.

Gopher Example

Let's look at one final example using a Gopher URL:

```
gopher://acs2.byu.edu/11
```

Using this URL with InetURL produces the results shown in Figure 3-7.

If you scroll around, you'll see the entire Gopher directory at Brigham Young University (BYU). Similar to the FTP example, using the URLs in the directory listing navigates you effectively through the Gopher hierarchy.

As you can see, this simple application opens the doors to all WinInet Internet protocols including HTTP, HTTPS, FTP, and Gopher. In fact, anything you can do with IE is also possible with InternetOpenUrl. If you're only interested in accessing resources associated with a URL and don't care about protocol specifics, using InternetOpenUrl is a good choice. You'll find out shortly that this approach is

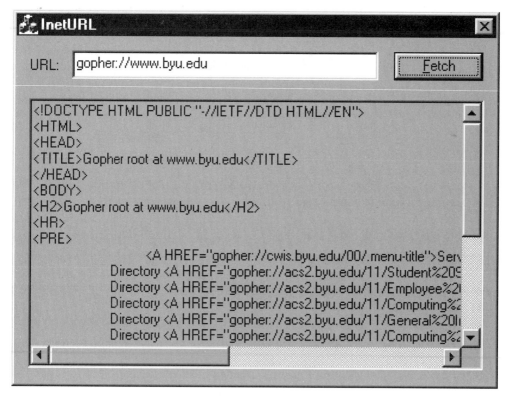

Figure 3-7 InetURL Gopher example

definitely easier than taking the InternetConnect path along with the protocol-specific functions.

I strongly recommend playing around with this sample program and trying to figure out how to use the various WinInet protocols with InternetOpenUrl. As we move forward in this book, I'll look at these protocols in much more detail. Becoming familiar with how they work now will help you understand what's ahead.

Conclusion

Using URLs is much simpler than using InternetConnect along with the protocol-specific functions. A URL really provides a nice encapsulation of all connection information required to download a resource located somewhere on the Internet. Since the Internet has become so popular, more and more of the general public is familiar with the concept of a URL. This makes working with URLs less of a challenge for the average user and a very acceptable solution for many WinInet applications.

No matter how you look at it, using InternetOpenUrl (as opposed to InternetConnect) saves you time, money, and energy. By now you should feel comfortable enough with the URL basics and how to use InternetOpenUrl to start using this powerful WinInet feature in your applications. Be sure to play around with the sample application in this chapter to become even more familiar with InternetOpenUrl.

The URL helper functions presented in this chapter were designed to simplify the process of working with URLs. Manipulating URLs manually can be very cumbersome. These functions help you crack, create, combine, and even canonicalize URLs according to the latest URL RFC specification.

As with all high-level abstractions, the main disadvantage to using InternetOpenUrl is the lack of control over the underlying protocol behavior. If you need more flexibility at the protocol level, you'll want to use InternetConnect along with the protocol-specific functions. The protocol-specific functions— covered in the next three chapters—give you direct control over the behavior of the given protocol.

II Part

WinInet
Protocol-Specific
Functions

4
Chapter

HTTP Functions

In this chapter, we'll look at the most widely used protocol on the Internet today—HTTP. First I'll cover the HTTP protocol specification and help you to understand how the protocol works. With that understanding in place I'll show you the WinInet HTTP functions and how to control various features of the HTTP protocol directly. These functions give you much more control over the protocol functionality than you'll get by using the tempting InternetOpenUrl.

Before leaving this chapter I'll walk you through the creation of a sample application that can download a Web page using the WinInet HTTP functions. This sample is very similar to the sample presented in the last chapter, except you'll be dealing with the HTTP protocol directly. You'll see that using the HTTP functions isn't much harder than using InternetOpenUrl, but you'll gain much more control over the protocol functionality.

By the time you're done with this chapter you should feel comfortable with the inner workings of HTTP and should be ready to start using the WinInet HTTP functions in your application. HTTP is really your application's gateway to the majority of the vast resources found on the Internet today.

The HTTP Protocol

Because of the Internet's recent popularity, HTTP is probably the most widely used application-level Internet protocol today. You'll probably find yourself using HTTP in your Internet applications more than any other Internet protocol. Since you'll be interfacing with it directly, you need a solid understanding of how the protocol works. Thus, this section is devoted to helping you to understand the ins and outs of the HTTP protocol specification.

HTTP is the protocol that makes the World Wide Web (WWW) work the way it does. When you navigate to a Web site using your Web browser (see Figure 4-1), the browser uses HTTP to communicate with the Web server and download all the files (text, images, sounds, ActiveX controls, and so forth) associated with the particular URL. Although HTTP is used mostly to transmit HTML files over the Internet, it can be used to transmit many types of data.

HTTP is a TCP/IP-based protocol. This means that HTTP uses TCP/IP to transmit data over the Internet. HTTP is a higher level protocol that simply defines how the data transmitted by TCP/IP should be formatted.

The HTTP Model

HTTP defines the format of a client request and a server response (both of which are discussed shortly). A basic HTTP transaction consists of the following four steps:

1. Establish a connection (TCP/IP).
2. The client sends a request to the server.
3. The server sends a response to the client.
4. The connection is closed (TCP/IP).

Figure 4-1 Microsoft Internet Explorer 4.0 Web browser

To establish a TCP/IP connection you must provide both a server (host name or IP address) and a port number. Remember that port 80 is reserved as the well-known HTTP port. Although you'll normally use port 80 to communicate via HTTP, other ports can be specified when establishing the connection. Now let's cover steps 2 and 3 of the basic HTTP transaction.

The HTTP Request

Unlike TCP and IP headers, HTTP request and response data is ASCII based, which makes it much easier to work with. An HTTP request consists of a method, uniform resource identifier (URI), protocol version, header, and data. Listing 4-1 contains a sample HTTP request.

Listing 4-1   Sample HTTP request

```
GET /cgi-bin/scripts/basketball-scores HTTP/1.0
Accept: text/plain; text/html
Accept: image/gif; image/jpeg
Accept-Encoding: x-compress; x-zip
Accept-Language: en
User-Agent: MSIE/4.0
If-Modified-Since: Mon, 10 Jan 1998 13:22:34 GMT
Pragma: no-cache
Content-Type: text/plain
Content-Length: 43

Team1=Utah Jazz&Team2=Portland Trailblazers
```

Now let's dissect the HTTP request and examine each component. Here is a breakdown of the HTTP request into components:

- Method URI ProtocolVersion
- Headers
- Carriage-return line-feed sequence (CRLF) (blank line)
- Entity-body

The CRLF is very important to the format of the HTTP request. The CRLF tells the HTTP server where the entity-body begins. Leaving out the CRLF character causes big problems when trying to communicate with an HTTP server. The following sections cover the HTTP method, URI, protocol version, headers, and entity-body.

The CRLF in the HTTP request tells the HTTP server where the headers end and the entity-body begins. Leaving out the CRLF sequence causes the server to process your request incorrectly.

Method

There are various methods that can be used in an HTTP request. Each provides different functionality. The brief method descriptions in Table 4-1 were taken from the World Wide Web Consortium's (W3C) specification on HTTP/1.0[2]. Table 4-1 describes three of the most commonly used HTTP methods.

The GET and POST methods are the most widely used HTTP methods on the Internet today. Nevertheless, there are many other methods that provide extended functionality. Also, HTTP isn't limited to the methods described here. The HTTP protocol is very extensible; by simply adding new methods, the protocol can grow logically.

Table 4-1   Common HTTP methods

HTTP Method	Description
GET	GET is probably the simplest and most used HTTP method. GET simply retrieves the data identified by the URL. If the URL refers to a script (CGI, ISAPI, and so on), it returns the data produced by the script and not the script itself. This method can also be used for searches.
HEAD	HEAD provides the same functionality as GET but only returns HTTP headers and no document body.
POST	Like GET, POST is another widely used HTTP method (typically used by HTML forms). POST creates a new object linked to the specified object. The message-id field of the new object may be set by the client or else is given by the server. A URL is allocated by the server and returned to the client. The new document is the data part of the request. It is considered to be subordinate to the specified object, in the way that a file is subordinate to a directory containing it, or a news article is subordinate to a newsgroup to which it is posted.

---

2. Source, *http://www.w3.org/Protocols/HTTP/Methods.html.*

URI

A URI specifies an Internet resource completely. A URL is actually a type of URI. However, for the most part in this book I treat URLs and URIs identically. For more information on URI specifics, see RFC2396 at *http://info.internet.isi.edu/in-notes/ rfe/files/rfc2396.txt/*.

A URI is usually interpreted as being relative to the server's root WWW directory. It should, however, always begin with a forward slash (/). Thus, a typical URI might look like this:

```
/cgi-bin/map-scripts/findzip.cgi
```

 If a URI doesn't contain a beginning forward slash, you might experience problems, depending on the HTTP server implementation.

Like URLs, URIs should also encode any unsafe characters (we discussed the standard encoding scheme in Chapter 3). Nevertheless, it's important enough (and caused enough developers grief) to cover again.

Have you ever navigated to a Web site and noticed a very long URL containing a bunch of % characters and numbers? This is what an encoded URL looks like. Typically, all unsafe characters should be "escaped" using the % character followed by two hexadecimal numbers representing the ASCII value of the given character (except for spaces, which are replaced with the + character).

For example, consider the following URI:

```
/query?value1=microsoft makes $$$&value2=lots
```

This URI contains nonalphanumeric characters that are potentially unsafe. After escaping these unsafe characters, the URI looks like this:

```
/query?value1=microsoft+makes+%24%24%24&value2=lots
```

Notice that the alphanumeric characters `microsoft` were not encoded because they are safe alphanumeric characters. But what about the space characters found in the URI? The space characters are encoded with the + character.

The ? character specifies where the address ends and the URI-specific data begins. Data is usually referred to in name/value pairs. For example, value1 is the first data element and contains a value of microsoft. The & character simply separates the name/value pairs.

Although you can pass data in the URI, this only works for the GET method. If you're using the POST method you'll pass the name/value pairs (or any other type of data you need to send) in the HTTP entity-body.

Protocol Version

The protocol version field of the request specifies the version of HTTP being used by the client sending the request. This is typically HTTP/1.0.

HTTP Headers

Every HTTP request or response contains a number of HTTP headers. There are four types of HTTP headers: general, entity, request, and response. In this section I discuss all of the HTTP header types except for the response headers, which I'll cover in the next section.

Now let's take a look at the possible header lines and their syntax. For more information on request header syntax, see RFC 822 at *http://info.internet.isi.edu/in-notes/ rfc/files/rfc822.txt.*

Table 4-2 General HTTP headers

Header	Description
Pragma	The Pragma general header is used to include implementation-specific directives that may apply to any recipient along the request/response chain. In other words, pragmas tell the servers that are used to send this request to behave in a certain way. The Pragma header may contain multiple values (the syntax is the same as for the Accept header). The following example tells all proxy servers that relay this request not to use a cached version of the object but to download the object from the specified location: `Pragma: no-cache`
Date	The Date general header represents the date and time at which the message was originated. For example, `Date: Tue, 15 Nov 1994 08:12:31 GMT`

General HTTP Headers   The general HTTP headers can be used with both HTTP requests and responses. General headers don't tell you anything about the requested entity but simply contain useful information that applies to all requests and responses. Table 4-2 describes the most common general HTTP headers.

Entity Headers   Like the general headers, the entity headers also apply to both HTTP requests and responses. The entity headers are used to provide information about the entity (data) being sent with the request or the response. If no data is being sent with the request, entity headers may be used to provide information about the requested object. The most common entity headers are described in Table 4-3.

Table 4-3   HTTP entity headers

Header	Description
Allow	The Allow header lists the set of methods supported by the resource identified by the requested URI. The purpose of this field is strictly to inform the recipient of valid methods associated with the resource. The Allow header is not permitted in a request using the POST method, and thus should be ignored if it is received as part of a POST entity. For example, `Allow: GET, HEAD`
Content-Encoding	The Content-Encoding entity header is used describe the type of encoding used on the entity. When present, its value indicates the decoding mechanism that must be applied to obtain the media type referenced by the Content-Type header. For example, `Content-Encoding: x-gzip`
Content-Length	The Content-Length entity header indicates the size of the entity-body, in decimal number of octets, sent to the recipient or, in the case of the HEAD method, the size of the entity-body that would have been sent had the request been a GET. Applications should use this field to indicate the size of the entity-body to be transferred, regardless of the media type of the entity. A valid Content-Length field value is required on all HTTP/1.0 request messages containing an entity-body. Any Content-Length header greater than or equal to zero is a valid value. For example, `Content-Length: 3495`

(continued)

Table 4-3 (continued)

Header	Description
Content-Type	The Content-Type header indicates the media type of the entity-body sent to the recipient or, in the case of the HEAD method, the media type that would have been sent had the request been a GET. For example, `Content-Type: text/html`
Expires	The Expires header gives the date and time after which the entity should be considered stale. This allows information providers to suggest the volatility of the resource or a date after which the information may no longer be valid. Applications must not cache this entity beyond the date given. The presence of an Expires field does not imply that the original resource will change or cease to exist at, before, or after that time. However, information providers that know or even suspect that a resource will change by a certain date should include an Expires header with that date. For example, `Expires: Thu, 01 Dec 1994 16:00:00 GMT`
Last-Modified	The Last-Modified header indicates the date and time at which the sender believes the resource was last modified. The exact semantics of this field are defined in terms of how the recipient should interpret it: If the recipient has a copy of this resource that is older than the date given by the Last-Modified field, that copy should be considered stale. For example, `Last-Modified: Tue, 15 Nov 1994 12:45:26 GMT`

Request Headers   Now that we have looked at all the general and entity headers that can be applied to both HTTP requests and responses, you're ready to look at the request-specific headers. Table 4-4 describes the headers that can be used with HTTP requests.

Entity-Body

Only requests (or responses) that need to send data (in addition to what is contained in the header) need to use an entity-body. The entity-body must be preceded by a blank line (CRLF), which separates it from the header. The HTTP entity headers describe the format and length of the data that make up the entity-body. For example, if the following entity headers were used in the request (or response)

```
Content-type: text/plain
Content-length: 45
```

Table 4-4 **HTTP request headers**

Header	Description
From	The From header specifies who is taking responsibility for the request. This field contains the e-mail address of the user submitting the request. For example, `From: skonnard@relia.net`

Accept	The Accept header contains a semicolon-separated list of MIME representation schemes that are accepted by the client. The server uses this information to determine which data types are safe to send to the client in the HTTP response. Although the Accept field can contain multiple values, the Accept line itself can also be used more than once to specify additional accept types (this has the same effect as specifying multiple accept types on a single line). If the Accept field is not used in the request header, the default accept types of text/plain and text/html are assumed. For example,
	
	`Accept: text/plain; text/html`
	`Accept: image/gif; image/jpeg`

Accept-Encoding	The Accept-Encoding header is very similar to the Accept header in syntax. However, it specifies the content-encoding schemes that are acceptable in the response. For example, `Accept-Encoding: x-compress; x-zip`
Accept-Language	The Accept-Language header is also similar to the Accept header. It specifies the preferred response language. The following example specifies English as the accepted language: `Accept-Language: en`
User-Agent	The User-Agent header (if present) specifies the name of the client software. The first word should be the name of the software followed by a slash and the version number (the version number is optional). Any other product names that are part of the complete software package may also be included. Each name/version pair should be separated by white space. This field is used mostly for statistical purposes. It allows servers to track software usage and protocol violations. For example, `User-Agent: MySoftware/1.0 YourSoftwareModule/2.0`

(continued)

Table 4-4 (continued)

Header	Description
Referer	The Referer header specifies the URI that contained the URI in the request header. In HTML, it would be the address of the page that contained the link to the requested object (the object, URI, being requested by this header). Like the User-Agent header, this header is not required but is mostly for the server's statistical and tracking benefit. For example, `Referer: default.html`
Authorization	The Authorization header contains authorization information. The first word contained in this header specifies the type of authorization system to use. Then, separated by white space, it should be followed by the authorization information such as a user name, password, and so forth. For example, `Authorization: user myusername:mypassword`
If-Modified-Since	The If-Modified-Since header is used with the GET method to make it conditional. Basically, if the object hasn't changed since the date and time specified by this header, the object is not sent. A local cached copy of the object is used instead. For example, `If-Modified-Since: Mon, 10 Jan 1998 13:22:34 GMT`

you would know that the entity-body contains 45 characters of plain text. For example, it could contain the following data:

```
The quick brown fox jumped over the lazy dog.
```

You only need to use an entity-body with an HTTP request when the requested object requires it. The entity-body is used the same way for HTTP responses, and it can be used to send different data formats back to the client. You can even use HTTP to send and receive binary data.

Request Summary

That pretty much wraps up what goes into an HTTP request. When we get to into using the WinInet HTTP functions, you'll notice that you don't even need to understand most of this information to handle simple HTTP requests. However, to leverage the full power of WinInet and HTTP, you need to understand the methods, headers, and data that make up the HTTP request. This section provides more than enough information on HTTP requests to get you started.

As I already alluded to, every HTTP request must be followed by an HTTP response. Although much of the information covered in this section also applies to HTTP responses, there are certain things you must understand about an HTTP response before diving into WinInet. The next section discusses the HTTP response in more detail.

The HTTP Response

The HTTP response format is much like the request format described earlier, with a few exceptions. In fact, notice that everything but the first line of the response header is exactly the same as the request header. Listing 4-2 contains a sample HTTP response.

Listing 4-2   Sample HTTP response

```
HTTP/1.0 200 OK
Server: Microsoft-IIS/2.0
Date: Mon, 3 Jan 1998 13:22:34 GMT
Content-Type: text/html
Last-Modified: Mon, 11 Jan 1998 13:22:34 GMT
Content-Length: 179

<html>
<head><title>Basketball Scores</title></head>
<body>
Utah Jazz vs. Chicago Bulls: 101-99<br>
Portland Trailblazers vs. Phoenix Suns: 113-88<br>
<br>
<b>GO JAZZ!</b>
</body>
</html>
```

Now let's dissect the HTTP response and examine each component. Here is a breakdown of the HTTP response into components:

- HTTP-Version Status-Code Reason-Phrase
- Headers
- CRLF (blank line)
- Entity-body

The first line in the response format is referred to as the response status line. This line contains important information about the status of the request. The headers section can contain all of the general and entity headers (described earlier in the HTTP request section) plus a few more response-specific headers. Finally, the entity-body is used in the same manner as described in the request section. Because I've already described the role of the entity-body sufficiently, the rest of this section focuses on the status line and the response-specific HTTP headers.

Response Status Line

The response status line is used to provide the requesting client with information on the status of its requests. Specifically, the status line offers three important pieces of information: an HTTP version number, a status code, and a reason phrase. The following is the exact format of the HTTP response status line:

```
HTTP-Version Status-Code Reason-Phrase
```

The HTTP-Version value defines the version of HTTP being used by the server processing the request. The Status-Code value is used to determine the status of the request. The status code tells you whether the request succeeded or failed (I'll cover status codes in more detail shortly). The Reason-Phrase value provides the client with a "human-readable" description of the status code. For example, take a look at the following status line:

```
HTTP/1.0 200 OK
```

This status line tells you that the server that processed the request is using HTTP version 1.0, the request succeeded (200 = success), and that everything went OK.

If you plan on using HTTP much, you need to be familiar with the HTTP status codes. HTTP status codes are organized into five categories. You can tell to which category the status code belongs by the first digit of the status code. Table 4-5 describes the different status code categories and what each of them represents.

For example, if a status code begins with a 5, you know that there was a server error. However, you need to look at last two digits of the status code to get more information about the specific error. HTTP status codes are extensible and can be used to provide application-specific status information. When I start to cover the WinInet HTTP functions, I'll present a detailed table containing all of the HTTP status codes and their descriptions.

Table 4-5   HTTP status code categories

Code	Description
1xx	Informational—reserved for future use
2xx	Success—the action was successful
3xx	Redirection—further action must be taken to complete the request
4xx	Client Error—the request contains bad syntax or cannot be fulfilled
5xx	Server Error—the server failed to fulfill an apparently valid request

Response Headers

Remember that the general and the entity headers described in the HTTP request section can be used as response headers as well. Besides the general and entity headers, there are only a few other headers that are specific to HTTP responses. Table 4-6 describes three of the most widely used response headers.

Response Summary

As you can see, the HTTP response format is very similar to the HTTP request. The response, however, provides the requester with important status information. Not only does the response provide specific status codes, it also provides the requesting client with information in response-specific headers. This information helps the requester figure out what it should do next. For example, the client may need to perform some type of authentication to continue, or it may simply need to retry the previous request that failed.

Using Telnet to Test HTTP

Both Windows 95 and Windows NT come with the Windows Telnet client (based on the Telnet protocol). With the Telnet client, you can establish a connection with a remote computer by specifying a host name and port number. On connection, you can send characters to the server on the specified port one character at a time.

This makes Telnet a great utility for learning and testing Internet application-level protocols. As you learn about HTTP, FTP, and Gopher (or any other Internet application-level protocol like Simple Mail Transfer Protocol, POP3, or NNTP), you should take advantage of the Telnet client while learning the given protocol.

Table 4-6   HTTP response headers

Header	Description
Location	The Location response header defines the exact location of the resource that was identified by the URI. For 3xx responses (which require redirection) the location must indicate the server's preferred URL for automatic redirection to the resource. Only one absolute URL is allowed. For example, `Location: http://www.w3.org/hypertext/WWW/NewLocation.html`
Server	The Server response header is like the User-Agent request header. It contains information about the software used by the originating server to handle the request. The header can contain multiple product tokens and comments that identify the server and any significant subproducts. For example, `Server: CERN/3.0 libwww/2.17`

WWW-Authenticate	The WWW-Authenticate response header must be included in 401 (unauthorized) response messages. The field value consists of at least one challenge that indicates the authentication schemes and parameters applicable to the URI. For example, consider the following response header:
	
	`WWW-Authenticate: Basic realm="SecureWebSite"`
	
	This tells the requester that to access the SecureWebSite realm, it needs to respond using the Basic authentication scheme. The requester could then respond using the Authorization header (as described earlier):
	
	`Authorization: Basic myusername:mypassword`
	
	These are the headers with which you need to be familiar to take advantage of HTTP authentication.

 Telnet is a great utility for learning application-level Internet protocols. To run Telnet, select the Start menu; then select Run. Then simply type `Telnet` and press Enter.

To use Telnet, press Run from the Windows Start menu. When the Run dialog appears, type `Telnet`. This should launch the Windows Telnet client. Choose

Remote System from the Connect menu and the Connect dialog should appear. Enter the server name and port to which you wish to connect. For example, to try out HTTP, connect to *www.microsoft.com* on port 80 (see Figure 4-2).

If you want to see what you're typing, select Terminal | Preferences from the menu and make sure Local Echo is turned on. Plus, you'll probably want to use VT100/ANSI for the terminal emulation. As soon as you connect to Microsoft's HTTP server on port 80, you'll see the cursor. At this point, you can type in a simple HTTP request.

For example, to download Microsoft's main Web page, type the HTTP request illustrated in Figure 4-3. After you press the Enter key, supplying the server with the CRLF delimiter, the Web page downloads, and you'll see the HTML text fill the Tel-

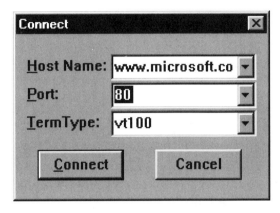

Figure 4-2 Telnet Connect dialog

Figure 4-3 Sample HTTP request using Telnet

net window. Only the HTML text is downloaded. If the downloaded HTML contains references to binary files (such as images or sounds), they are not downloaded.

A Complete HTTP Transaction

Listing 4-3 illustrates a complete HTTP transaction. The requested object (called basketball-scores) is capable of returning the most current basketball score for the requested teams.

Listing 4-3 Complete HTTP Transaction

Request
```
GET /cgi-bin/scripts/basketball-scores HTTP/1.0
Accept: text/plain, text/html
Accept: image/gif, image/jpeg
Accept-Encoding: x-compress; x-zip
Accept-Language: en
User-Agent: MSIE/4.0
If-Modified-Since: Mon, 10 Jan 1998 13:22:34 GMT
Pragma: no-cache
Content-Type: text/plain
Content-Length: 43


Team1=Utah Jazz&Team2=Portland Trailblazers
```

Response
```
HTTP/1.0 200 OK
Server: Microsoft-IIS/2.0
Date: Mon, 3 Jan 1998 13:22:34 GMT
Content-Type: text/html
Last-Modified: Mon, 1 Jan 1998 13:22:34 GMT
Content-Length: 179

<html>
<head><title>Basketball Scores</title></head>
<body>
Utah Jazz vs. Chicago Bulls: 101-99<br>
Portland Trailblazers vs. Phoenix Suns: 113-88<br>
<br>
<b>GO JAZZ!</b>
</body>
</html>
```

Notice how the names of the teams are passed in as plain text in the entity-body (or data) section of the request. Also, notice the blank line between the end of the request headers and the beginning of the entity-body. This blank line is crucial because it tells the server where the header ends and the data begins. After the server processes the request, it sends back the data shown in the response.

The status line is the first thing to come back, followed by the response headers. Once again, notice the blank line between the end of the headers and the beginning of the data. In case you're wondering, the data is formatted in HTML.

HTTP Protocol Summary

I've covered a great deal of information on the HTTP protocol in these sections. Hopefully HTTP is starting to make some sense by now. Because of its flexibility and power, HTTP is the most widely used Internet protocol today. In fact, HTTP is probably what you'll find yourself using most in your Internet applications.

It can be used as a solution to almost any communication problem. With this in mind, I've devoted a good portion of this chapter to HTTP specifics. Although the information that I've provided on HTTP is more than sufficient, there is plenty more where it came from.

 For the complete HTTP/1.0 specification, see RFC 1945 at *http://info.internet.isi.edu/in-notes/rfc/files/rfc1945.txt* and the HTTP documentation at the W3C, *http://www.w3.org/Protocols/HTTP.*

Now we're ready to dive into the WinInet HTTP functions and to learn how to unleash the power of this wonderful protocol.

WinInet HTTP Functions

One of the benefits of using the WinInet HTTP functions (or any of the WinInet protocol-specific functions for that matter) is the encapsulation of the underlying protocol. By using WinInet, you can safely ignore concerns about evolving protocol standards and let WinInet worry about the updates. Because IE is built on top of the WinInet layer, you can feel confident that Microsoft won't let this slip. So let your imagination run wild, and take advantage of HTTP at a much higher level—using the WinInet HTTP functions.

We've already covered how to establish an Internet session using InternetOpen. We also discussed how there are two paths leading away from InternetOpen. You can use either InternetOpenUrl or InternetConnect along with the protocol-specific functions. If you haven't already guessed, the second path is the topic of this chapter (covering the HTTP functions) and the two chapters to come (covering the FTP and Gopher functions).

HTTP Hierarchy

The handle hierarchy for the HTTP functions begins just like anything else—with InternetOpen and InternetConnect. After calling InternetConnect, the first HTTP function that you call is HttpOpenRequest. When you've called HttpOpenRequest, you can call any of the other HTTP functions. This HTTP handle hierarchy is illustrated in Figure 4-4.

HTTP Functions Overview

As you can see from Figure 4-4, there are only a handful of HTTP-specific functions. These functions allow you to open a connection with an HTTP server, add your own

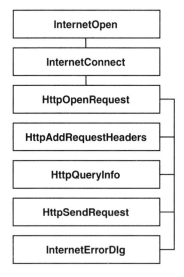

Figure 4-4   HTTP handle hierarchy

HTTP headers to the request, query information about a request, send data with the request, and use a common Internet error dialog. The HTTP functions are listed and described in Table 4-7.

Now let's take a look at each of these HTTP functions in more detail.

HttpOpenRequest

The first HTTP function that I'll cover is HttpOpenRequest. As you've learned, this is the first HTTP function that should be called after calling InternetConnect. Take a look at its function declaration:

```
HINTERNET HttpOpenRequest(
    IN HINTERNET hHttpSession,
    IN LPCSTR lpszVerb,
    IN LPCSTR lpszObjectName,
    IN LPCSTR lpszVersion,
    IN LPCSTR lpszReferer,
    IN LPCSTR FAR * lpszAcceptTypes,
    IN DWORD dwFlags,
    IN DWORD dwContext
);
```

hHttpSession is a handle to the HTTP session returned by InternetConnect. Remember that InternetConnect requires you to specify the type of session you wish

Table 4-7 HTTP functions

Function	Description
HttpOpenRequest	Opens an HTTP request handle. This function requires a handle created by InternetConnect.
HttpAddRequestHeaders	Adds HTTP request headers to the HTTP request handle. This function requires a handle created by HttpOpenRequest.
HttpSendRequest	Sends the specified HTTP request to the HTTP server. This function requires a handle created by HttpOpenRequest.
HttpQueryInfo	Queries information about an HTTP request. This function requires a handle created by the HttpOpenRequest or InternetOpenUrl function.
InternetErrorDlg	Displays predefined dialogs for common Internet error conditions. This function requires the handle used in the call to HttpSendRequest.

to create. For example, the following call to InternetConnect illustrates how you would establish an HTTP session:

```
HINTERNET hConnection = InternetConnect(hSession, "aarons.axtech.com",
        INTERNET_DEFAULT_HTTP_PORT, "aaron", "password",
        INTERNET_SERVICE_HTTP, 0, 0);
```

So after calling InternetConnect (as in the previous example), we've already established a connection handle with the specified HTTP server on the specified port. From here on, we can forget about the server and the port.

This is similar to the Telnet example. First you connect to the server on a particular port. Then you send the HTTP request along with any data. Calling InternetConnect logically accomplishes the same thing as the Telnet Connect dialog shown in Figure 4-2. From this point on we just supply the HINTERNET handle to our HTTP connection and call the appropriate HTTP functions.

Before discussing the next few parameters, let's quickly review the first line of every HTTP request:

```
Method URI ProtocolVersion
```

The next three parameters—lpszVerb, lpszObjectName, and lpszVersion—eventually make up this first line of the HTTP request. The second parameter, lpszVerb, is the address of a string containing the HTTP method you wish to use with this request. lpszVerb can contain any valid HTTP method (see Table 4-1). If you pass NULL, the GET method is used by default.

The next parameter, lpszObjectName, is the URI that you wish to access. This could be simply a file, a script, or even an executable. Remember that the URI specifies the network location of the resource.

For example, take a look at the following URL:

```
http://www.server.com:80/cgi-bin/search/find.cgi
```

Notice how the URL contains the server host name (*www.server.com*) and a port number (80). Because by the time you send the URI in the HTTP request you're already connected to an HTTP server on a particular port, a URI doesn't need to contain this information. On the contrary, the URI only needs to specify the network location of the resource. The URI should always begin with a forward slash (see the next tip). The URI associated with the previous URL would be as follows:

```
/cgi-bin/search/find.cgi
```

As you learned in the HTTP protocol section, the URI can also contain data associated with a GET request. For example, suppose you're sending a request to your favorite search engine. In this case, you would probably specify the search parameters as name/value pairs on the end of the URI like this:

```
/cgi-bin/search/find.cgi?name=Aaron&city=Layton
```

When I first began using WinInet I didn't always put the forward slash on the beginning of the URI. At first it didn't seem to cause any problems. Then one day a nasty bug came to life. All of a sudden my application's HTTP requests started failing with an HTTP server error on all machines using IE 3.x. Machines with IE 4.x didn't encounter the problem. (Don't you just love these kinds of bugs?) After a few hours of stepping through source code and checking file histories in Visual Source Safe, I came to the conclusion that none of my code changed. So what happened? To help figure this out, we wrote a little Perl script that would catch our WinInet requests and spit out all of the HTTP request text.

The day of the disaster, the server path for requests—which happened to be stored in the registry—was modified to look like this:

```
~myaccount/scripts/
```

When we tested a request on an IE 3.x machine, the first line of the HTTP request looked like this:

```
POST ~myaccount/scripts/object.cgi HTTP/1.0
```

But when we tested it on an IE 4.x machine, the first line looked like this:

```
POST /~myaccount/scripts/object.cgi HTTP/1.0
```

Apparently WinInet builds a URL out of the supplied components and later cracks it to get the path. During this process a leading slash is prepared if necessary. Most HTTP servers expect the URI to begin with a forward slash.

Most developers fall into the same trap I did by thinking in terms of relative and absolute paths. With HTTP, the server always interprets the URI relative to the root WWW directory, even with a beginning forward slash. So a safe rule of thumb is always to begin your URIs with a forward slash. Plus, if you're giving your users the ability to enter URIs, you probably want to validate that every URI begins with a forward slash on your own.

Finally, the lpszVersion parameter allows you to specify the version of HTTP you wish to use with this request. This value becomes the ProtocolVersion field of the first HTTP request line. If this parameter is NULL, HTTP/1.0 is used as the default value.

So in a nutshell, HttpOpenRequest gathers the data that is used to build the first line of the HTTP request. All three fields—Method, URI, and ProtocolVersion—that make up this crucial part of every HTTP request must be specified using this function. This is why HttpOpenRequest must be called before any other HTTP request.

HttpOpenRequest also allows you to specify a few HTTP request headers. The lpszReferer and lpszAcceptTypes parameters allow you to specify the Referer and Accept HTTP request headers, respectively. Remember these headers from our discussion of the HTTP protocol?

Specifying NULL for either of these parameters leaves these headers blank. You should note, however, that not specifying any accept types tells the HTTP server that your application is capable of receiving all data formats. Refer back to the section on the HTTP protocol for more information on these headers.

The last two HttpOpenRequest parameters are dwFlags and dwContext. dwContext, as you've learned, deals with asynchronous WinInet. dwFlags gives you an extra level of control over HttpOpenRequest behavior. To understand exactly what you can achieve with HttpOpenRequest, we need to look at the available flags in a little more detail. Table 4-8 describes all of the flags that can be used with HttpOpenRequest.

As you can see, the list of HttpOpenRequest flags is quite overwhelming. These flags really give you control over the behavior of the HTTP request. Let me just point out a few flags that I find very useful.

First, the INTERNET_FLAG_SECURE flag is probably my favorite flag offered by WinInet (if you hadn't already noticed). This is the same flag that you can use with InternetOpenUrl. Supplying this flag specifies that you wish to use SSL for this HTTP request. Once again, WinInet takes care of all the SSL functionality behind the scenes. I'll cover using SSL with HTTP in more detail shortly.

 If you're trying to use SSL by specifying INTERNET_FLAG_SECURE, you should also be aware of the INTERNET_FLAG_IGNORE_CERT_* flags. These flags tell WinInet to back off on the SSL digital certificate validation. If you've set up a test SSL HTTP server without valid certificates, these flags can really come in handy. Without them, your WinInet SSL requests always fail unless the server possesses a valid digital certificate.

Table 4-8   **HttpOpenRequest flags**

Flag	Description
INTERNET_FLAG_CACHE_IF_NET_FAIL	Returns the resource from the cache if the network request for the resource fails.
INTERNET_FLAG_DONT_CACHE	Does not add the returned entity to the cache. Identical to the preferred value, INTERNET_FLAG_NO_CACHE_WRITE.
INTERNET_FLAG_HYPERLINK	Forces a reload if there were no Expires time and no Last-Modified time returned from the server when determining whether to reload the item from the network.
INTERNET_FLAG_IGNORE_CERT_ CN_INVALID	Disables Win32 Internet function checking of SSL/PCT-based certificates that are returned from the server against the host name given in the request. Win32 Internet functions use a simple check against certificates by comparing for matching host names and simple wildcard rules.
INTERNET_FLAG_IGNORE_CERT_ DATE_INVALID	Disables Win32 Internet function checking of SSL/PCT-based certificates for proper validity dates.
INTERNET_FLAG_IGNORE_REDIRECT_ TO_HTTP	Disables the ability of the Win32 Internet functions to detect this special type of redirect. When this flag is used, Win32 Internet functions allow redirects transparently from HTTPS to HTTP URLs.
INTERNET_FLAG_IGNORE_REDIRECT_ TO_HTTPS	Disables the ability of the Win32 Internet functions to detect this special type of redirect. When this flag is used, Win32 Internet functions allow redirects transparently from HTTP to HTTPS URLs.
INTERNET_FLAG_KEEP_CONNECTION	Uses keep-alive semantics, if available, for the connection. This flag is required for MSN, NTLM, and other types of authentication.
INTERNET_FLAG_MUST_CACHE_ REQUEST	Causes a temporary file to be created if the file cannot be cached. Identical to the preferred value, INTERNET_FLAG_NEED_FILE.
INTERNET_FLAG_NEED_FILE	Causes a temporary file to be created if the file cannot be cached.

(continued)

Table 4-8   (continued)

Flag	Description
INTERNET_FLAG_NO_AUTH	Does not attempt authentication automatically.
INTERNET_FLAG_NO_AUTO_REDIRECT	Does not handle redirection automatically in HttpSendRequest
INTERNET_FLAG_NO_CACHE_WRITE	Does not add the returned entity to the cache.
INTERNET_FLAG_NO_COOKIES	Does not add cookie headers to requests automatically, and does not add returned cookies automatically to the cookie database.
INTERNET_FLAG_NO_UI	Disables the cookie dialog.
INTERNET_FLAG_PRAGMA_NOCACHE	Forces the request to be resolved by the originating server, even if a cached copy exists on the proxy.
INTERNET_FLAG_RELOAD	Forces a download of the requested file, object, or directory listing from the originating server, not from the cache.
INTERNET_FLAG_RESYNCHRONIZE	Reloads HTTP resources if the resource has been modified since the last time it was downloaded.
INTERNET_FLAG_SECURE	Uses SSL/PCT transaction semantics.

Another nice feature of WinInet's HTTP support is that of redirection. Unless you tell WinInet not to redirect automatically, it always redirects automatically under the covers. Because you may not always want this to happen, WinInet provided the INTERNET_FLAG_NO_AUTO_REDIRECT flag.

You may want to use the INTERNET_FLAG_RELOAD flag to make sure that WinInet always downloads the resource from the server and not from the local cache. Also, you may find INTERNET_FLAG_RESYNCHRONIZE useful because it only downloads the resource if it has been modified since the last time it was downloaded. (Remember the Last-Modified header? That's how WinInet keeps track.)

You can play around with the rest of these flags on your own. To help summarize everything we've learned about HttpOpenRequest, check out the following example:

```
HINTERNET hHttpRequest = HttpOpenRequest(hConnection, "GET",
        "/cgi-bin/object.cgi", NULL, NULL, INTERNET_FLAG_RELOAD, 0);
```

In this example, we've created an HTTP request with a first line that looks like this:

```
GET /cgi-bin/object.cgi HTTP/1.0
```

Neither the Referer nor the Accept headers are used by this request (unless you add them manually later with HttpAddRequestHeaders). Also, the flags specify that this request is sure to hit the server and not the cache.

Let's recap the steps up to this point. First, InternetOpen creates the application Internet session. Then, InternetConnect establishes the HTTP connection with a remote server. Finally, HttpOpenRequest creates an HTTP request that is sent over the established HTTP connection. Now let's look at how you can add headers to the request manually through HttpAddRequestHeaders.

HttpAddRequestHeaders

HttpAddRequestHeaders gives you the ability to add free-format headers to the HTTP request created by HttpOpenRequest before actually sending it. This function was added to the WinInet library for sophisticated HTTP applications that need precise control over the format of the HTTP request.

For the majority of HTTP requests, the default headers added by WinInet are sufficient and won't require modification. Nevertheless, if you do need to add, replace, or even remove HTTP headers from the request, HttpAddRequestHeaders is the key to making it happen. Let's take a look at the function declaration:

```
BOOL HttpAddRequestHeaders(
    IN HINTERNET hHttpRequest,
    IN LPCSTR lpszHeaders,
    IN DWORD dwHeadersLength,
    IN DWORD dwModifiers
);
```

lpszHeaders is the address of the string containing the headers with which you want to work; dwHeadersLength is simply the length of the header string. If you're trying to do anything but replace or remove a header you can pass in a list of headers (separated by a CRLF) to lpszHeaders. Otherwise, for replace/remove you can only pass in a single header.

The last parameter, dwModifiers, allows you to specify exactly what you want to happen with the provided headers. Table 4-9 describes the possible modifier values.

Notice how much control these modifiers give you over the final HTTP header configuration. Let's look at a few examples.

Suppose you wanted to add two new headers or replace the old ones (if they exist by default). The following example shows you would accomplish this:

Table 4-9   HttpAddRequestHeaders modifiers

Modifiers	Description
HTTP_ADDREQ_FLAG_ADD	Adds the header if it does not exist. Used with HTTP_ADDREQ_FLAG_REPLACE.
HTTP_ADDREQ_FLAG_ADD_IF_NEW	Adds the header only if it does not already exist; otherwise, an error is returned.
HTTP_ADDREQ_FLAG_COALESCE	Coalesces headers of the same name.
HTTP_ADDREQ_FLAG_COALESCE_ WITH_COMMA	Coalesces headers of the same name. For example, adding `Accept: text/*` followed by `Accept: audio/*` with this flag forms the single header `Accept: text/*, audio/*`, causing the first header found to be coalesced. It is up to the calling application to ensure a cohesive scheme with respect to coalesced/separated headers.
HTTP_ADDREQ_FLAG_COALESCE_ WITH_SEMICOLON	Coalesces headers of the same name using a semicolon.
HTTP_ADDREQ_FLAG_REPLACE	Replaces or removes a header. If the header value is empty and the header is found, it is removed. If the header value is not empty, the header value is replaced.

```
char *buffer = "Content-type: text/tdf\r\nContent-length: 158\r\n";
HttpAddRequestHeaders(hHttpRequest, buffer, -1, HTTP_ADDREQ_FLAG_ADD |
        HTTP_ADDREQ_FLAG_REPLACE);
```

Now suppose you want to coalesce a new Accept header to the default accept types that WinInet already knows. Depending on how you want the new header separated from the existing headers of the same type, you would use one of the HTTP_ADDREQ_FLAG_COALESCE* headers. If you want the new header to be separated by the existing headers with a semicolon, the code would look like this:

```
char *buffer = "Accept: image/*\r\n";
HttpAddRequestHeaders(hHttpRequest, buffer, -1, HTTP_ADDREQ_FLAG_COALESCE);
```

You probably won't find much need to use this function in most of your applications. But when the need does arise, it's comforting to know that the functionality is available. This is yet another example of how you really do need to understand the underlying WinInet protocols to take full advantage of WinInet's potential. In this case, if you're not familiar with the HTTP headers, this function does you absolutely no good. Although WinInet does a good job of hiding most of the protocol details, things like this pop up just to keep you on your toes.

HttpSendRequest

You use HttpOpenRequest to create the HTTP request, and HttpAddRequestHeaders to add additional headers to the request. When you're satisfied with the configuration of the HTTP request, you send it to the HTTP server by calling HttpSendRequest.

HttpSendRequest requires a handle created by HttpOpenRequest. Plus, it gives you one more chance to add more HTTP headers. Check out the HttpSendRequest function declaration:

```
BOOL HttpSendRequest(
    IN HINTERNET hHttpRequest,
    IN LPCSTR lpszHeaders,
    IN DWORD dwHeadersLength,
    IN LPVOID lpOptional,
    DWORD dwOptionalLength
);
```

The last two parameters, lpOptional and dwOptionalLength, are usually only used with HTTP methods that write data to the server, such as the POST method. The data passed in lpOptional becomes the entity-body of the HTTP request (refer to the HTTP request format). Let's take a look at an example.

Suppose you want to emulate an HTML form. To do so, you need to pass the form data to the server exactly like the form would. If the form contained three fields called name, phone, and id, you could emulate a form POST with the following code:

```
HINTERNET hHttpRequest = HttpOpenRequest(hConnection, "POST",
        "/cgi-bin/object.cgi", NULL, NULL, INTERNET_FLAG_RELOAD, 0);
CHAR szData[1024];
strcpy(szData, "name=Aaron&phone=7289813&id=1234");
if ( HttpSendRequest(hHttpRequest, NULL, 0, (LPVOID)szData, strlen(szData)) )
{
    //check the HTTP status code
}
```

After calling HttpSendRequest you need to check the HTTP status code returned by the server in the HTTP response (refer to the HTTP response format). I'll cover how to query the HTTP status code in the next section. Unless the HTTP status indicates an error, you're ready to read the data returned by the server. You can use InternetReadFile just like you would with a file returned by InternetOpenUrl.

Before continuing, let's take a step back and look at the underlying request for the previous example. The actual text sent to the server for the previous example would look something like this:

```
POST /cgi-bin/object.cgi HTTP/1.0
Content-Length: 32


name=Aaron&phone=7289813&id=1234
```

By now, the HTTP protocol should start making some sense. In the next section I'll cover how to access all the HTTP protocol information.

HttpQueryInfo

HttpQueryInfo allows you to retrieve information about a given HTTP request. You supply a buffer and specify which piece of information you wish to retrieve. For example, take a look at the following declaration:

```
BOOL HttpQueryInfo(
    IN HINTERNET hHttpRequest,
    IN DWORD dwInfoLevel,
    IN LPVOID lpvBuffer,
    IN LPDWORD lpdwBufferLength,
    IN OUT LPDWORD lpdwIndex,
);
```

As you learned from the handle hierarchy at the beginning of this chapter, hHttpRequest requires a handle returned by HttpOpenRequest. The second parameter, dwInfoLevel, specifies the type of information we're interested in retrieving for the supplied HTTP request. Although there are a plethora of possible dwInfoLevel values, I've listed the most commonly used values in Table 4-10. For information on all the possible dwInfoLevel values, see the WinInet documentation.

HttpQueryInfo is your gateway to information regarding a given HTTP request and response. One common use of HttpQueryInfo is to determine whether your HTTP request was successful or whether it generated an error.

Table 4-10 **Possible HttpQueryInfo dwInfoLevel values**

Value	Description
HTTP_QUERY_ALLOW	Receives the methods supported by the server.
HTTP_QUERY_CONTENT_DESCRIPTION	Receives the content description.
HTTP_QUERY_CONTENT_ID	Receives the content identification.
HTTP_QUERY_CONTENT_LENGTH	Receives the size of the resource in bytes.
HTTP_QUERY_CONTENT_TRANSFER_ ENCODING	Receives the additional content coding that has been applied to the resource.
HTTP_QUERY_CONTENT_TYPE	Receives the content type of the resource (such as text/html).
HTTP_QUERY_DATE	Receives the date and time at which the message originated.
HTTP_QUERY_EXPIRES	Receives the date and time after which the resource should be considered outdated.
HTTP_QUERY_LAST_MODIFIED	Receives the date and time at which the server believes the resource was last modified.
HTTP_QUERY_MIME_VERSION	Receives the version of the MIME protocol that was used to construct the message.
HTTP_QUERY_PRAGMA	Receives the implementation-specific directives that might apply to any recipient along the request/response chain.
HTTP_QUERY_PUBLIC	Receives the methods available from this server.
HTTP_QUERY_RAW_HEADERS	Receives all the headers returned by the server. Each header is terminated by \0. An additional \0 terminates the list of headers.
HTTP_QUERY_RAW_HEADERS_CRLF	Receives all the headers returned by the server. Each header is separated by a CRLF.
HTTP_QUERY_REQUEST_METHOD	Receives the verb that is being used in the request, typically GET or POST.
HTTP_QUERY_STATUS_CODE	Receives the status code returned by the server.
HTTP_QUERY_STATUS_TEXT	Receives any additional text returned by the server on the response line.
HTTP_QUERY_URL	Receives some or all of the URLs by which the Request URL resource can be identified.
HTTP_QUERY_VERSION	Receives the HTTP version used by the server.

Remember that the first line of every HTTP response looks like this:

```
HTTP-Version Status-Code Reason-Phrase
```

The following is an example of a typical HTTP response:

```
HTTP/1.0 200 OK
```

You can retrieve all three of these values by using the HTTP_QUERY_VERSION, HTTP_QUERY_STATUS_CODE, and HTTP_QUERY_STATUS_TEXT dwInfoLevel values, respectively.

Accessing the Raw HTTP Response Headers

You can access most of the HTTP headers directly—through a header-specific dwInfoLevel value—or you can ask for the complete raw header text and go trudging through it yourself. The following example demonstrates how to retrieve the raw HTTP response headers using HTTP_QUERY_RAW_HEADERS:

```
CHAR szBuffer[1024];
DWORD dwLen = 1024;
BOOL bRet;

bRet = HttpQueryInfo(hRequest, HTTP_QUERY_RAW_HEADERS, szBuffer, &dwLen, NULL);
```

 If you use HTTP_QUERY_RAW_HEADERS, the returned headers are separated by a NULL character (/0). You can also use HTTP_QUERY_RAW_HEADERS_CRLF if you would rather have the returned headers separated by a CRLF pair.

HttpQueryInfo Modifiers

There is also a set of modifier values that you can use in combination with the dwInfoLevel values to control the behavior of HttpQueryInfo. The modifier values should be OR-ed together with the dwInfoLevel value. Table 4-11 contains a list of the possible modifier values.

HTTP_QUERY_CUSTOM comes in handy if there isn't a dwInfoLevel value that returns the header in which you're interested and you don't want to parse through

Table 4-11   HttpQueryInfo modifier values

Modifier	Description
HTTP_QUERY_CUSTOM	Causes HttpQueryInfo to search for the ASCII header name specified in lpvBuffer and stores the header information in lpvBuffer.
HTTP_QUERY_FLAG_COALESCE	Combines the values from headers with the same name into the output buffer.
HTTP_QUERY_FLAG_NUMBER	Returns the data as a 32-bit number for headers with a value that is a number, such as the status code.
HTTP_QUERY_FLAG_REQUEST_HEADERS	Queries request headers only.
HTTP_QUERY_FLAG_SYSTEMTIME	Returns the header value as a standard Win32 SYSTEMTIME structure, which does not require the application to parse the data. Use for headers with a value that is a date/time string, such as Last-Modified-Time.

the raw headers yourself. The following example illustrates how you could look for a custom header called MyHeader.

```
CHAR szBuffer[1024];
DWORD dwLen = 1024;
BOOL bRet;

strcpy(szBuffer, "MyHeader");
bRet = HttpQueryInfo(hRequest, HTTP_QUERY_CUSTOM, szBuffer, &dwLen, NULL);
```

As described in Table 4-11, you can even make HttpQueryInfo return a number value for header values containing numbers, and Win32 SYSTEMTIME structures for headers containing dates. I'll show you an example of how to do this in the next section on HTTP status codes.

HTTP Status Codes

This seems like a good place to jump into HTTP status codes. I already described HTTP status codes briefly in the HTTP protocol section. Now, as I promised, I show you a complete list of the HTTP status codes along with their descriptions. Table 4-12 contains a list of HTTP status codes along with their corresponding WinInet value.

Table 4-12   HTTP status codes and WinInet values

Constant	Value	Description
HTTP_STATUS_OK	200	The request completed successfully.
HTTP_STATUS_CREATED	201	The request has been fulfilled and resulted in the creation of a new resource.
HTTP_STATUS_ACCEPTED	202	The request has been accepted for processing, but the processing has not been completed.
HTTP_STATUS_PARTIAL	203	The returned meta-information in the entity header is not the definitive set available from the originating server.
HTTP_STATUS_NO_CONTENT	204	The server has fulfilled the request, but there is no new information to send back.
HTTP_STATUS_RESET_CONTENT	205	The request has been completed, and the client program should reset the document view that caused the request to be sent to allow the user to initiate another input action easily.
HTTP_STATUS_PARTIAL_CONTENT	206	The server has fulfilled the partial GET request for the resource.
HTTP_STATUS_AMBIGUOUS	300	The server couldn't decide what to return.
HTTP_STATUS_MOVED	301	The requested resource has been assigned to a new, permanent URI, and any future references to this resource should be done using one of the returned URIs.
HTTP_STATUS_REDIRECT	302	The requested resource resides temporarily under a different URI.
HTTP_STATUS_REDIRECT_METHOD	303	The response to the request can be found under a different URI and should be retrieved using a GET method on that resource.
HTTP_STATUS_NOT_MODIFIED	304	The requested resource has not been modified.
HTTP_STATUS_USE_PROXY	305	The requested resource must be accessed through the proxy given by the location field.
HTTP_STATUS_REDIRECT_KEEP_ VERB	307	The redirected request keeps the same verb (HTTP/1.1 behavior).
HTTP_STATUS_BAD_REQUEST	400	The request could not be processed by the server due to invalid syntax.
HTTP_STATUS_DENIED	401	The requested resource requires user authentication.
HTTP_STATUS_PAYMENT_REQ	402	Not currently implemented in the HTTP protocol.
HTTP_STATUS_FORBIDDEN	403	The server understood the request, but is refusing to fulfill it.
HTTP_STATUS_NOT_FOUND	404	The server has not found anything matching the requested URI.

Constant	Value	Description
HTTP_STATUS_BAD_METHOD	405	The method used is not allowed.
HTTP_STATUS_NONE_ACCEPTABLE	406	No responses acceptable to the client were found.
HTTP_STATUS_PROXY_AUTH_REQ	407	Proxy authentication required.
HTTP_STATUS_REQUEST_TIMEOUT	408	The server experienced a timeout while waiting for the request.
HTTP_STATUS_CONFLICT	409	The request could not be completed due to a conflict with the current state of the resource. The user should resubmit with more information.
HTTP_STATUS_GONE	410	The requested resource is no longer available at the server, and no forwarding address is known.
HTTP_STATUS_LENGTH_REQUIRED	411	The server refuses to accept the request without a defined content length.
HTTP_STATUS_PRECOND_FAILED	412	The precondition given in one or more of the request header fields evaluted to false when it was tested on the server.
HTTP_STATUS_REQUEST_TOO_LARGE	413	The server is refusing to process a request because the request entity is larger than the server is willing or able to process.
HTTP_STATUS_URI_TOO_LONG	414	The server is refusing to service the request because the request URI is longer than the server is willing to interpret.
HTTP_STATUS_UNSUPPORTED_MEDIA	415	The server is refusing to service the request because the entity of the request is in a format not supported by the requested resource for the requested method.
HTTP_STATUS_SERVER_ERROR	500	The server encountered an unexpected condition that prevented it from fulfilling the request.
HTTP_STATUS_NOT_SUPPORTED	501	The server does not support the functionality required to fulfill the request.
HTTP_STATUS_BAD_GATEWAY	502	The server, while acting as a gateway or proxy, received an invalid response from the upstream server it accessed in attempting to fulfill the request.
HTTP_STATUS_SERVICE_UNAVAIL	503	The service is temporarily overloaded.
HTTP_STATUS_GATEWAY_TIMEOUT	504	The request encountered a timeout while waiting for a gateway.
HTTP_STATUS_VERSION_NOT_SUP	505	The server does not support, or refuses to support, the HTTP protocol version that was used in the request message.

Retrieving the status code is the most common task after calling HttpSendRequest. Calling HttpQueryInfo with the dwInfoLevel of HTTP_QUERY_STATUS_CODE is going to return the status value found in the HTTP response. Because this is something you'll be doing often with HTTP, let's write a function that encapsulates this functionality. Let's call the function QueryInfoStatusCode:

```
BOOL QueryInfoStatusCode(HINTERNET hRequest, DWORD& dwStatusCode)
{
    CHAR szBuffer[80];
    DWORD dwLen = 80;
    BOOL bRet;
    bRet = HttpQueryInfo(hRequest, HTTP_QUERY_STATUS_CODE, szBuffer,
            &dwLen, NULL);
    if (bRet)
        dwStatusCode = (DWORD) atol(szBuffer);
    return bRet;
}
```

That looks pretty straightforward. Notice, however, that I'm querying the status code as text and then converting it to a number. HTTP_QUERY_FLAG_NUMBER can help us avoid this extra step. Let's rewrite the function using this modifier:

```
BOOL QueryInfoStatusCode(HINTERNET hRequest, DWORD& dwStatusCode) const
{
    DWORD dwLen = sizeof(DWORD);
    return HttpQueryInfo(hRequest, HTTP_QUERY_STATUS_CODE |
            HTTP_QUERY_FLAG_NUMBER, (LPVOID)&dwStatusCode, &dwLen, NULL);
}
```

Notice how HTTP_QUERY_FLAG_NUMBER helps simplify this function. In general, the HttpQueryInfo modifiers are very helpful. Now let's look at how you would use this status helper function in your application:

```
HINTERNET hHttpRequest = HttpOpenRequest(hConnection, "GET",
        "/cgi-bin/object.cgi", NULL, NULL, INTERNET_FLAG_RELOAD, 0);
if (hHttpRequest)
{
    if ( HttpSendRequest(hHttpRequest, NULL, 0, NULL, 0) )
    {
        DWORD dwStatus;
```

```
    if ( QueryInfoStatusCode(hHttpRequest, dwStatus) )
    {
        switch(dwStatus)
        {
        case HTTP_STATUS_OK:
            //do something for success
            break;
        case HTTP_STATUS_DENIED:
            //do something for error
            break;
        ... //continue cases
        }
    }
}
```

HttpQueryInfo is another very powerful function that gives you a back door to the underlying HTTP protocol.

InternetErrorDlg

InternetErrorDlg is another valuable function that you can use in your HTTP code. Because InternetErrorDlg is a general Internet function, I covered the functional details in the previous chapter. Nevertheless, in the next section I'll show you an example of how to use InternetErrorDlg while handling HTTP authentication. This example should be sufficient in helping you understand this function.

HTTP Authentication Techniques

As you learned in the sections on the protocol specification, HTTP supports the concept of user authentication. If the HTTP server returns the WWW-Authenticate header, the HTTP client must send an additional request containing the user authentication information in the HTTP Authorization header. This allows an HTTP server to control who accesses its sites.

WinInet provides various mechanisms to support HTTP authentication. In this section I present a few of these methods and show you some examples. The first and easiest authentication method is tied to InternetConnect.

HTTP Authentication with InternetConnect

Remember that InternetConnect takes both user name and password parameters. These parameters are used automatically by WinInet to authenticate with secure Web sites. Suppose you call InternetConnect like this:

```
HINTERNET hConnection = InternetConnect(hSession, "aarons.axtech.com",
        INTERNET_DEFAULT_HTTP_PORT, "aaron", "password",
        INTERNET_SERVICE_HTTP, 0, 0);
```

If you then call HttpOpenRequest using this handle returned by InternetConnect and tried to access a secure Web site like

```
https://swww.etrade.com/cgi-bin/cgitrade/MainMenu
```

WinInet is going to pass `aaron` and `password` to the server in the HTTP Authorization header. If this authentication information is valid for the given Web site, the authentication process should succeed, and the resource associated with the URI (specified in HttpOpenRequest) should be returned.

This is by far the simplest method for handling HTTP authentication. The only problem, however, is that you're required to supply this information to InternetConnect. This means that if the authentication failed, you would have to close the HttpOpenRequest and InternetConnect handles, query the user for a new user name and password, and call both InternetConnect and HttpOpenRequest again. Wouldn't it be nice if you could just change the user name and password and call HttpOpenRequest again? Well, lucky for us—we can! The next two authentication methods describe how this is done.

HTTP Authentication with InternetErrorDlg

I'm finally going to show you how to use InternetErrorDlg. This function was designed specifically to assist in HTTP authentication. Not only does it provide a consistent UI for retrieving authentication information, it's also capable of storing the new user name and password values in your WinInet HTTP connection handle (see Figure 4-5).

Listing 4-4 demonstrates how to use InternetErrorDlg to handle authentication.

Listing 4-4   HTTP authentication with InternetErrorDlg

```
HINTERNET hOpenHandle,  hConnectHandle, hResourceHandle;
DWORD dwError, dwErrorCode, dwFlags;
```

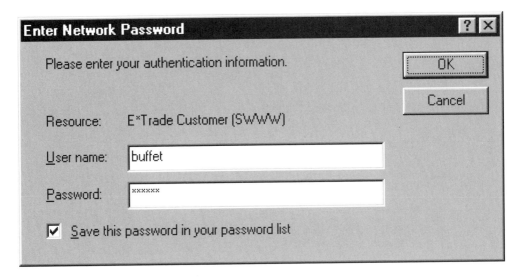

Figure 4-5   InternetErrorDlg authentication dialog

```
hOpenHandle = InternetOpen("Example", INTERNET_OPEN_TYPE_PRECONFIG,
        NULL, NULL, 0);


if (hOpenHandle)
{
    hConnectHandle = InternetConnect(hOpenHandle, "www.server.com",
            INTERNET_INVALID_PORT_NUMBER, NULL, NULL,
            INTERNET_SERVICE_HTTP,0,0);

    if (!hConnectHandle)
    {
        // clean-up resources
        return;
    }

    hResourceHandle = HttpOpenRequest(hConnectHandle, "GET",
            "/premium/default.htm", NULL, NULL, NULL,
            INTERNET_FLAG_KEEP_CONNECTION, 0);

    if (!hResourceHandle)
    {
        // clean-up resources
```

```
        return;
    }

    do
    {
        HttpSendRequest(hResourceHandle, NULL, 0, NULL, 0);

        //dwErrorCode stores the error code associated with
        //HttpSendRequest.
        dwErrorCode = hResourceHandle ? ERROR_SUCCESS : GetLastError();

        dwFlags = FLAGS_ERROR_UI_FILTER_FOR_ERRORS
                | FLAGS_ERROR_UI_FLAGS_CHANGE_OPTIONS
                | FLAGS_ERROR_UI_FLAGS_GENERATE_DATA;

        dwError = InternetErrorDlg(hwnd, hResourceHandle, dwErrorCode,
                        dwFlags, NULL);

    } while (ERROR_INTERNET_FORCE_RETRY == dwError)

    //  Insert code to read from the hResourceHandle at this point.
}
```

Although this code is pretty straightforward, there are a few tricky areas. First, because authentication errors don't cause HttpSendRequest to produce an error code, you must tell InternetErrorDlg to go through the response headers looking for hidden errors (like authentication errors and so on). You accomplish this by specifying the FLAGS_ERROR_UI_FILTER_FOR_ERRORS flag.

Also, to make sure that InternetErrorDlg updates the HTTP connection handle with the new authentication information, you must specify the FLAGS_ERROR_UI_FLAGS_CHANGE_OPTIONS flag. When InternetErrorDlg returns, you should be ready to resend the request.

Notice that we didn't have to close the HttpOpenRequest or InternetConnect handles. We simply call HttpSendRequest with the new authentication information stored in the HttpOpenRequest HINTERNET handle.

HTTP Authentication with InternetSetOption

The last WinInet authentication method deals with InternetSetOption. Like the InternetErrorDlg method, you can use InternetSetOption to change the user name and password associated with the HINTERNET handle after calling InternetConnect and

HttpOpenRequest. If you refer back to the section on Internet options in Chapter 2, you'll notice that two of the changeable options are INTERNET_OPTION_ USERNAME and INTERNET_OPTION_PASSWORD.

Listing 4-5 demonstrates how to use InternetSetOption to accomplish HTTP authentication. This example takes it a step further by showing you how to authenticate through a proxy server if required.

Listing 4-5   HTTP Authentication with InternetSetOption

```
HINTERNET hOpenHandle,  hResourceHandle;
DWORD dwError, dwStatus;
DWORD dwStatusSize = sizeof(dwStatus);
char strUsername[64], strPassword[64];

hOpenHandle = InternetOpen("Example", INTERNET_OPEN_TYPE_PRECONFIG,
        NULL, NULL, 0);

if (hOpenHandle)
{
    hConnectHandle = InternetConnect(hOpenHandle, "www.server.com",
            INTERNET_INVALID_PORT_NUMBER, NULL, NULL,
            INTERNET_SERVICE_HTTP,0,0);

    if (!hConnectHandle)
    {
        // clean-up resources
        return;
    }

    hResourceHandle = HttpOpenRequest(hConnectHandle, "GET",
            "/premium/default.htm", NULL, NULL, NULL,
            INTERNET_FLAG_KEEP_CONNECTION, 0);

    if (!hResourceHandle)
    {
        // clean-up resources
        return;
    }

    do
    {

        HttpSendRequest(hResourceHandle, NULL, 0, NULL, 0);
```

```
HttpQueryInfo(hResourceHandle, HTTP_QUERY_FLAG_NUMBER |
    HTTP_QUERY_STATUS_CODE, &dwStatus, &dwStatusSize, NULL);

switch (dwStatus)
{
    case HTTP_STATUS_PROXY_AUTH_REQ:
        // Proxy Authentication Required
        // Insert code to get strUsername and strPassword
        InternetSetOption(hResourceHandle,
                INTERNET_OPTION_PROXY_USERNAME,
                strUsername, strlen(strUsername)+1);
        InternetSetOption(hResourceHandle,
                INTERNET_OPTION_PROXY_PASSWORD,
                strPassword, strlen(strPassword)+1);
        break;

    case HTTP_STATUS_DENIED:
        // Server Authentication Required
        // Insert code to get strUsername and strPassword
        InternetSetOption(hResourceHandle,
                INTERNET_OPTION_USERNAME,
                strUsername, strlen(strUsername)+1);
        InternetSetOption(hResourceHandle,
                INTERNET_OPTION_PASSWORD,
                strPassword, strlen(strPassword)+1);
        break;

    default:
        break;
}
}while (dwStatus == HTTP_STATUS_PROXY_AUTH_REQ ||
    dwStatus == HTTP_STATUS_DENIED)

// Insert code to read from the hResourceHandle at this point.
}
```

This example is quite a bit different from the InternetErrorDlg example. First of all, this example calls HttpQueryInfo to determine whether proxy authentication is required or if server authentication is required. We could have called HttpQueryInfo in the previous example, but we didn't need to because InternetErrorDlg takes care of searching through the headers for us.

Second, in this example you must provide your own UI to query the user for correct authentication information. One of the advantages of using InternetErrorDlg is that you can leverage the same authentication dialog used by IE. Users of IE benefit from the consistent look and feel. With InternetSetOption you have to do this work yourself.

Third, after calling InternetSetOption to modify the user name and password values, you simply call HttpSendRequest again. Once again, we don't have to close and reopen any of the HINTERNET handles.

Using SSL with HTTP

Using SSL with the WinInet HTTP functions is just as simple as using SSL with InternetOpenUrl. You only need to do the following two things to make sure that your HTTP requests take advantage of SSL:

1. Specify INTERNET_FLAG_SECURE in your call to InternetConnect.
2. Use the default HTTPS port (INTERNET_DEFAULT_HTTPS_PORT; 443).

As long as you follow these two steps, all data sent by HttpSendRequest is encrypted using SSL. The nice thing is that you don't have to handle anything differently than you would if you weren't using SSL.

Web Page Retrieval Example

Now it's time to look at a sample program and see how everything fits together. The sample program associated with this chapter is called HttpApp. The sample program allows you to retrieve Web pages via HTTP. The application consists of a simple dialog with a read-only edit box for the downloaded text. To initiate an HTTP request, press the HTTP Request button and fill in the request information.

For example, take a look at Figure 4-6, which illustrates how to download Microsoft's default Web page at *www.microsoft.com*. In this first example I used the default HTTP port and method. The default Microsoft Web site is called *ie40.htm* and is located in the root directory. Assuming that you enter the information as shown in Figure 4-6, you should see a result similar to the one shown in Figure 4-7.

All of the WinInet code for this sample program is isolated in CHttpAppDlg::OnOK except for the two helper functions QueryInfoStatusCode and QueryInfoStatusText. The CHttpAppDlg::OnOK handler gets called each time the user presses the HTTP Request button. Take a look at Listing 4-6:

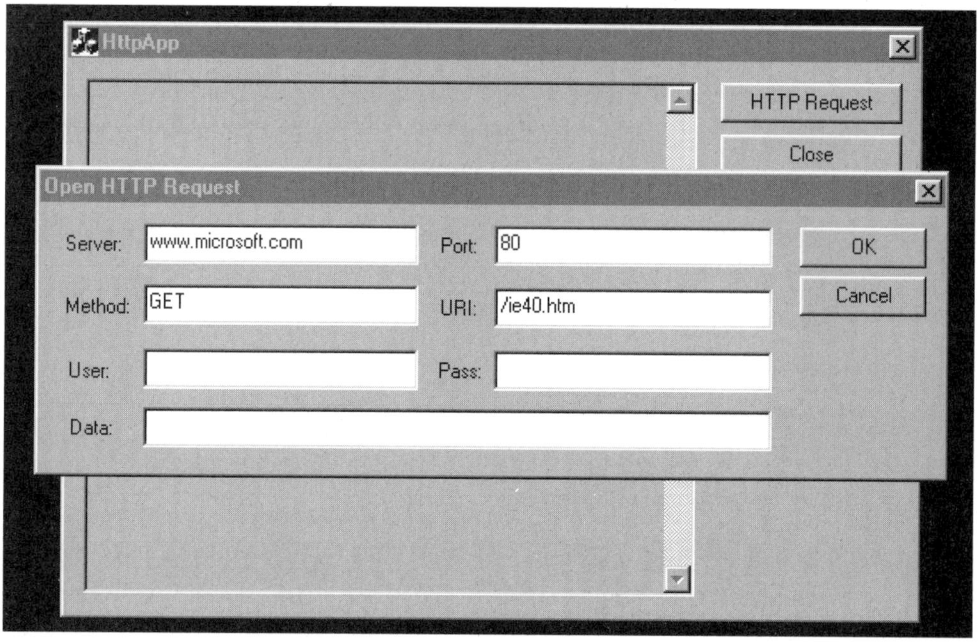

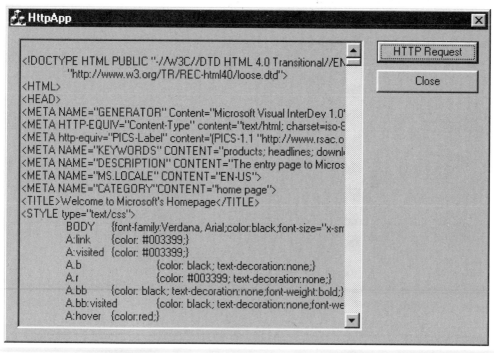

Figure 4-6   HttpApp GET example

Figure 4-7   HttpApp GET example result

Listing 4-6 CHttpAppDlg::OnOK

```
BOOL QueryInfoStatusCode(HINTERNET hRequest, DWORD& dwStatusCode)
{
    DWORD dwLen = sizeof(DWORD);
    return HttpQueryInfo(hRequest, HTTP_QUERY_STATUS_CODE |
            HTTP_QUERY_FLAG_NUMBER, (LPVOID)&dwStatusCode, &dwLen, NULL);
}

BOOL QueryInfoStatusText(HINTERNET hRequest, CString& strStatus)
{
    DWORD dwLen = 255;
    CHAR szBuffer[255];
    BOOL bRet = HttpQueryInfo(hRequest, HTTP_QUERY_STATUS_TEXT,
            (LPVOID)szBuffer, &dwLen, NULL);
    if (bRet) strStatus = szBuffer;
    return bRet;
}

void CHttpAppDlg::OnOK()
{
    HINTERNET hOpenHandle,  hConnectHandle, hResourceHandle;
    DWORD dwError = ERROR_INTERNET_FORCE_RETRY, dwErrorCode;
    CHAR lpszBuffer[256];
    DWORD dwRead, dwFlags, dwStatus;
    CString strStatus;
    CHttpRequestDlg dlg;

    if (IDCANCEL == dlg.DoModal())
        return;

    m_strResult.Empty();

    // Initialize WinInet and create the Internet session
    hOpenHandle = InternetOpen("HttpApp/1.0", INTERNET_OPEN_TYPE_PRECONFIG,
            NULL, NULL, 0);

    if (!hOpenHandle)
        return;

    // check to see if the user wants to use SSL
    dwFlags = (dlg.m_nPort == 443) ? INTERNET_FLAG_SECURE : 0;
```

```cpp
// establish the connection with the HTTP server
hConnectHandle = InternetConnect(hOpenHandle, dlg.m_strServer,
        dlg.m_nPort, dlg.m_strUserName, dlg.m_strPassword,
        INTERNET_SERVICE_HTTP, 0, 0);

if (!hConnectHandle)
{
    InternetCloseHandle(hOpenHandle);
    return;
}

// create the HTTP request
hResourceHandle = HttpOpenRequest(hConnectHandle, dlg.m_strMethod,
    dlg.m_strURI, NULL, NULL, NULL, dwFlags, 0);

if (!hResourceHandle)
{
    InternetCloseHandle(hConnectHandle);
    InternetCloseHandle(hOpenHandle);
    return;
}

// keep sending until authentication is successful
while ( ERROR_INTERNET_FORCE_RETRY == dwError)
{
    HttpSendRequest(hResourceHandle, NULL, 0,
        (LPVOID)dlg.m_strData.GetBuffer(0), dlg.m_strData.GetLength());

    dlg.m_strData.ReleaseBuffer();
    dwErrorCode = hResourceHandle ? ERROR_SUCCESS : GetLastError();


    dwError = InternetErrorDlg(GetSafeHwnd(), hResourceHandle,
            dwErrorCode, FLAGS_ERROR_UI_FILTER_FOR_ERRORS |
            FLAGS_ERROR_UI_FLAGS_CHANGE_OPTIONS |
            FLAGS_ERROR_UI_FLAGS_GENERATE_DATA, NULL);
}

if (!QueryInfoStatusCode(hResourceHandle, dwStatus))
    AfxMessageBox("Error in QueryInfoStatusCode");
else
```

```
{
    if (HTTP_STATUS_OK != dwStatus)
    {
        CString strMsgFormat("HTTP Status Code: %d, Reason: %s");
        CString strMsg;

        if (!QueryInfoStatusText(hResourceHandle, strStatus))
            strMsg = "Unknown";
        strMsg.Format(strMsgFormat, dwStatus, strStatus);
        AfxMessageBox(strMsg);
    }
    else
    {
        while (InternetReadFile(hResourceHandle, lpszBuffer, 255, &dwRead))
        {
            if (dwRead == 0)
                break;
            lpszBuffer[dwRead]=0;
            m_strResult += lpszBuffer;
        }
    }
}
//clean up
InternetCloseHandle(hResourceHandle);
InternetCloseHandle(hConnectHandle);
InternetCloseHandle(hOpenHandle);

//update dialog
UpdateData(FALSE);
}
```

Notice how I use QueryInfoStatusCode and QueryInfoStatusText to determine the problem with an erroneous HTTP request. If you retry the example shown in Figure 4-6 but this time type in ie40.html (instead of ie40.htm) for the URI, you get the error dialog shown in Figure 4-8, telling you that the server couldn't find the file. Notice that the text Object Not Found was returned by the HTTP server.

Suppose you want to do a POST request. You can do so by imitating an HTML form submit. For example, browse to *http://quote.yahoo.com* and let's imitate the stock quote look-up form. Using HttpApp, type in the information shown in Figure 4-9.

Figure 4-8   HttpApp error dialog

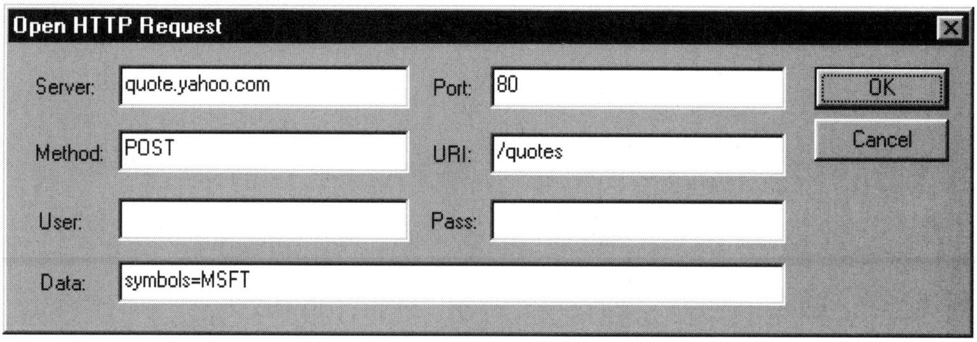

Figure 4-9   HttpApp POST example

So how did I know what to type in here to imitate the form? If you select View | Source from the menu, you can look at the form values. The form action is what you want to enter for the URI. Then you simply need to identify the name values for the form fields. In this case there is only one form field called symbols. For this example, let's only enter one stock symbol—MSFT (Microsoft). If we were to use more than one symbol and there was more than one form field, the POST data line would look something like this:

```
Symbols=MSFT+INTC+SEEK&QuoteType=Full
```

Notice that the stock symbols are separated by the + symbol, which corresponds to user-typed spaces. Also, the name/value pairs are separated by the & character. The example shown in Figure 4-9 should produce the result shown in Figure 4-10. This HTML shown in this result produces the Web page illustrated in Figure 4-11.

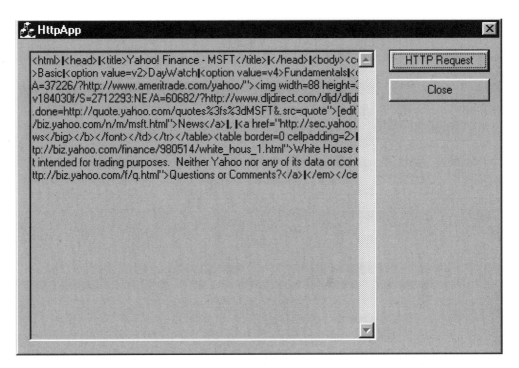

Figure 4-10   HttpApp POST example result

If the user enters 443—the default HTTPS port—for the port value, I use the INTERNET_FLAG_SECURE flag in the call to HttpOpenRequest. Also, notice that I use the InternetErrorDlg method for handling user authentication. The code used in this example is virtually identical to the code presented in the previous section.

If the user doesn't enter a user name or password and the URI identifies a resource that requires authentication, InternetErrorDlg gets called and the dialog shown in Figure 4-5 is presented to the user. Otherwise, if the user enters a valid user name and password in the Open HTTP Request dialog, InternetErrorDlg won't do anything.

Let's take a look at one final example of accessing a secure Web site (SSL) that requires user authentication. Take a look at Figure 4-12, which demonstrates how to access ETrade Securities secure Web site. ETrade's site requires user authentication. You won't be able to test this unless you have an account with ETrade, but you can do the same thing with any secure Web site.

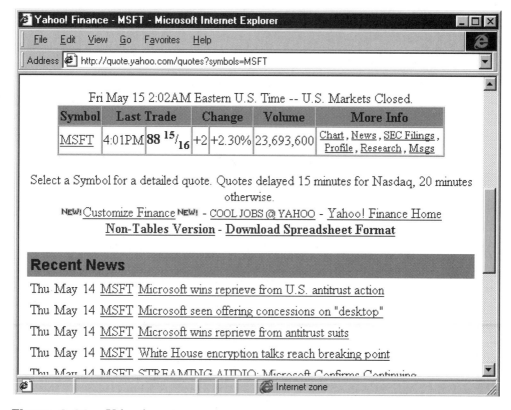

Figure 4-11 Yahoo! quotes

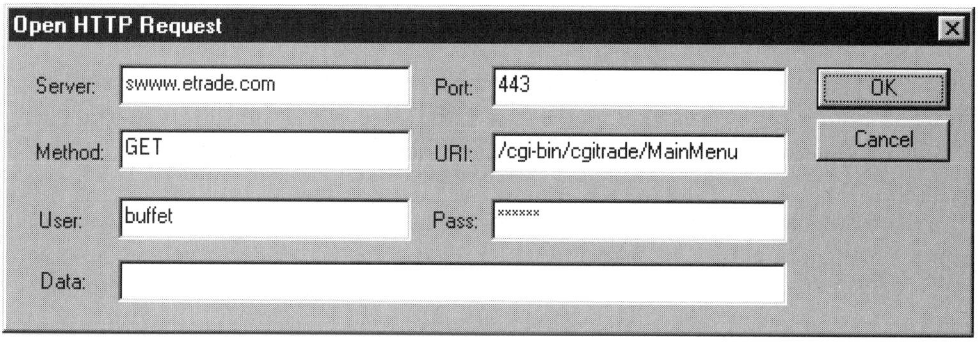

Figure 4-12 HttpApp SSL example

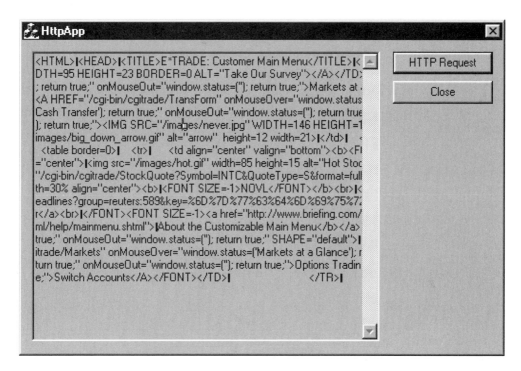

Figure 4-13   HttpApp SSL example result

As long as the user name and password entered are valid, you get a result similar to the one shown in Figure 4-13.

This example differs from the rest because it transmits all data via SSL. Notice, however, that our code didn't have to do any special handling besides setting the appropriate flag and port number. By the time we read the data using InternetReadFile, the response has already been decrypted back to plain text.

Conclusion

As you've learned, the HTTP protocol opens up the doors to powerful and flexible communications. You can use HTTP to access any of the vast resources found on the WWW. These resources not only extend your application's functionality, but also improve your application's maintainability. By now you should feel comfortable enough with the HTTP protocol to take full advantage of the WinInet HTTP functions.

The WinInet HTTP functions provide an easy-to-use interface to the HTTP protocol. Tasks that were once a chore using technologies like Winsock are now considered a "cakewalk" with the WinInet HTTP functions. For example, WinInet makes HTTP user authentication and SSL as simple as specifying a few values.

The sample program HttpApp should help solidify the concepts you learned in this chapter. Be sure to play around with the sample code and retrieve resources from the Web using various HTTP methods, ports, URIs, and authentication values.

5
Chapter

FTP Functions

In this chapter, we'll look at the commonly used protocol for transferring files between computers—FTP. The format of this chapter is very similar to that of the HTTP chapter. First I'll walk you through the FTP protocol specification. Then I'll present the WinInet FTP functions and show you how you can use them to leverage the underlying FTP protocol. Finally I'll help you create a sample FTP program that uses the concepts presented in this chapter.

The FTP Protocol

FTP was designed for transferring files between computers over the Internet. You're probably familiar with the command-based FTP client that comes with Windows 95 and Windows NT (see Figure 5-1). FTP was developed with the following goals in mind:

- To promote the sharing of files
- To encourage the use of remote computers
- To shield a user from variations in file storage systems among hosts
- To transfer data reliably and efficiently

Although HTTP is designed around using somewhat complicated headers, FTP is built on a much simpler command-based design. Like HTTP, FTP also relies on TCP/IP to manage connections and to transfer data. To understand FTP, you must understand the FTP model along with the set of FTP commands that make everything happen.

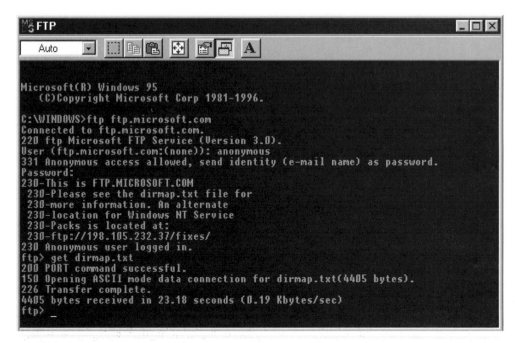

Figure 5-1   Windows 95 FTP client

The FTP Model

Figure 5-2 illustrates the FTP model. First, through some type of UI (like the one in Figure 5-1), the user needs to establish a connection with a remote FTP server. FTP servers listen on the well-known FTP port (21). When the connection is established through TCP/IP on port 21, the user sends FTP commands to the FTP server. The FTP protocol interpreter on the remote server processes the user's commands and takes the appropriate action.

Notice that all data is transferred via TCP/IP, which interfaces directly with the file system on each end of the connection. For example, suppose that I want to download a file from Microsoft's FTP server. After establishing a connection with the server I type

```
ftp> get dirmap.txt
```

The local FTP client translates the get command into the appropriate FTP command (RECV) and sends it to the remote FTP interpreter. After the remote FTP interpreter processes the command and realizes that it needs to send dirmap.txt, it locates the file, sends a reply, and begins sending the data over the TCP/IP connection. After

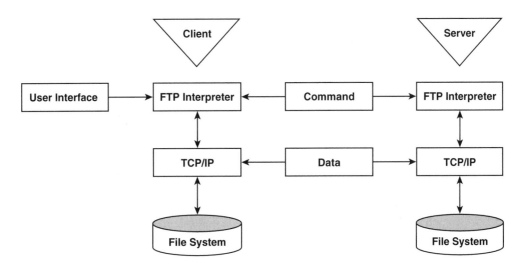

Figure 5-2 The FTP model

my computer receives the reply, it begins receiving the data and saves the file to my local file system.

Although there are certain problem areas dealing with differences in file and data structures across systems, the overall FTP model is quite simple. Lucky for us, WinInet takes care of most of the problem areas and lets us focus on the higher level FTP commands. A good understanding of the FTP commands is more than sufficient preparation for what's ahead.

FTP Commands

There are three types of FTP commands: access control, transfer parameter, and FTP service. First, the access control commands deal with establishing the FTP connection and identifying the client's access privileges. Second, the transfer parameter commands provide a way for the client to change certain transfer properties, such as the data port, file structure, and data representation type. Third, the FTP service commands define specific file transfer functions.

All FTP commands must conform to the defined command syntax. The command syntax defines what the server expects the command to look like. Before looking at the specific commands, let's briefly cover the command syntax rules.

Command Syntax

There are a few important things to keep in mind about FTP command syntax. First, all commands are treated with case insensitivity. This means that PWD, Pwd, and pwd are all treated the same by the protocol interpreter. Second, space and CRLF characters play crucial roles in delimiting a command. Take a look at the following command syntax:

```
<command> <SP> <parameter> <SP> <parameter> <CRLF>
```

Every command line begins with the command code (see the FTP command tables). The command code is followed by a space (<SP>). If the command requires a parameter, the parameter follows the space. (If the command requires more than one parameter, they are all separated by spaces.) Finally, a CRLF follows the last parameter and signals the server to begin processing the given command line.

Access Control Commands

Table 5-1 describes the FTP access control commands. Like their name suggests, these FTP commands deal with access control on the remote file system. Commands like USER, PASS, and ACCT allow a client to provide user name and password authentication information for a specific account on the remote system. CWD and CDUP allow the user to change the working directory on the remote file system without having to reconnect. REIN and QUIT provide a way to wipe out all access information and terminate the connection.

The four-letter code in parentheses next to the command name represents the actual command text. The description for each command specifies the parameters that are needed (if any) and gives a brief description of the command functionality.

Transfer Parameter Commands

The transfer parameter commands (see Table 5-2) allow the client to modify the data transfer properties or parameters. Although every transfer parameter has a default value, the default functionality may not fit your needs exactly. Therefore, these commands give you control over certain aspects of the data transfer properties.

For example, you can change the default data port by using the PORT command. Or you can use other commands such as TYPE, STRU, MODE, and PASV to change other properties like the representation type (ASCII, EBDIC, or Image), file structure (file, record, or page), transfer mode (stream, block, or compressed), or the way the server listens to the data port.

THE FTP PROTOCOL • 143

Table 5-1   FTP access control commands

Command	Description
USER NAME (USER)	The argument field is a string identifying the user to the file system. It's normally the first command transmitted by the user after the control connections are made. Some servers may also require additional identification information such as a password and/or an account command.
PASSWORD (PASS)	The argument field is a Telnet string specifying the user password. It must be preceded by the USER command.
ACCOUNT (ACCT)	The argument field is a Telnet string identifying the user account. Some servers may require this command for certain operations, such as storing files.
CHANGE WORKING DIRECTORY (CWD)	The argument field is a path name specifying the new directory on the remote file system. Changes the working directory on the remote file system to the specified path.
CHANGE TO PARENT DIRECTORY (CDUP)	No argument. Simply makes the parent directory the current directory on the remote file system.
STRUCTURE MOUNT (SMNT)	The argument is a pathname specifying a directory or other system-dependent file group designator. Mounts the specified file system structure.
REINITIALIZE (REIN)	No argument. This command terminates USER, flushing all input/output and account information, except to allow any transfer in progress to be completed.
LOGOUT (QUIT)	No argument. This command terminates USER and, if file transfer is not in progress, the server closes the control connection.

FTP Service Commands

The FTP service commands define a specific file transfer function requested by the user. Normally the parameter for these commands is a pathname to a file. Because the commands are fairly self-explanatory, I'll let you peruse Table 5-3 on your own.

Table 5-2   FTP transfer parameter commands

Command	Description
DATA PORT (PORT)	The argument is a HOST-PORT specification for the data port to be used in data connection.
PASSIVE (PASV)	This command requests the server to "listen" on a data port (which is not its default data port) and to wait for a connection rather than initiate one on receipt of a transfer command.
REPRESENTATION TYPE (TYPE)	The argument specifies the representation type, such as ASCII, EBDIC, or Image. The default is ASCII.
FILE STRUCTURE (STRU)	The argument is a single character describing the file structure (F, File; R, Record; P, Page structure). The default is File.
TRANSFER MODE (MODE)	The argument is a single character describing the transfer mode (S, Stream; B, Block; C, Compressed). The default is Stream.

Table 5-3   FTP service commands

Command	Description
RETRIEVE (RETR)	Retrieves the specified file and transfers it to the local file system.
STORE (STOR)	Stores the data being transferred as a file on the remote file system. If the specified file already exists on the server, the file is overwritten. If it doesn't already exist, a new file is created with the supplied file name.
STORE UNIQUE (STOU)	Works like STOR except it ensures that files on the remote system are given unique names (in other words, files aren't overwritten).
APPEND (APPE)	Stores the data being transferred as a file on the remote file system. If the specified file already exists, the new data is appended to the file; otherwise, a new file is created.
ALLOCATE (ALLO)	Reserves sufficient storage to accommodate the new file to be transferred.
RESTART (REST)	Represents the server marker at which file transfer is to be restarted.

Command	Description
RENAME FROM (RNFR)	Specifies the old pathname of the file being renamed. This command must be immediately followed by RNTO, specifying the new file pathname.
RENAME TO (RNTO)	Specifies the new pathname of the file specified in the immediately preceding RNFR command. Together the two commands cause a file to be renamed.
ABORT (ABOR)	Aborts the previous FTP service command and any associated transfer of data.
DELETE (DELE)	Deletes the file specified in the pathname at the server site.
REMOVE DIRECTORY (RMD)	Removes the specified directory.
MAKE DIRECTORY (MKD)	Creates the specified directory.
PRINT WORKING DIRECTORY (PWD)	Returns the name of the current working directory in the reply.
LIST (LIST)	Lists a directory of files or specific file information. If the pathname specifies a directory or other group of files, the server should transfer a list of files in the specified directory. If the pathname specifies a file, then the server should send current information on the file. A null argument implies the user's current working or default directory.
NAME LIST (NLST)	Lists a directory of files. The pathname should specify a directory or other system-specific file group descriptor. A null argument implies the current directory. The server returns a stream of names of files and no other information.
SITE PARAMETERS (SITE)	This command is used by the server to provide services specific to its system that are essential to file transfer but not sufficiently universal to be included as commands in the protocol.
SYSTEM (SYST)	Returns the type of operating system at the server.
STATUS (STAT)	Sends a status response over the control connection in the form of a reply.
HELP (HELP)	Sends helpful information regarding its implementation status over the control connection to the user. The command may take an argument (for example, any command name) and return more specific information as a response.
NOOP (NOOP)	This command does not affect any parameters or previously entered commands. If it succeeds, the server simply returns OK in the response.

FTP Replies

Every FTP command generates one or more server replies. The reply gives the status of the submitted command and defines what further action, if any, is necessary. As you can see from the FTP command tables, certain commands can only be processed if a previous command has succeeded. USER and PASS are a perfect example of this. If USER succeeds, PASS also succeeds. In sequential command scenarios, replies give the user information about the state of a given operation. If a command in a sequence fails, the state is corrupted and the user must start over, from the beginning of the command sequence.

Like commands, replies must also conform to the reply syntax. The reply syntax defines what the client expects the reply to look like. Before moving on to the specific reply codes, let's look briefly at the general reply syntax.

Reply Syntax

The reply syntax is a great deal like the command syntax. In fact, the same delimiters used by the command syntax (<SP> and <CRLF>) are also employed by the reply syntax. The following is how the general FTP reply syntax looks:

```
<reply code> <SP> <text> <CRLF>
```

Interestingly, the reply code is the only essential piece of information returned by the server. The reply code contains enough information for the client to figure out what happened and, more importantly, what should happen next. The text field is for user-friendly purposes. The client FTP interpreter doesn't do anything with this information except pass it back to the application (if desired). This text can be displayed to keep the user informed of the status of each operation. Notice that a space must separate the reply code and text fields; also, the end of the reply line must end with a CRLF.

I should also mention that the text field could be more than one line long. In this case, the syntax changes a bit to help the client figure out where the reply begins and ends. For more information on this anomaly, see the FTP specification outlined in RFC 959 at *http://info.internet.isi.edu/in-notes/rfc/files/rfc959.txt.*

Reply Codes

Reply codes are three-digit numbers. Similar to the HTTP status codes, each digit of the reply code has significance. This arrangement enables the client to look for general or more specific information on the results of an action request.

The first digit of the reply code tells the user whether the reply is good, bad, or incomplete. A well-designed FTP client should be able to figure out what to do next simply by examining the first digit of the reply code. The second digit contains information about the specific error that occurred. The third digit is used to represent the most specific error information. To understand this better, let's look at the possible meanings for both the first and second digits.

First Digit Like I said, the first digit of the reply code is used to determine whether the reply is successful, unsuccessful, or incomplete. Table 5-4 describes each first-digit value of the reply code. For example, all reply codes beginning with the digit 2 mean that the requested action completed successfully. The first digit of the reply code is generally used to determine quickly the general success of the command.

Second Digit The second digit contains more specific information about the command and reply. For example, commands that contain syntax errors receive a reply with a second-digit value of 0. All replies that refer to the control and data connections have a second-digit value of 2. Examine Table 5-5 for details of the second digits.

Third Digit—Specific Reply Code Meanings The third digit of the reply code offers the most specific information about what happened or needs to happen with a given command. If you can remember the meanings of the first and second digits, it will make your life much easier when dealing with FTP replies. Nevertheless, in most cases you'll need to examine the entire reply code for an exact status. Therefore, I've organized the most common FTP reply codes into functional groups, with a short description to the right of each code. Codes within a group are similar in meaning (because they contain the same first two digits) and only differ by the third digit of the code. Skim Table 5-6 to see how codes within the same group are related with slightly different meanings.

Table 5-4 FTP reply code first-digit values

Value	Meaning
1 X X	The requested action is being initiated; expect another reply before proceeding with a new command.
2 X X	The requested action has been completed successfully. A new request may be initiated.
3 X X	The command has been accepted, but the requested action is being held in abeyance, pending receipt of further information. The user should send another command specifying this information. This reply is used in command sequence groups.
4 X X	The command was not accepted and the requested action did not take place, but the error condition is temporary and the action may be requested again. The user should return to the beginning of the command sequence, if any.
5 X X	The command was not accepted and the requested action did not take place. The user process is discouraged from repeating the exact request (in the same sequence).

Table 5-5   FTP reply code second-digit values

Value	Meaning
X 0 X	Syntax—Replies that refer to syntax errors, syntactically correct commands that don't fit any functional category, or unimplemented or superfluous commands
X 1 X	Information—Replies to requests for information, such as status or help
X 2 X	Connections—Replies that refer to the control and data connections
X 3 X	Authentication and accounting—Replies for the log-in process and accounting procedures
X 4 X	Unspecified as yet
X 5 X	File system—Replies that indicate the status of the server file system vis-à-vis the requested transfer or other file system action

Table 5-6   FTP reply codes by group

Group	Examples	
1 1 X	110	Restart marker reply. In this case, the text is exact and not left to the particular implementation; it must read: MARK yyyy = mmmm Where yyyy is User-process data stream marker, and mmmm server's equivalent marker. (Note the spaces between markers and =).
1 2 X	120	Service ready in nnn minutes.
	125	Data connection already open; transfer starting.
1 5 X	150	File status okay; about to open data connection.
2 0 X	200	Command okay.
	202	Command not implemented, superfluous at this site.
2 1 X	211	System status, or system help reply.
	212	Directory status.
	213	File status.
	214	Help message regarding how to use the server, or the meaning of a particular nonstandard command. This reply is useful only to the human user.
	215	NAME system type, where NAME is an official system name from the list in the Assigned Numbers document.
2 2 X	220	Service ready for new user.
	221	Service closing control connection; logged out if appropriate.

Group	Examples	
	225	Data connection open; no transfer in progress.
	226	Closing data connection; requested file action successful (for example, file transfer or file abort).
	227	Entering passive mode (h1, h2, h3, h4, p1, p2).
2 3 X	230	User logged in; proceed.
2 5 X	250	Requested file action okay; completed.
	257	PATHNAME created.
3 3 X	331	User name okay; need password.
	332	Need account for login.
3 5 X	350	Requested file action pending further information.
4 2 X	421	Service not available; closing control connection. This may be a reply to any command if the service knows it must shut down.
	425	Can't open data connection.
	426	Connection closed; transfer aborted.
4 5 X	450	Requested file action not taken; file unavailable (for example, file busy).
	451	Requested action aborted; local error in processing.
	452	Requested action not taken; insufficient storage space in system.
5 0 X	500	Syntax error; command unrecognized. This may include errors such as command line too long.
	501	Syntax error in parameters or arguments.
	502	Command not implemented.
	503	Bad sequence of commands.
	504	Command not implemented for that parameter.
5 3 X	530	Not logged in.
	532	Need account for storing files.
5 5 X	550	Requested action not taken; file unavailable (for example, file not found, no access).
	551	Requested action aborted; page type unknown.
	552	Requested file action aborted; exceeded storage allocation for current directory or dataset.
	553	Requested action not taken; file name not allowed.

Command-Specific Replies and Sequences

For each command there is a set of possible replies. Knowing which reply codes are possible for a given command helps the client-side developer write more solid and efficient code. Additionally, there is even a defined sequence for the reply codes for a given command. For example, let's look at the possible reply codes for the LIST command.

Figure 5-3 illustrates the LIST command's possible reply codes along with their sequence. As you can see, after executing the LIST command, there are three types (or groups) of replies that can be used. The first group of replies (125, 150) represents success (refer to Table 5-6 for exact meanings). However, if either 125 or 150 are received, additional replies will follow. The second group (450) represents temporary errors. In this case, no additional reply codes follow. The command should be tried again because the error is only temporary. The final group (421, 500, 501, 502, and 530) represents error conditions that aren't temporary. Once again, no additional reply codes are necessary.

Why is this important? Well, the client processing the reply needs to know when it needs to take action and when it needs to wait for additional replies. In a way, each command has its own state diagram of replies. In the LIST example in Figure 5-3, after receiving a reply of 450, the client can continue (with a new command) because no more reply codes are possible. The final state of the command has been determined. On the other hand, if the client receives 125, it must wait for additional reply codes before it can determine the final state of the command.

Minimum Implementation

If you have some experience with different FTP clients and/or servers, you may be wondering why you've never heard of many of the commands described in the previous tables. Well, the answer is simple: because the client or the server that you're used to may not support them. You mean an FTP client/server isn't required to

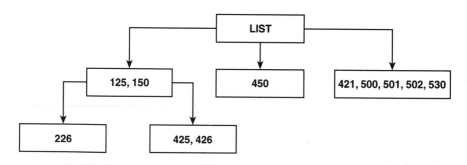

Figure 5-3 LIST command reply sequence

Table 5-7   FTP minimum implementation standard

Functionality	Minimum Level of Support
TYPE	ASCII
MODE	Stream
STRUCTURE	File, Record
COMMANDS	USER, QUIT, PORT, TYPE, MODE, STRU, RETR, STOR, NOOP

implement all the commands described earlier? That is correct. However, servers are required to adhere to a minimum implementation standard (see Table 5-7).

Without this minimum level of functionality, clients would have to deal with endless error messages while trying to figure out which commands are supported. This standard gives clients a set of functionality that can be expected from all FTP servers.

 Most FTP clients/servers don't support all of the FTP protocol commands.

A Typical FTP Scenario

Let's look at a typical FTP scenario to help you understand how the different FTP commands are used to accomplish a specific task. Suppose you need to download a file called file.txt from *ftp.server.com* using a standard FTP client. Figure 5-4 illustrates the communication between the FTP client and the server. The box on the left represents the FTP client, and the box on the right represents the FTP server. The text inside the client box represents the FTP commands entered by the user. The arrows going toward the server contain the FTP commands sent to the server by the FTP client. The arrows going toward the client contain the FTP replies sent to the client by the FTP server.

Using Telnet to Test FTP

You can use Telnet to play around with FTP just like you can with HTTP. For example, try connecting to *ftp.microsoft.com* on port 21 and type in the commands shown in Figure 5-5. For more information on using Telnet refer to the previous chapter on HTTP.

FTP Protocol Summary

Although FTP is a little easier to digest than HTTP, there is still a great deal of information to absorb. A basic understanding of the FTP model, commands, and replies is

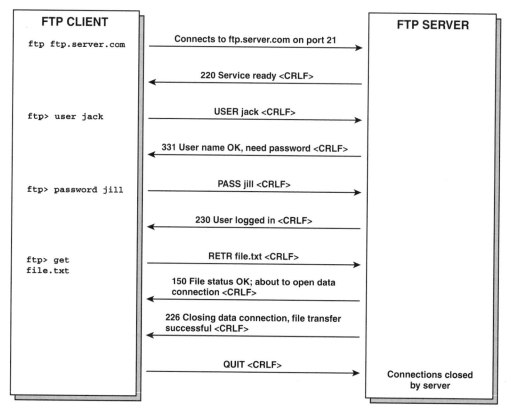

Figure 5-4 FTP typical scenario

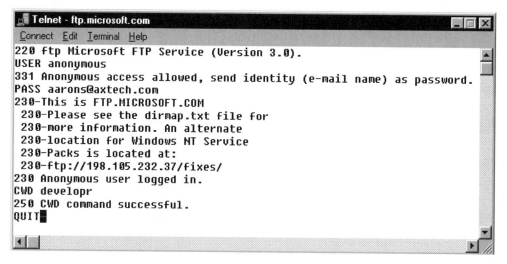

Figure 5-5 Sample FTP request using Telnet

all you need to start developing FTP-based applications. The information I've presented here is also more than enough to prepare you for using the WinInet FTP functions. Refer to RFC 959 at *http://info.internet.isi.edu/in-notes/rfc/files/rfc959.txt* for more information.

WinInet FTP Functions

The WinInet FTP functions allow you to forget about most of the underlying FTP protocol details. As you'll see shortly, most of the FTP functions encapsulate one of the FTP service commands. Establishing an FTP session is just like establishing an HTTP session, with a few minor modifications. Let's take a look at the handle hierarchy for using the FTP functions.

FTP Hierarchy

The FTP handle hierarchy is illustrated in Figure 5-6. Notice that the first two steps are the same as with the HTTP handle hierarchy. You must first call InternetOpen and then InternetConnect with the INTERNET_SERVICE_FTP service flag. After you receive a valid HINTERNET handle from InternetConnect, you can do just about anything that the FTP functions have to offer.

Let's briefly review how you would take care of the first two steps: InternetOpen and InternetConnect. Here is an example:

```
HINTNERNET hOpenHandle = InternetOpen("MyFTP/1.0",
        INTERNET_OPEN_TYPE_PRECONFIG, NULL, NULL, 0);


if (hOpenHandle)
{
    HINTERNET hConnectHandle = InternetConnect(hOpenHandle, "ftp.server.com",
            INTERNET_DEFAULT_FTP_PORT, "anonymous", "email",
            INTERNET_SERVICE_FTP, 0, 0);
}
```

Notice that everything looks pretty much the same as with the HTTP example. Nothing really changed in the call to InternetOpen (besides the User-Agent text). There are, however, a few changes to the call to InternetConnect. This time I used INTERNET_SERVICE_FTP and INTERNET_DEFAULT_FTP_PORT for the port number in the call to InternetConnect.

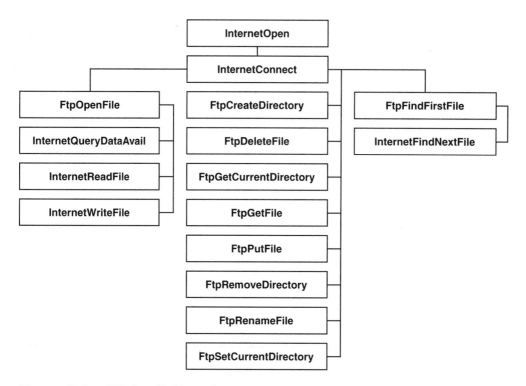

Figure 5-6 FTP handle hierarchy

Also notice that I supplied `anonymous` for my user name and my e-mail address for the password. If you've used FTP servers much, you'll be familiar with this concept. If you pass in NULL for both of these parameters, InternetConnect uses your log-on user name and your e-mail address for these parameters by default. In the section on InternetConnect in Chapter 2, I covered all the possible values for the user name and password parameters when using INTERNET_SERVICE_FTP. For more information on these values, refer back to that section.

When you get to this point, you're ready to start calling the WinInet FTP functions. Let's look at each of the available functions in more detail.

FTP Functions Overview

Table 5-8 describes each of the WinInet FTP functions. If you review these functions and then look back to the section on the FTP protocol commands, you'll notice many similarities. As we look at each of these functions in more detail, you'll see how easy it is to take advantage of the FTP protocol in your applications.

Table 5-8   WinInet FTP functions

Function	Description
FtpCreateDirectory	Creates a new directory on the server. This function requires a handle created by InternetConnect.
FtpDeleteFile	Deletes a file from the server. This function requires a handle created by InternetConnect.
FtpFindFirstFile	Starts file enumeration or file search in the current directory. This function requires a handle created by InternetConnect.
FtpGetCurrentDirectory	Returns the client's current directory on the server. This function requires a handle created by InternetConnect.
FtpGetFile	Retrieves a file from the server. This function requires a handle created by InternetConnect.
FtpOpenFile	Initiates access to a file on the server for either reading or writing. This function requires a handle created by InternetConnect.
FtpPutFile	Writes a file to the server. This function requires a handle created by InternetConnect.
FtpRemoveDirectory	Deletes a directory on the server. This function requires a handle created by InternetConnect.
FtpRenameFile	Renames a file on the server. This function requires a handle created by InternetConnect.
FtpSetCurrentDirectory	Changes the client's current directory on the server. This function requires a handle created by InternetConnect.
InternetWriteFile	Writes data to an open file on the server. This function requires a handle created by InternetConnect.
FtpCommand	Issues an arbitrary command to the FTP server.

Sample FTP Client

In this section I show you how to build a graphical FTP client using the WinInet FTP functions. As we cover each of the functions listed in Table 5-8, I show you a practical example of how to use it in the sample application. First let me give you a brief overview of the sample and how to get started.

I wrote the sample application on Windows 95 using Visual C++ 5.0 (the sample is linked against the IE 4.0 version of WinInet). I recommend that you browse the source code before continuing with this chapter. This will give you a chance to get confused and formulate questions that, hopefully, I'll answer throughout the rest of the chapter. No matter how frustrating it may be, getting confused ahead of time always seems to help solidify concepts. Now let's walk through the steps of creating the MyFTP skeleton, which we'll use throughout the rest of this chapter.

Creating the Project

For the purpose of this example I wanted to keep the UI as simple as possible. In Visual C++ 5.0, create a new project by going to the File menu and pressing New. In the list of new project types, choose MFC AppWizard (exe). Then, in step 1 of the MFC AppWizard, choose Dialog-based application. Finish the rest of the Wizard using the default settings (it really doesn't matter what you choose for the rest of the steps) and press Finish to generate the project and its associated files.

The wizard should generate the normal project files that you're used to seeing. However, the files we're going to be dealing with the most in this application are described in Table 5-9.

We'll implement all the FTP functionality in the CMyFTPDlg class found in MyFTPDlg.h and MyFTPDlg.cpp. The CWinApp-derived application object does nothing more than create and show the one and only CMyFTPDlg instance. As you can see, the sample design is purposely quite simple. This allows us to focus all of our attention on the WinInet FTP implementation.

Dialog Template

The main window of this sample is simply a dialog. If you're following along at home, you'll want to make your dialog look like the one in Figure 5-7. Each of the buttons takes care of a piece of FTP functionality. Throughout the rest of this chapter I'll show you how to implement the code behind each of these buttons.

CMyFTPDlg

Take a look at the CMyFTPDlg class declaration (see Listing 5-1). This should look very familiar if you've done much MFC programming. There are, however, a few things of which to be aware. First, the member variable m_lMode holds the current

Table 5-9 MyFTP project files

Wizard-Generated File	Description
MyFTP.rc	Resource file
MyFTPDlg.h	Main dialog header file
MyFTPDlg.cpp	Main dialog implementation file

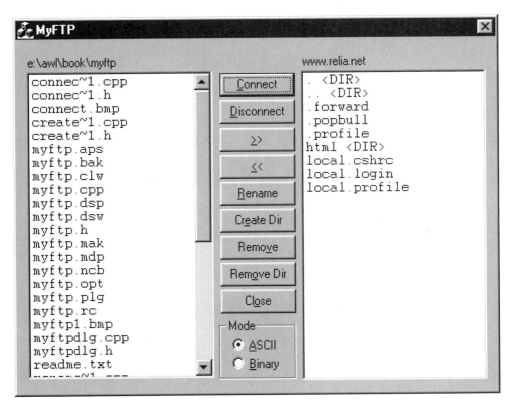

Figure 5-7   MyFTP dialog screen shot

transfer mode that is selected for the FTP GET and PUT commands. The m_strLocalDir contains the path to the current directory with the contents that are displayed in the left list box control. And m_font simply contains the current font used to display the contents of the list boxes.

Listing 5-1   CMyFTPDlg

```
//////////////////////////////////////////////////////////////////////////
// CMyFTPDlg dialog

class CMyFTPDlg : public CDialog
{
// Construction
public:
    CMyFTPDlg(CWnd* pParent = NULL);    // standard constructor
    ~CMyFTPDlg();
```

```
        LONG m_lMode;
        CString m_strLocalDir;
        CFont m_font;

        void FillLocalList();
        void FillRemoteList();

// Dialog Data
        //{{AFX_DATA(CMyFTPDlg)
        enum { IDD = IDD_MYFTP_DIALOG };
        CListBox m_RemoteList;
        CListBox m_LocalList;
        CString m_strStatus;
        CString m_strRemote;
        //}}AFX_DATA

        // ClassWizard generated virtual function overrides
        //{{AFX_VIRTUAL(CMyFTPDlg)
        protected:
        virtual void DoDataExchange(CDataExchange* pDX);     // DDX/DDV support
        //}}AFX_VIRTUAL

// Implementation
protected:
        HICON m_hIcon;

        // Generated message map functions
        //{{AFX_MSG(CMyFTPDlg)
        virtual BOOL OnInitDialog();
        afx_msg void OnSysCommand(UINT nID, LPARAM lParam);
        afx_msg void OnPaint();
        afx_msg HCURSOR OnQueryDragIcon();
        afx_msg void OnConnect();
        afx_msg void OnCreate();
        afx_msg void OnGet();
        afx_msg void OnPut();
        afx_msg void OnRename();
        virtual void OnCancel();
        afx_msg void OnRemove();
        afx_msg void OnDblclkListRemote();
        afx_msg void OnDblclkListLocal();
```

```
afx_msg void OnRemovedir();
afx_msg void OnRadioAscii();
afx_msg void OnRadioBinary();
afx_msg void OnDisconnect();
//}}AFX_MSG
DECLARE_MESSAGE_MAP()
};
```

```
#endif
```

As you'll notice, there are two helper member functions used to fill the contents of the list boxes: FillLocalList and FillRemoteList. The first method, FillLocalList, uses the CWnd::DlgDirList function to enumerate automatically the directory specified by m_strLocalDir. By default, the program begins with m_strLocalDir set to the system TEMP directory. The following code shows how m_strLocalDir is initialized:

```
//fill local list with TEMP directory
GetTempPath(BUFFLEN, m_strLocalDir.GetBuffer(BUFFLEN));
m_strLocalDir.ReleaseBuffer();
m_strLocalDir += "*.*";
FillLocalList();
```

When m_strLocalDir contains the starting directory, FillLocalList simply calls DlgDirList in the following manner:

```
void CMyFTPDlg::FillLocalList()
{
    m_LocalList.ResetContent();
    DlgDirList( m_strLocalDir.GetBuffer(BUFFLEN), IDC_LIST_LOCAL,
            IDC_STATIC_LOCAL, DDL_READWRITE|DDL_DIRECTORY|DDL_DRIVES );
    m_strLocalDir.ReleaseBuffer();
}
```

The second method, FillRemoteList, is a bit more complicated. I'll look at it in more detail shortly.

The rest of the methods are command handlers for the various buttons contained in the dialog template (IDD_MYFTP_DIALOG) shown in Figure 5-7. Now that we have this project skeleton in place, it's just a matter of implementing the code for each of the various buttons. Before we dive into the FTP functions, let me quickly show you how the first two buttons work: Connect and Disconnect.

Connect

First of all, the application uses a single global Internet session. The global HINTERNET handle is stored in g_hSession, which is initialized in CMyFTPDlg::OnInitDialog like this:

```
g_hSession = InternetOpen("MyFTP", INTERNET_OPEN_TYPE_PRECONFIG, NULL, NULL,0);
```

When the user presses the Connect button, CMyFTPDlg::OnConnect is called (see Listing 5-2).

Listing 5-2   CMyFTPDlg::OnConnect

```
void CMyFTPDlg::OnConnect()
{
    CConnectDlg dlg;
    if (IDOK == dlg.DoModal())
    {
        //if already connected, disconnect
        if (g_hConnection)
            InternetCloseHandle(g_hConnection);

        //connect to FTP server
        g_hConnection = InternetConnect(g_hSession, dlg.m_strServer,
                INTERNET_DEFAULT_FTP_PORT, dlg.m_strUser, dlg.m_strPassword,
                INTERNET_SERVICE_FTP, INTERNET_FLAG_PASSIVE, 0);

        if (g_hConnection)
        {
            //enumerates remote directory using FtpFindFirstFile
            FillRemoteList();
        }
        else ProcessInternetError();
        m_strRemote = dlg.m_strServer;
        UpdateData(FALSE);
    }
}
```

OnConnect shows a dialog (CConnectDlg) to query the user for server, user name, and password values (see Figure 5-8).

If the user presses OK, OnConnect continues the connection process; otherwise, it does nothing. If the user is already connected to another FTP server, the previous connection is closed. Then OnConnect calls InternetConnect with the values entered by

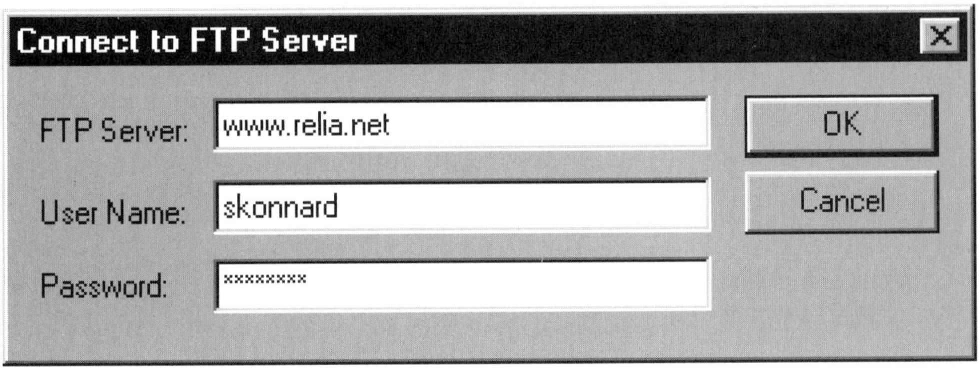

Figure 5-8 Connect dialog

the user. The resulting HINTERNET handle is stored in another global HINTERNET variable—g_hConnection.

Remember the FTP protocol commands. Which commands do you think are being used by the previous call to InternetConnect? The USER and PASS commands should come to mind. Also, since I specified INTERNET_FLAG_PASSIVE, the PASV command is probably also being used behind the scenes.

If the connection succeeded (g_hConnection contains a valid HINTERNET handle), OnConnect calls FillRemoteList to enumerate the remote directory. I'll look at how to do this shortly. The rest of the FTP functions use the HINTERNET handle contained in g_hConnection.

Disconnect

The Disconnect button is much simpler than Connect. When the user presses Disconnect, we simply want to close the g_hConnection handle (see Listing 5-3). Calling InternetCloseHandle on an FTP connection corresponds to the protocol QUIT command.

Listing 5-3 **CMyFTPDlg::OnDisconnect**

```
void CMyFTPDlg::OnDisconnect()
{
    if (g_hConnection)
    {
        InternetCloseHandle(g_hConnection);
        g_hConnection = NULL;
    }
    m_RemoteList.ResetContent();
}
```

Processing Errors

One more thing I want to mention is how the sample application handles errors. Whenever any of the functions discovers a WinInet error, it simply calls ProcessInternetError:

```
void ProcessInternetError()
{
    DWORD dwError = GetLastError();
    CString strMsg;
    strMsg.Format("GetLastError returned %d", dwError);
    AfxMessageBox(strMsg);
}
```

FTP Function Descriptions

We now have an FTP application in place that is capable of connecting to FTP servers with user-provided information, as well as disconnecting. From here on we look at how each of the FTP functions fits into this sample application.

FtpFindFirstFile and InternetFindNextFile

FtpFindFirstFile and InternetFindNextFile encapsulate the behavior of the FTP protocol LIST command, which returns a list of files and directories on the remote FTP server.

FtpFindFirstFile behaves just like the Win32 FindFirstFile function. The only difference is that FtpFindFirstFile enumerates remote directories and files. You would use FtpFindFirstFile to enumerate a directory and display its contents. This is exactly what we want to do in the sample application.

FtpFindFirstFile does exactly what its name suggests—it finds the first file on the remote FTP site that matches the provided criteria. After calling FtpFindFirstFile, you continue the enumeration by calling InternetFindNextFile, which uses the same criteria passed to FtpFindFirstFile.

To begin, let's look at FtpFindFirstFile's function declaration:

```
HINTERNET FtpFindFirstFile(
    IN HINTERNET hFtpSession,
    IN LPCSTR lpszSearchFile,
    OUT LPWIN32_FIND_DATA lpFindFileData,
    IN DWORD dwFlags,
```

```
    IN DWORD dwContext
);
```

hFtpSession takes the HINTERNET handle returned by InternetConnect. lpszSearchFile takes your search criteria for this enumeration. lpszSearchFile specifies the path and file search string. For example, take a look at the following string:

```
/pub/windows/apps/office*.*
```

If you passed this in lpszSearchFile, FtpFindFirstFile looks in /pub/windows/apps/ and enumerates all files that match `office*.*`. If you pass NULL or an empty string, FtpFindFirstFile simply returns the first file in the root directory.

 When calling FtpFindFirstFile, if lpszSearchFile is NULL or an empty string, FtpFindFirstFile enumerates the root FTP directory.

Notice that FtpFindFirstFile returns the file information in the standard WIN32_FIND_DATA structure. This is the same structure used by the Win32 FindFirstFile function. Examining the WIN32_FIND_DATA structure tells you exactly what kind of information you can retrieve for a single file:

```
typedef struct _WIN32_FIND_DATA { // wfd
    DWORD dwFileAttributes;
    FILETIME ftCreationTime;
    FILETIME ftLastAccessTime;
    FILETIME ftLastWriteTime;
    DWORD nFileSizeHigh;
    DWORD nFileSizeLow;
    DWORD dwReserved0;
    DWORD dwReserved1;
    TCHAR cFileName[ MAX_PATH ];
    TCHAR cAlternateFileName[ 14 ];
} WIN32_FIND_DATA;
```

As you can see, you can retrieve file attributes, times, sizes, and names. Because FtpFindFirstFile and FindFirstFile are so similar, working with local and remote files can, and should, be transparent to the user.

Table 5-10 describes the flags that can be used with FtpFindFirstFile.

Table 5-10   FtpFindFirstFile flags

Flag	Description
INTERNET_FLAG_DONT_CACHE	Does not add the returned entity to the cache. Identical to the preferred value, INTERNET_FLAG_NO_CACHE_WRITE.
INTERNET_FLAG_HYPERLINK	Forces a reload if there was no Expires time and no Last-Modified time returned from the server when determining whether to reload the item from the network.
INTERNET_FLAG_MUST_CACHE_ REQUEST	Causes a temporary file to be created if the file cannot be cached. Identical to INTERNET_FLAG_NEED_FILE.
INTERNET_FLAG_NEED_FILE	Causes a temporary file to be created if the file cannot be cached.
INTERNET_FLAG_NO_CACHE_WRITE	Does not add the returned entity to the cache.
INTERNET_FLAG_RELOAD	Forces a download of the requested file, object, or directory listing from the originating server, not from the cache.
INTERNET_FLAG_RESYNCHRONIZE	Causes the FTP resource to be reloaded from the server.

One nuance found in the FTP protocol is that it only allows a single directory enumeration at a given time per session. In other words, if you call FtpFindFirstFile on a given FTP connection handle and then try to call it again on the same handle, you get an error (ERROR_FTP_TRANSFER_IN_PROGRESS). Hence, before calling FtpFindFirstFile again, you must call InternetCloseHandle.

 Another problem is the lack of an enumeration standard across FTP servers. Most FTP servers handle file and directory enumeration differently. Because of this, some of the data returned in the WIN32_ FIND_DATA structure may be invalid or incorrect. For the most part, WinInet tries to make a best guess at what the data should be if it doesn't receive anything from the server. For example, if the creation time comes back empty, it will probably end up containing the last write time and so forth.

InternetFindNextFile is responsible for continuing the enumeration started by FtpFindFirstFile. Take a look at its function declaration:

```
BOOL InternetFindNextFile( IN HINTERNET hFind, OUT LPVOID lpvFindData);
```

If you refer back to the FTP handle hierarchy (see Figure 5-6), you'll notice that InternetFindNextFile requires a handle returned by FtpFindFirstFile; hFind takes the handle created by FtpFindFirstFile. lpvFindData is simply a pointer to a WIN32_FIND_DATA structure that contains the next file (or directory) found.

InternetFindNextFile returns TRUE if it succeeds or FALSE if it fails. When it reaches the end of the enumeration, InternetFindNextFile returns FALSE, and GetLastError returns ERROR_NO_MORE_FILES.

Now it's time to look at how to use this function in the sample program. Remember that CMyFTPDlg::OnConnect calls FillRemoteList after establishing the connection successfully. CMyFTPDlg::FillRemoteList handles all of the remote file enumeration (see Listing 5-4).

Listing 5-4   CMyFTPDlg::FillRemoteList

```
void CMyFTPDlg::FillRemoteList()
{
    CString strFileName;
    WIN32_FIND_DATA FindFileData;
    HINTERNET hFindFile;

    m_RemoteList.ResetContent();

    if (hFindFile)
        InternetCloseHandle(hFindFile);

    hFindFile = FtpFindFirstFile(g_hConnection, NULL, &FindFileData,
            INTERNET_FLAG_RELOAD, 0);

    if (hFindFile)
    {
        // if it's a directory, add <DIR> to description
        if ( (FindFileData.dwFileAttributes & FILE_ATTRIBUTE_DIRECTORY) ==
                FILE_ATTRIBUTE_DIRECTORY )
            strFileName.Format("%s <DIR>", FindFileData.cFileName);
        else
            strFileName = FindFileData.cFileName;
```

```
    m_RemoteList.AddString(strFileName);

    while(InternetFindNextFile(hFindFile, &FindFileData))
    {
        // if it's a directory, add <DIR> to description
        if ( (FindFileData.dwFileAttributes &
                FILE_ATTRIBUTE_DIRECTORY) == FILE_ATTRIBUTE_DIRECTORY )
            strFileName.Format("%s <DIR>", FindFileData.cFileName);
        else
            strFileName = FindFileData.cFileName;

        m_RemoteList.AddString(strFileName);
    }
    InternetCloseHandle(hFindFile);
    }
    else ProcessInternetError();
}
```

You can check to see whether the returned item is a file or directory by looking at the attribute field in WIN32_FIND_DATA. In this sample I tack on <DIR> to the items that are directories to help distinguish them from files.

 As we cover the rest of the FTP functions, any time we modify data on the remote server you'll see a call to FillRemoteList. The call to InternetCloseHandle(hFindFile) is very crucial to making this work. Because only one enumeration is allowed per session, it's a good practice always to close the enumeration handles after they're complete.

FtpSetCurrentDirectory and FtpGetCurrentDirectory

While we're on the subject of file/directory enumeration, let's look at how to navigate to a new directory once we've found it. Using the FTP protocol, you would use CWD (change directory) and CDUP (change to parent directory). With WinInet, however, you use FtpSetCurrentDirectory.

To determine the current directory, the FTP protocol provides the PWD (print working directory) command. WinInet's FtpGetCurrentDirectory encapsulates this functionality.

Because both of these WinInet functions are so straightforward, I'm not going to cover them in any detail. For more details on these functions, refer to the online documentation.

In the sample application, I want the user to be able to double click on a directory to make it the new working directory. To accomplish this, I trap the list box double-click notification and call it CMyFTPDlg::OnDblclkListRemote (see Listing 5-5).

Listing 5-5   CMyFTPDlg::OnDblclkListRemote

```
void CMyFTPDlg::OnDblclkListRemote()
{
    CString strFile;
    int iIndex;
    char szDir[255];
    DWORD dwLen = 255;

    if (!g_hConnection)
    {
        AfxMessageBox("You must first connect to an FTP server");
        return;
    }

    iIndex = m_RemoteList.GetCurSel();
    if (LB_ERR == iIndex)
        return;

    //get directory that user double clicked
    m_RemoteList.GetText(iIndex, strFile);
    iIndex = strFile.Find(" <DIR>");
    if (-1 != iIndex)
        strFile = strFile.Left(iIndex);
    else
        return;

    //get the current remote directory
    if (!FtpGetCurrentDirectory(g_hConnection, szDir, &dwLen))
        ProcessInternetError();

    //build the new directory
    CString strNewDir;
    strNewDir = szDir;
    strNewDir += "/" + strFile;
```

```
//set the new remote working directory
if (!FtpSetCurrentDirectory(g_hConnection, strFile))
    ProcessInternetError();

//refill the remote list with new directory
FillRemoteList();
}
```

Because I concatenated <DIR> to the end of the every directory string, I must remember to strip it off before calling FtpSetCurrentDirectory. Notice that I call FtpGetCurrentDirectory and then create the new directory string with the resulting absolute path. Finally, with the new absolute directory, I'm ready to call FtpSetCurrentDirectory.

FtpGetFile

FtpGetFile encapsulates the underlying RETR FTP command. Using the FTP protocol you would normally set the data transfer parameters, such as TYPE, before using RETR. With FtpGetFile you can specify certain parameters through WinInet flags. Take a look at the following declaration:

```
BOOL FtpGetFile(
    IN HINTERNET hFtpSession,
    IN LPCSTR lpszRemoteFile,
    IN LPCSTR lpszNewFile,
    IN BOOL fFailIfExists,
    IN DWORD dwLocalFlagsAndAttributes,
    IN DWORD dwInternetFlags,
    IN DWORD dwContext
);
```

The name of the file you want to download is specified by lpszRemoteFile, whereas the name of the new local file is specified by lpszNewFile. You can control whether or not you want a local file of the same name to be overwritten. For example, if fFailIfExists is set to TRUE and a local file exists with the name specified by lpszNewFile, FtpGetFile fails. If fFailIfExists is set to FALSE, files of the same name are overwritten.

 Both lpszRemoteFile and lpszNewFile can be either partially or fully qualified file names relative to the current directory. A backslash (\) or forward slash (/) can be used as the directory separator for either name. FtpGetFile translates the directory name separators to the appropriate character before they are used.

The dwLocalFlagsAndAttributes parameter allows you to specify the file attributes for the new local file. You can use any of the FILE_ATTRIBUTE_* flags that are used by the Win32 CreateFile function.

Table 5-11 describes the flags that can be used with FtpGetFile.

The sample program has a button labeled <<, which causes the selected file to be downloaded (see Listing 5-6).

Table 5-11 FtpGetFile flags

Flag	Description
FTP_TRANSFER_TYPE_ASCII	Transfers the file using FTP's ASCII (type A) transfer method. Control and formatting information is converted to local equivalents.
FTP_TRANSFER_TYPE_BINARY	Transfers the file using FTP's Image (type I) transfer method. The file is transferred exactly as it exists, with no changes. This is the default transfer method.
FTP_TRANSFER_TYPE_UNKNOWN	Defaults to FTP_TRANSFER_TYPE_BINARY.
INTERNET_FLAG_TRANSFER_ASCII	Transfers the file as ASCII.
INTERNET_FLAG_TRANSFER_BINARY	Transfers the file as binary.
INTERNET_FLAG_DONT_CACHE	Does not add the returned entity to the cache. Identical to the preferred value, INTERNET_FLAG_NO_CACHE_WRITE.
INTERNET_FLAG_HYPERLINK	Forces a reload if there was no Expires time and no Last-Modified time returned from the server when determining whether to reload the item from the network.
INTERNET_FLAG_MUST_CACHE_REQUEST	Causes a temporary file to be created if the file cannot be cached. Identical to the preferred value, INTERNET_FLAG_NEED_FILE.
INTERNET_FLAG_NEED_FILE	Causes a temporary file to be created if the file cannot be cached.
INTERNET_FLAG_NO_CACHE_WRITE	Does not add the returned entity to the cache.
INTERNET_FLAG_RELOAD	Forces a download of the requested file, object, or directory listing from the originating server, not from the cache.
INTERNET_FLAG_RESYNCHRONIZE	Causes the FTP resource to be reloaded from the server.

Listing 5-6   CMyFTPDlg::OnGet

```
void CMyFTPDlg::OnGet()
{
    if (!g_hConnection)
    {
        AfxMessageBox("You must first connect to an FTP server");
        return;
    }

    CString strFile;
    int iIndex = m_RemoteList.GetCurSel();
    if (LB_ERR == iIndex)
    {
        AfxMessageBox("You must select a remote file first");
        return;
    }

    m_RemoteList.GetText(iIndex, strFile);

    DWORD dwFlags;

    if (m_lMode == MODE_ASCII)
        dwFlags = FTP_TRANSFER_TYPE_ASCII;
    else
        dwFlags = FTP_TRANSFER_TYPE_BINARY;

    BOOL bRet = FtpGetFile(g_hConnection, strFile, strFile, FALSE,
            FILE_ATTRIBUTE_NORMAL, dwFlags, 0);

    if (bRet)
    {
        FillLocalList();
    }
    else ProcessInternetError();
}

void CMyFTPDlg::OnRadioAscii()
{
    m_lMode = MODE_ASCII;
}
```

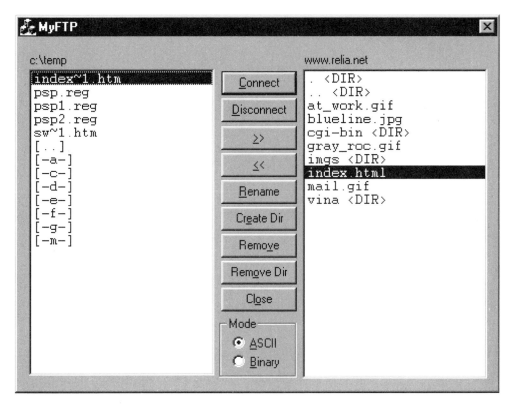

Figure 5-9 MyFTP get example

```
void CMyFTPDlg::OnRadioBinary()
{
    m_lMode = MODE_BINARY;
}
```

The function first checks to see which radio button is selected before determining the transfer type (ASCII or Binary). When FtpGetFile returns successfully, the call to FillLocalList should cause the new file to appear in the local directory (see Figure 5-9).

FtpPutFile

The FTP protocol command for uploading a file is STOR, and the WinInet function is called FtpPutFile. Uploading a file to an FTP server using FtpPutFile is almost identical to getting a file. Obviously the local file issues are no longer applicable, but the user must have write permissions on the server for FtpPutFile to succeed. Take a look at the function declaration:

```
BOOL FtpPutFile(
    IN HINTERNET hFtpSession,
    IN LPCSTR lpszLocalFile,
    IN LPCSTR lpszNewRemoteFile,
    IN DWORD dwFlags,
    IN DWORD dwContext
);
```

 Most FTP sites don't allow anonymous users to upload files. However, users with an FTP account, such as with their ISP, should be able to upload files to their account.

Because this function is almost identical to FtpGetFile, I'm not going to cover it in any more detail. Instead, I'll show you how it fits into our sample application. The button labeled >> causes a local file to be uploaded to the FTP server (see Listing 5-7).

Listing 5-7   CMyFTPDlg::OnPut

```
void CMyFTPDlg::OnPut()
{
    if (!g_hConnection)
    {
        AfxMessageBox("You must first connect to an FTP server");
        return;
    }

    CString strFile;
    int iIndex = m_LocalList.GetCurSel();
    if (LB_ERR == iIndex)
    {
        AfxMessageBox("You must select a local file first");
        return;
    }

    m_LocalList.GetText(iIndex, strFile);

    DWORD dwFlags;

    if (m_lMode == MODE_ASCII)
        dwFlags = FTP_TRANSFER_TYPE_ASCII;
```

```
    else
        dwFlags = FTP_TRANSFER_TYPE_BINARY;

    BOOL bRet = FtpPutFile(g_hConnection, strFile, strFile, dwFlags, 0);

    if (bRet)
    {
        FillRemoteList();
    }
    else ProcessInternetError();
}
```

When the file has been uploaded successfully, calling FillRemoteList should now cause the uploaded file to appear in the working directory.

FtpCreateDirectory

FtpCreateDirectory creates a new directory on the FTP server. The underlying protocol command is MKD (make directory). Check out the FtpCreateDirectory function declaration:

```
BOOL FtpCreateDirectory(
    IN HINTERNET hFtpSession,
    IN LPCSTR lpszDirectory
);
```

The lpszDirectory parameter contains the name of the new directory to be created. This can be either an absolute or relative path. The same rules that applied to FtpSetCurrentDirectory and FtpGetCurrentDirectory apply to all FTP directory-related functions, including this one.

There is a button on the sample application dialog labeled Create Dir. The handler for this button is shown in Listing 5-8.

Listing 5-8 CMyFTPDlg::OnCreate

```
void CMyFTPDlg::OnCreate()
{
    if (!g_hConnection)
    {
        AfxMessageBox("You must first connect to an FTP server");
        return;
```

```
    }

    CCreateDirectoryDlg dlg;

    if (IDOK == dlg.DoModal())
    {
        if (!FtpCreateDirectory(g_hConnection, dlg.m_strNewDirName))
            ProcessInternetError();
    }
    FillRemoteList();
}
```

Before calling FtpCreateDirectory we have to query the user for the new directory name. In this example let's assume that the user always wants to create the directory under the current working directory, so we can simply use relative paths. CCreateDirectoryDlg is shown in Figure 5-10.

Assuming no errors, the call to FillRemoteList at the end of the function should cause the new directory to appear.

FtpRemoveDirectory

FtpRemoveDirectory removes a directory from the FTP server. The underlying protocol command is RMD (remove directory). Take a look at the FtpRemoveDirectory function declaration:

```
BOOL FtpRemoveDirectory(
    IN HINTERNET hFtpSession,
    IN LPCSTR lpszDirectory
);
```

Once again, simple and sweet. You simply provide the directory name that you wish to remove, and the rest is history. Listing 5-9 demonstrates how I implemented the Remove Dir button in the sample application.

Figure 5-10   CCreateDirectoryDlg

Listing 5-9 CMyFTPDlg::OnRemovedir

```
void CMyFTPDlg::OnRemovedir()
{
    if (!g_hConnection)
    {
        AfxMessageBox("You must first connect to an FTP server");
        return;
    }

    CString strFile;
    int iIndex = m_RemoteList.GetCurSel();

    if (LB_ERR == iIndex)
    {
        AfxMessageBox("You must select a remote directory first");
        return;
    }

    m_RemoteList.GetText(iIndex, strFile);
    iIndex = strFile.Find(" <DIR>");
    if (-1 != iIndex)
        strFile = strFile.Left(iIndex);

    if (IDOK == AfxMessageBox("Delete selected directory from ftp server",
        MB_YESNO|MB_ICONQUESTION))
    {
        if (!FtpRemoveDirectory(g_hConnection, strFile))
            ProcessInternetError();
    }
    FillRemoteList();
}
```

The bulk of this function is validating the connection, selection, and the user's intent. Plus, don't forget we need to strip off <DIR> from the directory name before calling FtpRemoveDirectory. The call to FillRemoteList should cause the deleted directory to be removed from the remote directory list.

FtpDeleteFile

Like FtpRemoveDirectory, FtpDeleteFile deletes a file from the FTP server. The underlying protocol command for delete is DELE. Take a look at the function declaration:

```
BOOL FtpDeleteFile(
    IN HINTERNET hFtpSession,
    IN LPCSTR lpszFileName
);
```

You simply supply the name of the file you wish to delete and it is gone for good. It's a good idea to warn users before deleting the file just to make sure they realize what they're about to do. Listing 5-10 shows how I implemented the dialog's Remove button.

Listing 5-10   CMyFTPDlg::OnRemove

```
void CMyFTPDlg::OnRemove()
{
    if (!g_hConnection)
    {
        AfxMessageBox("You must first connect to an FTP server");
        return;
    }

    CString strFile;
    int iIndex = m_RemoteList.GetCurSel();
    if (LB_ERR == iIndex)
    {
        AfxMessageBox("You must select a remote file first");
        return;
    }

    m_RemoteList.GetText(iIndex, strFile);

    if (IDOK == AfxMessageBox("Delete selected file from FTP server",
        MB_YESNO|MB_ICONQUESTION))
    {
        if (!FtpDeleteFile(g_hConnection, strFile))
            ProcessInternetError();
    }
    FillRemoteList();
}
```

FtpRenameFile

FtpRenameFile allows you to rename a file on the FTP server. In the underlying FTP protocol, renaming a file is a two-step process. You use the RNFR (rename from) command immediately followed by the RNTO (rename to) command. Here is an example:

```
RNFR oldname.txt
RNTO newname.txt
```

Lucky for us, FtpRenameFile encapsulates this whole process. You simply provide both the existing file name and the new file name. Here is the function declaration:

```
BOOL FtpRenameFile(
    IN HINTERNET hFtpSession,
    IN LPCSTR lpszExisting,
    IN LPCSTR lpszNew
);
```

The sample application contains a button labeled Rename, which brings up the dialog shown in Figure 5-11 to query the user for the new file name.

Check out the function implementation in Listing 5-11.

Listing 5-11   CMyFTPDlg::OnRename

```
void CMyFTPDlg::OnRename()
{
    if (!g_hConnection)
    {
        AfxMessageBox("You must first connect to an FTP server");
        return;
    }

    CString strFile;
    int iIndex = m_RemoteList.GetCurSel();
    if (LB_ERR == iIndex)
```

Figure 5-11   CRenameDlg

```
    {
        AfxMessageBox("You must select a remote file first");
        return;
    }


    m_RemoteList.GetText(iIndex, strFile);


    CRenameDlg dlg;
    if (IDOK == dlg.DoModal())
    {
        if (!FtpRenameFile(g_hConnection, strFile, dlg.m_strNewName))
            ProcessInternetError();
    }
    FillRemoteList();
}
```

Have all these functions started to look the same to you? That's because they are very similar. When you've established the FTP connection, the rest of the FTP functionality is very simple, using the WinInet FTP functions.

Now I'll cover two functions that are not implemented in the sample program: FtpOpenFile and FtpCommand.

FtpOpenFile

Most people familiar with FTP understand the concept of downloading and uploading a file using FtpGetFile and FtpPutFile, but what about FtpOpenFile? When would you want to use FtpOpenFile instead of the previous two? To help answer this question I went directly to Microsoft's online documentation. FtpOpenFile should be used in the following situations:

- When an application has data it needs to send to an FTP server to be created as a file on the FTP server, but the application does not have a local file containing the data. After the file is opened with FtpOpenFile, the application uses InternetWriteFile to send the FTP file data to the server.

- When an application needs to retrieve a file from the server into application-controlled memory, instead of writing the file to disk. The application uses InternetReadFile after using FtpOpenFile to open the file.

- When an application needs a fine level of control over a file transfer. For example, the application may need to display a progress indicator when downloading a file to indicate to the user that the file transfer is or is not proceeding correctly.

Take a look at the FtpOpenFile declaration:

```
HINTERNET FtpOpenFile(
    IN HINTERNET hFtpSession,
    IN LPCSTR lpszFileName,
    IN DWORD fdwAccess,
    IN DWORD dwFlags,
    IN DWORD dwContext
);
```

Using FtpOpenFile is much like using either FtpGetFile or FtpPutFile. Most of the flags that apply to both of those functions also apply to FtpOpenFile. The fdwAccess parameter tells FtpOpenFile how to access the file on the remote server. This value can be either GENERIC_READ or GENERIC_WRITE (but it can't be both).

When you call FtpOpenFile successfully, you can use InternetReadFile or InternetWriteFile, depending on what you're doing. This function adds a new level of flexibility to the WinInet FTP functions and was introduced to help simplify application development. Most serious FTP-based applications might find a need for using FtpOpenFile instead of FtpGetFile and FtpPutFile.

FtpCommand

A very common question on the WinInet newsgroups is the following: *Isn't there an FTP function that allows you to execute any FTP protocol command?*

Currently, there isn't. If you start digging around in the latest WinInet.h (that comes with Visual C++ 5.0), you'll notice a function called FtpCommand. When I first saw the function declaration, I was really excited. But when I started looking for documentation on the function, my enthusiasm faded. I did a search on Microsoft's Web site and found a page that contained the function spec. However, when I tried using it, link errors followed.

Using dumpbin.exe (found in the Visual C++ 5.0 bin directory), I delved into the lib files to see if the function was exported in the latest WinInet.lib. Unfortunately, it doesn't appear to be supported in the IE 4.0 version of WININET.DLL. Take a look at the proposed function declaration:

```
BOOL FtpCommand(
    IN HINTERNET hFtpConnect,
    IN BOOL fExpectResponse,
    IN DWORD dwFlags,
```

```
    IN LPCTSTR lpszCommand,
    IN DWORD dwContext
);
```

You supply the handle returned by InternetConnect in hFtpConnect. You can execute any underlying FTP protocol command by supplying the raw command text in lpszCommand. This is the same text that you would use if you were using the FTP protocol through Telnet.

When you use Telnet, you must press the Enter key for the command to be executed. When you press the Enter key, a CRLF is sent to the FTP server, which tells it to process the command. Hence, when using FtpCommand, you must supply the CRLF ($\r\n$) on the end of the command string.

For example, if you wanted to change directories to newdir, you would supply the following text:

```
"CWD newdir\r\n"
```

You can also control whether the data is transmitted using the ASCII or Binary transfer type by using FTP_TRANSFER_TYPE_ASCII and FTP_TRANSFER_TYPE_BINARY for the flags.

So how do you know when to read data from the server? Suppose you execute the LIST command. After executing the command, you'll want to read the data returned by the server. Apparently, fExpectResponse tells the server whether you're interested in reading data after the command. If fExpectResponse is TRUE, you can follow the call to FtpCommand with InternetReadFile. Otherwise, FtpCommand assumes that you won't be attempting to read data.

Because I haven't been able to test FtpCommand, this is all hypothetical. Nonetheless, look for this valuable addition to the FTP function set. Hopefully it should be coming soon.

Conclusion

In this chapter I covered the FTP protocol and showed you how the WinInet FTP functions hide the details. The WinInet FTP functions provide a powerful and flexible mechanism for adding file transfer capabilities to your Windows applications. The sample application presented in this chapter should help you understand how you might go about adding similar functionality to your own applications.

6
Chapter

Gopher Functions

Although most developers perceive the Gopher protocol as being extinct, it continues to flourish on the Web, especially in academia. Newer protocols like HTTP make it hard for Gopher to continue its growth. Nevertheless, by including Gopher in the WinInet library, Microsoft believes that Gopher, even today, plays an important role.

The format of this chapter is much like the previous two. After introducing you to the Gopher protocol I'll dive into the WinInet Gopher functions and show you how to take advantage of them in a sample program.

The Gopher Protocol

A gopher is a burrowing rodent with a stout body, short tail, and external cheek pouches (Webster's dictionary). Don't worry, this chapter isn't about that particular member of the rodent family. On the contrary, this chapter is about another sophisticated application-level Internet protocol—Gopher—which carries a well-suited name. Like it's furry little counterpart, the Gopher protocol does its share of burrowing. However, instead of burrowing through the dirt, Gopher makes it possible to burrow through the Internet and locate documents that could reside anywhere in the world.

Gopher was designed and developed in the university setting to act as a simple document retrieval system. Using Gopher, both professors and students can make documents available to everyone at the university (and the world for that matter) by simply publishing the documents on one of the university's Gopher servers. Anyone with appropriate rights can connect to a Gopher server, browse the hierarchy of documents, and perform document searches.

Like file systems, Gopher servers are organized into a hierarchy of items and directories. Because most users are familiar with how to locate documents on a local file system, the Gopher paradigm should be easy for most to grasp. In fact, the only difference between browsing files and directories on your local system and those on a Gopher server is the physical location of the files. Whether a particular document resides on a server in the South Pacific or in Russia, it is transparent to the user of the Gopher client.

Figure 6-1 illustrates a typical Gopher client application called WSGopher32 (developed by the Idaho National Engineering Laboratory). When the application started, I told it to connect to *www.byu.edu* (BYU) at port 70. The directory structure in Figure 6-1 is the result of that request. The Gopher server returned the BYU Gopher server's main menu. At this point I can browse directories (in the left pane) and view files by double clicking on them (in the right pane). Notice the UI for this Gopher client is very similar to that of Windows Explorer.

The user of this Gopher client doesn't care where the files ultimately reside. Although the files displayed here could sit physically on any Gopher server, they are displayed in a topic-oriented structure, which makes it easier for users to navigate and find what they're looking for. Although the structure and hierarchy is obviously up to the particular Gopher server, Figure 6-1 is a typical example of how most Gopher servers are organized. The client and server interaction shown in Figure 6-1 is exactly what the Gopher protocol was designed to facilitate.

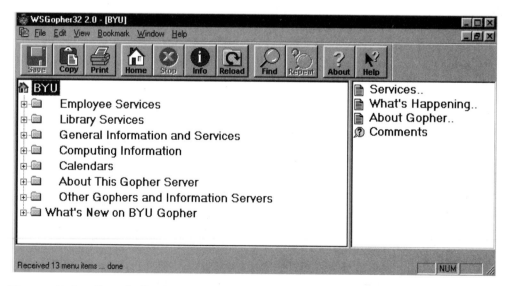

Figure 6-1   Sample Gopher client

The Gopher Model

Like HTTP (but unlike FTP), Gopher is a stateless protocol. Gopher servers listen on the well-known Gopher port (70). A Gopher client connects to the Gopher server on port 70 and sends a simple selector string, which identifies what the client is looking for. The server then responds to the client by sending a list of Gopher items. The last line in the Gopher response contains a period and nothing else (this tells the client that the server is finished sending items).

As you can see, a Gopher transaction consists of a request (consisting of the Gopher selector string) and a response (consisting of the Gopher items). Really, the beauty of the Gopher protocol lies in its simplicity. Client programming for the Gopher protocol is probably one of the easiest areas of Internet application development to learn and master quickly.

Let's look briefly at a simple Gopher transaction. Referring back to Figure 6-1, let's examine the first transaction made by WSGopher32, which was used to display the directory hierarchy and files:

WSGopher32:   Connects to *www.byu.edu* on port 70.

Server: Accepts the connection.

WSGopher32:   Sends an empty selector string to the server: CRLF. (An empty selector string tells the server to list its main menu.)

Server: Sends a series of lines to the client (see Listing 6-1).

Listing 6-1   Sample Gopher response

```
0Services..    0/.menu-title    cwis.byu.edu     70
1    Employee Services    1/Employee Services    acs2.byu.edu    70
1    Library Services    1/Computing Information/Library    acs2.byu.edu    70
1    General Info. and Services    1/General Information    acs2.byu.edu    70
1    Computing Information    1/Computing Information    acs2.byu.edu    70
0What's Happening..    0/.menu-title    cwis.byu.edu    70
1    Calendars  1/Calendars    acs2.byu.edu    70
0About Gopher..  0/.menu-title    cwis.byu.edu    70
1    About This Gopher Server    1/gopi  acs2.byu.edu    70
1    Other Gophers and Information Servers    1/gop    acs2.byu.edu    70
0Comments    0/Comments    acs2.byu.edu    70
1What's New on BYU Gopher    1/What's New on    acs2.byu.edu    70
.
```

After scanning the response lines you'll notice some striking similarities between the actual response line and what is displayed to the user in the WSGopher32 application.

This is no surprise. In fact, the Gopher client uses these response lines to build its UI and associated functionality. The Gopher response items, which I discuss shortly, contain all the information the client needs to function as a Gopher client. Also, notice the period on the final line of the response. The client uses this period to identify the end of the response items.

Gopher Response Items

The Gopher response items are really what make the Gopher protocol tick. Each item contains the necessary information to select the particular item. The following represents a typical response item:

```
TYPE <TAB> DISPLAY-STRING <TAB> SELECTOR-STRING <TAB> HOST <TAB> PORT <CRLF>
```

With that in mind, let's take another look at one of the line items from the previous example:

```
1    Employee Services    1/Employee Services    acs2.byu.edu    70
```

Now these response items are probably starting to make a little more sense. A TAB character separates all subitems and a CRLF terminates each item. In this example, the 1 represents the item type (1 means directory in this case). Gopher clients usually display the second subitem, the display string, to the user. If you look at Figure 6-1 again, you'll notice that Employee Services is the name of one of the directories displayed in the left pane. The third subitem is the selector string that should be sent to the server to request the particular item. Finally, the fourth and fifth subitems identify the server and port number with which the client should communicate to retrieve the particular item.

For example, if I were to click on the Employee Services directory in Figure 6-1, the client, WSGopher32, would establish a connection with *acs2.byu.edu* on port 70 and send 1/Employee Services as the selector string.

The type field of a Gopher response item consists of a single ASCII character. This character identifies the type of item. For example, a particular item may represent a file, directory, image, error, or a handful of other Gopher types (see Table 6-1).

Although the file and directory types are by far the most commonly used, the Gopher protocol is capable of handling many different types of information retrieval.

Table 6-1   **Gopher type characters**

Character	Meaning
0	File
1	Directory
2	CSO phonebook server
3	Error
4	Bin-hexed Macintosh file
5	DOS binary archive
6	Unix uuencoded file
7	Index-search server
8	Text-based Telnet session
9	Binary file
+	Redundant server
T	Text-based tn3270 session
G	GIF format graphics file
I	Image file

Gopher Selector String

The Gopher selector string identifies something, somewhere, on some server. Selector strings typically represent a path to a file or directory, but they may also represent a script, application, or a search query.

The intelligence behind the selector string is built into the Gopher server. Remember, from the previous example, the very first selector string that I sent was a blank line with only a CRLF. This blank selector string tells the server to tell me about its root hierarchy, which is displayed in Figure 6-1.

From that point on, when the user navigates around the hierarchy and selects a certain item, the selector string associated with the item (which, by the way, was originally sent to the client by the server) is used in the request.

We know from the original response that the selector string for Employee Services is 1/Employee Services. If you connect to *www.byu.edu* and use 1/Employee Services as the selector string instead of the blank selector string, you get the response shown in Listing 6-2.

Listing 6-2   **Sample Gopher response for selector 1/Employee Services**

```
2BYU Directory (sample, experimental, incomplete)    ucs2.byu.edu    4002
1Find employees at other institutions   1/Employee Services/.otheremp
acs2.byu.edu    70
```

```
0Directory Access (Off-Campus)   0/Employee Services/Directory Access
acs2.byu.edu     70
1Handbook        1/Handbook/     acs2.byu.edu     71
0Registering and Modifying EMail Alias   0/Employee Services/Registering and
Modifying EMail Alias        acs2.byu.edu     70
.
```

Using Telnet to Test Gopher

You can try this for yourself by using Telnet to connect to *www.byu.edu* on port 70. This returns the same response as shown in Figure 6-2.

Hence, the format of the Gopher selector string for a given item is at the discretion of the Gopher server. This allows different servers to organize and to identify items in a way that best fits their needs while still conforming to a protocol that allows all clients to communicate identically.

Gopher Protocol Summary

The beauty of Gopher lies in its simplicity. It is probably one of the easiest protocols to program on the client side because the intelligence is contained in the server. Understanding the format of Gopher items and how to use the information contained within them is the only requirement for producing Gopher applications. Furthermore, the higher level interface provided by WinInet makes using the Gopher protocol in your applications a breeze. Refer to RFC 1436 at

Figure 6-2   Gopher selector string using Telnet

http://info.internet.isi.edu/in-notes/rfc/files/rfc1436.txt for complete information
on the Gopher protocol.

Gopher+

Gopher+ is the second-generation Gopher protocol (just when you thought that you
had Gopher licked!). Although Gopher+ does maintain backward compatibility with
original Gopher servers, it also provides an enhanced attribute information system.
Servers usually accomplish this by sending the extra information on the end of the
standard Gopher format. Hence, clients that only understand standard Gopher won't
even know that the extra information is there, whereas Gopher+-enabled clients can
use it however they desire.

Let's look at an example. The following Gopher+ item contains various attributes
that provide the client with powerful information about the document:

```
+INFO:0Welcome 0/Welcome server.school.edu 70 +
+ADMIN
 Admin: Aaron Skonnard +1 801 777-7777
 Mod-Date: Tue May 19 20:10:42 1998
+VIEWS:
 Text/plain En_US: <.3k>
 Text/plain De_DE: <.6k>
 Text/plain Es_ES: <.8k>
 Text/plain Fr_FR: <.7k>
+ABSTRACT:
This file is maintained in 4 languages!
```

Gopher+ allows the server to provide valuable meta-information about an item to
the client. In the previous example, the client could use this information to download
files found in French. Or, when the user prompts to download the file, the client could
ask the user to choose a language. I wanted at least to mention Gopher+ because
WinInet provides Gopher+ attribute information support.

WinInet Gopher Functions

Like both the HTTP and FTP functions, the WinInet Gopher functions allow you to
forget about most of the underlying Gopher protocol details. As you'll see shortly,
most of the Gopher functions revolve around the concept of a Gopher locator.

A Gopher locator is equivalent to the Gopher response item format described in the previous section. Let's take a look at the handle hierarchy for using the Gopher functions.

Gopher Hierarchy

The Gopher handle hierarchy is illustrated in Figure 6-3. Notice that the first two steps are the same as both the HTTP and FTP handle hierarchies. You must first call InternetOpen and then call InternetConnect with the INTERNET_SERVICE_GOPHER service flag. When you receive a valid HINTERNET handle from InternetConnect, you can do just about anything that the Gopher functions have to offer.

Let's briefly review how you would take care of the first two steps: InternetOpen and InternetConnect. Here is an example:

```
HINTNERNET hOpenHandle = InternetOpen("MyGopher/1.0",
        INTERNET_OPEN_TYPE_PRECONFIG, NULL, NULL, 0);


if (hOpenHandle)
{
    HINTERNET hConnectHandle = InternetConnect(hOpenHandle,
            "gopher.server.com", INTERNET_DEFAULT_GOPHER_PORT, "", "",
            INTERNET_SERVICE_GOPHER, 0, 0);
}
```

Notice that everything looks pretty much the same as the HTTP and FTP examples. Nothing really changed in the call to InternetOpen (besides the User-Agent text). There are, however, a few changes to the call to InternetConnect. This time I used

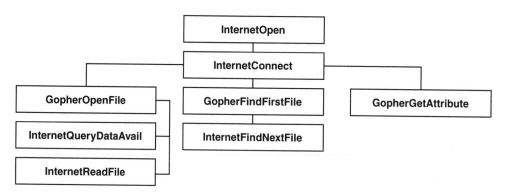

Figure 6-3   Gopher handle hierarchy

INTERNET_SERVICE_GOPHER and INTERNET_DEFAULT_GOPHER_PORT for the port number in the call to InternetConnect.

When you get to this point, you're ready to start calling the WinInet Gopher functions. Now let's look at each of the available functions in more detail.

Gopher Functions Overview

Table 6-2 describes each of the WinInet Gopher functions. If you review these functions and then look back to the section on the Gopher protocol, you'll notice many similarities. As we look at each of these functions in more detail, you'll see how easy it is to take advantage of the Gopher protocol in your applications.

Sample Gopher Application

In this chapter I show you how to build a graphical Gopher client—like WSGopher32 shown in Figure 6-1—using the WinInet Gopher functions. As we cover each of the functions listed in Table 6-2, I'll show you a practical example of how to use it in the sample application. First, let me give you a brief overview of the sample and how to get started.

Once again, I wrote the sample application using Visual C++ 5.0 (the sample is linked against the IE 4.0 version of WinInet). Now let's walk through the steps of creating the MyGopher skeleton, which we'll use throughout the rest of this chapter.

Table 6-2   WinInet Gopher functions

Function	Description
GopherAttributeEnumerator	Defines a callback function that processes attribute information from a Gopher server.
GopherCreateLocator	Forms a Gopher locator for use in other Gopher function calls.
GopherFindFirstFile	Starts enumerating a Gopher directory listing. This function requires a handle created by InternetConnect.
GopherGetAttribute	Retrieves attribute information on the Gopher object. This function requires a handle created by InternetConnect.
GopherGetLocatorType	Parses a Gopher locator and determines its attributes.
GopherOpenFile	Starts retrieving a Gopher object. This function requires a handle created by InternetConnect.

Creating the Project

In Visual C++ 5.0, create a new project by going to the File menu and pressing New. In the list of new project types, choose MFC AppWizard (exe). Then, in step 1 of the MFC AppWizard, choose Dialog-based application. Finish the rest of the Wizard using the default settings (it really doesn't matter what you choose for the rest of the steps), and press Finish to generate the project and its associated files.

The files we're going to be dealing with in this application are described in Table 6-3.

We'll implement all of the Gopher functionality in the CMyGopherDlg class found in MyGopherDlg.h and MyGopherDlg.cpp. The CWinApp-derived application object does nothing more than create and show the one and only CMyGopherDlg instance. As you can see, the sample design is quite simple. This allows us to focus all our attention on the WinInet Gopher implementation.

Dialog Template

The CMyGopherDlg dialog template looks like Figure 6-4. Each of the buttons and controls takes care of a piece of Gopher functionality. Throughout the rest of this chapter, I'll show you how everything in this dialog fits together.

CMyGopherDlg

The class declaration for CMyGopherDlg is shown in Listing 6-3. The two member variables m_hSession and m_hConnection are designed to contain the HINTERNET handles returned by InternetOpen and InternetConnect, respectively. The three main functions, besides the command handlers, that encapsulate most of the application's Gopher functionality are FindGopherFiles, Search, and GetFile. I'll cover each of these functions along with most of the command handlers as I discuss the individual Gopher functions.

Table 6-3 MyGopher project files

Wizard-Generated File	Description
MyGopher.rc	Resource file
MyGopherDlg.h	Main dialog header file
MyGopherDlg.cpp	Main dialog implementation file

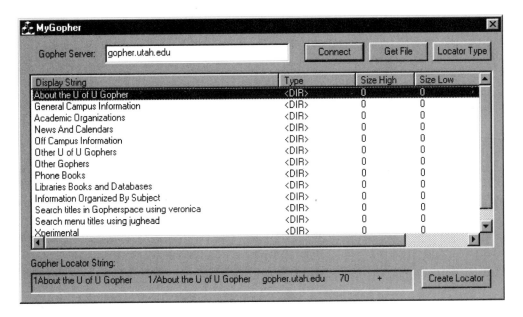

Figure 6-4   MyGopher dialog

Listing 6-3   CMyGopherDlg

```
#include <wininet.h>


/////////////////////////////////////////////////////////////////////////////
// CMyGopherDlg dialog

class CMyGopherDlg : public CDialog
{
// Construction
public:
    CMyGopherDlg(CWnd* pParent = NULL);     // standard constructor

// Methods
public:
    void FindGopherFiles(LPCTSTR lpszLocator, LPCTSTR lpszSearch=NULL);
    void Search(CString& strLocator);
    void GetFile(CString& strLocator);
```

```
// Data Members
public:
    HINTERNET m_hSession;
    HINTERNET m_hConnection;

// Dialog Data
    //{{AFX_DATA(CMyGopherDlg)
    enum { IDD = IDD_MYGOPHER_DIALOG };
    CListCtrl    m_List;
    CString      m_strServer;
    CString      m_strLocator;
    //}}AFX_DATA

    // ClassWizard generated virtual function overrides
    //{{AFX_VIRTUAL(CMyGopherDlg)
    protected:
    virtual void DoDataExchange(CDataExchange* pDX);      // DDX/DDV support
    //}}AFX_VIRTUAL

// Implementation
protected:
    HICON m_hIcon;

    // Generated message map functions
    //{{AFX_MSG(CMyGopherDlg)
    virtual BOOL OnInitDialog();
    afx_msg void OnSysCommand(UINT nID, LPARAM lParam);
    afx_msg void OnPaint();
    afx_msg HCURSOR OnQueryDragIcon();
    virtual void OnOK();
    afx_msg void OnClose();
    afx_msg void OnDblclkListResult(NMHDR* pNMHDR, LRESULT* pResult);
    afx_msg void OnClickListResult(NMHDR* pNMHDR, LRESULT* pResult);
    afx_msg void OnGet();
    afx_msg void OnType();
    afx_msg void OnCreateLocator();
    //}}AFX_MSG
    DECLARE_MESSAGE_MAP()
};
```

Establishing the Gopher Session (InternetOpen)

Let's look at the first two steps of establishing a Gopher session—InternetOpen and InternetConnect (refer back to Figure 6-3). First of all, the application must call InternetOpen and store the resulting HINTERNET in m_hSession. CMyGopherDlg::OnInitDialog takes care of this with the following line of code:

```
g_hSession = InternetOpen("MyGopher/1.0", INTERNET_OPEN_TYPE_PRECONFIG, NULL,
        NULL,0);
```

When the user presses the Connect button, CMyGopherDlg::OnConnect is called (see Listing 6-4) to establish the connection with the supplied Gopher server.

Listing 6-4   CMyGopherDlg::OnConnect

```
void CMyGopherDlg::OnConnect()
{
    UpdateData(TRUE);

    // if already connected, disconnect
    if (!m_hConnection)
        InternetCloseHandle(m_hConnection);

    // connect to Gopher server using default Gopher port
    m_hConnection = InternetConnect(m_hSession, m_strServer,
            INTERNET_DEFAULT_GOPHER_PORT, NULL, NULL, INTERNET_SERVICE_GOPHER,
            0, 0);

    // enumerate Gopher items using empty locator
    FindGopherFiles("");
    UpdateData(FALSE);
}
```

Notice that if m_hConnection already contains a handle, InternetCloseHandle is used to close the connection before attempting a new connection. Also, when the dialog is closed, InternetCloseHandle is used to free the handle stored in m_hSession.

Function Descriptions

Now we have an application skeleton that is capable of connecting to a Gopher server and disconnecting. We have the dialog template ready along with the dialog class command handlers. At this point, we're ready to look at the individual Gopher functions and see how they fit into this sample application.

GopherFindFirstFile

GopherFindFirstFile is much like FtpFindFirstFile. GopherFindFirstFile begins an enumeration of items returned by the Gopher server. After calling GopherFindFirstFile, you use InternetFindNextFile (just like with FTP). You use a Gopher locator string and possibly some search criteria (if the locator describes a search index) to specify the types of Gopher items you're interested in enumerating. Let's quickly review the concept of a Gopher locator string.

If you remember back to the section on the Gopher protocol, we defined the format of a Gopher response item to be the following:

```
TYPE <TAB> DISPLAY-STRING <TAB> SELECTOR-STRING <TAB> HOST <TAB> PORT <CRLF>
```

This is essentially what the WinInet Gopher functions refer to as a Gopher locator. For example, the following string could be used as a WinInet locator (look familiar?):

```
1    Employee Services   1/Employee Services     acs2.byu.edu    70
```

Now the function declaration for GopherFindFirstFile should make more sense:

```
HINTERNET GopherFindFirstFile(
    IN HINTERNET hGopherSession,
    IN LPCSTR lpszLocator,
    IN LPCSTR lpszSearchString,
    OUT LPGOPHER_FIND_DATA lpFindData,
    IN DWORD dwFlags,
    IN DWORD dwContext
);
```

hGopherSession refers to the handle returned by InternetConnect. The next two parameters, lpszLocator and lpszSearchString, specify the type of Gopher items in which you're interested. The locator string shown here could be used for lpszLocator;

this example refers to a directory. If the locator referred to a Gopher index server, you can supply a search string in lpszSearchString.

GopherFindFirstFile returns the item information in the GOPHER_FIND_DATA structure, which looks like this:

```
typedef struct {
    TCHAR DisplayString[MAX_GOPHER_DISPLAY_TEXT + 1];
    DWORD GopherType;
    DWORD SizeLow;
    DWORD SizeHigh;
    FILETIME LastModificationTime;
    TCHAR Locator[MAX_GOPHER_LOCATOR_LENGTH + 1];
} GOPHER_FIND_DATA, FAR *LPGOPHER_FIND_DATA;
```

If you're like me and have to know to what the macros expand, you can find the following in WinInet.h:

```
#define MAX_GOPHER_DISPLAY_TEXT      128
#define MAX_GOPHER_SELECTOR_TEXT     256
#define MAX_GOPHER_HOST_NAME         INTERNET_MAX_HOST_NAME_LENGTH
#define MAX_GOPHER_LOCATOR_LENGTH    (1                                  \
                                     + MAX_GOPHER_DISPLAY_TEXT           \
                                     + 1                                 \
                                     + MAX_GOPHER_SELECTOR_TEXT          \
                                     + 1                                 \
                                     + MAX_GOPHER_HOST_NAME              \
                                     + 1                                 \
                                     + INTERNET_MAX_PORT_NUMBER_LENGTH   \
                                     + 1                                 \
                                     + 1                                 \
                                     + 2                                 \
                                     )
```

As you can see, the GOPHER_FIND_DATA structure is quite different than the WIN32_FIND_DATA structure used for files. The DisplayString field is what you would normally display to the user. The GopherType field tells you what type of item this really is. And finally, the Locator field makes it possible for you to retrieve this item by calling either GopherFindFirstFile again or GopherOpenFile.

Back in Table 6-1 I listed the most common Gopher protocol types. Here in Table 6-4 is a complete list of WinInet Gopher type values and their descriptions.

Table 6-4   **WinInet Gopher type values**

Gopher Type	Description
GOPHER_TYPE_ASK	Ask+ item
GOPHER_TYPE_BINARY	Binary file
GOPHER_TYPE_BITMAP	Bitmap file
GOPHER_TYPE_CALENDAR	Calendar file
GOPHER_TYPE_CSO	CSO telephone book server
GOPHER_TYPE_DIRECTORY	Directory of additional Gopher items
GOPHER_TYPE_DOS_ARCHIVE	MS-DOS archive file
GOPHER_TYPE_ERROR	Indicator of an error condition
GOPHER_TYPE_GIF	GIF graphics file
GOPHER_TYPE_GOPHER_PLUS	Gopher+ item
GOPHER_TYPE_HTML	HTML document
GOPHER_TYPE_IMAGE	Image file
GOPHER_TYPE_INDEX_SERVER	Index server
GOPHER_TYPE_INLINE	Inline file
GOPHER_TYPE_MAC_BINHEX	Macintosh file in BINHEX format
GOPHER_TYPE_MOVIE	Movie file
GOPHER_TYPE_PDF	PDF file
GOPHER_TYPE_REDUNDANT	Indicator of a duplicated server. The information contained within is a duplicate of the primary server. The primary server is defined as the last directory entry that did not have a GOPHER_TYPE_ REDUNDANT type.
GOPHER_TYPE_SOUND	Sound file
GOPHER_TYPE_TELNET	Telnet server
GOPHER_TYPE_TEXT_FILE	ASCII text file
GOPHER_TYPE_TN3270	tn3270 server
GOPHER_TYPE_UNIX_UUENCODED	UUENCODED file
GOPHER_TYPE_UNKNOWN	Item type is unknown

The rest of the fields in the GOPHER_FIND_DATA structure are used to provide useful information like sizes and dates. However, because not all Gopher servers use equivalent enumeration schemes, some of the information contained in these helper fields may be invalid or meaningless.

Table 6-5 describes the flags that can be used with GopherFindFirstFile.

Now we're ready to see how GopherFindFirstFile fits into the sample application. There are a few places in the application that we want to enumerate Gopher items.

Table 6-5 **GopherFindFirstFile flags**

Flag	Description
INTERNET_FLAG_DONT_CACHE	Does not add the returned entity to the cache. Identical to the preferred value, INTERNET_FLAG_NO_CACHE_WRITE.
INTERNET_FLAG_HYPERLINK	Forces a reload if there was no Expires time and no Last-Modified time returned from the server when determining whether to reload the item from the network.
INTERNET_FLAG_MUST_CACHE_REQUEST	Causes a temporary file to be created if the file cannot be cached. Identical to INTERNET_FLAG_NEED_FILE.
INTERNET_FLAG_NEED_FILE	Causes a temporary file to be created if the file cannot be cached.
INTERNET_FLAG_NO_CACHE_WRITE	Does not add the returned entity to the cache.
INTERNET_FLAG_RELOAD	Forces a download of the requested file, object, or directory listing from the originating server, not from the cache.
INTERNET_FLAG_RESYNCHRONIZE	Causes the FTP resource to be reloaded from the server.

First, we want to enumerate the root Gopher items found on the server after we establish a connection. If you noticed in the CMyGopherDlg::OnConnect method, there is a call to FindGopherFiles passing an empty string.

Also, if the user double clicks on a directory, we want to use GopherFindFirstFile to enumerate that directory and display its contents. If the user creates a Gopher locator manually (using the Create Locator button) that specifies a Gopher directory, we want to enumerate the new directory items. And finally if the user performs a search, GopherFindFirstFile should also be used to enumerate the items returned by the server that match the search criteria.

Because there are so many places that we need to use this enumeration functionality, I created a function called FindGopherFiles that takes a locator string and a search string. This function can be used for all cases discussed earlier. Take a look at Listing 6-5, which shows the FindGopherFiles implementation along with the double-click and search functionality.

Listing 6-5   CMyGopherDlg::FindGopherFiles

```
void CMyGopherDlg::FindGopherFiles(LPCTSTR lpszLocator, LPCTSTR
        lpszSearch/*=NULL*/)
{
    // make sure there is a connection
    if (!m_hConnection)
        return;

    m_List.DeleteAllItems();

    HINTERNET hFind;
    GOPHER_FIND_DATA file;

    // begin Gopher enumeration, using search string if available
    if (strlen(lpszLocator))
        hFind = GopherFindFirstFile(m_hConnection, lpszLocator, lpszSearch,
                &file, 0, 0);
    else
        hFind = GopherFindFirstFile(m_hConnection, NULL, lpszSearch, &file,
                0, 0);

    if (hFind)
    {
        CString strText;
        UINT index = 0;

        //insert main item
        LV_ITEM item;
        item.mask = LVIF_TEXT;
        item.iItem = index++;
        item.iSubItem = 0;
        item.pszText = file.DisplayString;
        m_List.InsertItem(&item);

        //insert subitems
        strText = GetGopherTypeString(file.GopherType);
        m_List.SetItemText(item.iItem, 1, strText);
        strText.Format("%d", file.SizeLow);
        m_List.SetItemText(item.iItem, 2, strText);
        strText.Format("%d", file.SizeHigh);
```

```
        m_List.SetItemText(item.iItem, 3, strText);
        strText = file.Locator;
        m_List.SetItemText(item.iItem, 4, strText);
        // continue enumeration using InternetFindNextFile
        while (InternetFindNextFile(hFind, &file))
        {
            item.mask = LVIF_TEXT;
            item.iItem = index++;
            item.iSubItem = 0;
            item.pszText = file.DisplayString;
            m_List.InsertItem(&item);

            strText = GetGopherTypeString(file.GopherType);
            m_List.SetItemText(item.iItem, 1, strText);
            strText.Format("%d", file.SizeLow);
            m_List.SetItemText(item.iItem, 2, strText);
            strText.Format("%d", file.SizeHigh);
            m_List.SetItemText(item.iItem, 3, strText);
            strText = file.Locator;
            m_List.SetItemText(item.iItem, 4, strText);
        }
        // close enumeration handle
        InternetCloseHandle(hFind);
    }
}

void CMyGopherDlg::Search(CString& strLocator)
{
    // query user for search string
    CSearchDlg dlg;
    if (IDOK==dlg.DoModal())
    {
        // enumerate Gopher items returned by search index
        FindGopherFiles(strLocator, dlg.m_strSearch);
    }
}

void CMyGopherDlg::OnDblclkListResult(NMHDR* pNMHDR, LRESULT* pResult)
{
    // make sure there is a connection
    if (!m_hConnection)
        return;
```

```
    // get selected item
    UINT index = m_List.GetNextItem(-1 , LVNI_SELECTED);
    if (index == -1)
        return;

    // get locator type string for selected item
    CString strType = m_List.GetItemText(index, 1);
    // get locator string for selected item
    CString strLocator = m_List.GetItemText(index, 4);

    // enumerate, search, or download depending on type
    if (strType.Compare("<DIR>") == 0)
        FindGopherFiles(strLocator);
    else if (strType.Compare("Index") == 0)
        Search(strLocator);
    else if (strType.Compare("File") == 0)
        GetFile(strLocator);

    //update dialog
    m_strLocator.Empty();
    UpdateData(FALSE);
    *pResult = 0;
}
```

The FindGopherFiles method simply fills in the list control with the information contained in the GOPHER_FIND_DATA structure. However, there is one mystery function, GetGopherTypeString, that I'll look at shortly. This gets the type string, such as <DIR>, for the directory and stores it in the list control.

Notice that if the user double clicks on a directory, FindGopherFiles is called. If the user double clicks on a search index, the Search method is called, which queries the user for a search string (see Figure 6-5) and then calls FindGopherFiles with that

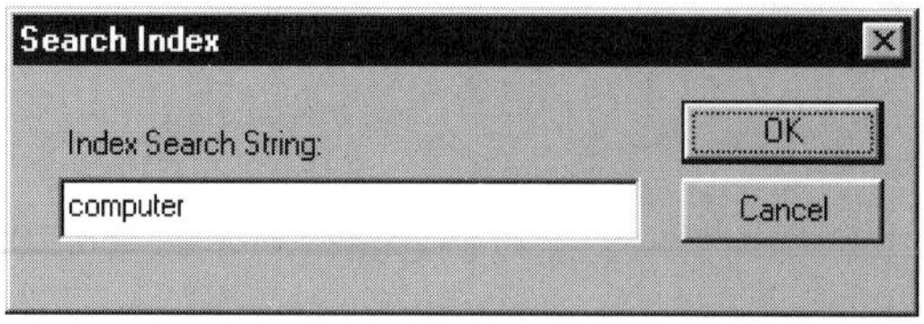

Figure 6-5   MyGopher search dialog

value. If the user double clicks on a file, the GetFile method is called to download the file and display it to the user.

GopherOpenFile

Like FtpOpenFile, GopherOpenFile opens a remote file that can be read using InternetReadFile. There are, however, a few subtle differences. First, you obviously need to provide a Gopher locator string instead of a file name. Second, you can also provide a file view. Check out the function declaration:

```
HINTERNET GopherOpenFile(
    IN HINTERNET hGopherSession,
    IN LPCSTR lpszLocator,
    IN LPCSTR lpszView,
    IN DWORD dwFlags,
    IN DWORD dwContext
);
```

If you remember back to the brief discussion on Gopher+, I gave an example of a Gopher+ file that contained multiple views—one in each of four languages. This is a Gopher+ attribute that may not be supported by all Gopher servers. Passing NULL for this value retrieves the default view (if more than one exists). The same flags used with GopherFindFirstFile can also be used with GopherOpen.

In the sample application, if the user double clicks on a file or presses the Get File button, OnGet is called, which then calls the GetFile method to download the file (see Listing 6-6).

Listing 6-6   CMyGopherDlg::GetFile

```
void CMyGopherDlg::GetFile(CString& strLocator)
{
    DWORD dwToRead=4095, dwRead;
    char szBuffer[4096];
    CString strFile;

    // open the remote Gopher file
    HINTERNET hFile = GopherOpenFile(m_hConnection, strLocator, NULL, 0, 0);

    // read the file until finished
    while (InternetReadFile(hFile, szBuffer, dwToRead, &dwRead))
    {
```

```
        if (dwRead == 0)
            break;
        szBuffer[dwRead]=0;
        strFile += szBuffer;
    }


    // show downloaded test in dialog
    CFileDownloadDlg dlg;
    dlg.m_strFileText = strFile;
    dlg.DoModal();
}


void CMyGopherDlg::OnGet()
{
    // get selected item information
    UINT index = m_List.GetNextItem(-1, LVNI_SELECTED);
    if (index == -1)
        return;

    CString strType = m_List.GetItemText(index, 1);
    if (strType.Compare("File") != 0)
        return;
    CString strLocator = m_List.GetItemText(index, 4);

    // download file
    GetFile(strLocator);
}
```

Notice that the same InternetReadFile logic used with HTTP and FTP is also used here. When the file has been downloaded, the result is displayed in a dialog. For example, if I double click on the University of Utah Campus Calendar Gopher item, the dialog in Figure 6-6 appears.

GopherGetLocatorType

GopherGetLocatorType is simple and straightforward. It takes a Gopher locator string and tells you which WinInet Gopher type it represents. The WinInet Gopher type values are listed in Table 6-4.

```
BOOL GopherGetLocatorType(
IN LPCSTR lpszLocator,
```

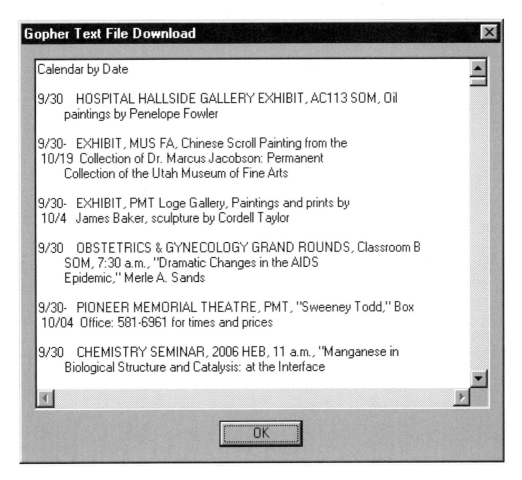

Figure 6-6 Gopher Text File Download dialog

```
OUT LPDWORD lpdwGopherType
);
```

There are some Gopher type helper macros hidden away in WinInet.h that simplify the process of determining general Gopher types. Because they aren't documented, most developers don't even know they exist. Here's how they are defined in WinInet.h:

```
//
// Gopher type macros
//
```

```
#define IS_GOPHER_FILE(type)
        (BOOL)(((type) & GOPHER_TYPE_FILE_MASK) ? TRUE : FALSE)

#define IS_GOPHER_DIRECTORY(type)
        (BOOL)(((type) & GOPHER_TYPE_DIRECTORY) ? TRUE : FALSE)

#define IS_GOPHER_PHONE_SERVER(type)
        (BOOL)(((type) & GOPHER_TYPE_CSO) ? TRUE : FALSE)

#define IS_GOPHER_ERROR(type)
        (BOOL)(((type) & GOPHER_TYPE_ERROR) ? TRUE : FALSE)

#define IS_GOPHER_INDEX_SERVER(type)
        (BOOL)(((type) & GOPHER_TYPE_INDEX_SERVER) ? TRUE : FALSE)

#define IS_GOPHER_TELNET_SESSION(type)
        (BOOL)(((type) & GOPHER_TYPE_TELNET) ? TRUE : FALSE)

#define IS_GOPHER_BACKUP_SERVER(type)
        (BOOL)(((type) & GOPHER_TYPE_REDUNDANT) ? TRUE : FALSE)

#define IS_GOPHER_TN3270_SESSION(type)
        (BOOL)(((type) & GOPHER_TYPE_TN3270) ? TRUE : FALSE)

#define IS_GOPHER_ASK(type)
        (BOOL)(((type) & GOPHER_TYPE_ASK) ? TRUE : FALSE)

#define IS_GOPHER_PLUS(type)
        (BOOL)(((type) & GOPHER_TYPE_GOPHER_PLUS) ? TRUE : FALSE)

#define IS_GOPHER_TYPE_KNOWN(type)
        (BOOL)(((type) & GOPHER_TYPE_UNKNOWN) ? FALSE : TRUE)

//
// GOPHER_TYPE_FILE_MASK - use this to determine if a locator identifies a
// (known) file type
//

#define GOPHER_TYPE_FILE_MASK        (GOPHER_TYPE_TEXT_FILE           \
                                     | GOPHER_TYPE_MAC_BINHEX         \
```

```
| GOPHER_TYPE_DOS_ARCHIVE       \
| GOPHER_TYPE_UNIX_UUENCODED    \
| GOPHER_TYPE_BINARY            \
| GOPHER_TYPE_GIF               \
| GOPHER_TYPE_IMAGE             \
| GOPHER_TYPE_BITMAP            \
| GOPHER_TYPE_MOVIE             \
| GOPHER_TYPE_SOUND             \
| GOPHER_TYPE_HTML              \
| GOPHER_TYPE_PDF               \
| GOPHER_TYPE_CALENDAR          \
| GOPHER_TYPE_INLINE            \
)
```

I took advantage of these macros in the sample program to determine quickly the type of a given Gopher locator. The OnType method is called when the user presses the Locator Type button; it simply displays the DWORD type value. GetGopherTypeString is used by FindGopherFiles to retrieve the type string that is shown in the list control (see Listing 6-7). Figure 6-7 shows an example of different locator types.

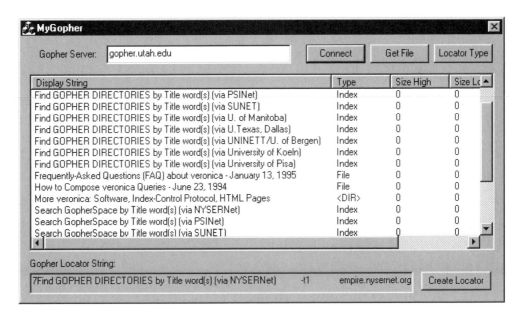

Figure 6-7 MyGopher dialog with different locator types

Listing 6-7   MyGopher type functions

```
void CMyGopherDlg::OnType()
{
    DWORD dwType;
    CString strType;

    // get selected item information
    UINT index = m_List.GetNextItem(-1, LVNI_SELECTED);
    if (index == -1)
        return;
    CString strLocator = m_List.GetItemText(index, 4);

    // display locator type number
    if (!GopherGetLocatorType(strLocator, &dwType))
        return;
    strType.Format("Locator type = %lu", dwType);
    AfxMessageBox(strType);
}


CString GetGopherTypeString(DWORD type)
{
    CString strType;

    // Get the Gopher type string
    // using utility macros
    if (IS_GOPHER_FILE(type))
        strType = "File";
    else if (IS_GOPHER_DIRECTORY(type))
        strType = "<DIR>";
    else if (IS_GOPHER_PHONE_SERVER(type))
        strType = "Phone";
    else if (IS_GOPHER_ERROR(type))
        strType = "Error";
    else if (IS_GOPHER_INDEX_SERVER(type))
        strType = "Index";
    else if (IS_GOPHER_TELNET_SESSION(type))
        strType = "Telnet";
    else if (IS_GOPHER_BACKUP_SERVER(type))
        strType = "Backup";
```

```
    else if (IS_GOPHER_TN3270_SESSION(type))
        strType = "TN3270";
    else if (IS_GOPHER_ASK(type))
        strType = "Ask";
    else if (IS_GOPHER_PLUS(type))
        strType = "Gopher+";
    return strType;
}
```

GopherCreateLocator

GopherCreateLocator gives you the ability to create Gopher or Gopher+ locator strings manually to use with the other Gopher functions. The parameters represent the various locator string components:

```
BOOL GopherCreateLocator(
    IN LPCSTR lpszHost,
    IN INTERNET_PORT nServerPort,
    IN LPCSTR lpszDisplayString,
    IN LPCSTR lpszSelectorString,
    IN DWORD dwGopherType,
    OUT LPCSTR lpszLocator,
    IN OUT LPDWORD lpdwBufferLength
);
```

The resulting locator string is copied to the supplied buffer—lpszLocator. To help illustrate how this might be useful, I added a button to the dialog called Create Locator. This button brings up the dialog shown in Figure 6-8 and allows you to enter the Gopher locator information.

After you press OK, the Gopher locator is created and retrieved based on the type (see Listing 6-8). If you created the locator shown in Figure 6-8, the MyGopher list box would be populated with the items shown in Figure 6-9.

Listing 6-8   CMyGopherDlg::OnCreateLocator

```
void CMyGopherDlg::OnCreateLocator()
{
    // query user for locator parameters
    CCreateLocatorDlg dlg;
    if (IDCANCEL == dlg.DoModal())
        return;
```

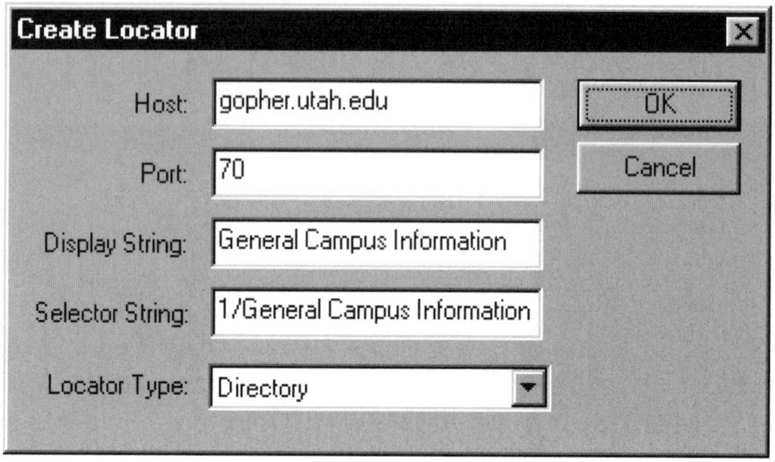

Figure 6-8   MyGopher Create Locator dialog

```
DWORD dwType, dwLen=4096;
char szBuffer[4096];

// figure out the WinInet Gopher type value
switch (dlg.m_nType)
{
case 0:
    dwType = GOPHER_TYPE_ASK;
    break;
case 1:
    dwType = GOPHER_TYPE_BINARY;
    break;
case 2:
    dwType = GOPHER_TYPE_BITMAP;
    break;
case 3:
    dwType = GOPHER_TYPE_CALENDAR;
    break;
case 4:
    dwType = GOPHER_TYPE_CSO;
    break;
case 5:
    dwType = GOPHER_TYPE_DIRECTORY;
```

```
        break;
case 6:
        dwType = GOPHER_TYPE_DOS_ARCHIVE;
        break;
case 7:
        dwType = GOPHER_TYPE_ERROR;
        break;
case 8:
        dwType = GOPHER_TYPE_GIF;
        break;
case 9:
        dwType = GOPHER_TYPE_GOPHER_PLUS;
        break;
case 10:
        dwType = GOPHER_TYPE_HTML;
        break;
case 11:
        dwType = GOPHER_TYPE_IMAGE;
        break;
case 12:
        dwType = GOPHER_TYPE_INDEX_SERVER;
        break;
case 13:
        dwType = GOPHER_TYPE_INLINE;
        break;
case 14:
        dwType = GOPHER_TYPE_MAC_BINHEX;
        break;
case 15:
        dwType = GOPHER_TYPE_MOVIE;
        break;
case 16:
        dwType = GOPHER_TYPE_PDF;
        break;
case 17:
        dwType = GOPHER_TYPE_REDUNDANT;
        break;
case 18:
        dwType = GOPHER_TYPE_SOUND;
        break;
case 19:
```

```
        dwType = GOPHER_TYPE_TELNET;
        break;
    case 20:
        dwType = GOPHER_TYPE_TEXT_FILE;
        break;
    case 21:
        dwType = GOPHER_TYPE_TN3270;
        break;
    case 22:
        dwType = GOPHER_TYPE_UNIX_UUENCODED;
        break;
    default:
        dwType = GOPHER_TYPE_UNKNOWN;
        break;
    }

    // create the locator string
    if (GopherCreateLocator(dlg.m_strHost, dlg.m_nPort, dlg.m_strDisplay,
        dlg.m_strSelector, dwType, szBuffer, &dwLen))
    {
        // enumerate, search, or download depending on type
        m_strLocator = szBuffer;
        switch(dwType)
        {
        case GOPHER_TYPE_DIRECTORY:
            FindGopherFiles(m_strLocator);
            break;
        case GOPHER_TYPE_HTML:
        case GOPHER_TYPE_TEXT_FILE:
            GetFile(m_strLocator);
            break;
        case GOPHER_TYPE_INDEX_SERVER:
            Search(m_strLocator);
            break;
        default:
            break;
        }
        UpdateData(FALSE);
    }
}
```

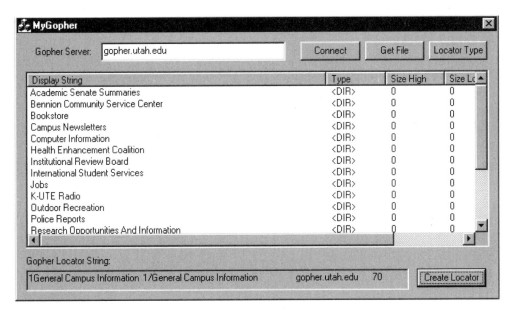

Figure 6-9 MyGopher dialog after using GopherCreateLocator

GopherGetAttribute and GopherAttributeEnumerator

GopherGetAttribute and GopherAttributeEnumerator are specific to Gopher+. These functions allow you to retrieve attribute information for a given Gopher+ locator. Typically you call GopherGetAttribute and supply the locator in which you're interested. If you're interested in all of the item's attributes, you can even specify a callback function in your call to GopherGetAttribute.

The callback function must match the definition of GopherAttributeEnumerator. Your GopherAttributeEnumerator callback function will be called once for each attribute of the Gopher+ locator. It provides the attribute information in a GOPHER_ATTRIBUTE_TYPE structure. This information simply helps you, as a Gopher client application, make better decisions about Gopher locators and what they have to offer. After you make a decision, however, you'll use the other Gopher functions presented throughout this chapter to create a new enumeration or download a file.

Conclusion

In this chapter I covered the Gopher protocol and showed you how the WinInet Gopher functions hide the details. The WinInet Gopher functions make it easy to add document retrieval functionality to your Windows applications. The sample application presented throughout this chapter should help you understand how you might go about adding similar functionality to your own applications.

III Part

MFC and Visual Basic

7
Chapter

WinInet MFC Internet Classes

I mentioned at the beginning of this book that WinInet provides tools for both Win32 and MFC developers. Up to this point I've been strictly covering the WinInet Win32 API. Now it's time to cover the MFC Internet classes, which encapsulate the underlying API.

Learning MFC without understanding the underlying Windows SDK is a difficult task. In my opinion, it's best to learn the underlying API before diving into the MFC classes. If you understand the API, the MFC classes are easier to use. The same rules apply to the Win32 WinInet API and the MFC Internet classes. This is the main reason behind the organization of the book.

At this point I've covered the most common Win32 WinInet API functions. By now you should feel comfortable with writing a simple WinInet application using the Win32 functions described throughout this book. If you're an MFC programmer, read on. In this chapter I'll cover how the MFC Internet classes encapsulate the WinInet API and how to rewrite some of the sample applications we've already covered. If you're not interested in using WinInet and MFC together, you may want to skip ahead.

Benefits

There are plenty of advantages to using the MFC WinInet classes. Not only do the classes use standard MFC file classes, but they also take advantage of other object-oriented features like default parameters and exception handling. Plus, the classes help take care of cleaning up open Internet handles and connections. Besides these nice features, the MFC Internet classes do nothing more than call the corresponding WinInet API function.

If you write your Windows applications in MFC, you'll probably want to take advantage of the MFC Internet classes instead of the straight WinInet API; the MFC classes will fit nicely into your design. However, even if you don't commonly use MFC, you may still want to consider using the MFC Internet classes because of their object-oriented approach.

It's your choice. You can use WinInet with either the standard Win32 API or the MFC class wrappers. Just like with Windows programming, you may even want to use bits and pieces of each interface. As you'll learn throughout the rest of this chapter, the MFC classes accomplish the same result as using the underlying API.

WinInet MFC Classes

Beginning with Visual C++ 4.1, Microsoft introduced a new set of classes into the MFC class hierarchy. Figure 7-1 illustrates how the MFC Internet classes fit into the overall MFC class hierarchy.

As you can see, all of the MFC Internet classes derive from CObject, which is at the top of the MFC class hierarchy. If you're familiar with MFC, you'll also notice a few other MFC classes sprinkled throughout this diagram. For example, all of the MFC Internet file classes derive from the standard MFC classes CFile and CStdioFile. Also, both CFtpFileFind and CGopherFind derive from the standard MFC class CFileFind.

In the upcoming sections I'll cover each of these MFC Internet classes in detail. I'll show you the MFC Internet class declarations, along with examples of how they encapsulate the underlying API.

Getting Started with MFC WinInet Support

To begin using the MFC Internet classes you only need to do one thing: include afxinet.h in your project. The best place to do this is in stdafx.h. If you include afxinet.h in stdafx.h, you'll never have to worry about including it anywhere else (assuming that each source file already includes stdafx.h).

The afxinet.h header file contains all of the MFC Internet class declarations. Plus, it takes care of including WinInet.h if you haven't already done so. It accomplishes this with the following lines at the beginning of the file:

```
#ifndef _WININET_
#include <wininet.h>
#endif
```

Then, inside WinInet.h at the beginning of the file, you'll find the following lines of code:

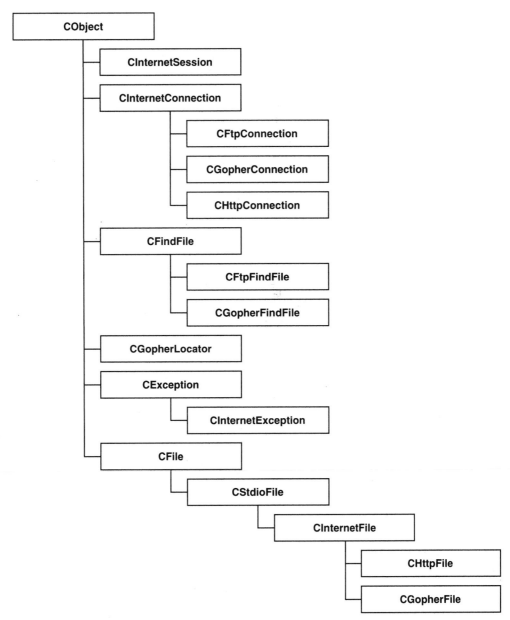

Figure 7-1   MFC Internet class hierarchy

```
#if !defined(_WININET_)
#define _WININET_
```

Thus, if you've already included WinInet.h in your project somewhere, it won't be included multiple times. However, if you haven't included it, afxinet.h takes care of this task for you. Afxinet.h also takes care of linking in wininet.lib with the following statement:

```
#pragma comment(lib, "WININET.LIB")
```

So as you can see, afxinet.h takes care of all the pesky details involved in using WinInet in your applications. When you're using the WinInet API, as we've done up to this point in this book, you have to make sure to manage these details yourself. When you're using the MFC Internet classes, however, simply add afxinet.h to your precompiled header file (usually stdafx.h) and away you go.

 To use the MFC Internet classes, include afxinet.h in your project (usually in stdafx.h).

CInternetSession

Let's start our MFC class investigation by looking at CInternetSession. I want to start with CInternetSession because it encapsulates the functionality of InternetOpen. You've learned that every WinInet application must call InternetOpen before using any other WinInet function. Likewise, every MFC application must create an instance of CInternetSession before using the other MFC Internet classes.

Before going any further, look over Listing 7-1, which contains the CInternetSession class declaration. As you do, you should notice many similarities to things that we have already discussed.

Listing 7-1   CInternetSession class declaration

```
class CInternetSession : public CObject
{
public:
    CInternetSession(LPCTSTR pstrAgent = NULL,
        DWORD dwContext = 1,
        DWORD dwAccessType = PRE_CONFIG_INTERNET_ACCESS,
        LPCTSTR pstrProxyName = NULL,
        LPCTSTR pstrProxyBypass = NULL,
        DWORD dwFlags = 0);

    BOOL QueryOption(DWORD dwOption, LPVOID lpBuffer,
        LPDWORD lpdwBufLen) const;
    BOOL QueryOption(DWORD dwOption, DWORD& dwValue) const;
    BOOL QueryOption(DWORD dwOption, CString& refString) const;
```

```
    BOOL SetOption(DWORD dwOption, LPVOID lpBuffer, DWORD dwBufferLength,
        DWORD dwFlags = 0);
    BOOL SetOption(DWORD dwOption, DWORD dwValue, DWORD dwFlags = 0);

    CStdioFile* OpenURL(LPCTSTR pstrURL,
        DWORD dwContext = 1, DWORD dwFlags = INTERNET_FLAG_TRANSFER_ASCII,
        LPCTSTR pstrHeaders = NULL, DWORD dwHeadersLength = 0);

    CFtpConnection* GetFtpConnection(LPCTSTR pstrServer,
        LPCTSTR pstrUserName = NULL, LPCTSTR pstrPassword = NULL,
        INTERNET_PORT nPort = INTERNET_INVALID_PORT_NUMBER,
        BOOL bPassive = FALSE);

    CHttpConnection* GetHttpConnection(LPCTSTR pstrServer,
        INTERNET_PORT nPort = INTERNET_INVALID_PORT_NUMBER,
        LPCTSTR pstrUserName = NULL, LPCTSTR pstrPassword = NULL);
    CHttpConnection* GetHttpConnection(LPCTSTR pstrServer, DWORD dwFlags,
        INTERNET_PORT nPort = INTERNET_INVALID_PORT_NUMBER,
        LPCTSTR pstrUserName = NULL, LPCTSTR pstrPassword = NULL);

    CGopherConnection* GetGopherConnection(LPCTSTR pstrServer,
        LPCTSTR pstrUserName = NULL, LPCTSTR pstrPassword = NULL,
        INTERNET_PORT nPort = INTERNET_INVALID_PORT_NUMBER);

    BOOL EnableStatusCallback(BOOL bEnable = TRUE);
    DWORD ServiceTypeFromHandle(HINTERNET hQuery);

// operations

    DWORD GetContext() const;
    operator HINTERNET() const;
    virtual void Close();

// overridables
    virtual void OnStatusCallback(DWORD dwContext, DWORD dwInternetStatus,
        LPVOID lpvStatusInformation, DWORD dwStatusInformationLength);

// implementation
    DECLARE_DYNAMIC(CInternetSession)
    ~CInternetSession();

protected:
    DWORD m_dwContext;
    HINTERNET m_hSession;
    INTERNET_STATUS_CALLBACK m_pOldCallback;
```

```
    BOOL m_bCallbackEnabled;

public:
#ifdef _DEBUG
    virtual void Dump(CDumpContext& dc) const;
#endif
};
```

Looking at this class declaration should help you realize that CInternetSession is the gateway to all WinInet protocols. Whether you want to establish an HTTP, FTP, or Gopher session, using CInternetSession is the first step.

CInternetSession Construction

Probably the most important thing to point out about the CInternetSession class declaration is the protected member variable m_hSession. This member variable holds the HINTERNET handle returned by InternetOpen. Because you're probably wondering when this actually occurs, let's look into the CInternetSession constructor (see Listing 7-2).

Listing 7-2   CInternetSession constructor

```
CInternetSession::CInternetSession(LPCTSTR pstrAgent /* = NULL */,
    DWORD dwContext /* = 1 */,
    DWORD dwAccessType /* = PRE_CONFIG_INTERNET_ACCESS */,
    LPCTSTR pstrProxyName /* = NULL */,
    LPCTSTR pstrProxyBypass /* = NULL */,
    DWORD dwFlags /* = 0 */)
{
    m_bCallbackEnabled = FALSE;
    m_pOldCallback = NULL;

    m_dwContext = dwContext;
    if (pstrAgent == NULL)
        pstrAgent = AfxGetAppName();
    m_hSession = InternetOpen(pstrAgent, dwAccessType,
        pstrProxyName, pstrProxyBypass, dwFlags);

    if (m_hSession == NULL)
        AfxThrowInternetException(m_dwContext);
    else
        _afxSessionMap.SetAt(m_hSession, this);
}
```

The CInternetSession constructor illustrates many important concepts related to using the MFC Internet classes. First of all, notice all the default constructor comments. These defaults help simplify the process of creating a CInternetSession object. Because of these defaults, you can create an instance of CInternetSession in the following manner:

```
CInternetSession session;
```

If you pass NULL in pstrAgent, the constructor actually uses the application name in the InternetOpen User-Agent parameter by calling AfxGetAppName. These are some of the typical benefits of using C++ and classes in general.

After properly initializing all of its member variables, the CInternetSession constructor calls InternetOpen and saves the resulting HINTERNET in m_hSession. Because we've already covered InternetOpen and its functionality in detail, I'll concentrate on the MFC class wrapper functionality.

The constructor also handles some error checking for us. Notice that if m_hSession is NULL after calling InternetOpen, it calls AfxThrowInternetException using the context value. We'll look at AfxThrowInternetException in more detail shortly, but it basically constructs a CInternetException object and throws it. Because it's possible for the CInternetSession object to throw an exception, you need to set up the appropriate catch statements. There is one more thing that I want to point out about the CInternetSession constructor. Check out the following line:

```
_afxSessionMap.SetAt(m_hSession, this);
```

If you've done much MFC programming, you should be familiar with the concept of handle maps. MFC uses maps to associate the CWnd objects with the underlying Window handle with which it's associated. Similarly, MFC keeps a map of all CInternetSession objects and their underlying HINTERNET handles. This is how MFC keeps track of which CInternetSession object belongs to a given HINTERNET handle. Throughout the MFC source code you'll see MFC using _afxSessionMap to look up handles or CInternetSession objects.

Establishing a Status Callback Function

The task of establishing a status callback function through CInternetSession can be confusing. If you look back at Listing 7-1, you'll notice the following method that enables the status callback:

```
BOOL EnableStatusCallback(BOOL bEnable = TRUE);
```

The only problem is that you can't specify the callback function you wish to register. If you look at the overridable section of Listing 7-1, you'll see the following virtual function declaration:

```
// overridables
    virtual void OnStatusCallback(DWORD dwContext, DWORD dwInternetStatus,
        LPVOID lpvStatusInformation, DWORD dwStatusInformationLength);
```

Hence, to establish a status callback function using CInternetSession, you must derive your own class from CInternetSession and override OnStatusCallback. Then you must be sure to call CInternetSession::EnableStatusCallback. Inside of your derived class you can implement OnStatusCallback to fit your needs.

Let's look at a typical example of how you might derive your own class from CInternetSession. Listing 7-3 shows the class declaration CMyInternetSession, which derives from CInternetSession and overrides OnStatusCallback.

Listing 7-3   CMyInternetSession declaration

```
class CMyInternetSession : public CInternetSession
{
public:
    CMyInternetSession(LPCTSTR pstrAgent = NULL, DWORD dwContext = 1, DWORD
        dwAccessType = INTERNET_OPEN_TYPE_PRECONFIG, LPCTSTR pstrProxyName =
        NULL, LPCTSTR pstrProxyBypass = NULL, DWORD dwFlags = 0 )
        : CInternetSession(pstrAgent, dwContext, dwAccessType, pstrProxyName,
            pstrProxyBypass, dwFlags) { }

    //override OnStatusCallback
    virtual void OnStatusCallback(DWORD dwContext, DWORD dwInternetStatus,
        LPVOID lpvStatusInformation, DWORD dwStatusInformationLength )
    { AfxmessageBox("OnStatusCallback Called"); }
};
```

In this example I want my version of OnStatusCallback simply to pop up a message box indicating that it was called. Now to use my derived class, I need to declare an instance of it and call CInternetSession::EnableStatusCallback like this:

```
CMyInternetSession session;
Session.EnableStatusCallback(TRUE);
```

As soon as I start using my session object and the underlying WinInet functionality, CMyInternetSession::OnStatusCallback is called to indicate the status of my Internet session.

How CMyInternetSession::OnStatusCallback gets called seems like magic, but digging into the MFC code helps you understand how it all works. First of all, notice that there are a few status-callback related member variables inside the CInternetSession class declaration:

```
protected:
    INTERNET_STATUS_CALLBACK m_pOldCallback;
    BOOL m_bCallbackEnabled;
```

The CInternetSession constructor initializes m_pOldCallback to NULL and m_bCallbackEnabled to FALSE, which basically means status callback support is turned off to begin with. The key to most of the MFC status callback support is hidden in CInternetSession::EnableStatusCallback (see Listing 7-4).

Listing 7-4   CInternetSession::EnableStatusCallback

```
BOOL CInternetSession::EnableStatusCallback(BOOL bEnable /* = TRUE */)
{
    ASSERT(bEnable == FALSE || m_hSession != NULL);
    if (m_hSession == NULL)
        return FALSE;

    BOOL bResult = TRUE;
    if (bEnable)
    {
        ASSERT(!m_bCallbackEnabled);
        if (!m_bCallbackEnabled)
        {
            INTERNET_STATUS_CALLBACK pRet =
                InternetSetStatusCallback(m_hSession,
                    AfxInternetStatusCallback);

            if (pRet != INTERNET_INVALID_STATUS_CALLBACK)
            {
                m_pOldCallback = pRet;
                m_bCallbackEnabled = TRUE;
            }
            else AfxThrowInternetException(m_dwContext);
        }
    }
    else
```

```
    {
        ASSERT(m_bCallbackEnabled);
        if (m_bCallbackEnabled)
        {
            InternetSetStatusCallback(m_hSession, NULL);
            m_bCallbackEnabled = FALSE;
        }
    }
    return bResult;
}
```

EnableStatusCallback is used to hook and to unhook the status callback function (depending on bEnable). If bEnable is TRUE, it calls InternetSetStatusCallback with m_hSession and AfxInternetStatusCallback. As long as it succeeds, m_pOldCallback saves off the old callback function and m_bCallbackEnabled gets set to TRUE. If bEnable is FALSE, it simply calls InternetSetStatusCallback with NULL and sets m_bCallbackEnabled to FALSE.

The big question is why did InternetSetStatusCallback set the callback function to AfxInternetStatusCallback and not our derived class' OnStatusCallback method? The answer to this deals with how WinInet calls the status callback functions. WinInet calls status callback functions based on an HINTERNET handle and is oblivious to our CMyInternetSession class. Hence, MFC needs to take care of this for us behind the scenes. Take a look at AfxInternetStatusCallback in Listing 7-5.

Listing 7-5 AfxInternetStatusCallback

```
void AFXAPI AfxInternetStatusCallback(HINTERNET hInternet, DWORD dwContext,
    DWORD dwInternetStatus, LPVOID lpvStatusInformation,
    DWORD dwStatusInformationLength)
{
    CInternetSession* pSession;

#ifdef _DEBUG
    if (afxTraceFlags & traceInternet)
        AfxInternetStatusCallbackDebug(hInternet, dwContext,
            dwInternetStatus, lpvStatusInformation, dwStatusInformationLength);
#endif

    if (_afxSessionMap.Lookup(hInternet, pSession))
```

```
{
    pSession->OnStatusCallback(dwContext, dwInternetStatus,
            lpvStatusInformation, dwStatusInformationLength);
}

    // note that an entry we can't match is simply ignored as
    // WinInet can send notifications for handles that we can't
    // see-such as when using InternetOpenURL()
}
```

AfxInternetStatusCallback matches the INTERNET_STATUS_CALLBACK
definition, which we've already covered. This global callback method is registered
for all MFC CInternetSession-derived classes in the call to EnableStatusCallback.

Because WinInet passes the HINTERNET handle, MFC can use the handle
map (_afxSessionMap) to find the CInternetSession object associated with the
HINTERNET handle. If it finds one, it calls OnStatusCallback on the CInternetSession
pointer. Because OnStatusCallback is a virtual function, the OnStatusCallback function in the derived class—CMyInternetSession::OnStatusCallback in the previous
example—is called. This is a great example of how MFC uses maps to manage the
interaction between the API and the MFC class wrappers.

AfxInternetStatusCallback acts as a dispatch center for all MFC-based status callback functions. One benefit of allowing MFC to intercept the call like this is the diagnos-
tic support it provides. Notice that if you're in debug mode (_DEBUG is defined) and the
traceInternet flag is turned on, it calls AfxInternetStatusCallbackDebug first and then
continues. AfxInternetStatusCallbackDebug simply outputs relevant status information
to the Visual C++ development environment debug output window (see Listing 7-6).

You can turn on the Internet trace flags in the development environment from the
Tools menu. Choosing MFC Tracer from the Tools menu displays the dialog shown in
Figure 7-2. If you check the Internet Client Tracing option, the traceInternet flag is set
properly and you should begin to see status information show up in the debug output
window.

Listing 7-6   AfxInternetStatusCallbackDebug

```
#ifdef _DEBUG
void AFXAPI AfxInternetStatusCallbackDebug(HINTERNET hInternet,
    DWORD dwContext, DWORD dwInternetStatus, LPVOID lpvStatusInformation,
    DWORD dwStatusInformationLength)
```

```
{
    UNUSED_ALWAYS(hInternet);
    TRACE1("Internet ctxt=%d: ", dwContext);

    switch (dwInternetStatus)
    {
    case INTERNET_STATUS_RESOLVING_NAME:
        TRACE1("resolving name for %s\n", lpvStatusInformation);
        break;

    case INTERNET_STATUS_NAME_RESOLVED:
        TRACE1("resolved name for %s!\n", lpvStatusInformation);
        break;

    case INTERNET_STATUS_HANDLE_CREATED:
        TRACE1("handle %8.8X created\n", hInternet);
        break;

    // continued for all status values
    // ...

    default:
        TRACE1("Unknown status: %d\n", dwInternetStatus);
        break;
    }

    return;
}
#endif // _DEBUG
```

Accessing Internet Options

Do you remember the InternetSetOption and InternetQueryOption WinInet functions? CInternetSession encapsulates these functions as well. The CInternetSession::SetOption and CInternetSession::QueryOption methods do nothing more than assumption validation along with a call to the corresponding underlying WinInet function (see Listing 7-7).

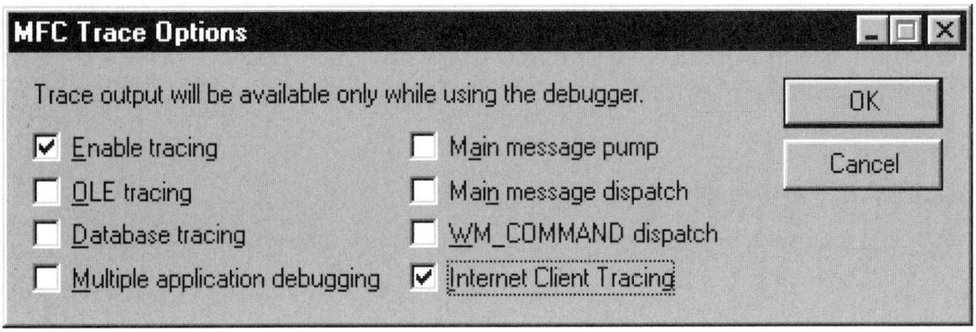

Figure 7-2 MFC Trace Options dialog

Listing 7-7 **CInternetSession SetOption and QueryOption**

```
BOOL CInternetSession::SetOption(DWORD dwOption, LPVOID lpBuffer,
    DWORD dwBufferLength, DWORD dwFlags /* = 0 */)
{
    ASSERT(dwOption >= INTERNET_FIRST_OPTION &&
        dwOption <= INTERNET_LAST_OPTION);
    ASSERT(lpBuffer != NULL);
    ASSERT(dwBufferLength != 0);

    // bogus flag?
    ASSERT(dwFlags == 0 || ((dwFlags & ISO_VALID_FLAGS) == dwFlags));

    return InternetSetOptionEx(m_hSession, dwOption,
        lpBuffer, dwBufferLength, dwFlags);
}


BOOL CInternetSession::QueryOption(DWORD dwOption, LPVOID lpBuffer,
    LPDWORD lpdwBufferLength) const
{
    ASSERT(dwOption >= INTERNET_FIRST_OPTION &&
        dwOption <= INTERNET_LAST_OPTION);
    ASSERT(lpBuffer != NULL);
    ASSERT(lpdwBufferLength != NULL);
    ASSERT(*lpdwBufferLength != 0);

    return InternetQueryOption(m_hSession, dwOption,
        lpBuffer, lpdwBufferLength);
}
```

However, you'll notice that each of these methods has at least one overloaded version of itself that makes working with DWORD and CString option values easier. For example, Listing 7-8 shows the two overloaded QueryOption methods and their implementations.

Listing 7-8   Overloaded QueryOption methods

```
BOOL CInternetSession::QueryOption(DWORD dwOption, DWORD& dwValue) const
{
    DWORD dwLen = sizeof(DWORD);
    return InternetQueryOption(m_hSession, dwOption,
        &dwValue, &dwLen);
}

BOOL CInternetSession::QueryOption(DWORD dwOption, CString& refString) const
{
    ASSERT(dwOption >= INTERNET_FIRST_OPTION &&
        dwOption <= INTERNET_LAST_OPTION);

    return _AfxQueryCStringInternetOption(m_hSession, dwOption, refString);
}
```

Using OpenURL

CInternetSession::OpenURL encapsulates InternetOpenUrl. Besides calling InternetOpenUrl, CInternetSession::OpenURL also creates the appropriate MFC file object and returns a pointer to it. Because all of the MFC Internet file classes are derived from CStdioFile, OpenURL can return a pointer to CStdioFile (the base class) regardless of which file class is actually being returned.

Listing 7-9 contains the implementation for CInternetSession::OpenURL. Notice that if pstrURL identifies a local file, a call to InternetOpenUrl is not needed. Thus, it simply creates, opens, and returns a pointer to an instance of CStdioFile for the local file.

If it's not a local file, InternetOpenUrl is called immediately. Then, based on the WinInet protocol being used (HTTP, FTP, or Gopher), the appropriate Internet file object is created. For example, if pstrURL specifies an HTTP resource, a CHttpFile object is created based on the HINTERNET handle returned by InternetOpenUrl.

Listing 7-9   CInternetSession::OpenURL

```
CStdioFile* CInternetSession::OpenURL(LPCTSTR pstrURL,
        DWORD dwContext /* = 0 */, DWORD dwFlags /* =
```

```
        INTERNET_FLAG_TRANSFER_BINARY */, LPCTSTR pstrHeaders /* = NULL */, DWORD
        dwHeadersLength /* = 0 */)
{
    //asserts removed...

    if (dwContext == 1)
        dwContext = m_dwContext;

    DWORD dwServiceType;
    CString strServer;
    CString strObject;
    INTERNET_PORT nPort;
    CStdioFile* pReturn;

    BOOL bParsed = AfxParseURL(pstrURL, dwServiceType, strServer,  strObject,
        nPort);

    // if it turns out to be a file...
    if (bParsed && dwServiceType == AFX_INET_SERVICE_FILE)
    {
        int nMode = CFile::modeRead | CFile::shareCompat;
        if (dwFlags & INTERNET_FLAG_TRANSFER_BINARY)
            nMode |= CFile::typeBinary;
        else
            nMode |= CFile::typeText;

        pReturn = new CStdioFile(strObject, nMode);
    }
    else
    {
        HINTERNET hOpener;

        hOpener = InternetOpenUrl(m_hSession, pstrURL, pstrHeaders,
            dwHeadersLength, dwFlags, dwContext);

        if (hOpener == NULL)
            AfxThrowInternetException(m_dwContext);

        if (!bParsed)
            dwServiceType = AfxGetInternetHandleType(hOpener);
```

```
    switch (dwServiceType)
    {
        case INTERNET_HANDLE_TYPE_GOPHER_FILE:
        case AFX_INET_SERVICE_GOPHER:
        //WINBUG: WININET supplies no way to
        // convert from a URL to a Gopher locator
            pReturn = new CGopherFile(hOpener, m_hSession,
                                     _T(""),0, dwContext);
            _afxSessionMap.SetAt(hOpener, this);
            break;

        case INTERNET_HANDLE_TYPE_FTP_FILE:
        case AFX_INET_SERVICE_FTP:
            pReturn = new CInternetFile(hOpener, m_hSession,
                    strObject, strServer, dwContext, TRUE);
            _afxSessionMap.SetAt(hOpener, this);
            break;

        case INTERNET_HANDLE_TYPE_HTTP_REQUEST:
        case AFX_INET_SERVICE_HTTP:
        case AFX_INET_SERVICE_HTTPS:
            pReturn = new CHttpFile(hOpener, m_hSession, strObject,
              strServer,
              CHttpConnection::szHtmlVerbs[CHttpConnection::HTTP_VERB_GET],
              dwContext);
            _afxSessionMap.SetAt(hOpener, this);
            break;

        default:
            TRACE1("Error: Unidentified service type: %8.8X\n",
                    dwServiceType);
            pReturn = NULL;
    }
}
return pReturn;
}
```

Because you won't know which file object was actually created and returned, you'll have to take advantage of some of C++'s runtime support. First of all, most of the CFile, CStdioFile, and CInternetFile methods are declared as virtual. So as long as you call virtual functions on the pointer returned by OpenURL, the correct method should be called.

> If you would like to determine the type of object programmatically, you can use C++'s dynamic_cast. dynamic_cast actually checks the object type to verify that the pointer cast is valid. If the cast is invalid, dynamic_cast returns NULL. The following example illustrates how you can determine if the pointer returned by OpenURL really points to a CHttpFile object:

```
CInternetSession session;
CStdioFile* pFile = session.OpenURL("http://www.microsoft.com");
CHttpFile* pHttpFle = dynamic_cast<CHttpFile*>(pFile);
if (pHttpFile)
{
    // it really is a CHttpFile object
}
```

After calling OpenURL you use the file object to read the remote file. I'll look at this more closely when we get to CInternetFile.

Establishing a Protocol-Specific Connection

CInternetSession is also your gateway to creating the protocol-specific MFC Internet connection objects. In other words, you should never create a connection object directly. For example, you should never have to write the following line of code:

```
CHttpConnection* pHttpConnection = new CHttpConnection(/* params */);
```

Instead, you should use the CInternetSession GetHttpConnection, GetFtpConnection, and GetGopherConnection methods, which create the corresponding MFC connection object for you. Take a look at Listing 7-10, which illustrates how this is accomplished.

Listing 7-10   GetHttpConnection, GetFtpConnection, and GetGopherConnection

```
CHttpConnection* CInternetSession::GetHttpConnection(LPCTSTR pstrServer,
    DWORD dwFlags, INTERNET_PORT nPort /* = INTERNET_INVALID_PORT_NUMBER  */,
    LPCTSTR pstrUserName /* = NULL */, LPCTSTR pstrPassword /* = NULL */)
{
    ASSERT(pstrServer != NULL);
    CHttpConnection* pReturn = new CHttpConnection(this, pstrServer,
            dwFlags, nPort, pstrUserName, pstrPassword, m_dwContext);
    return pReturn;
}


CFtpConnection* CInternetSession::GetFtpConnection(LPCTSTR pstrServer,
    LPCTSTR pstrUserName /* = NULL */, LPCTSTR pstrPassword /* = NULL */,
    INTERNET_PORT nPort /* = INTERNET_INVALID_PORT_NUMBER */,
    BOOL bPassive /* = FALSE */)
{
    ASSERT(pstrServer != NULL);
    CFtpConnection* pReturn = new CFtpConnection(this,
        pstrServer, pstrUserName, pstrPassword, m_dwContext,
        nPort, bPassive);
    return pReturn;
}


CGopherConnection* CInternetSession::GetGopherConnection(LPCTSTR pstrServer,
    LPCTSTR pstrUserName /* = NULL */, LPCTSTR pstrPassword /* = NULL */,
    INTERNET_PORT nPort /* = INTERNET_INVALID_PORT_NUMBER */)
{
    ASSERT(pstrServer != NULL);
    CGopherConnection* pReturn = new CGopherConnection(this,
        pstrServer, pstrUserName, pstrPassword, m_dwContext, nPort);
    return pReturn;
}
```

These methods simply create the corresponding MFC Internet connection object and return the object pointer. Although I'll look at each of the individual connection objects in more detail shortly, the following example illustrates how to use GetHttpConnection:

```
CInternetSession session;
CHttpFile* pHttpFle = session.GetHttpConnection("www.microsoft.com", 0);
if (pHttpFile)
{
    // use the CHttpFile object
}
```

CInternetSession Cleanup

One of the benefits of using the MFC WinInet classes is that the classes automatically clean up the HINTERNET handles for you. For example, take a look at Listing 7-11, which shows the CInternetSession destructor and Close method.

Listing 7-11   CInternetSession destructor and Close method

```
CInternetSession::~CInternetSession()
{
    Close();
}
void CInternetSession::Close()
{
    if (m_bCallbackEnabled)
        EnableStatusCallback(FALSE);

    if (m_hSession != NULL)
    {
        InternetCloseHandle(m_hSession);
        _afxSessionMap.RemoveKey(m_hSession);
        m_hSession = NULL;
    }
}
```

Notice that the destructor calls Close, and Close calls InternetCloseHandle. So instead of worrying about closing all of the underlying handles, you only need to manage the higher level objects.

CInternetSession Summary

CInternetSession clearly plays an important role in MFC WinInet support. Like InternetOpen, an instance of CInternetSession must exist in every MFC-based WinInet application. Furthermore, CInternetSession acts as a gateway to establishing Internet connections with any of the WinInet supported protocols.

CInternetFile

CInternetFile encapsulates the remote Internet file functionality. It's the base class for both CHttpFile and CGopherFile. When using HTTP and Gopher, you never create an instance of CInternetFile directly. On the contrary, you create CHttpFile and CGopherFile objects by calling CHttpConnection::OpenRequest and CGopherConnection::OpenFile. When you call CFtpConnection::OpenFile, however, you get a CInternetFile object.

The CInternetFile class derives from CStdioFile, which derives from CFile. The CInternetFile functionality is modeled after these standard Win32 file classes. Listing 7-12 shows the CInternetFile class declaration. If you look over the class, you'll notice that using this class to work with remote files is much like using CFile or CStdioFile to work with local files.

Listing 7-12   CInternetFile class declaration

```
class CInternetFile : public CStdioFile
{
// Constructors
protected:
    CInternetFile(HINTERNET hFile, LPCTSTR pstrFileName,
        CInternetConnection* pConnection, BOOL bReadMode);
    CInternetFile(HINTERNET hFile, HINTERNET hSession,
        LPCTSTR pstrFileName, LPCTSTR pstrServer, DWORD dwContext,
        BOOL bReadMode);

// Attributes
protected:
    HINTERNET m_hFile;
public:
    operator HINTERNET() const;
    DWORD GetContext() const;
// Operations
    BOOL SetWriteBufferSize(UINT nWriteSize);
    BOOL SetReadBufferSize(UINT nReadSize);
    BOOL QueryOption(DWORD dwOption, LPVOID lpBuffer,
            LPDWORD lpdwBufLen) const;
    BOOL QueryOption(DWORD dwOption, DWORD& dwValue) const;
    BOOL QueryOption(DWORD dwOption, CString& refString) const;
    BOOL SetOption(DWORD dwOption, LPVOID lpBuffer, DWORD dwBufferLength,
        DWORD dwFlags = 0);
    BOOL SetOption(DWORD dwOption, DWORD dwValue, DWORD dwFlags = 0);
```

```cpp
// Overridables
    virtual LONG Seek(LONG lOffset, UINT nFrom);
    virtual UINT Read(void* lpBuf, UINT nCount);
    virtual void Write(const void* lpBuf, UINT nCount);
    virtual void Abort();
    virtual void Flush();
    virtual void Close();
    virtual DWORD GetLength() const;
    virtual BOOL ReadString(CString& rString);
    virtual LPTSTR ReadString(LPTSTR pstr, UINT nMax);
    virtual void WriteString(LPCTSTR pstr);
    // Not supported by CInternetFile
    void LockRange(DWORD dwPos, DWORD dwCount);
    void UnlockRange(DWORD dwPos, DWORD dwCount);
    CFile* Duplicate() const;
    virtual void SetLength(DWORD dwNewLen);
// Implementation
public:
    virtual ~CInternetFile();
protected:
    BOOL m_bReadMode;
    DWORD m_dwContext;
    HINTERNET m_hConnection;
    CString m_strServerName;
    UINT m_nWriteBufferSize;
    UINT m_nWriteBufferPos;
    LPBYTE m_pbWriteBuffer;
    UINT m_nReadBufferSize;
    UINT m_nReadBufferPos;
    LPBYTE m_pbReadBuffer;
    UINT m_nReadBufferBytes;
#ifdef _DEBUG
    virtual void AssertValid() const;
    virtual void Dump(CDumpContext& dc) const;
#endif
    friend class CInternetSession;
    friend class CFtpConnection;
    friend class CHttpConnection;
    friend class CGopherConnection;
    DECLARE_DYNAMIC(CInternetFile)
};
```

One of the most obvious differences is that CInternetFile contains a bunch of methods for querying and setting Internet options. These methods are very similar to the ones found in the CInternetSession class except they take care of reading and setting the Internet options on the file handle (instead of the session handle). Like CInternetSession, these methods are implemented by using the InternetSetOption and InternetQueryOption WinInet API functions.

Let's take a look at both CInternetFile::Read and CInternetFile::Write. As you would probably guess, they're implemented using the underlying WinInet InternetReadFile and InternetWriteFile functions. Take a look at Listing 7-13.

Listing 7-13   CInternetFile Read and Write

```
UINT CInternetFile::Read(LPVOID lpBuf, UINT nCount)
{
    ASSERT_VALID(this);
    ASSERT(m_hFile != NULL);
    ASSERT(m_bReadMode);

    DWORD dwBytes;

    if (!m_bReadMode || m_hFile == NULL)
        AfxThrowInternetException(m_dwContext, ERROR_INVALID_HANDLE);

    if (m_pbReadBuffer == NULL)
    {
        if (!InternetReadFile(m_hFile, (LPVOID) lpBuf, nCount, &dwBytes))
                AfxThrowInternetException(m_dwContext);
        return dwBytes;
    }

    LPBYTE lpbBuf = (LPBYTE) lpBuf;

    // if the requested size is bigger than our buffer,
    // then handle it directly

    if (nCount >= m_nReadBufferSize)
    {
        DWORD dwMoved = max(0, (long)m_nReadBufferBytes -
                (long)m_nReadBufferPos);
        memcpy(lpBuf, m_pbReadBuffer + m_nReadBufferPos, dwMoved);
        m_nReadBufferPos = m_nReadBufferSize;
```

```
        if (!InternetReadFile(m_hFile, lpbBuf+dwMoved, nCount-dwMoved,
                &dwBytes))
                AfxThrowInternetException(m_dwContext);
        dwBytes += dwMoved;
    }
    else
    {
        if (m_nReadBufferPos + nCount >= m_nReadBufferBytes)
        {
            DWORD dwMoved = max(0, (long)m_nReadBufferBytes -
                    (long)m_nReadBufferPos);
            memcpy(lpbBuf, m_pbReadBuffer + m_nReadBufferPos, dwMoved);
            DWORD dwRead;
            if (!InternetReadFile(m_hFile, m_pbReadBuffer,
                    m_nReadBufferSize, &dwRead))
                AfxThrowInternetException(m_dwContext);
            m_nReadBufferBytes = dwRead;

            dwRead = min(nCount - dwMoved, m_nReadBufferBytes);
            memcpy(lpbBuf + dwMoved, m_pbReadBuffer, dwRead);
            m_nReadBufferPos = dwRead;
            dwBytes = dwMoved + dwRead;
        }
        else
        {
            memcpy(lpbBuf, m_pbReadBuffer + m_nReadBufferPos, nCount);
            m_nReadBufferPos += nCount;
            dwBytes = nCount;
        }
    }
    return dwBytes;
}


void CInternetFile::Write(const void* lpBuf, UINT nCount)
{
    ASSERT_VALID(this);
    ASSERT(m_hFile != NULL);
    ASSERT(!m_bReadMode);

    if (m_bReadMode || m_hFile == NULL)
        AfxThrowInternetException(m_dwContext, ERROR_INVALID_HANDLE);
```

```
DWORD dwBytes;
if (m_pbWriteBuffer == NULL)
{
    if (!InternetWriteFile(m_hFile, lpBuf, nCount, &dwBytes))
        AfxThrowInternetException(m_dwContext);

    if (dwBytes != nCount)
        AfxThrowInternetException(m_dwContext);

}
else
{
    if ((m_nWriteBufferPos + nCount) >= m_nWriteBufferSize)
    {
        // write what is in the buffer just now

        if (!InternetWriteFile(m_hFile, m_pbWriteBuffer,
                m_nWriteBufferPos, &dwBytes))
            AfxThrowInternetException(m_dwContext);

        // reset the buffer position since it is now clean

        m_nWriteBufferPos = 0;
    }

    // if we can't hope to buffer the write request,
    // do it immediately ... otherwise, buffer it!

    if (nCount >= m_nWriteBufferSize)
    {
        if (!InternetWriteFile(m_hFile, (LPVOID) lpBuf, nCount,
                &dwBytes))
            AfxThrowInternetException(m_dwContext);
    }
    else
    {
        memcpy(m_nWriteBufferPos + m_pbWriteBuffer, lpBuf, nCount);
        m_nWriteBufferPos += nCount;
    }
}
}
```

I also want to point out how CInternetFile::Seek is implemented. Remember when we covered InternetSetFilePointer at the beginning of the book? This is one place where it comes in handy. Check out Listing 7-14.

Listing 7-14   CInternetFile::Seek

```
LONG CInternetFile::Seek(LONG lOffset, UINT nFrom)
{
    ASSERT_VALID(this);
    ASSERT(m_hFile != NULL);
    ASSERT(m_bReadMode == TRUE);
    ASSERT(m_pbReadBuffer == NULL);

    // can't do this on a file for writing
    // can't do this on a file that's got a buffer
    if (!m_bReadMode || m_pbReadBuffer != NULL)
        AfxThrowInternetException(m_dwContext, ERROR_INVALID_HANDLE);

    switch (nFrom)
    {
        case begin:
            nFrom = FILE_BEGIN;
            break;

        case current:
            nFrom = FILE_CURRENT;
            break;

        case end:
            nFrom = FILE_END;
            break;

        default:
            ASSERT(FALSE);   // got a bogus nFrom value
            AfxThrowInternetException(m_dwContext, ERROR_INVALID_PARAMETER);
            break;
    }

    LONG lRet;
    lRet = InternetSetFilePointer(m_hFile, lOffset, NULL, nFrom, m_dwContext);
```

```
    if (lRet == -1)
        AfxThrowInternetException(m_dwContext);

    return lRet;
}
```

CInternetFile also takes care of cleaning up its associated HINTERNET handle. The destructor calls Close and Close calls InternetCloseHandle (see Listing 7-15). However, because CInternetFile objects are created dynamically, you have to remember to call `delete` on the object pointer.

Listing 7-15   CInternetFile cleanup

```
CInternetFile::~CInternetFile()
{
    if (m_hFile != NULL)
    {
#ifdef _DEBUG
        USES_CONVERSION;
        LPCTSTR pszName = A2CT(GetRuntimeClass()->m_lpszClassName);
        TRACE2("Warning: destroying an open %s with handle %8.8X\n",
            pszName, m_hFile);
#endif
        Close();
    }

    if (m_pbReadBuffer != NULL)
        delete m_pbReadBuffer;

    if (m_pbWriteBuffer != NULL)
        delete m_pbWriteBuffer;
}

void CInternetFile::Close()
{
    if (m_hFile != NULL)
    {
        Flush();
        InternetCloseHandle(m_hFile);
        _afxSessionMap.RemoveKey(m_hFile);
        m_hFile = NULL;

        if (m_pbWriteBuffer != NULL)
        {
```

```
        delete [] m_pbWriteBuffer;
        m_pbWriteBuffer = NULL;
    }

    if (m_pbReadBuffer != NULL)
    {
        delete [] m_pbReadBuffer;
        m_pbReadBuffer = NULL;
    }
  }
}
```

Once again, the CInternetFile class was designed to behave like the CFile and CStdioFile classes. If you're familiar with these standard MFC file classes, you should have no problem working with the CInternetFile, CHttpFile, and CGopherFile classes. I'll look at how to use both CHttpFile and CGopherFile shortly.

CInternetConnection

CInternetConnection is the base class for all protocol-specific connection classes, including CHttpConnection, CFtpConnection, and CGopherConnection. The class declaration (see Listing 7-16) is simple. Like the other classes we've looked at so far, CInternetConnection also has methods to set and to query the Internet options for the connection handle.

Probably the most important member of CInternetConnection is m_hConnection, which holds HINTERNET returned by InternetConnect. If you look in the source code for CInternetConnection, you won't find it calling InternetConnect anywhere. So where does m_hConnection get set? We'll see the answer to this when we look at each protocol-specific connection class. The constructor for each of these classes calls InternetConnect and sets m_hConnection to the returned handle.

Listing 7-16   **CInternetConnection class declaration**

```
class CInternetConnection : public CObject
{
public:
    CInternetConnection(CInternetSession* pSession, LPCTSTR pstrServer,
        INTERNET_PORT nPort = INTERNET_INVALID_PORT_NUMBER,
        DWORD dwContext = 1);
```

```
// Operations
    operator HINTERNET() const;
    DWORD GetContext() const;
    CInternetSession* GetSession() const;

    CString GetServerName() const;

    BOOL QueryOption(DWORD dwOption, LPVOID lpBuffer,
            LPDWORD lpdwBufLen) const;
    BOOL QueryOption(DWORD dwOption, DWORD& dwValue) const;
    BOOL QueryOption(DWORD dwOption, CString& refString) const;

    BOOL SetOption(DWORD dwOption, LPVOID lpBuffer, DWORD dwBufferLength,
        DWORD dwFlags = 0);
    BOOL SetOption(DWORD dwOption, DWORD dwValue, DWORD dwFlags = 0);

// Implementation
protected:
    HINTERNET m_hConnection;
    DWORD m_dwContext;
    CInternetSession* m_pSession;
    virtual void Close();

    CString m_strServerName;
    INTERNET_PORT m_nPort;

public:
    ~CInternetConnection();
    DECLARE_DYNAMIC(CInternetConnection)

#ifdef _DEBUG
    virtual void Dump(CDumpContext& dc) const;
    void AssertValid() const;
#endif
};
```

The only thing that I want to show you about CInternetConnection is how it takes care of cleanup. Take a look at Listing 7-17, which shows the CInternetConnection destructor and Close method. As you can see, these look a lot like the other classes we've looked at up to this point.

Listing 7-17 CInternetConnection::Close

```
CInternetConnection::~CInternetConnection()
{
    if (m_hConnection != NULL)
    {
#ifdef _DEBUG
        USES_CONVERSION;
        LPCTSTR pszName = A2CT(GetRuntimeClass()->m_lpszClassName);
        TRACE3("Warning: Disconnecting %s handle %8.8X in context %8.8X at
                destruction.\n",
            pszName, m_hConnection, m_dwContext);
#endif
        Close();
    }
}

void CInternetConnection::Close()
{
    if (m_hConnection != NULL)
    {
        InternetCloseHandle(m_hConnection);
        _afxSessionMap.RemoveKey(m_hConnection);
        m_hConnection = NULL;
    }
}
```

 Because CInternetFile and CInternetConnection objects are created dynamically by other methods (CFtpConnection::OpenFile and CInternetSession::GetHttpConnection, for example), you must call delete to free them from memory.

HTTP Classes

Now we're ready to look at the HTTP protocol-specific classes. There are two HTTP classes that take care of HTTP protocol functionality: CHttpConnection and CHttpFile.

CHttpConnection

Let's begin by looking at CHttpConnection's class declaration (see Listing 7-18).

Listing 7-18   CHttpConnection class declaration

```
class CHttpConnection : public CInternetConnection
{
public:
    enum {
        _HTTP_VERB_MIN      = 0,
        HTTP_VERB_POST      = 0,
        HTTP_VERB_GET       = 1,
        HTTP_VERB_HEAD      = 2,
        HTTP_VERB_PUT       = 3,
        HTTP_VERB_LINK      = 4,
        HTTP_VERB_DELETE    = 5,
        HTTP_VERB_UNLINK    = 6,
        _HTTP_VERB_MAX      = 6,
    };

public:
    CHttpConnection(CInternetSession* pSession, HINTERNET hConnected,
        LPCTSTR pstrServer, DWORD dwContext);
    CHttpConnection(CInternetSession* pSession, LPCTSTR pstrServer,
        INTERNET_PORT nPort = INTERNET_INVALID_PORT_NUMBER,
        LPCTSTR pstrUserName = NULL, LPCTSTR pstrPassword = NULL,
        DWORD dwContext = 1);
    CHttpConnection(CInternetSession* pSession, LPCTSTR pstrServer,
        DWORD dwFlags, INTERNET_PORT nPort = INTERNET_INVALID_PORT_NUMBER,
        LPCTSTR pstrUserName = NULL, LPCTSTR pstrPassword = NULL,
        DWORD dwContext = 1);

    CHttpFile* OpenRequest(LPCTSTR pstrVerb,    LPCTSTR pstrObjectName,
        LPCTSTR pstrReferer = NULL,DWORD dwContext = 1,
        LPCTSTR* ppstrAcceptTypes = NULL, LPCTSTR pstrVersion = NULL,
        DWORD dwFlags = INTERNET_FLAG_EXISTING_CONNECT);

    CHttpFile* OpenRequest(int nVerb, LPCTSTR pstrObjectName,
        LPCTSTR pstrReferer = NULL, DWORD dwContext = 1,
        LPCTSTR* ppstrAcceptTypes = NULL, LPCTSTR pstrVersion = NULL,
        DWORD dwFlags = INTERNET_FLAG_EXISTING_CONNECT);
```

```
// implementation
    ~CHttpConnection();
    virtual void Close();

protected:
    CString m_strServerName;
    static const LPCTSTR szHtmlVerbs[];

public:
#ifdef _DEBUG
    virtual void Dump(CDumpContext& dc) const;
    virtual void AssertValid() const;
#endif

    friend class CInternetSession;  // just to access szHtmlVerbs
    DECLARE_DYNAMIC(CHttpConnection)
};
```

There are several versions of the CHttpConnection constructor. The first constructor assumes that the connection handle already exists. Thus, it takes an HINTERNET handle in hConnected (this should be a handle returned by InternetConnect). Because the first constructor assumes that you've already called InternetConnect, it doesn't attempt to call InternetConnect.

The only difference between the second and third constructors is the existence of a dwFlags parameter in the third constructor. The third constructor allows you to specify the dwFlags parameter, which is used in the call to InternetConnect. The second constructor, which doesn't accept dwFlags, simply uses zero for dwFlags in its call to InternetConnect.

Remember that CInternetSession::GetHttpConnection dynamically creates an instance of CHttpConnection using the third version of the constructor. Let's take a look at this constructor in more detail (see Listing 7-19). As you'll notice, this is where InternetConnect gets called.

Listing 7-19   CHttpConnection constructor

```
CHttpConnection::CHttpConnection(CInternetSession* pSession,
    LPCTSTR pstrServer, DWORD dwFlags,
    INTERNET_PORT nPort /* = INTERNET_INVALID_PORT_NUMBER */,
    LPCTSTR pstrUserName /* = NULL */,
    LPCTSTR pstrPassword /* = NULL */,
```

```
        DWORD dwContext /* = 1 */)
        : CInternetConnection(pSession, pstrServer, nPort, dwContext)
{

    ASSERT(pSession != NULL);
    ASSERT_KINDOF(CInternetSession, pSession);

    m_hConnection = InternetConnect((HINTERNET) *pSession, pstrServer,
        nPort, pstrUserName, pstrPassword, INTERNET_SERVICE_HTTP,
        dwFlags, m_dwContext);

    if (m_hConnection == NULL)
        AfxThrowInternetException(m_dwContext);
    else
        _afxSessionMap.SetAt(m_hConnection, m_pSession);
}
```

There are also two versions of OpenRequest, which encapsulates the functionality of the HttpOpenRequest function. The only difference between the two versions is that the first allows you to specify the method string yourself whereas the second lets you use an enum value that represents a standard method string. Let's look at how this works (see Listing 7-20).

Listing 7-20   CHttpConnection::OpenRequest

```
const LPCTSTR CHttpConnection::szHtmlVerbs[] = {
    _T("POST"),
    _T("GET"),
    _T("HEAD"),
    _T("PUT"),
    _T("LINK"),
    _T("DELETE"),
    _T("UNLINK"),
};

CHttpFile* CHttpConnection::OpenRequest(LPCTSTR pstrVerb,
    LPCTSTR pstrObjectName, LPCTSTR pstrReferer, DWORD dwContext,
    LPCTSTR* ppstrAcceptTypes, LPCTSTR pstrVersion, DWORD dwFlags)
{
    ASSERT_VALID(this);
    ASSERT(m_hConnection != NULL);

    if (dwContext == 1)
        dwContext = m_dwContext;
```

```
    if (pstrVersion == NULL)
        pstrVersion = HTTP_VERSION;


    HINTERNET hFile;
    hFile = HttpOpenRequest(m_hConnection, pstrVerb, pstrObjectName,
        pstrVersion, pstrReferer, ppstrAcceptTypes, dwFlags, dwContext);


    CHttpFile* pRet = new CHttpFile(hFile, pstrVerb, pstrObjectName, this);
    pRet->m_dwContext = dwContext;
    return pRet;
}


CHttpFile* CHttpConnection::OpenRequest(int nVerb,
    LPCTSTR pstrObjectName, LPCTSTR pstrReferer, DWORD dwContext,
    LPCTSTR* ppstrAcceptTypes, LPCTSTR pstrVersion, DWORD dwFlags)
{
    ASSERT_VALID(this);
    ASSERT(m_hConnection != NULL);

    ASSERT(nVerb >= _HTTP_VERB_MIN && nVerb <= _HTTP_VERB_MAX);

    LPCTSTR pstrVerb;
    if (nVerb >= _HTTP_VERB_MIN && nVerb <= _HTTP_VERB_MAX)
        pstrVerb = szHtmlVerbs[nVerb];
    else
        pstrVerb = _T("");

    return OpenRequest(pstrVerb, pstrObjectName, pstrReferer,
        dwContext, ppstrAcceptTypes, pstrVersion, dwFlags);
}
```

The second version of OpenRequest looks up the method string in szHtmlVerbs and then calls the first version of OpenRequest. The first version does two important things. First, it calls HttpOpenRequest using the connection handle stored in m_hConnection along with the other specified parameters. Then it creates an instance of CHttpFile using the handle returned by HttpOpenRequest and returns a pointer to the new object.

Before looking at CHttpFile, I want to make one observation about CHttpConnection cleanup. Notice that in Listing 7-21 the CHttpConnection destructor does nothing and the CHttpConnection::Close method simply calls the base class. Although this can be confusing at first, once you think about it, it makes perfect sense. Don't forget that in C++ the base class destructor is called implicitly. Hence, the CInternetConnection destructor is called automatically, as is CInternetConnection::Close. And because the connection handle is stored in CInternetConnection, CHttpConnection has nothing else to free.

Listing 7-21   CHttpConnection cleanup

```
CHttpConnection::~CHttpConnection()
{
}
void CHttpConnection::Close()
{
    CInternetConnection::Close();
}
```

CHttpFile

The CHttpFile class encapsulates the rest of the WinInet HTTP functionality. After looking at the class declaration in Listing 7-22, you can probably guess the WinInet HTTP function encapsulated by a particular method. For example, if you guessed that AddRequestHeaders encapsulates HttpAddRequestHeaders, you're correct. Or if you guessed that QueryInfo encapsulates HttpQueryInfo, you're also correct. This class and its implementation are very straightforward.

Listing 7-22   CHttpFile class declaration

```
class CHttpFile : public CInternetFile
{
// Constructors
protected:
    CHttpFile(HINTERNET hFile, HINTERNET hSession, LPCTSTR pstrObject,
        LPCTSTR pstrServer, LPCTSTR pstrVerb, DWORD dwContext);
    CHttpFile(HINTERNET hFile, LPCTSTR pstrVerb, LPCTSTR pstrObject,
        CHttpConnection* pConnection);

// Operations
public:
    BOOL AddRequestHeaders(LPCTSTR pstrHeaders, DWORD dwFlags =
        HTTP_ADDREQ_FLAG_ADD_IF_NEW, int dwHeadersLen = -1);
    BOOL AddRequestHeaders(CString& str,
        DWORD dwFlags = HTTP_ADDREQ_FLAG_ADD_IF_NEW);
```

```
    BOOL SendRequest(LPCTSTR pstrHeaders = NULL, DWORD dwHeadersLen = 0,
        LPVOID lpOptional = NULL, DWORD dwOptionalLen = 0);
    BOOL SendRequest(CString& strHeaders,
        LPVOID lpOptional = NULL, DWORD dwOptionalLen = 0);

    BOOL QueryInfo(DWORD dwInfoLevel, LPVOID lpvBuffer,
        LPDWORD lpdwBufferLength, LPDWORD lpdwIndex = NULL) const;
    BOOL QueryInfo(DWORD dwInfoLevel, CString& str,
        LPDWORD dwIndex = NULL) const;
    BOOL QueryInfo(DWORD dwInfoLevel, SYSTEMTIME* pSysTime,
        LPDWORD dwIndex = NULL) const;
    BOOL QueryInfo(DWORD dwInfoLevel, DWORD& dwResult,
        LPDWORD dwIndex = NULL) const;
    BOOL QueryInfoStatusCode(DWORD& dwStatusCode) const;

    DWORD ErrorDlg(CWnd* pParent = NULL, DWORD dwError =
        ERROR_INTERNET_INCORRECT_PASSWORD,
        DWORD dwFlags = FLAGS_ERROR_UI_FLAGS_GENERATE_DATA |
        FLAGS_ERROR_UI_FLAGS_CHANGE_OPTIONS, LPVOID* lppvData = NULL);

// Attributes
public:
    CString GetVerb() const;
    CString GetObject() const;
    virtual CString GetFileURL() const;
    virtual void Close();

// Implementation
public:
    virtual ~CHttpFile();
protected:
    CString m_strObject;
    CString m_strVerb;

#ifdef _DEBUG
    virtual void AssertValid() const;
    virtual void Dump(CDumpContext& dc) const;
#endif

    friend class CHttpConnection;
    friend class CInternetSession;
    DECLARE_DYNAMIC(CHttpFile)
};
```

The overloaded QueryInfo methods provide a convenient interface to get the type of HTTP information you're looking for. As you've learned, the HttpQueryInfo method can return various types of information. Each QueryInfo overload returns one of the possible types to save you from the details.

There is even a QueryInfoStatusCode method (see Listing 7-23), which gets one of the most common pieces of HTTP status information—the HTTP status code. This should look very familiar. Remember the status code function that we implemented back in Chapter 4?

Listing 7-23   CHttpFile::QueryInfoStatusCode

```
BOOL CHttpFile::QueryInfoStatusCode(DWORD& dwStatusCode) const
{
    ASSERT_VALID(this);
    ASSERT(m_hFile != NULL);

    TCHAR szBuffer[80];
    DWORD dwLen = _countof(szBuffer);
    BOOL bRet;

    bRet = HttpQueryInfo(m_hFile, HTTP_QUERY_STATUS_CODE,
            szBuffer, &dwLen, NULL);

    if (bRet)
        dwStatusCode = (DWORD) _ttol(szBuffer);
    return bRet;
}
```

AddRequestHeaders, SendRequest, and ErrorDlg call HttpAddRequestHeaders, HttpSendRequest, and InternetErrorDlg, respectively. These methods do nothing more than call the underlying HTTP function (along with some validation and error handling of course). Nevertheless, I would encourage you to browse the implementation of this class if you plan on using it.

HTTP Example

To help put this in perspective, the example in Listing 7-24 illustrates a simple HTTP session that downloads the ie40.htm file located at *www.microsoft.com*. This example should help you understand how these HTTP classes are used together.

WININET MFC CLASSES • 251

Listing 7-24 Http example

```
CString GetMicrosoftWebPage()
{
    CString strResponse;
    try
    {
        CInternetSession session;

        CHttpConnection* pConnection =
                session.GetHttpConnection("www.microsoft.com");

        CHttpFile* pFile = pConnection->OpenRequest(HTTP_VERB_GET, "ie40.htm");

        if (pFile->SendRequest())
        {
            DWORD dwStatus;

            pFile->QueryInfoStatusCode(dwStatus);
            if (HTTP_STATUS_OK == dwStatus)
            {
                char szBuffer[BUFFLEN];
                DWORD dwRead=0;

                for (;;)
                {
                    dwRead = pFile->Read(szBuffer, BUFFLEN-1);
                    strResponse += szBuffer;
                    if (dwRead == 0)
                        break;
                }
            }
        }
    }
    catch(CInternetException* e)
    {
        e->ReportError();
        e->Delete();
    }
    return strResponse;
}
```

FTP Classes

There are also two FTP-specific MFC classes: CFtpConnection and CFtpFindFile. In this section I'll show how to use these classes to take advantage of WinInet's FTP functionality.

CFtpConnection

Like CHttpConnection, CFtpConnection encapsulates the functionality of InternetConnect. CFtpConnection, however, also encapsulates most of the WinInet FTP functions. Just about anything that you would want to do with FTP can be accomplished through this class. Take a look at Listing 7-25, which contains the CFtpConnection class declaration.

Listing 7-25   **CFtpConnection class declaration**

```
class CFtpConnection : public CInternetConnection
{
public:
    CFtpConnection(CInternetSession* pSession, HINTERNET hConnected,
        LPCTSTR pstrServer, DWORD dwContext);
    CFtpConnection(CInternetSession* pSession, LPCTSTR pstrServer,
        LPCTSTR pstrUserName = NULL, LPCTSTR pstrPassword = NULL,
        DWORD dwContext = 0,
        INTERNET_PORT nPort = INTERNET_INVALID_PORT_NUMBER,
        BOOL bPassive = FALSE);

    BOOL SetCurrentDirectory(LPCTSTR pstrDirName);

    BOOL GetCurrentDirectory(CString& strDirName) const;
    BOOL GetCurrentDirectory(LPTSTR pstrDirName, LPDWORD lpdwLen) const;
    BOOL GetCurrentDirectoryAsURL(LPTSTR pstrName, LPDWORD lpdwLen) const;
    BOOL GetCurrentDirectoryAsURL(CString& strDirName) const;

    BOOL RemoveDirectory(LPCTSTR pstrDirName);
    BOOL CreateDirectory(LPCTSTR pstrDirName);
    BOOL Rename(LPCTSTR pstrExisting, LPCTSTR pstrNew);
    BOOL Remove(LPCTSTR pstrFileName);

    BOOL PutFile(LPCTSTR pstrLocalFile, LPCTSTR pstrRemoteFile,
        DWORD dwFlags = FTP_TRANSFER_TYPE_BINARY, DWORD dwContext = 1);
```

```
    BOOL GetFile(LPCTSTR pstrRemoteFile, LPCTSTR pstrLocalFile,
        BOOL bFailIfExists = TRUE,
        DWORD dwAttributes = FILE_ATTRIBUTE_NORMAL,
        DWORD dwFlags = FTP_TRANSFER_TYPE_BINARY, DWORD dwContext = 1);

    CInternetFile* OpenFile(LPCTSTR pstrFileName,
        DWORD dwAccess = GENERIC_READ,
        DWORD dwFlags = FTP_TRANSFER_TYPE_BINARY, DWORD dwContext = 1);

    virtual void Close();

// implementation
    ~CFtpConnection();

protected:
    CString m_strServerName;

public:
#ifdef _DEBUG
    virtual void Dump(CDumpContext& dc) const;
    virtual void AssertValid() const;
#endif

    DECLARE_DYNAMIC(CFtpConnection)
};
```

The design of CFtpConnection is very similar to that of CHttpConnection. In fact, the constructor and destructor for CFtpConnection are almost identical to those in CHttpConnection. Because these aspects of the class are so similar, I won't go over them in more detail.

Most of the methods in this class should look familiar. Almost every WinInet FTP function has a corresponding method in this class. For example, the function FtpGetFile corresponds to CFtpConnection::GetFile. You can probably imagine how these methods are implemented.

Listing 7-26 shows the implementation for most of the CFtpConnection methods. I removed all Asserts to make them easier to read.

Listing 7-26   CFtpConnection implementation

```
BOOL CFtpConnection::Remove(LPCTSTR pstrFileName)
{
```

```
    return FtpDeleteFile(m_hConnection, pstrFileName);
}


BOOL CFtpConnection::Rename(LPCTSTR pstrExisting, LPCTSTR pstrNew)
{
    return FtpRenameFile(m_hConnection, pstrExisting, pstrNew);
}


BOOL CFtpConnection::CreateDirectory(LPCTSTR pstrDirName)
{
    return FtpCreateDirectory(m_hConnection, pstrDirName);
}


BOOL CFtpConnection::RemoveDirectory(LPCTSTR pstrDirName)
{
    return FtpRemoveDirectory(m_hConnection, pstrDirName);
}


BOOL CFtpConnection::SetCurrentDirectory(LPCTSTR pstrDirName)
{
    return FtpSetCurrentDirectory(m_hConnection, pstrDirName);
}


BOOL CFtpConnection::GetCurrentDirectory(LPTSTR pstrDirName,
    LPDWORD lpdwLen) const
{
    return FtpGetCurrentDirectory(m_hConnection, pstrDirName, lpdwLen);
}

BOOL CFtpConnection::GetCurrentDirectoryAsURL(CString& strDirName) const
{
    CString strDirectory;
    if (!GetCurrentDirectory(strDirectory))
        return FALSE;

    strDirName = szURLftp;
    strDirName += GetServerName();

    if (strDirectory[0] != '/')
        strDirName += '/';
```

```
        strDirName += strDirectory;
        return TRUE;
}


BOOL CFtpConnection::GetCurrentDirectoryAsURL(LPTSTR pstrName,
        LPDWORD lpdwLen) const
{
        CString strTemp;

        if (lpdwLen == NULL || !GetCurrentDirectoryAsURL(strTemp))
            return FALSE;

        if (pstrName == NULL)
            *lpdwLen = strTemp.GetLength();
        else
            lstrcpyn(pstrName, (LPCTSTR) strTemp, max(0, *lpdwLen -1));

        return TRUE;
}


BOOL CFtpConnection::GetCurrentDirectory(CString& strDirName) const
{
        DWORD dwLen = INTERNET_MAX_PATH_LENGTH;
        LPTSTR pstrTarget = strDirName.GetBufferSetLength(dwLen);
        BOOL bRet = FtpGetCurrentDirectory(m_hConnection, pstrTarget, &dwLen);

        if (bRet)
            strDirName.ReleaseBuffer(dwLen);
        else
            strDirName.ReleaseBuffer(0);

        return bRet;
}


CInternetFile* CFtpConnection::OpenFile(LPCTSTR pstrFileName,
        DWORD dwAccess /* = GENERIC_READ */,
        DWORD dwFlags /* = FTP_TRANSFER_TYPE_BINARY */,
        DWORD dwContext /* = 1 */)
{
        HINTERNET hFile;
```

```
    if (dwContext == 1)
        dwContext = m_dwContext;


    hFile = FtpOpenFile(m_hConnection, pstrFileName, dwAccess,
        dwFlags, dwContext);
    if (hFile == NULL)
        AfxThrowInternetException(dwContext);


    CInternetFile* pFile = new CInternetFile(hFile, pstrFileName, this,
        (dwAccess == GENERIC_READ));
    return pFile;
}


BOOL CFtpConnection::PutFile(LPCTSTR pstrLocalFile, LPCTSTR pstrRemoteFile,
    DWORD dwFlags /* = FTP_TRANSFER_TYPE_BINARY */,
    DWORD dwContext /* = 1 */)
{
    if (dwContext == 1)
        dwContext = m_dwContext;


    return FtpPutFile(m_hConnection, pstrLocalFile, pstrRemoteFile,
        dwFlags, dwContext);
}


BOOL CFtpConnection::GetFile(LPCTSTR pstrRemoteFile, LPCTSTR pstrLocalFile,
    BOOL bFailIfExists /* = TRUE */,
    DWORD dwAttributes /* = FILE_ATTRIBUTE_NORMAL */,
    DWORD dwFlags /* = FTP_TRANSFER_TYPE_BINARY */, DWORD dwContext /* = 1 */)
{
    if (dwContext == 1)
        dwContext = m_dwContext;


    return FtpGetFile(m_hConnection, pstrRemoteFile, pstrLocalFile,
        bFailIfExists, dwAttributes, dwFlags, dwContext);
}
```

As you can see, the implementation of this class is very predictable. It does nothing more than call the corresponding WinInet FTP function and manage state. Regardless of its simplicity, this class greatly simplifies the process of using the WinInet FTP functions.

You may have noticed that CFtpConnection doesn't contain any method that resembles FtpFindFirstFile. This is because the concept of enumerating files warrants its own class: CFtpFileFind.

CFtpFileFind

CFtpFileFind encapsulates the process of enumerating remote FTP directories and files. We accomplished this using the WinInet API by using FtpFindFirstFile and InternetFindNextFile. Let's take a look at the CFtpFileFind class declaration (see Listing 7-27).

Listing 7-27   CFtpFileFind class declaration

```
class CFtpFileFind : public CFileFind
{
public:
    CFtpFileFind(CFtpConnection* pConnection, DWORD dwContext = 1);
    virtual ~CFtpFileFind();

    virtual BOOL FindFile(LPCTSTR pstrName = NULL,
        DWORD dwFlags = INTERNET_FLAG_RELOAD);
    virtual BOOL FindNextFile();
    CString GetFileURL() const;

// implementation
protected:
    virtual void CloseContext();
    CFtpConnection* m_pConnection;
    DWORD m_dwContext;

public:
#ifdef _DEBUG
    virtual void Dump(CDumpContext& dc) const;
    virtual void AssertValid() const;
#endif

    DECLARE_DYNAMIC(CFtpFileFind)
};
```

The constructor and destructor (and most of the other methods) don't do anything worth mentioning. The two CFtpFileFind methods that make things happen are FindFile and FindNextFile. Let's look at these methods in more detail (see Listing 7-28).

Listing 7-28   **CFtpFileFind::FindFile and CFtpFileFind::FindNextFile**

```
BOOL CFtpFileFind::FindFile(LPCTSTR pstrName /* = NULL */,
    DWORD dwFlags /* = INTERNET_FLAG_RELOAD */)
{
    ASSERT(m_pConnection != NULL);
    ASSERT_VALID(m_pConnection);

    if (m_pConnection == NULL)
        return FALSE;

    Close();
    m_pNextInfo = new WIN32_FIND_DATA;
    m_bGotLast = FALSE;

    if (pstrName == NULL)
        pstrName = _T("*");
    _tcscpy(((LPWIN32_FIND_DATA) m_pNextInfo)->cFileName, pstrName);

    m_hContext = FtpFindFirstFile((HINTERNET) *m_pConnection,
        pstrName, (LPWIN32_FIND_DATA) m_pNextInfo, dwFlags, m_dwContext);

    if (m_hContext == NULL)
    {
        Close();
        return FALSE;
    }

    LPCTSTR pstrRoot = _tcspbrk(pstrName, _T("\\/"));
    CString strCWD;
    m_pConnection->GetCurrentDirectory(strCWD);

    if (pstrRoot == NULL)
    {
        if (m_pConnection->SetCurrentDirectory(pstrName))
        {
            m_pConnection->GetCurrentDirectory(m_strRoot);
            m_pConnection->SetCurrentDirectory(strCWD);
        }
        else
            m_strRoot = strCWD;
```

```
        }
        else
        {
            // find the last forward or backward whack

            int nLast;
            LPCTSTR pstrOther = _tcsrchr(pstrName, '\\');
            pstrRoot = _tcsrchr(pstrName, '/');

            if (pstrRoot == NULL)
                pstrRoot = pstrName;
            if (pstrOther == NULL)
                pstrOther = pstrName;

            if (pstrRoot >= pstrOther)
                nLast = pstrRoot - pstrName;
            else
                nLast = pstrOther - pstrName;

            // from the start to the last whack is the root

            if (nLast == 0)
                nLast++;

            m_strRoot = pstrName;
            m_strRoot = m_strRoot.Left(nLast);
        }

        return TRUE;
}

BOOL CFtpFileFind::FindNextFile()
{
    ASSERT(m_hContext != NULL);
    if (m_hContext == NULL)
        return FALSE;

    if (m_pFoundInfo == NULL)
        m_pFoundInfo = new WIN32_FIND_DATA;
```

```
    ASSERT_VALID(this);
    void* pTemp = m_pFoundInfo;
    m_pFoundInfo = m_pNextInfo;
    m_pNextInfo = pTemp;

    return InternetFindNextFile(m_hContext, m_pNextInfo);
}
```

Notice that one of the first things CFtpFileFind::FindFile does is call Close. Remember that there can only be one FtpFindFirstFile enumeration handle open in a given session. Hence, each time you call CFtpFileFind::FindFirst to begin a new enumeration, the method takes care of this nasty detail for you.

Another nice benefit of this class is the memory management. It takes care of allocating and freeing the memory used by the WIN32_FIND_DATA structures. All you need to do is call FindFile or FindNextFile and then you can call any of the CFileFind (base class) methods, such as CFileFind::GetFileName.

FTP Example

The example in this section shows you how to use both CFtpConnection and CFtpFileFind. The example assumes that there is a dialog class called CMyDialog, which contains a CListCtrl called m_RemoteList and a CListCtrl called m_LocalList. The OnGet method is called when the user selects a remote file and presses the dialog's Get button (see Listing 7-29).

Listing 7-29   FTP example

```
// global initialization
/////////////////////////////
CInternetSession session;

CFtpConnection* g_pFTPConnection session.GetFtpConnection ( "www.server.com",
        "anonymous", "myemail@server.com", INTERNET_DEFAULT_FTP_PORT);

// enumerates files and fills in dialog's CListCtrl
void CMyDialog::EnumerateFiles()
{
    m_RemoteList.ResetContent();

    CFtpFileFind FtpFileFind(g_pFTPConnection);
    if (FtpFileFind.FindFile())
```

```
    {
        while(FtpFileFind.FindNextFile())
            m_RemoteList.AddString(FtpFileFind.GetFileName());
        m_RemoteList.AddString(FtpFileFind.GetFileName());
    }
    FtpFileFind.Close();
}


// gets the selected remote file
void CMyDialog::OnGet()
{
    CString strFile;
    int iIndex = m_RemoteList.GetCurSel();
    if (LB_ERR == iIndex)
    {
        AfxMessageBox("You must select a remote file first");
        return;
    }
    m_RemoteList.GetText(iIndex, strFile);
    g_pFTPConnection->GetFile(strFile, strFile, FALSE);
    FillLocalList();
}
```

Gopher Classes

Interestingly, there are more Gopher-specific classes than HTTP or FTP classes. Like
the other connection classes, there is a CGopherConnection class, which encapsulates
the Gopher connection functionality. Like CHttpFile, there is a CGopherFile class.
Like CFtpFileFind, there is a CGopherFileFind class. And finally, there is a class
unique to Gopher called CGopherLocator, which encapsulates the Gopher locator
functionality.

CGopherConnection

The CGopherConnection class is designed like CHttpConnection and
CFtpConnection. There are, however, a few Gopher-specific methods that make
up this class such as CreateLocator and GetAttribute (see Listing 7-30).

Listing 7-30   CGopherConnection class declaration

```
class CGopherConnection : public CInternetConnection
{
public:
    CGopherConnection(CInternetSession* pSession,
        HINTERNET hConnected, LPCTSTR pstrServer, DWORD dwContext);
    CGopherConnection(CInternetSession* pSession, LPCTSTR pstrServer,
        LPCTSTR pstrUserName = NULL, LPCTSTR pstrPassword = NULL,
        DWORD dwContext = 0,
        INTERNET_PORT nPort = INTERNET_INVALID_PORT_NUMBER);

    CGopherFile* OpenFile(CGopherLocator& refLocator, DWORD dwFlags = 0,
        LPCTSTR pstrView = NULL, DWORD dwContext = 1);

    CGopherLocator CreateLocator(LPCTSTR pstrDisplayString,
        LPCTSTR pstrSelectorString, DWORD dwGopherType);

    BOOL CGopherConnection::GetAttribute(CGopherLocator& refLocator,
        CString strRequestedAttributes, CString& strResult);

    static CGopherLocator CreateLocator(LPCTSTR pstrLocator);
    static CGopherLocator CreateLocator(LPCTSTR pstrServerName,
        LPCTSTR pstrDisplayString,
        LPCTSTR pstrSelectorString, DWORD dwGopherType,
        INTERNET_PORT nPort = INTERNET_INVALID_PORT_NUMBER);

// implementation
    ~CGopherConnection();
    virtual void Close();

public:
#ifdef _DEBUG
    virtual void Dump(CDumpContext& dc) const;
    virtual void AssertValid() const;
#endif
    DECLARE_DYNAMIC(CGopherConnection)
};
```

Hence, the CGopherConnection class gives you an easy interface to create CGopherLocator objects that can be used by the other Gopher classes. As you learned in the section on the Gopher protocol, the locator string is really what makes everything happen.

CGopherLocator

CGopherLocator is nothing more than a helper class that knows a little about a Gopher locator string. The class contains a CString member that holds the locator string. Plus, it contains the GetLocatorType method that knows how to determine the locator type from the locator string (see Listing 7-31).

Listing 7-31   CGopherLocator class declaration

```
class CGopherLocator : public CObject
{

public:
    ~CGopherLocator();
    operator LPCTSTR() const;
    CGopherLocator(const CGopherLocator& ref);
    BOOL GetLocatorType(DWORD& dwRef) const;

private:
    // this only created by CGopherConnection::CreateLocator or by
serialization
    CGopherLocator(LPCTSTR pstrLocator, DWORD dwLocLen);

    CString m_Locator;  // _not_ a zero-terminated string!
    DWORD m_dwBufferLength;

    friend class CGopherConnection;
    friend class CGopherFile;
};
```

CGopherFile

The CGopherFile class is only used after a call to CGopherConnection::OpenFile. As you can see, CGopherFile derives from CInternetFile and is very similar to CHttpFile. You would use this class when you've found a file that you wish to read or if you wish to write to a remote Gopher file (see Listing 7-32).

Listing 7-32 CGopherFile class declaration

```
class CGopherFile : public CInternetFile
{

// Constructors
protected:
    CGopherFile(HINTERNET hFile, CGopherLocator& refLocator,
        CGopherConnection* pConnection);
    CGopherFile(HINTERNET hFile, HINTERNET hSession,
        LPCTSTR pstrLocator, DWORD dwLocLen, DWORD dwContext);
// Operations
public:
    virtual void Close();
    virtual void Write(const void* lpBuf, UINT nCount);
    void WriteString(LPCTSTR pstr);

// Implementation
protected:
    CGopherLocator m_Locator;
public:
    virtual ~CGopherFile();

#ifdef _DEBUG
    virtual void AssertValid() const;
    virtual void Dump(CDumpContext& dc) const;
#endif

    friend class CInternetSession;
    friend class CGopherConnection;
    DECLARE_DYNAMIC(CGopherFile)
};
```

CGopherFileFind

Finally, the CGopherFileFind class accomplishes the same task as CFtpFileFind—it enumerates remote Gopher files and directories. Look at the class declaration in Listing 7-33, and notice that it also has FindFile and FindNextFile methods. The main difference, however, is that FindFile and FindNextFile need a CGopherLocator object.

Listing 7-33   **CGopherFileFind class declaration**

```
class CGopherFileFind : public CFileFind
{
public:
    CGopherFileFind(CGopherConnection* pConnection, DWORD dwContext = 1);
    virtual ~CGopherFileFind();

    virtual BOOL FindFile(CGopherLocator& refLocator, LPCTSTR pstrString,
        DWORD dwFlags = INTERNET_FLAG_RELOAD);
    virtual BOOL FindFile(LPCTSTR pstrString,
        DWORD dwFlags = INTERNET_FLAG_RELOAD);
    virtual BOOL FindNextFile();

    virtual BOOL IsDots() const;

    virtual BOOL GetLastWriteTime(FILETIME* pTimeStamp) const;
    virtual BOOL GetLastAccessTime(FILETIME* pTimeStamp) const;
    virtual BOOL GetCreationTime(FILETIME* pTimeStamp) const;
    virtual BOOL GetLastWriteTime(CTime& refTime) const;
    virtual BOOL GetLastAccessTime(CTime& refTime) const;
    virtual BOOL GetCreationTime(CTime& refTime) const;

    CGopherLocator GetLocator() const;
    CString GetScreenName() const;

    virtual DWORD GetLength() const;
#if defined(_X86_) || defined(_ALPHA_)
    virtual __int64 GetLength64() const;
#endif

protected:
    virtual void CloseContext();
    CGopherConnection* m_pConnection;
    DWORD m_dwContext;

// implementation
public:
    // Unsupported APIs
```

```
    CString GetFileName() const;
    CString GetFilePath() const;
    CString GetFileTitle() const;
    CString GetFileURL() const;
    CString GetRoot() const;

#ifdef _DEBUG
    virtual void Dump(CDumpContext& dc) const;
    virtual void AssertValid() const;
#endif
    DECLARE_DYNAMIC(CGopherFileFind)
};
```

Also notice that CGopherFileFind encapsulates the GOPHER_FIND_DATA structure by supplying various data retrieval methods like GetLastWriteTime, GetLastAccessTime, and so forth. By now you should be comfortable enough with how the MFC classes encapsulate the underlying API that you shouldn't have a problem working with the Gopher classes.

CInternetException

The last MFC Internet class that I want to cover briefly is CInternetException, which is used by most of the other classes that we've covered up to this point. CInternetException derives from CException and works like any standard exception class. You can use CInternetException with the standard try/catch blocks or with the MFC TRY/CATCH macros. Here is an example:

```
TRY
{
    // do some stuff with MFC Internet classes
}
CATCH(CInternetException, e)
{
    e->ReportError();
}
END_CATCH
```

If you're using the MFC Internet classes, you'll want to make sure that you understand which methods can throw CInternetException and handle it appropriately. The best place to find this information is in the MFC online documentation.

Global MFC Internet Functions

There are four global MFC Internet functions (see Table 7-1) that can be very helpful if you're using the MFC Internet classes. AfxParseURL and AfxParseURLEx both take care of parsing a URL string into its various components. If you look back at the code for CInternetSession::OpenURL (see Listing 7-9), you'll see that it uses this helper function to take care of business.

AfxGetInternetHandleType can take any HINTERNET handle and determine what type of Internet handle it really is. Finally, AfxThrowInternetException simplifies the process of throwing a CInternetException object manually. Refer to the MFC online documentation for more information on these global helper functions.

Table 7-1   Global MFC Internet functions

Name	Description
AfxParseURL	Parses a URL string and returns the type of service and its components.
AfxParseURLEx	Parses a URL string and returns the type of service and its components (including user name, password, and flags).
AfxGetInternetHandleType	Determines the type of Internet handle.
AfxThrowInternetException	Constructs and throws a CInternetException object.

Conclusion

In this chapter I covered all of the MFC Internet classes and looked at how these classes fit into the existing MFC class hierarchy. Instead of just walking you through the steps of how to use these classes, I showed you how these classes were implemented using the underlying WinInet API. If you have a solid understanding of how an API works and how MFC encapsulates the API, you should have no problem taking advantage of the MFC classes in your applications. This is not only true with the standard Win32 API, but also with the WinInet API. When you start looking at the code behind the MFC Internet classes, all the pieces start falling into place.

Once again, whether you use the standard WinInet API or the MFC Internet classes makes no difference. They are simply two different interfaces to the same functionality and, hence, to the same results. If you're a Win32 developer, you'll probably want to stick with the WinInet Win32 functions. However, if you're an object-oriented MFC enthusiast, the MFC Internet classes will surely brighten your day.

For a complete sample application written with the MFC Internet classes, see the Stock Watcher sample presented in Chapter 10.

8
Chapter

WinInet in Visual Basic

Because the number of Microsoft VB maniacs seems to be growing every day, I decided to include a chapter that discusses how to take advantage of WinInet in the VB environment. I've heard plenty of complaints and received too much e-mail from VB programmers trying to use WinInet in their applications. Although using the WinInet API is no different than using the Win32 API from within VB, it seems that it's still a point of much confusion.

There are really two ways to take advantage of WinInet in VB. First, you can use the Microsoft Internet Transfer Control, which encapsulates a subset of the WinInet API in the form of an ActiveX control. Or you can call the API functions found in wininet.dll directly, using standard VB/DLL techniques. In this chapter I'll show you how to take advantage of both methods.

This chapter is specifically for developers who want to use WinInet in VB. If you're a VB adversary and have no plans to touch WinInet outside the Visual C++ arena, you may want to skip this chapter. However, if VB is a definite possibility in your WinInet future, stay tuned—this chapter may save you some headaches.

VB 5.0

Everything that I discuss in this chapter assumes that you're using Microsoft VB 5.0. Both of the sample applications were written using VB 5.0 and the Microsoft IE 4.0 version of the WinInet library.

Microsoft Internet Transfer Control

The Microsoft Internet Transfer Control is an ActiveX control that encapsulates a subset of the WinInet API. This subset includes InternetOpenUrl functionality along with portions of the HTTP and FTP protocol functionality. Unfortunately, the Gopher protocol isn't included in this control. Nevertheless, the most commonly used portions of the WinInet API are accessible.

Although you can use the WinInet API directly, the Microsoft Internet Transfer Control fits nicely into the VB paradigm and is, therefore, much easier to use. You can begin using this control by selecting the Project | Components menu and selecting Microsoft Internet Transfer Control, as shown in Figure 8-1.

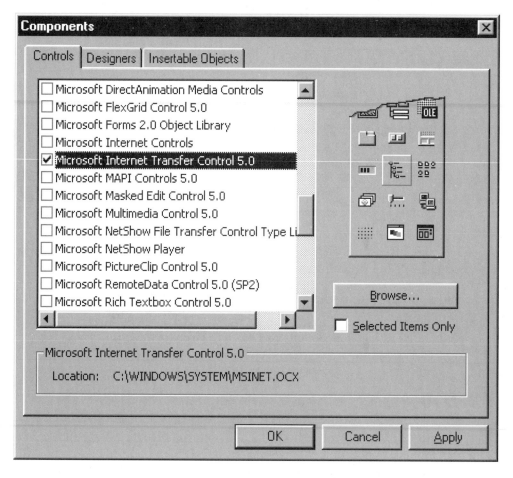

Figure 8-1   Selecting the Microsoft Internet Transfer Control

When you select the control and press OK, the Microsoft Internet Transfer Control shows up in the general control toolbar (see Figure 8-2). At this point you simply click on the control and place it on your form. This control is hidden at runtime even though you see an icon on the form.

If you double click on the icon, you should see the Microsoft Internet Transfer Control property pages that allow you to specify how you would like the control to behave. These property pages are illustrated in Figures 8-3 and 8-4.

As you look at these property pages, you should see things that look very familiar to you (now that we've covered the WinInet API in such depth). For example, the access type, proxy, host, port, user name, and password properties should be like second nature to you.

In this chapter I do not cover what these properties mean—that's what the rest of this book is about. I'm simply going to show you what is available and how to begin using the tools. If you're jumping headfirst into this chapter and are a bit lost in the WinInet details, refer back to the first few chapters, which cover the WinInet API completely.

Before looking at the sample application, let's look briefly at Microsoft Internet Transfer Control's properties, methods, and events.

Figure 8-2   VB general control toolbar

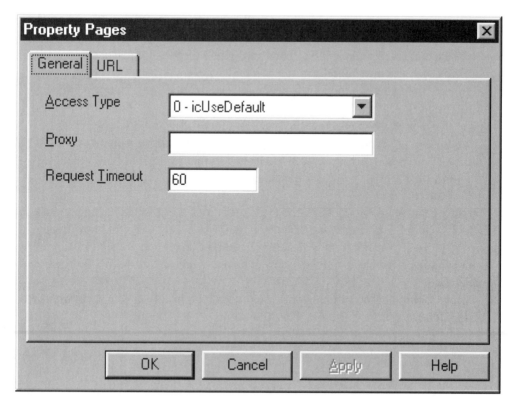

Figure 8-3   Microsoft Internet Transfer Control general property page

Properties

Table 8-1 describes the Microsoft Internet Transfer Control properties. Although some of these apply to most ActiveX controls, you should quickly notice the WinInet-specific properties and understand what they represent. Notice the hInternet property, which returns the HINTERNET handle for the underlying WinInet API. This is probably the most obvious link between the WinInet API and this higher level control.

Methods

Table 8-2 describes the Microsoft Internet Transfer Control methods. Can you guess what OpenURL encapsulates? If not, you'd better go back and review the beginning chapters again. One thing you should know is that OpenURL always behaves synchronously, and the Execute method always behaves asynchronously. Take a look at the VB online documentation for more information regarding these methods.

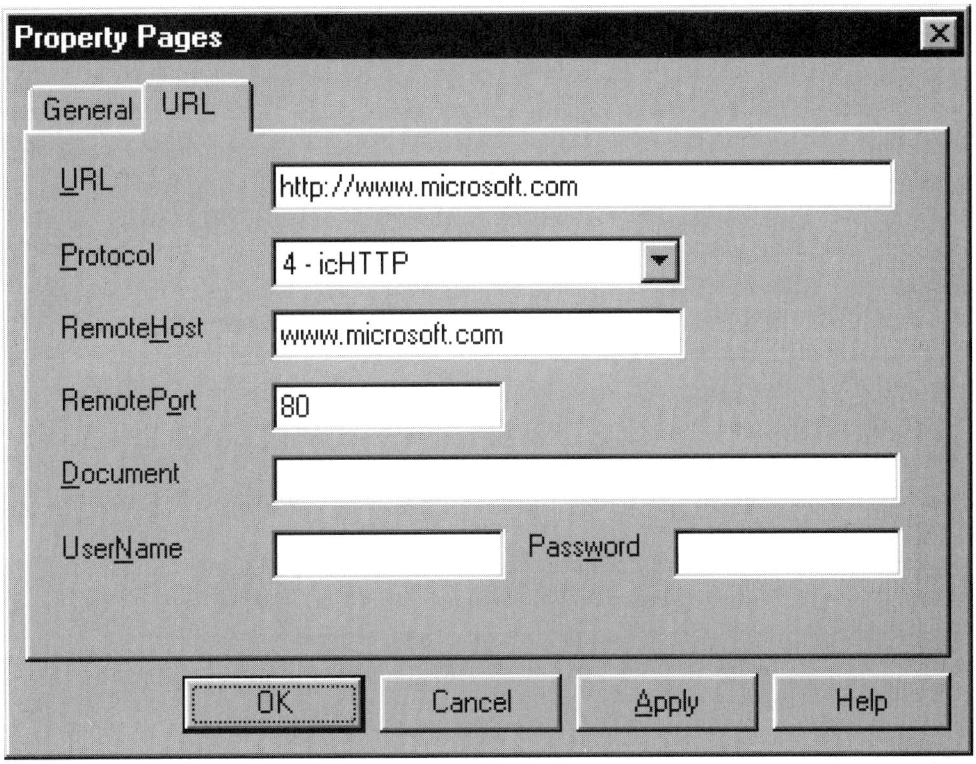

Figure 8-4   Microsoft Internet Transfer Control URL property page

Events

Table 8-3 describes the Microsoft Internet Transfer Control events, or should I say event. That's right—there is only one event for this control, called StateChanged. This event takes care of the underlying WinInet InternetStatusCallback mechanism.

As you can see, Microsoft Internet Transfer Control simplifies the process of using WinInet in VB. Now that we've covered the basics, let's walk through the process of using this control in a simple VB sample program that uses OpenURL.

Sample Application Using OpenURL

To begin, create a new project and insert the Microsoft Internet Transfer Control into the default project form (I called the control instance Inet1). Then design your form to look like the one in Figure 8-5. I called the URL text box TextURL and the gray result text box TextResult. Plus, the static text at the bottom of the dialog is called Status.

Table 8-1 Microsoft Internet Transfer Control properties

Name	Description
AccessType	Returns or sets the type of Internet access (direct or through a proxy, for example).
Document	Returns or sets the document to be retrieved or written to on the server.
hInternet	Returns the HINTERNET handle from the underlying WinInet API.
Index	Identifies an object in a collection uniquely.
Name	Returns the name/identifier of the control.
Object	Specifies the object you want to use in an automation task.
Parent	Returns the parent of the control.
Password	Returns or sets the password that is sent with the request to log on to remote computers.
Protocol	Returns or sets the protocol that is used with the Execute method.
Proxy	Returns or sets the name of the proxy server used to communicate with the Internet.
RemoteHost	Returns or sets the remote machine to which a control sends or receives data.
RemotePort	Returns or sets the remote port number to which to connect.
RequestTimeout	Returns or sets the length, in seconds, to wait before a timeout expires.
ResponseCode	Returns the error code from the connection when the icError (11) state occurs in the StateChanged event.
ResponseInfo	Returns the text of the last error that occurred.
StillExecuting	Returns a value that specifies if the Internet Transfer Control is busy.
Tag	Returns or sets an expression that stores any extra data needed for your program.
URL	Returns or sets the URL that is used by the Execute or OpenURL methods.
UserName	Returns or sets the name that is sent with requests to remote computers.

Table 8-2 Microsoft Internet Transfer Control methods

Name	Description
Cancel	Cancels the current request and closes any connections currently established.
Execute	Executes a request to a remote server. You can only send requests that are valid for the particular protocol.
GetChunk	Retrieves data from in the StateChanged event. Use this method after invoking the Execute method as a GET operation.
GetHeader	Retrieves header text from an HTTP file.
OpenURL	Opens and returns the document at the specified URL. The document is returned as a variant. When the method has completed, the URL properties (and portions of the URL, such as the protocol) are updated to reflect the current URL.

Table 8-3   **Microsoft Internet Transfer Control events**

Name	Description
StateChanged	Occurs whenever there is a state change in the connection.

The code that makes everything work is in the command handler for the Get button. Plus, I added an event handler for StatusChanged. Take a look at the implementation of this sample in Listing 8-1.

Listing 8-1   **Internet Transfer Control example implementation**

```
Private Sub CommandGet_Click()
TextResult.Text = Inet1.OpenURL(TextURL.Text)
End Sub
```

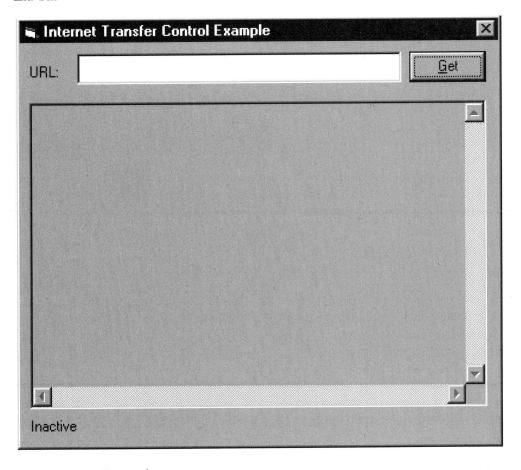

Figure 8-5   Format layout

```
Private Sub Inet1_StateChanged(ByVal State As Integer)
    Select Case State
    Case icNone
        Status.Caption = "No state to report"
    Case icHostResolvingHost
        Status.Caption = "Looking up IP address..."
    Case icHostResolved
        Status.Caption = "Found IP address"
    Case icConnecting
        Status.Caption = "Connecting to host..."
    Case icConnected
        Status.Caption = "Connected to host"
    Case icRequesting
        Status.Caption = "Sending request..."
    Case icRequestSent
        Status.Caption = "Sent request"
    Case icReceivingResponse
        Status.Caption = "Receiving response..."
    Case icResponseReceived
        Status.Caption = "Received response"
    Case icDisconnecting
        Status.Caption = "Disconnecting from host..."
    Case icDisconnected
        Status.Caption = "Disconnected from host"
    Case icError
        Status.Caption = "An error occurred"
    Case icResponseCompleted
        Status.Caption = "Request complete!"
    End Select
End Sub
```

With a few lines of code, you have implemented an application that is capable of downloading files over the Internet. In fact, the following single line of code takes care of all Internet transfer functionality:

```
TextResult.Text = Inet1.OpenURL(TextURL.Text)
```

The rest of the code is simply for displaying the current status to the user in the static text at the bottom of the dialog. If you run the sample application and type in `http://www.microsoft.com`, you should see a result similar to the one in Figure 8-6.

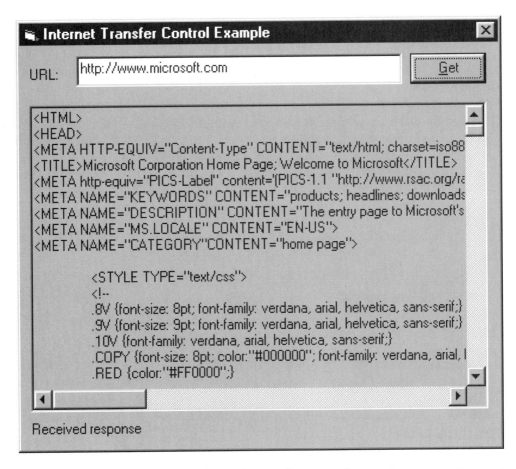

Figure 8-6 Internet Transfer Control example screen shot

You have to admit that using high-level tools like VB and the Microsoft Internet Transfer Control make writing WinInet-based applications a breeze. However, as with any high-level tool, you lose a significant degree of flexibility.

Using WinInet Directly

Even though the Microsoft Internet Transfer Control is the easiest interface using WinInet in VB, there are times when you'll need to access the underlying API functions directly. You can accomplish this by calling into the WinInet library directly. In this section I'll cover how to accomplish this and show you how to rewrite the previous sample program using InternetOpen, InternetOpenUrl, InternetReadFile, and InternetCloseHandle.

Declarations

VB makes it possible to call procedures found in any DLL. However, because DLL procedures are external to your application, you must tell VB where to find the procedure and what the arguments look like. You accomplish this in VB by using the Declare statement.

For example, take at look at the Win32 ASCII declaration for InternetOpen:

```
INTERNETAPI
HINTERNET
WINAPI
InternetOpenA(
    IN LPCSTR lpszAgent,
    IN DWORD dwAccessType,
    IN LPCSTR lpszProxy OPTIONAL,
    IN LPCSTR lpszProxyBypass OPTIONAL,
    IN DWORD dwFlags
    );
```

To use this function from within your VB application, you would need the following declare statement in your VB code:

```
Private Declare Function InternetOpen Lib "wininet.dll" _
    Alias "InternetOpenA" (ByVal sAgent As String, _
    ByVal lAccessType As Long, ByVal sProxyName As String, _
    ByVal sProxyBypass As String, ByVal lFlags As Long) As Long
```

Notice that the Declare statement tells VB where to find the function. In this case it tells it to look for InternetOpenA in wininet.dll. Throughout our VB code, we can now refer to it as InternetOpen. You have to do this for all WinInet functions that you wish to use in your VB application.

What about all of the WinInet constant values and flags? You have to do the same thing for them as well. Each WinInet constant that you need to use also requires a VB declaration.

VB offers some tools to make interacting with the Win32 API much easier. There is a set of text files that contain the declarations for various APIs. With my installation of VB 5.0, I received text files for the Win32 API and the Messaging Application Programming Interface (MAPI) API. You can open these files either manually or through a viewer application called API Text Viewer (see Figure 8-7). The API Text Viewer helps you find the declaration in which you're interested and copies it to the clipboard. Then you can easily paste the declaration into your VB code.

Unfortunately, at this point Microsoft hasn't provided the declarations for the WinInet API. However, keep your eyes peeled. They will probably be available sometime in the near future.

Revamped Sample Application Using InternetOpenUrl

Now let's look at how to rewrite the previous sample application using the WinInet API directly. We'll use the same project and the same form with a few exceptions. In

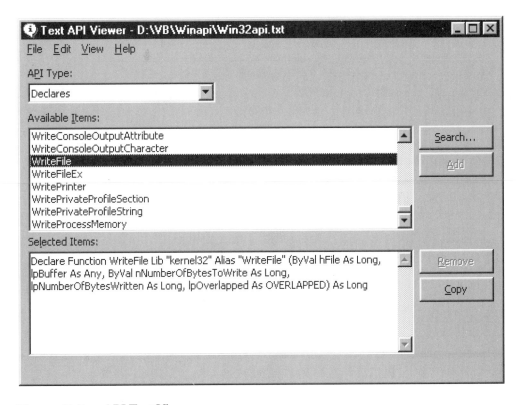

Figure 8-7   API Text Viewer

this example I'm not going to implement a status callback function so I removed the static text at the bottom of the dialog called Status. Also, because we're going to use the WinInet API directly, we don't need the Microsoft Internet Transfer Control in the form. Besides those two changes, everything else remains the same.

Listing 8-2 contains the implementation of the revamped sample that uses the WinInet DLL directly. To use InternetOpenUrl, we'll also need to use InternetOpen, InternetReadFile, and InternetCloseHandle. We'll also need to declare a few VB constants for the WinInet constants we plan on using, such as INTERNET_FLAG_ RELOAD and INTERNET_OPEN_TYPE_PRECONFIG.

Listing 8-2   Revamped sample application using the WinInet DLL

```
Private Declare Function InternetOpen Lib "wininet.dll" _
    Alias "InternetOpenA" (ByVal sAgent As String, _
    ByVal lAccessType As Long, ByVal sProxyName As String, _
    ByVal sProxyBypass As String, ByVal lFlags As Long) As Long

Private Declare Function InternetOpenUrl Lib "wininet.dll" _
    Alias "InternetOpenUrlA" (ByVal hInternetSession As Long, _
    ByVal sUrl As String, ByVal sHeaders As String, _
    ByVal lHeadersLength As Long, ByVal lFlags As Long, _
    ByVal lContext As Long) As Long

Private Declare Function InternetReadFile Lib "wininet.dll" _
    (ByVal hFile As Long, ByVal sBuffer As String, _
    ByVal lNumberOfBytesToRead As Long, _
    lNumberOfBytesRead As Long) As Integer

Private Declare Function InternetCloseHandle Lib "wininet.dll" _
        (ByVal hInet As Long) As Integer

Private Const INTERNET_OPEN_TYPE_PRECONFIG = 0
Private Const INTERNET_FLAG_RELOAD = &H80000000

Private hSession            As Long
Private hFile               As Long
Private Result              As String
Private Buffer              As String * 1024
```

```
Private bResult          As Boolean
Private lRead            As Long


Private Sub CommandGet_Click()
hSession = InternetOpen("VBandWinInet/1.0", INTERNET_OPEN_TYPE_PRECONFIG, "",
        "", 0)

If hSession Then
    hFile = InternetOpenUrl(hSession, TextURL.Text, "", 0,
                INTERNET_FLAG_RELOAD, 0)

    If hFile Then
        lRead = 1
        While lRead
            If InternetReadFile(hFile, Buffer, Len(Buffer), lRead) Then
                Result = Result + Buffer
            End If
        Wend
        TextResult.Text = Result
        InternetCloseHandle (hFile)
    End If
    InternetCloseHandle (hSession)
End If
End Sub
```

When you have the declarations in place, implementing the functionality is just like using the WinInet API in a Win32 application. In fact, CommandGet_Click should look very similar to the sample code I presented while covering the InternetOpenUrl function.

 Besides the obvious syntactical differences, everything that you learn about WinInet in this book can also be leveraged in VB.

Conclusion

In this chapter I covered how to use the WinInet API in VB applications. You can use either the WinInet API directly by calling into the WinInet DLL or the higher level Microsoft Internet Transfer Control (ActiveX). Although the latter fits better into the VB way of doing things, the former is more powerful and flexible. Everything that I cover in this book is also applicable in the VB environment.

IV
Part

Advanced
WinInet

9
Chapter

Asynchronous WinInet

Any application that tries to take advantage of the Internet is forced to deal with one big problem: The Internet is slow! Before the Internet came into play, most applications only dealt with resources found on the user's local machine. Accessing resources located on the same machine as the application is typically lightning fast. This makes for a very pleasant programming model and very content developers. However, when you want to make your application access a resource on a computer miles away, things get a little more complicated.

Imagine the following scenario. You just installed a new Internet browser called LightningFast and heard about a new Web site halfway across the world from you. So you point your Web browser to *http://www.newsite.com* and press the Enter key. Then you notice something strange; the browser window seems dead. It looks like most windows normally do before executing the End Task command or even worse, the three-finger salute (Ctrl-Alt-Delete). You try pressing buttons and menus, but to no avail. Nothing happens. Everything is dead. Then you get called to dinner for the fifth time and decide you'd better go. While eating dinner, you get entrapped in one of your all-time favorite Seinfield episodes and don't make it back to the computer for almost a couple of hours. When you deactivate the screen saver you notice something even odder than before: The new Web site is loaded, and LightingFast is back from the dead. What happened?

LightningFast used a synchronous programming model. In other words, when you told LightningFast to download the file, the function that handled the request didn't return (it blocked) until it finished downloading the file. This results in an unresponsive UI and confused users. A better approach is to give the user status feedback (indicating how much of the file has been downloaded, how much is left, and so on) and allow the user to continue working and using the program's other features while waiting for the download to finish. This asynchronous model is how virtually all Internet-centric applications behave today.

In this chapter I'll give you a brief overview of asynchronous programming and show you how to take advantage of the built-in asynchronous features of WinInet. Then I'll show you how to convert the MyFTP sample application (from Chapter 5) so that it takes advantage of asynchronous WinInet calls. The sample helps clear up the common questions encountered while implementing asynchronous WinInet. By the time you're done with this chapter, you'll be ready to make your WinInet applications competitive with today's asynchronous Internet applications. I'll also show you how to accomplish similar functionality using the alternative to WinInet's asynchronous support—Win32 threads.

Synchronous versus Asynchronous

In programming terms, if you make a synchronous function call, the program does not continue until the function returns. This is often referred to as a *blocking function*. In contrast, if you make an asynchronous function call, the program begins to execute the function's code and at the same time continues with its previous path of execution, producing two simultaneous paths of execution within the program. This is often referred to as a *nonblocking function*.

Although at first glance the terms *synchronous/asynchronous* and *blocking/nonblocking* seem to be synonymous, they have slightly different meanings (even though everyone uses them interchangeably).

Asynchronous functions are nonblocking. Nonblocking function calls, however, are not necessarily asynchronous. An asynchronous function call begins the execution of a separate code path and returns immediately. When the asynchronous function finishes executing, the primary thread is notified through a callback mechanism (usually through a Windows message or a registered callback function).

A nonblocking function, on the other hand, doesn't have to be asynchronous. A nonblocking function first checks to see if the process can be completed immediately. If it can, it executes the code and returns. However, if the process cannot be completed immediately, the nonblocking function can begin a separate thread of execution (making the call asynchronous), or it can simply return an error that indicates that the function would take too long to complete (satisfying the definition of nonblocking). Hence, an asynchronous function always completes, even if it must use a secondary thread, whereas a nonblocking function only guarantees that the function will not block.

The whole idea of asynchronous function calls began in the 16-bit world. Before 32-bit operating systems like Windows 95, Windows NT, and multithread capabilities, using asynchronous function calls was the only way to keep the UI alive while making time-consuming function calls. Windows produces asynchronous behavior through hidden windows and calls to PeekMessage. In other words, if a Windows API function claims to support asynchronous behavior, the operating system monitors the separate paths of execution under the scenes through sly Windows messages.

Figure 9-1 illustrates the difference between synchronous and asynchronous function calls. In Figure 9-1, the box on the left represents the main code, and the box on the right represents a function. Notice that with the synchronous call, the main code doesn't continue executing (it blocks) until all the function code is executed and the function returns. With the asynchronous call, on the other hand, the main code continues to execute as soon as the call is made to the function. It does not block. When the asynchronous function finishes, it normally notifies the primary thread through a callback mechanism (usually implemented with Windows messages or registered callback functions).

Pros and Cons

There are pros and cons to both methods of programming. Although synchronous programming is very easy to implement, it is also very limited. Most Internet-related

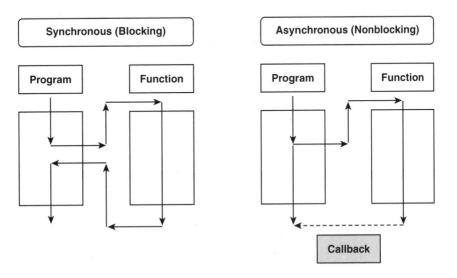

Figure 9-1   Synchronous versus asynchronous function calls

functions take a considerable amount of time to complete. If you use a synchronous strategy, your program will not be able to continue until the time-consuming operation completes. This is very undesirable to say the least. A user-friendly program allows the user to do other things while processing the download in the background. Although asynchronous communication is much more desirable from the user's perspective, it's more difficult to implement.

Asynchronous communication requires you, the programmer, to handle the synchronization between the different channels of communication. This can get quite complex very quickly. If you've ever dealt with asynchronous programming, you'll appreciate what I'm talking about.

You're responsible for monitoring the progress and completion of the asynchronous channel, and for notifying any interested clients. It's easy to understand how the program can monitor the success of a synchronous call because it waits for it to return. But with asynchronous calls, the main code continues to execute at the same time the function executes. When the function completes executing, you don't know where you'll be in the main thread.

WinInet's Built-in Asynchronous Support

WinInet offers a simple built-in asynchronous communication mechanism that helps reduce many of the complexities described earlier. To make WinInet requests asynchronous, your application only needs to do three things:

1. Use INTERNET_FLAG_ASYNC in the call to InternetOpen.
2. Register a callback function with WinInet through InternetSetStatusCallback (for notification purposes).
3. Specify a context value other than zero for any asynchronous function call.

The rest is taken care of behind the scenes. All WinInet requests on handles derived from the asynchronous session handle (created with InternetOpen) are made asynchronously (unless a context value of zero is specified). The application simply needs to monitor the callback function to determine when the asynchronous request finishes and whether it was successful.

With that high-level overview of asynchronous functions and WinInet's built-in asynchronous support, we're ready to convert MyFTP into an asynchronous FTP client. MyFTP illustrates in detail how to accomplish the three steps listed earlier. Walking through the process of converting the synchronous sample will help you understand how to take advantage of asynchronous WinInet in your own applications.

MyFTP: Asynchronous FTP Sample Application

The MyFTP sample should already be familiar to you unless you skipped Chapter 5. If this is the case, you may want to quickly review the MyFTP sample presented in Chapter 5 before diving in here.

Remember that this sample was compiled using Visual C++ 5.0 and linked against the IE 4.0 version of WinInet.

Figure 9-2 illustrates the dialog that is used in this asynchronous version of MyFTP. The only difference from the synchronous version is the addition of the status bar. We'll be using this status bar to provide the user with request status information.

We'll use the same project skeleton (same callbacks and so forth) for this asynchronous example. To make this sample behave asynchronously, we'll make tweaks to

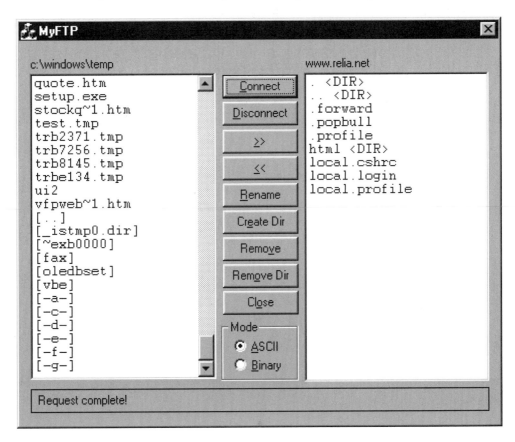

Figure 9-2   MyFTP sample application

the established code. Once again, if you run across anything confusing, you may want to refer back to the synchronous version of MyFTP, which is explained in detail in Chapter 5.

Establishing the Asynchronous Internet Session

The first step in establishing an asynchronous session of any type is to use the asynchronous flag in the call to InternetOpen (INTERNET_FLAG_ASYNC). For example, take a look at Listing 9-1, which illustrates how InternetOpen is called from within the CMyFTPDlg::OnInitDialog method.

Listing 9-1   **CMyFTPDlg::OnInitDialog code segment**

```
g_hSession = InternetOpen("MyFTP", INTERNET_OPEN_TYPE_PRECONFIG, NULL, NULL,
                    INTERNET_FLAG_ASYNC);

if (g_hSession)
{
    INTERNET_STATUS_CALLBACK dwStatusCallback;
    dwStatusCallback = InternetSetStatusCallback(g_hSession,
            MyStatusCallback);

    if (INTERNET_INVALID_STATUS_CALLBACK == dwStatusCallback)
    {
        AfxMessageBox("Error setting status callback");
    }
}
```

Remember that g_hSession is a global HINTERNET handle declared in MyFTPDlg.cpp. g_hSession receives the return value of InternetOpen. Because INTERNET_FLAG_ASYNC is passed to InternetOpen, all subsequent WinInet functions that use g_hSession can behave asynchronously (if they are capable of behaving asynchronously, that is).

This first step is quite simple. It sets the stage for asynchronous WinInet operations in your application. The rest of the work is tied to the WinInet-registered callback function that gets notified of the progress of the particular WinInet operation. We are particularly interested in being notified when asynchronous operations finish.

InternetStatusCallback

The second step to establishing an asynchronous WinInet session is to register a status callback function. A callback function provides a way for you to inform the user of the operation in progress. Although we will be looking at how to use this callback function in an asynchronous session, a status callback function can be used by a synchronous WinInet session as well. In the next chapter I'll cover how to use a status callback function with synchronous/blocking WinInet calls from within a multithreaded application.

You establish the callback function the same way whether you're using synchronous or asynchronous calls. The only difference is you don't use INTERNET_FLAG_ ASYNC in your call to InternetOpen.

You probably noticed in Listing 9-1 the call to InternetSetStatusCallback, which takes care of registering a callback function on a specific handle. Take a look at the declaration of InternetSetStatusCallback:

```
INTERNET_STATUS_CALLBACK InternetSetStatusCallback(
    IN HINTERNET hInternet,
    IN INTERNET_STATUS_CALLBACK lpfnInternetCallback
);
```

InternetSetStatusCallback sets up a callback function that WinInet calls as progress is made during an operation. It returns the previously defined status callback function if successful, NULL if there was no previously defined status callback function, or INTERNET_INVALID_STATUS_CALLBACK if the callback function is not valid (refer back to Listing 9-1).

The parameter lpfnInternetCallback should contain the address of the callback function to call when progress is made. To remove the current callback function, pass NULL in this parameter. In Listing 9-1, the call to InternetSetStatusCallback looks like this:

```
dwStatusCallback = InternetSetStatusCallback(g_hSession, MyStatusCallback);
```

MyStatusCallback is the callback function being registered, which must be of type INTERNET_STATUS_CALLBACK.

INTERNET_STATUS_CALLBACK

INTERNET_STATUS_CALLBACK defines the signature of the callback function WinInet expects you to define. Take a look at the following declaration of INTERNET_STATUS_CALLBACK:

```
VOID (CALLBACK * INTERNET_STATUS_CALLBACK)(
    IN HINTERNET hInternet,
```

```
    IN DWORD dwContext,
    IN DWORD dwInternetStatus,
    IN LPVOID lpvStatusInformation,
    IN DWORD dwStatusInformationLength
);
```

With this in mind, the callback function MyStatusCallback is defined in MyFTPDlg.h as follows:

```
VOID CALLBACK MyStatusCallback(
    HINTERNET hInternet,
    DWORD dwContext,
    DWORD dwInternetStatus,
    LPVOID lpvStatusInformation,
    DWORD dwStatusInformationLength
);
```

The first parameter, hInternet, is the handle for which the callback function is being called. In other words, this is the handle that was used in the call to InternetSetStatusCallback. The second parameter, dwContext, is an application-defined context value for the particular handle. This value gives you a way to determine which asynchronous operation initiated the callback function.

For example, suppose your application calls FtpGetFile and FtpPutFile, both of which are asynchronous. The callback function should behave differently for each operation. However, because both functions are called on the same HINTERNET handle, you need some other way to determine which operation initiated the callback function. The only way to determine this is through a context value—hence the parameter dwContext.

I defined three context values in MyFTPDlg.h that will be used for the following three asynchronous FTP operations: InternetConnect, FtpGetFile, and FtpPutFile. The following shows how these context values are defined:

```
#define CONTEXT_CONNECT     1
#define CONTEXT_GET         2
#define CONTEXT_PUT         3
```

When I call FtpPutFile, I pass in the context value CONTEXT_PUT (which happens to be the third and final step for establishing an asynchronous session). Then, if MyStatusCallback is called with a dwContext value of CONTEXT_PUT, I know that it's being called on behalf of FtpPutFile.

The third parameter, dwInternetStatus, contains a status code that indicates why the callback function is being called. dwInternetStatus can be any one of the values described in Table 9-1.

Table 9-1 **dwInternetStatus values**

dwInternetStatus Value	Description
INTERNET_STATUS_CLOSING_ CONNECTION	Closes the connection to the server. The lpvStatusInformation parameter is NULL.
INTERNET_STATUS_CONNECTED_TO_ SERVER	Connects successfully to the socket address (SOCKADDR) pointed to by lpvStatusInformation.
INTERNET_STATUS_CONNECTING_TO_ SERVER	Connects to the socket address (SOCKADDR) pointed to by lpvStatusInformation.
INTERNET_STATUS_CONNECTION_ CLOSED	Closes the connection to the server successfully. The lpvStatusInformation parameter is NULL.
INTERNET_STATUS_CTL_RESPONSE_ RECEIVED	Not currently implemented.
INTERNET_STATUS_HANDLE_CLOSING	Terminates this handle value.
INTERNET_STATUS_HANDLE_CREATED	Used by InternetConnect to indicate it has created the new handle. This lets the application call InternetCloseHandle from another thread if the connect is taking too long.
INTERNET_STATUS_INTERMEDIATE_ RESPONSE	Receives an intermediate (100 level) status code message from the server.
INTERNET_STATUS_NAME_RESOLVED	Finds the IP address of the name contained in lpvStatusInformation successfully.
INTERNET_STATUS_PREFETCH	Not currently implemented.
INTERNET_STATUS_RECEIVING_ RESPONSE	Waiting for the server to respond to a request. The lpvStatusInformation parameter is NULL.
INTERNET_STATUS_REDIRECT	An HTTP request is about to redirect the request automatically. The lpvStatusInformation parameter points to the new URL. At this point, the application can read any data returned by the server with the redirect response and can query the response headers. It can also cancel the operation by closing the handle. This callback is not made if the original request specified INTERNET_FLAG_NO_AUTO_REDIRECT.
INTERNET_STATUS_REQUEST_ COMPLETE	An asynchronous operation has been completed. See InternetOpen for details on INTERNET_FLAG_ASYNC.

(continued)

Table 9-1 (continued)

dwInternetStatus Value	Description
INTERNET_STATUS_REQUEST_SENT	Sends the information request successfully to the server. The lpvStatusInformation parameter points to a DWORD containing the number of bytes sent.
INTERNET_STATUS_RESOLVING_NAME	Looks up the IP address of the name contained in lpvStatusInformation.
INTERNET_STATUS_RESPONSE_RECEIVED	Receives a response successfully from the server. The lpvStatusInformation parameter points to a DWORD containing the number of bytes received.
INTERNET_STATUS_SENDING_REQUEST	Sends the information request to the server. The lpvStatusInformation parameter is NULL.
INTERNET_STATUS_STATE_CHANGE	Indicates a change between online/offine state.

As you can see, the value of lpvStatusInformation depends on the value of dwInternetStatus (and in some cases isn't used at all). In this asynchronous scenario, the values of most interest to us are INTERNET_STATUS_REQUEST_COMPLETE, INTERNET_STATUS_HANDLE_CREATED, and INTERNET_STATUS_HANDLE_CLOSING.

When INTERNET_STATUS_HANDLE_CREATED is received, lpvStatusInformation contains the HINTERNET value for the newly created handle. Your application can store this value for later use. For example, if the user wants to cancel the operation before INTERNET_STATUS_REQUEST_COMPLETE is received, you can call InternetCloseHandle with the value received by the callback on INTERNET_STATUS_HANDLE_CREATED. Calling InternetCloseHandle on the handle effectively cancels the operation.

INTERNET_STATUS_HANDLE_CLOSING, on the contrary, is the final status notification you receive for a handle. The callback function is called with this value right before the handle is terminated.

The last status of interest is INTERNET_STATUS_REQUEST_COMPLETE. This status is used to determine when an asynchronous operation finishes. When the callback function receives this status, the application can find out if the asynchronous request was successful by looking at the INTERNET_ASYNC_RESULT structure. The following is a description of the INTERNET_ASYNC_RESULT structure:

```
typedef struct {
    DWORD dwResult;
```

```
    DWORD dwError;
} INTERNET_ASYNC_RESULT, * LPINTERNET_ASYNC_RESULT;
```

dwResult is an HINTERNET, DWORD, or BOOL return code from an asynchronous function. dwError is an error message if dwResult indicates that the function failed. If the operation succeeds, this member usually contains ERROR_SUCCESS.

The dwResult field contains the HINTERNET, DWORD, or BOOL return value from the asynchronous request. For example, if the asynchronous function normally returns an HINTERNET, dwResult contains the resulting HINTERNET value. If dwResult indicates an error, the dwError field contains the error code; otherwise, it usually contains ERROR_SUCCESS.

 Because callbacks are made during asynchronous operation, you should spend as little time as possible in the callback function. For example, displaying any modal (blocking) UI in the callback function would defeat the purpose of your asynchronous operation .

I'll cover the implementation of MyStatusCallback shortly. First we need to look at how the asynchronous operations are initiated.

OnConnect

As you've learned, the first two steps in establishing an FTP session are (1) calling InternetOpen and (2) calling InternetConnect. In this example we used InternetOpen the same way we always have, except this time we passed in the INTERNET_FLAG_ ASYNC flag. This makes the Internet session created by InternetOpen asynchronous. All future calls on the handle returned from InternetOpen may behave asynchronously (if possible). InternetOpen, however, never behaves asynchronously, so there is nothing to worry about there.

InternetConnect, on the other hand, is the first function that you call in an asynchronous session that can and does behave asynchronously. I created a dialog called CConnectDlg to gather the connection information from the user. In particular, we need to know the FTP server, user name, and password for the FTP account to which the user wishes to connect. When the user presses the Connect button on the main dialog (CMyFTPDlg), the CMyFTPDlg::OnConnect command handler is called (see Listing 9-2).

Displaying CConnectDlg, as illustrated in Figure 9-3, is the first thing that happens in CMyFTPDlg::OnConnect. If the user presses OK, the method continues processing the connection; otherwise, the function returns immediately.

CMyFTPDlg::OnConnect then checks to see if there is already a global g_hConnection handle (this global HINTERNET handle is also declared in MyFTPDlg.cpp). If a valid g_hConnection handle already exists, the method closes it before opening the new connection. After making that quick check, the method proceeds to call InternetConnect.

The call to InternetConnect should look very familiar to you by now. It simply takes the information we gathered from CConnectDlg and specifies INTERNET_SERVICE_FTP using INTERNET_DEFAULT_FTP_PORT. The only thing different from before is that this time I used a context value of CONTEXT_CONNECT.

Remember that I defined three context values that I use throughout this sample application. Once again, these values are defined as follows:

```
#define CONTEXT_CONNECT        1
#define CONTEXT_GET            2
#define CONTEXT_PUT            3
```

Specifying a context value in InternetConnect is crucial to the success of our application. If InternetConnect decides to behave asynchronously, it returns NULL. This causes a problem in the standard synchronous approach because we can't continue without a valid HINTERNET handle. Thus, in the asynchronous approach, we must rely on MyStatusCallback to set the value of g_hConnection to the result of InternetConnect when it receives the INTERNET_STATUS_REQUEST_COMPLETE status value along with a context value of CONTEXT_CONNECT. I'll look at how MyStatusCallback accomplishes this shortly.

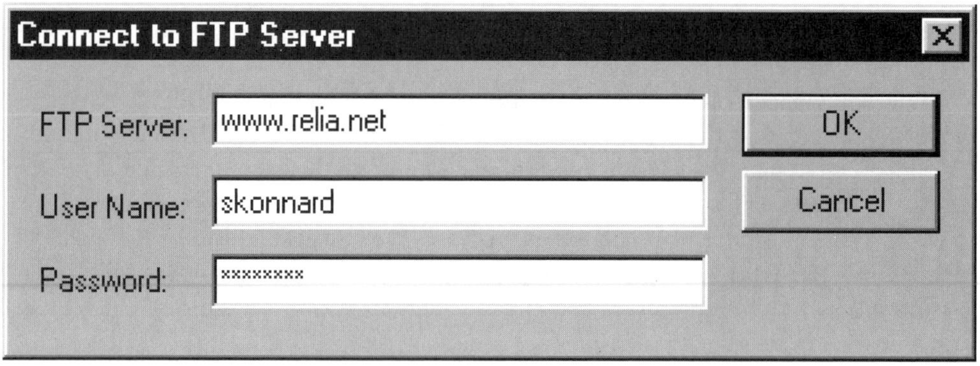

Figure 9-3   Connect to FTP Server dialog

If InternetConnect behaves synchronously and returns an HINTERNET handle, we can go ahead and call FillRemoteList, which requires a valid HINTERNET handle returned by InternetConnect. If InternetConnect returns NULL, we must call GetLastError to determine the cause of failure. If GetLastError returns ERROR_ IO_PENDING, the function was executed asynchronously, and the result is still pending. In this case we can continue, assuming MyStatusCallback will take care of the details from here. Otherwise, if there is another error, we should notify the user and handle the error immediately.

Listing 9-2   OnConnect

```
void CMyFTPDlg::OnConnect()
{
    CConnectDlg dlg;
    if (IDOK == dlg.DoModal())
    {
        //if already connected, disconnect
        if (g_hConnection)
            InternetCloseHandle(g_hConnection);

        //connect
        g_hConnection = InternetConnect(g_hSession, dlg.m_strServer,
                INTERNET_DEFAULT_FTP_PORT, dlg.m_strUser, dlg.m_strPassword,
                INTERNET_SERVICE_FTP, INTERNET_FLAG_PASSIVE , CONTEXT_CONNECT);

        if (g_hConnection)
        {
            FillRemoteList();
        }
        else
        {
            DWORD dwError = GetLastError();
            if (ERROR_IO_PENDING != dwError)
            {
                CString strMsg;
                strMsg.Format("GetLastError returned %d", dwError);
                AfxMessageBox(strMsg);
            }
        }
    }
```

```
        m_strRemote = dlg.m_strServer;
        UpdateData(FALSE);
    }
}
```

OnDisconnect

OnDisconnect is much simpler than OnConnect. OnDisconnect simply checks for a valid g_hConnection handle, calls InternetCloseHandle, and resets the contents of the remote list box (see Listing 9-3). Because InternetCloseHandle never behaves asynchronously, we don't have to worry about asynchronous complexities. There is, however, one problem with calling InternetCloseHandle on a handle with outstanding asynchronous requests.

If asynchronous requests are pending for g_hConnection or any of its child handles (in other words, a handle returned from FtpFindFirstFile), g_hConnection cannot be closed immediately. InternetCloseHandle will, however, invalidate the handle waiting for the pending asynchronous requests to finish. If g_hConnection has been invalidated by a call to InternetCloseHandle and you try to use it with a new request, you get an ERROR_INVALID_HANDLE error.

Listing 9-3   OnDisconnect

```
void CMyFTPDlg::OnDisconnect()
{
    if (g_hConnection)
    {
        InternetCloseHandle(g_hConnection);
        g_hConnection = NULL;
    }
    m_RemoteList.ResetContent();
}
```

OnGet

OnGet first makes sure that g_hConnection contains a valid HINTERNET handle (see Listing 9-4). Then it gets the selected transfer mode from the radio buttons on the dialog. Finally, it calls FtpGetFile.

Like InternetConnect, FtpGetFile can take a substantial amount of time to complete, especially if you're downloading a 20-MB file. Because FtpGetFile is mostly likely to behave asynchronously, we need to pass the context value CONTEXT_GET to FtpGetFile.

If FtpGetFile returns TRUE, the function completed successfully (and synchronously). In this case we can go ahead and file the local list; otherwise, we need to check the return error and make sure the error was ERROR_IO_PENDING. If the error was ERROR_IO_PENDING, once again we can assume that MyStatusCallback will take care of the rest.

Listing 9-4   OnGet

```
void CMyFTPDlg::OnGet()
{
    if (!g_hConnection)
    {
        AfxMessageBox("You must first connect to an FTP server");
        return;
    }

    CString strFile;
    int iIndex = m_RemoteList.GetCurSel();
    if (LB_ERR == iIndex)
    {
        AfxMessageBox("You must select a remote file first");
        return;
    }
    m_RemoteList.GetText(iIndex, strFile);

    DWORD dwFlags;
    if (m_lMode == MODE_ASCII)
        dwFlags = FTP_TRANSFER_TYPE_ASCII;
    else
        dwFlags = FTP_TRANSFER_TYPE_BINARY;

    BOOL bRet = FtpGetFile(g_hConnection, strFile, strFile, FALSE,
            FILE_ATTRIBUTE_NORMAL, dwFlags, CONTEXT_GET);

    if (bRet)
    {
        FillLocalList();
    }
    else
```

```
    {

        DWORD dwError = GetLastError();
        if (ERROR_IO_PENDING != dwError)
        {
            CString strMsg;
            strMsg.Format("GetLastError returned %d", dwError);
            AfxMessageBox(strMsg);
        }
    }
}
```

OnPut

OnPut (see Listing 9-5) is almost identical to OnGet. The main difference is that OnPut calls FtpPutFile with a context value of CONTEXT_PUT. If OnPut behaves synchronously and returns TRUE, it calls FillRemoteList. Otherwise, it counts on MyStatusCallback to complete the functionality.

Listing 9-5   OnPut

```
void CMyFTPDlg::OnPut()
{
    if (!g_hConnection)
    {
        AfxMessageBox("You must first connect to an FTP server");
        return;
    }

    CString strFile;
    int iIndex = m_LocalList.GetCurSel();
    if (LB_ERR == iIndex)
    {
        AfxMessageBox("You must select a local file first");
        return;
    }

    m_LocalList.GetText(iIndex, strFile);
    DWORD dwFlags;
    if (m_lMode == MODE_ASCII)
        dwFlags = FTP_TRANSFER_TYPE_ASCII;
```

```
    else
        dwFlags = FTP_TRANSFER_TYPE_BINARY;

    BOOL bRet = FtpPutFile(g_hConnection, strFile, strFile, dwFlags,
            CONTEXT_PUT);

    if (bRet)
    {
        FillRemoteList();
    }
    else
    {
        DWORD dwError = GetLastError();
        if (ERROR_IO_PENDING != dwError)
        {
            CString strMsg;
            strMsg.Format("GetLastError returned %d", dwError);
            AfxMessageBox(strMsg);
        }
    }
}
```

MyStatusCallback Implementation

Finally, it's time to look at the implementation of MyStatusCallback—the glue that holds this asynchronous FTP application together (see Listing 9-6). I've already covered how to register MyStatusCallback using InternetSetStatusCallback. Now it's time to look at how the implementation makes asynchronous WinInet possible and provides a more user-friendly application.

First let's look at how to use MyStatusCallback to complete the asynchronous WinInet operations we've already discussed. So far, we've looked at OnConnect, OnGet, and OnPut, which call InternetConnect, FtpGetFile, and FtpPutFile on an asynchronous HINTERNET handle. We passed CONTEXT_CONNECT, CONTEXT_GET, and CONTEXT_PUT in the dwContext parameter for each of these functions respectively. These same context values are passed to MyStatusCallback.

MyStatusCallback contains one large switch statement on dwInternetStatus. When an asynchronous operation finishes, MyStatusCallback is called with a status of INTERNET_STATUS_REQUEST_COMPLETE.

Inside the case block for INTERNET_STATUS_REQUEST_COMPLETE we need to take additional steps to finish the asynchronous operation specified by dwContext. The switch statement shown in Listing 9-6 is used to handle the three context values used by this application.

Listing 9-6   **MyStatusCallback INTERNET_STATUS_
REQUEST_COMPLETE case**

```
case INTERNET_STATUS_REQUEST_COMPLETE:
{
    strStatus="Request complete!";
    switch(dwContext)
    {
    case CONTEXT_GET:
        pDlg->FillLocalList();
        break;
    case CONTEXT_PUT:
        pDlg->FillRemoteList();
        break;
    case CONTEXT_CONNECT:
    {
        if (!g_hConnection)
        {
            LPINTERNET_ASYNC_RESULT pResult =
                    (LPINTERNET_ASYNC_RESULT)(lpvStatusInformation);

            g_hConnection = (HINTERNET)pResult->dwResult;
        }
        pDlg->FillRemoteList();
    }
    break;
    default:
        // handle error/
        break;
    }
}
break;
```

The cases for CONTEXT_GET and CONTEXT_PUT are simple. If dwContext is CONTEXT_GET, we need to fill the local list, which should now contain the down-loaded file, by calling CMyFTPDlg::FillLocalList. If dwContext is CONTEXT_PUT, we need to fill the remote list, which should now contain the uploaded file, by calling CMyFTPDlg::FillRemoteList.

In the case of CONTEXT_CONNECT, we need to save the newly created HINTERNET handle in g_hConnection. The new handle can be retrieved from the dwResult field of the INTERNET_ASYNC_RESULT structure stored in lpvStatusInformation. After storing the handle, a call to CMyFTPDlg::FillRemoteList should be able to populate the list box successfully with the files on the remote server.

There is one tricky thing to watch for here. Notice that before I try to save the result handle to g_hConnection, I check to see if g_hConnection is NULL. This is necessary because it's possible that this code may be executed for other WinInet operations that share the CONTEXT_CONNECT context value.

 The context value used with InternetConnect becomes the default context value for all operations that use the g_hConnection handle. If a context value isn't specified explicitly, as with FtpGetFile and FtpPutFile, the default context value is used. There are many FTP operations used in this sample application that don't even accept a context value, such as FtpDeleteFile and FtpRenameFile to name a few. When these operations complete, even though they behave synchronously, MyStatusCallback is still called with a status of INTERNET_STATUS_REQUEST_COMPLETE and a context value of CONTEXT_CONNECT—the default context value.

g_hConnection should only be NULL when fulfilling an InternetConnect request. In this case only, we need to look for the resulting HINTERNET value. If g_hConnection already contains a valid value, MyStatusCallback has been called for another request using the default context value. In this case we simply reload the remote list box by calling CMyFTPDlg::FillRemoteList.

For any other dwInternetStatus value, MyStatusCallback simply sets the appropriate status message and displays it in the dialog status window. Listing 9-7 demonstrates how this is accomplished.

Listing 9-7   MyStatusCallback

```
VOID CALLBACK MyStatusCallback(
    HINTERNET hInternet,
    DWORD dwContext,
    DWORD dwInternetStatus,
    LPVOID lpvStatusInformation,
```

```
    DWORD dwStatusInformationLength
)
{

    CString strStatus;
    CMyFTPDlg* pDlg = (CMyFTPDlg*)AfxGetMainWnd();
    if (!pDlg)
        return;

    switch(dwInternetStatus)
    {
    case INTERNET_STATUS_RESOLVING_NAME:
        strStatus="Resolving name...";
        break;
    case INTERNET_STATUS_NAME_RESOLVED:
        strStatus="Resolved name!";
        break;
    case INTERNET_STATUS_CONNECTING_TO_SERVER:
        strStatus="Connecting to server...";
        break;
    case INTERNET_STATUS_CONNECTED_TO_SERVER:
        strStatus="Connected to server!";
        break;
    case INTERNET_STATUS_SENDING_REQUEST:
        strStatus="Sending request...";
        break;
    case INTERNET_STATUS_REQUEST_SENT:
        strStatus="Request sent!";
        break;
    case INTERNET_STATUS_RECEIVING_RESPONSE:
        strStatus="Receiving response...";
        break;
    case INTERNET_STATUS_RESPONSE_RECEIVED:
        strStatus="Response received!";
        break;
    case INTERNET_STATUS_CLOSING_CONNECTION:
        strStatus="Closing connection...";
        break;
    case INTERNET_STATUS_CONNECTION_CLOSED:
        strStatus="Connection closed!";
        break;
    case INTERNET_STATUS_HANDLE_CREATED:
        strStatus="Handle created!";
```

```
            break;
    case INTERNET_STATUS_HANDLE_CLOSING:
        strStatus="Closing handle...";
        break;
    case INTERNET_STATUS_REQUEST_COMPLETE:
        {
            strStatus="Request complete!";
            switch(dwContext)
            {
            case CONTEXT_GET:
                pDlg->FillLocalList();
                break;
            case CONTEXT_PUT:
                pDlg->FillRemoteList();
                break;
            case CONTEXT_CONNECT:
                {
                    if (!g_hConnection)
                    {
                        LPINTERNET_ASYNC_RESULT pResult =
                            (LPINTERNET_ASYNC_RESULT)(lpvStatusInformation);
                        g_hConnection = (HINTERNET)pResult->dwResult;
                    }
                    pDlg->FillRemoteList();
                }
                break;
            default:
                break;
            }
        }
        break;
    default:
        strStatus="";
        break;
    }
    CWnd* pText = NULL;
    if (pDlg)
        pText = pDlg->GetDlgItem(IDC_STATIC_STATUS);
    if (pText)
        pText->SetWindowText(strStatus);
}
```

For example, when the status INTERNET_STATUS_RECEIVING_RESPONSE is received, the text "Receiving response . . ." is displayed in the status window, as shown in Figure 9-4.

MyStatusCallback is the key to providing a user-friendly FTP application. It makes it possible to keep the user informed of the status of each FTP operation. Furthermore, it makes it possible to make asynchronous WinInet requests. If you connect to an FTP server and start a GET command by pressing the button labeled <<, the dialog is still alive (meaning you can initiate new commands). In fact, you can press the Disconnect button to cancel the GET request. This functionality is impossible to achieve in a standard synchronous WinInet application.

FillRemoteList

FillRemoteList is responsible for enumerating the files on the remote server through the functions FtpFindFirstFile and InternetFindNextFile. Although FtpFindFirstFile

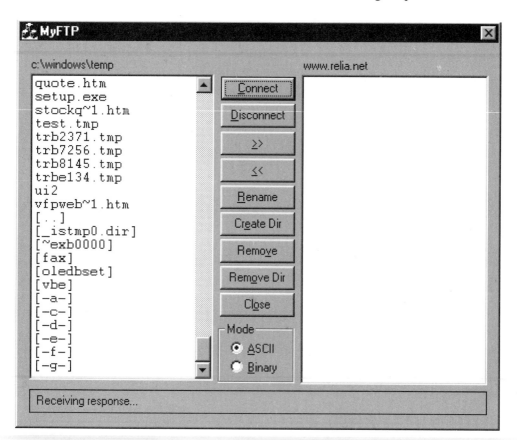

Figure 9-4   Status bar

can behave asynchronously, I decided always to make this function behave synchronously for this example. To accomplish this you only need to do one thing—pass a dwContext value of zero to FtpFindFirstFile. Any requests that specify a context value of zero are forced to behave synchronously.

Listing 9-8 contains the implementation of CMyFTPDlg::FillRemoteList. Because you're already familiar with FTP file enumeration, I'll let you peruse this function on your own.

 Use a context value of zero to force synchronous execution of an operation on an asynchronous HINTERNET handle.

Listing 9-8   FillRemoteList

```
void CMyFTPDlg::FillRemoteList()
{
    CString strFileName;
    WIN32_FIND_DATA FindFileData;
    HINTERNET hFindFile;

    m_RemoteList.ResetContent();

    if (hFindFile)
        InternetCloseHandle(hFindFile);

    hFindFile = FtpFindFirstFile(g_hConnection, NULL, &FindFileData,
            INTERNET_FLAG_RELOAD, 0);

    if (hFindFile)
    {
        if ( (FindFileData.dwFileAttributes & FILE_ATTRIBUTE_DIRECTORY) ==
                FILE_ATTRIBUTE_DIRECTORY)
            strFileName.Format("%s <DIR>", FindFileData.cFileName);
        else
            strFileName = FindFileData.cFileName;
        m_RemoteList.AddString(strFileName);

        while(InternetFindNextFile(hFindFile, &FindFileData))
        {
```

```
            if ( (FindFileData.dwFileAttributes & FILE_ATTRIBUTE_DIRECTORY) ==
                  FILE_ATTRIBUTE_DIRECTORY )
                strFileName.Format("%s <DIR>", FindFileData.cFileName);
            else
                strFileName = FindFileData.cFileName;
            m_RemoteList.AddString(strFileName);
        }
        InternetCloseHandle(hFindFile);
    }
    else
    {
        DWORD dwError = GetLastError();
        if (ERROR_IO_PENDING != dwError)
        {
            CString strMsg;
            strMsg.Format("GetLastError returned %d", dwError);
            AfxMessageBox(strMsg);
        }
    }
}
```

The Rest of the Details

The rest of the MyFTP sample application implementation details are pretty self-explanatory. Listing 9-9 contains the code for the rest of the FTP operations that make up the application. The only thing I want to point out is that none of these functions calls CMyFTPDlg::FillRemoteList directly. This is because none of these functions specifies a context value.

As we covered in the previous sections, MyStatusCallback is still called for these operations even though they behave synchronously. The case block for CONTEXT_CONNECT (for INTERNET_STATUS_REQUEST_COMPLETE) acts as a catchall for operations that don't specify a context value and call CMyFTPDlg::FillRemoteList. Hence, these methods don't need to worry about calling CMyFTPDlg::FillRemoteList themselves.

Listing 9-9   MyFTPDlg.cpp

```
void CMyFTPDlg::OnCreate()
{
    if (!g_hConnection)
    {
```

```
            AfxMessageBox("You must first connect to an FTP server");
            return;
        }

        CCreateDirectoryDlg dlg;
        if (IDOK == dlg.DoModal())
        {
            if (!FtpCreateDirectory(g_hConnection, dlg.m_strNewDirName))
                ProcessInternetError();
        }
    }

void CMyFTPDlg::OnRename()
{
    if (!g_hConnection)
    {
        AfxMessageBox("You must first connect to an FTP server");
        return;
    }

    CString strFile;
    int iIndex = m_RemoteList.GetCurSel();
    if (LB_ERR == iIndex)
    {
        AfxMessageBox("You must select a remote file first");
        return;
    }

    m_RemoteList.GetText(iIndex, strFile);

    CRenameDlg dlg;
    if (IDOK == dlg.DoModal())
    {
        if (!FtpRenameFile(g_hConnection, strFile, dlg.m_strNewName))
            ProcessInternetError();
    }
}

void CMyFTPDlg::OnRemove()
{
    if (!g_hConnection)
```

```
    {
        AfxMessageBox("You must first connect to an FTP server");
        return;
    }

    CString strFile;
    int iIndex = m_RemoteList.GetCurSel();
    if (LB_ERR == iIndex)
    {
        AfxMessageBox("You must select a remote file first");
        return;
    }

    m_RemoteList.GetText(iIndex, strFile);

    if (IDOK == AfxMessageBox("Delete selected file from ftp server",
            MB_YESNO|MB_ICONQUESTION))
    {
        if (!FtpDeleteFile(g_hConnection, strFile))
            ProcessInternetError();
    }
}
void CMyFTPDlg::OnDblclkListRemote()
{
    if (!g_hConnection)
    {
        AfxMessageBox("You must first connect to an FTP server");
        return;
    }

    CString strFile;
    int iIndex = m_RemoteList.GetCurSel();
    if (LB_ERR == iIndex)
        return;

    m_RemoteList.GetText(iIndex, strFile);
    iIndex = strFile.Find(" <DIR>");
    if (-1 != iIndex)
        strFile = strFile.Left(iIndex);
```

```
        if (!FtpSetCurrentDirectory(g_hConnection, strFile))
            ProcessInternetError();
}


void CMyFTPDlg::OnDblclkListLocal()
{
    CString strFile;
    int iIndex = m_LocalList.GetCurSel();
    if (LB_ERR == iIndex)
        return;

    if (!DlgDirSelectEx(GetSafeHwnd(), strFile.GetBuffer(BUFFLEN), BUFFLEN,
            IDC_LIST_LOCAL))
        return;

    strFile.ReleaseBuffer();
    m_strLocalDir = strFile;
}


void CMyFTPDlg::OnRemovedir()
{
    if (!g_hConnection)
    {
        AfxMessageBox("You must first connect to an FTP server");
        return;
    }

    CString strFile;
    int iIndex = m_RemoteList.GetCurSel();
    if (LB_ERR == iIndex)
    {
        AfxMessageBox("You must select a remote directory first");
        return;
    }

    m_RemoteList.GetText(iIndex, strFile);

    iIndex = strFile.Find(" <DIR>");
    if (-1 != iIndex)
        strFile = strFile.Left(iIndex);
```

```
if (IDOK == AfxMessageBox("Delete selected directory from ftp server",
    MB_YESNO|MB_ICONQUESTION))
{
    if (!FtpRemoveDirectory(g_hConnection, strFile))
        ProcessInternetError();
}
}


void CMyFTPDlg::OnRadioAscii()
{
    m_lMode = MODE_ASCII;
}


void CMyFTPDlg::OnRadioBinary()
{
    m_lMode = MODE_BINARY;
}
```

Conclusion

In this chapter I walked you through converting the synchronous MyFTP sample into an asynchronous version. By now you should understand the details of using WinInet asynchronously. In particular, I covered how to establish an asynchronous Internet session by using INTERNET_FLAG_ASYNC in the call to InternetOpen. I also discussed how to use InternetSetStatusCallback to register a status callback function with your Internet session. Finally, I showed you how context values are used to communicate with the registered callback function as the progress of an FTP request changes.

These three steps simplify the process of establishing an asynchronous Internet session, which ultimately makes your application more user friendly. Although you might run into problems the first time you try to use WinInet asynchronously, don't worry—it's really not that bad.

10
Chapter

Reusable WinInet COM

Components

The more I use WinInet in my applications, the more it seems like I'm writing the same lines of code over and over again. In fact, every time I write a new WinInet-based function, it looks just like the last one I wrote, with a few minor modifications. After thorough investigation, I've decided that this is mostly due to the general nature of Internet application development. Typically, every data transmission on a given Internet protocol is going to follow the same high-level logic. On the other hand, there are certain aspects of an Internet transaction that will always need to be customized for a given task.

For example, suppose you want to create an application that uses HTTP to communicate via TCP/IP with different servers across the Internet. The natural approach would be to write WinInet-based functions to handle the transmission of data. Most developers would look for ways to make the functions reusable and generic. Object-oriented developers may even develop their own C++ classes to encapsulate the desired transmission functionality. However, regardless of the transmission implementation, every task potentially is going to require different HTTP methods, headers, input data formats, host names, port numbers, and parsing routines to handle the various HTTP response formats. To add even another layer of complexity, some requests may require SSL and some form of authentication whereas others may not.

Although you can find ways to solve this design problem using more generic functions or C++ classes, isn't there a better approach that allows more reusable and extensible WinInet code? If you haven't already guessed, the solution at which I'm hinting is COM. Whether you're in the business of selling shrink-wrapped products, customized applications, or software components, finding better ways to write reusable code makes everyone around you (including yourself) happier.

By now, you've surely heard of COM. In fact, COM has become such the word on the street lately that you're probably feeling the pressure of joining the COM ranks. As most developers begin their pursuit of COM Zen, they are often discouraged by what Kraig Brockschmidt termed the "mental fog" that often follows. To help break through this mental fog, most developers need simple, concise examples that help put the concepts in practice. The COM-based approach to developing WinInet code presented in this chapter will help you to get one step closer to this higher plane of existence.

It's exciting to find a good design fit for COM. As you'll see shortly, COM is the perfect solution for writing reusable WinInet components that are easily extensible and reusable by multiple clients and applications. Breaking the functionality described in the HTTP scenario into multiple COM objects allows developers to reuse the more generic components and rewrite the more task-specific components on a case-per-case basis. This approach allows developers to leverage well-written and tested components while minimizing the amount of code required for a new WinInet-related task. Furthermore, the COM approach offers dynamic application extensibility by simply adding new components to the user's system at runtime.

In this chapter I'll present an example that illustrates how to write reusable WinInet HTTP COM components. I'll show you how to define and implement two COM interfaces: IHttpRequest and IQuoteProvider. Plus, I'll show you how to tie it all together in a sample application that I wrote called Stock Watcher. Stock Watcher downloads stock quotes from different Internet stock quote providers and displays them to the user. If you get nothing else from this chapter, you'll at least get a nifty application for monitoring your portfolio.

This chapter assumes that you have some knowledge of COM and ATL. The Stock Watcher tutorial walks you step-by-step through the process of creating WinInet COM/ATL components. However, it's presented in more of a how-to fashion as opposed to presenting the theory behind what makes it all work. I chose to do it this way because (1) there isn't space in this book to cover COM and ATL, and (2) it's not what this book is about fundamentally. Appendix E contains a list of my favorite COM and ATL references. However, in my opinion, the two best references on COM and ATL are

- *Essential COM* by Don Box (Reading, MA: Addison Wesley Longman, 1998)
- *ATL Internals* by Brent E. Rector and Chris Sells (Reading, MA: Addison Wesley Longman, 1999)

Of all the books on COM, no one explains it like Don Box. Be sure to keep your eye on his column in *Microsoft Systems Journal,* which covers the latest COM/ATL technologies.

Stock Watcher Sample Application

Stock Watcher, the sample application that I wrote for this chapter, illustrates many interesting WinInet concepts. In particular, Stock Watcher uses the WinInet MFC classes CInternetSession, CHttpConnection, and CHttpFile to implement the HTTP transaction functionality. It also illustrates how to derive your own class from CInternetSession to override the CInternetSession::OnStatusCallback method.

In addition to the WinInet concepts, Stock Watcher also demonstrates how to generate powerful and reusable COM components using ATL. The Stock Watcher components implement the following COM interfaces: IUnknown, IConnectionPointContainer, and IConnectionPoint, and the application-specific interfaces IQuoteProvider and IHttpRequest. Stock Watcher also illustrates a practical example of using COM component categories.

The functionality of the Stock Watcher application is intentionally quite simple. It's an MFC-based single document interface (SDI) application with a single view. The view consists of a single CListCtrl that displays the user-entered stock portfolio (see Figure 10-1).

This sample allows users to add stock symbols to their portfolios, save their portfolio to a file, and refresh their portfolios data by connecting to an Internet stock quote provider and downloading the current stock information (price, change, open, volume, and so on).

I wrote Stock Watcher using Microsoft Visual C++ 5.0 and some of the new common control features provided by the new IE 3.02 version of the Windows common control library. You can download the sample code from the *Essential WinInet* Web site.

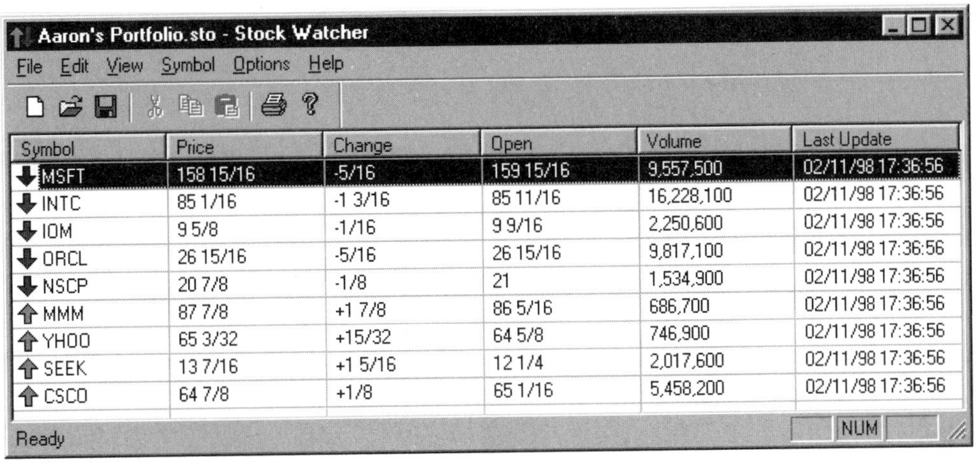
Aaron's Portfolio.sto - Stock Watcher
File Edit View Symbol Options Help
Symbol Price Change Open Volume Last Update
MSFT 158 15/16 -5/16 159 15/16 9,557,500 02/11/98 17:36:56
INTC 85 1/16 -1 3/16 85 11/16 16,228,100 02/11/98 17:36:56
IOM 9 5/8 -1/16 9 9/16 2,250,600 02/11/98 17:36:56
ORCL 26 15/16 -5/16 26 15/16 9,817,100 02/11/98 17:36:56
NSCP 20 7/8 -1/8 21 1,534,900 02/11/98 17:36:56
MMM 87 7/8 +1 7/8 86 5/16 686,700 02/11/98 17:36:56
YHOO 65 3/32 +15/32 64 5/8 746,900 02/11/98 17:36:56
SEEK 13 7/16 +1 5/16 12 1/4 2,017,600 02/11/98 17:36:56
CSCO 64 7/8 +1/8 65 1/16 5,458,200 02/11/98 17:36:56
Ready
NUM

Figure 10-1 Stock Watcher sample application screen shot

If you compile the workspace, all the COM components should be registered for you properly. If you would like to run the executable without compiling the project, however, you'll need to run SW.BAT to register the components properly.

If you open stock watcher.dsw in Developer Studio, you should see the following three projects: Stock Watcher, HttpObjectServer, and QuoteProviders. Stock Watcher is an MFC AppWizard-generated application that implements the UI. The HttpObjectServer and QuoteProviders projects are both ATL COM AppWizard-generated projects that implement the IHttpRequest and IQuoteProvider interfaces.

Figure 10-2 illustrates a high-level view of the Stock Watcher design model. When the user initiates the HTTP request, the MFC application creates an instance of the CHttpRequest component and the CQuoteProvider component. The MFC application establishes an event sink between the CQuoteProvider component and its own CQuoteProviderEventSink component. At this point the MFC application passes the IQuoteProvider interface pointer to the CHttpRequest component, which from that point on interfaces with it directly. Because the CHttpRequest component needs quote provider-specific information for the request, it simply queries the IQuoteProvider interface. Finally, when CQuoteProvider is finished parsing the HTTP result, it fires an event notifying the MFC application.

As far as memory management is concerned, the MFC application only needs to track the IHttpRequest interface pointers. After the MFC application passes the IQuoteProvider interface pointer to the CHttpRequest component, the CHttpRequest component first calls IUnknown::AddRef, which is followed by the MFC application calling IUnknown::Release. Thus, the CQuoteProvider component remains in memory until the CHttpRequest destructor releases the IQuoteProvider interface.

Now let's look at each of the interfaces and components in more detail.

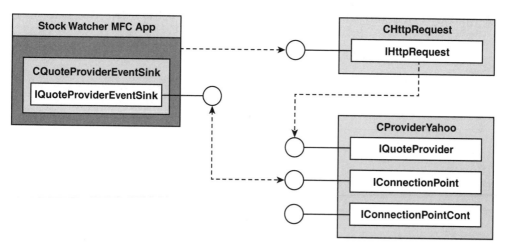

Figure 10-2   Stock Watcher design model

The QuoteProvider Component

First, let's examine QuoteProviders' project and components. To begin, I created a new ATL COM AppWizard project called QuoteProviders (see Figure 10-3) and added it to the blank Stock Watcher workspace.

The ATL COM AppWizard currently only consists of one step. This step allows you to specify the following: (1) the COM server type, (2) whether you want to allow merging of proxy/stub code, and (3) whether you want to support MFC. To keep things simple for this project, let's make QuoteProviders an in-process COM server (DLL) and add support for MFC (see Figure 10-4).

When you press Finish, the wizard generates the files for an ATL project without any initial objects. The wizard generates the main DLL entry points needed for a COM server including DllCanUnloadNow, DllGetClassObject, DllRegisterServer, and DllUnregisterServer. These functions are implemented in QuoteProviders.cpp and are exported in QuoteProviders.def.

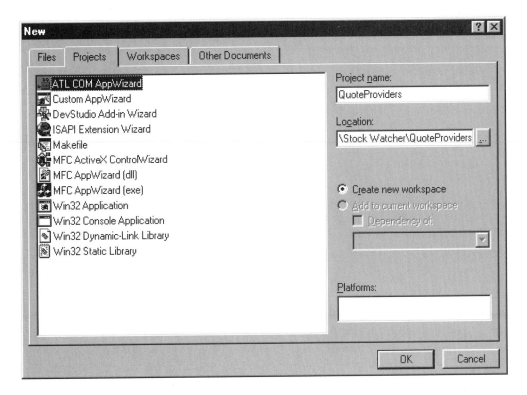

Figure 10-3 New project wizard

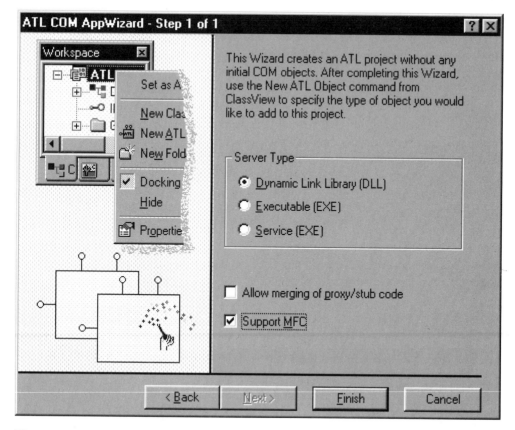

Figure 10-4   ATL COM AppWizard

The wizard also generates QuoteProviders.idl and QuoteProviders.rgs. The Interface Definition Language (IDL) file contains the interface and component descriptions whereas the registry scripts (RGS) file contains information about how the component is configured in the registry. I'll cover these files in a little more detail when they contain more interesting interface information. After creating the ATL project, you add new interfaces and components through the ATL Object Wizard.

To MFC or not to MFC
Complicated module state issues arise when using MFC in both a COM server and its client application. These issues result from being able to link dynamically the MFC DLL to both regular DLLs (COM servers, by the way, are implemented as regular DLLs) and an application executable that loads the DLL.

The problem with this configuration deals with how MFC manages its global data. MFC global data consists of the current CWinApp and CWinThread pointers, the resource handle, and the temporary and permanent Window maps (the Window maps correlate the MFC Window classes, like CWnd, with their corresponding HWND).

Each process using a Win32 DLL gets its own copy of the DLL's data. The problem is rooted in the AFXDLL model, which assumed that there would be only one CWinApp object and only one set of handle maps in the process. Based on that assumption, these items could be tracked in the MFC DLL itself.

However, now it's possible to have more than one CWinApp object in a process. The application executable owns a CWinApp object, and any dynamically linked regular DLL also owns a CWinApp object. Thus, a call to AfxGetApp in the DLL should return a pointer to the DLL's CWinApp object instead of the CWinApp object belonging to the executable. To maintain the correct MFC module state, a mechanism is required to switch the module state as module boundaries are crossed.

The AFX_MANAGE_STATE macro implements this module state switching. You need to make sure that all DLL entry points set the module state explicitly by calling AFX_MANAGE_STATE. Message handlers, however, are taken care of for you automatically by MFC. Because we specified in the QuoteProviders project that we want to support MFC, every wizard-generated entry point is going to contain the following line of code automatically:

```
AFX_MANAGE_STATE(AfxGetStaticModuleState( ))
```

After the AFX_MANAGE_STATE macro goes out of scope, the previous module state is reset. Although the ATL wizards take care of most of the details, you must manage this manually for any entry points not generated by ATL. This is especially true for connection points and their corresponding event sink handlers. However, if you're thinking that this gyration is more than you care to deal with, you can simply choose to avoid using MFC in your COM server.

The CProviderYahoo Component

Because both the IHttpRequest interface and the MFC application depend on the IQuoteProvider interface, it makes sense to start here. Let's let the ATL Object Wizard take care of most of the implementation details for us. Then we'll go in and tweak the code manually to make it fit our exact needs.

The first step is to initiate the ATL Object Wizard. You can find the New ATL Object menu item under the main Insert menu. After the ATL Object Wizard is displayed, you should see the dialog illustrated in Figure 10-5. As you can see, the ATL Object Wizard offers many different types of ATL components (Objects, Controls, Miscellaneous, and Data Access). Plus, for each component type, it offers many different functional choices.

Once again, to learn more about ATL in general and these different ATL component types, refer to the recommended readings at the beginning of this chapter and in Appendix E. Also, check out Don Box's article entitled "The Active Template Library Makes Building Compact COM Objects a Joy" in the June 1997 issue of *Microsoft Systems Journal.* For our purposes, the Simple Object does just fine.

The one and only step of the wizard allows you to specify names for the C++ classes and the COM interface it implements. If you're following along at home, simply fill in the data as shown in Figures 10-6 and 10-7.

The wizard generates a C++ class called CProviderYahoo that implements the IProviderYahoo interface. In this example, CProviderYahoo provides information that deals with connecting to the Yahoo! quote server and parsing the files returned by the stock quote request. Notice that I also changed the interface type from Dual to Custom. As a general rule of thumb, if you ever plan on using a component from

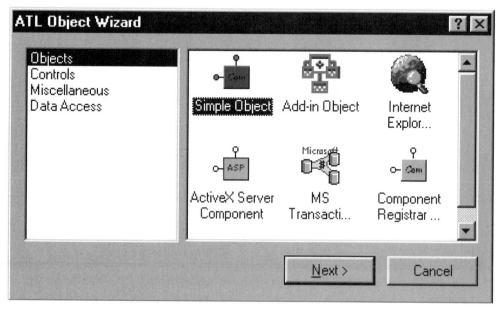

Figure 10-5   ATL Object Wizard

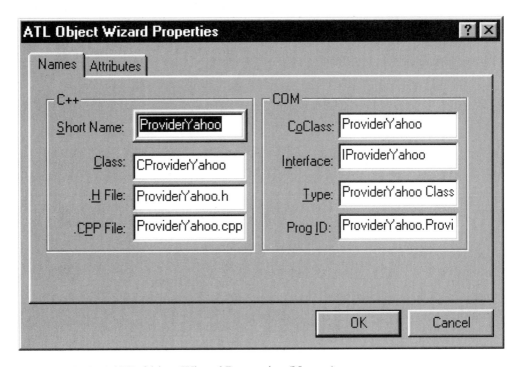

Figure 10-6   ATL Object Wizard Properties (Names)

a scripting language (like VB), you should stick with a dual interface. However, if you know that the component will only be used in the C++ arena, custom interfaces are much more flexible.

I also checked the Support Connection Points option. This does nothing more than add a few extra lines of code to your class declaration file, which we'll look at shortly. After pressing OK, the wizard performs its magic and generates the files and code required by this new component.

At this point the CProviderYahoo class and the IProviderYahoo interface should show up in the Developer Studio class view. First take a look at the wizard-generated IProviderYahoo interface defined in quoteproviders.idl (see Listing 10-1). If you're unfamiliar with IDL, refer to the Visual C++ online documentation.

Listing 10-1   QuoteProviders.idl

```
// QuoteProviders.idl : IDL source for QuoteProviders.dll
// This file will be processed by the MIDL tool to
// produce the type library (QuoteProviders.tlb) and  marshalling code.
```

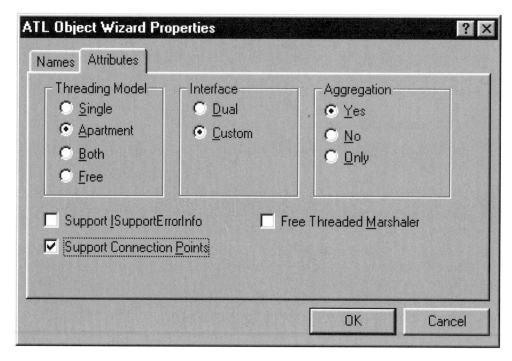

Figure 10-7 ATL Object Wizard Properties (Attributes)

```
import "oaidl.idl";
import "ocidl.idl";

    [
        uuid(F02EAD3F-9F0C-11D1-B2B2-006008ACADF7),
        helpstring("IProviderYahoo Interface"),
        pointer_default(unique)
    ]
    interface IProviderYahoo : IUnknown
    {
    };
[

    uuid(F02EAD31-9F0C-11D1-B2B2-006008ACADF7),
    version(1.0),
    helpstring("QuoteProviders 1.0 Type Library")
]
```

```
library QUOTEPROVIDERSLib
{
    importlib("stdole32.tlb");
    importlib("stdole2.tlb");

    [
        uuid(F02EAD40-9F0C-11D1-B2B2-006008ACADF7),
        helpstring("ProviderYahoo Class")
    ]
    coclass ProviderYahoo
    {
        [default] interface IProviderYahoo;
    };
};
```

As we add methods to interfaces and even new interfaces, the ATL wizards continue to modify this file. The complete quoteproviders.idl is shown in Listing 10-3. Each time you compile the project, Visual C++ uses the Microsoft IDL (MIDL) compiler to process QuoteProviders.idl. The MIDL compiler generates the type library (quoteproviders.tlb) and various other helper files that are used by this and other projects. Table 10-1 describes the MIDL-generated files in more detail.

Now take a look at the CProviderYahoo declaration file (see Listing 10-2).

Listing 10-2   ProviderYahoo.h

```
#ifndef __PROVIDERYAHOO_H_
#define __PROVIDERYAHOO_H_


#include "resource.h"        // main symbols
```

Table 10-1   MIDL Generated Files

MIDL-generated files

QuoteProviders.tlb	The QuoteProvider type library.
DllData.c	Implements a DLL containing the proxy/stub code.
QuoteProviders_i.c	Defines the Globally unique indentifiers (GUIDs) used in the IDL file.
QuoteProviders_p.c	Implements the proxy/stub code.
QuoteProviders.h	A header file that contains the declarations for all of the interfaces defined in the IDL file.

```
/////////////////////////////////////////////////////////////////////////
// CProviderYahoo
class ATL_NO_VTABLE CProviderYahoo :
    public CComObjectRootEx<CComSingleThreadModel>,
    public CComCoClass<CProviderYahoo, &CLSID_ProviderYahoo>,
    public IConnectionPointContainerImpl<CProviderYahoo>,
    public IProviderYahoo
{
public:
    CProviderYahoo()
    {
    }
    ~CProviderYahoo()
    {
    }

DECLARE_REGISTRY_RESOURCEID(IDR_PROVIDERYAHOO)

BEGIN_COM_MAP(CProviderYahoo)
    COM_INTERFACE_ENTRY(IQuoteProvider)
    COM_INTERFACE_ENTRY_IMPL(IConnectionPointContainer)
END_COM_MAP()

BEGIN_CONNECTION_POINT_MAP(CProviderYahoo)
END_CONNECTION_POINT_MAP()

// IProviderYahoo
public:
};


#endif //__PROVIDERYAHOO_H_
```

CProviderYahoo derives from some of the standard ATL base template classes (CComObjectRootEx and CComCoClass). These templates take care of the class factory and IUnknown implementations for CProviderYahoo. Because we chose to support connection points in the ATL Object Wizard, CProviderYahoo also inherits from IConnectionPointContainerImpl. (I'll cover the rest of the connection point code when we implement the event interface.) Finally, CProviderYahoo also inherits from the IProviderYahoo interface that we looked at earlier.

Like the IDL file, as we add methods to interfaces and even new interfaces, the ATL wizards also continue to modify this file.

Adding Interface Methods

At this point we're ready to start adding methods to the IProviderYahoo interface. Begin by right clicking on IProviderYahoo in class view and select Add Method. The dialog in Figure 10-8 is displayed. Adding a method to the interface in this manner adds the method definition to the IDL file (quoteproviders.idl) and a CProviderYahoo method implementation stub to provideryahoo.cpp.

Before adding methods wildly to the IProviderYahoo interface, let's take a step back and look once again at the purpose of this module. The CHttpRequest component is going to interface with the quote provider components to get information about a given quote server and to parse the data returned from the same quote server.

Obviously every quote server is going to have different host names and potentially different HTTP port numbers. Furthermore, different quote servers will have different server-side script names (which we'll be invoking) and will require different input parameters. Additionally, because we don't control the server-side scripts, we must take special care in parsing the results from the different stock quote providers.

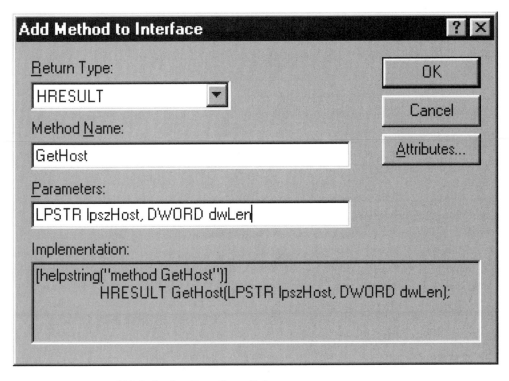

Figure 10-8   Add Method to Interface dialog

We want to make the IProviderYahoo component intelligent enough to tell the IHttpRequest component everything it needs to know about connecting to the Yahoo! quote server and parsing the data it returns. Table 10-2 describes the methods that I decided to make part of IProviderYahoo.

Most of these methods simply return information needed by WinInet to complete an HTTP transaction (all except for InitializeData and ParseResult). You can easily add new methods to this interface if they are common to all components that will share the interface. When we start looking at IHttpRequest, you'll see how these methods are actually used. However, if you're anxious to see how they're implemented, refer to provideryahoo.cpp.

Didn't We Mean IQuoteProvider?

If you look back at Figure 10-2, you might be wondering why the IProviderYahoo interface isn't anywhere in the application design. Furthermore, the design model shows that the CProviderYahoo component implements the IQuoteProvider interface. So what's going on? Shouldn't we have called it IQuoteProvider?

Yes. The goal of this application design is to allow runtime extensibility by simply plugging in additional quote provider components that implement the same interface. It would make more sense to have the standard quote provider interface called something like IQuoteProvider instead of IProviderYahoo.

Table 10-2   IProviderYahoo methods

Method	Description
GetHost	Provides the Yahoo! quote server's host name (quote.yahoo.com).
GetPort	Provides the Yahoo! quote server's port number.
GetMethod	Provides the HTTP method for the quote request (GET, POST, and so on).
GetURL	Provides the identifier for the quote request.
GetHttpVersion	Provides the HTTP version (HTTP/1.0).
GetHeaders	Provides additional HTTP headers that should be used in the quote request.
GetAcceptTypes	Provides additional HTTP accept types that should be used in the quote request.
GetData	Provides properly formatted input data for the quote request.
GetFlags	Provides additional WinInet-specific flags that should be used in the quote request.
InitializeData	Passes in a string of stock symbols; used by the client.
LoginIsRequired	Determines if this quote provider requires HTTP authentication.
ParseResult	Parses the HTML response returned by the Yahoo! server

However, because the ATL wizards kindly generate IDL code, it makes sense to implement the first component using the wizards and then to generalize the resulting IDL interface description. (This approach beats writing the IDL code by hand.) In other words, the IProviderYahoo interface found in quoteproviders.idl needs to be renamed to IQuoteProvider. You can do this by simply replacing all occurrences of IProviderYahoo with IQuoteProvider in the quoteproviders.idl file. The next time you compile the project, quoteproviders.h will contain the new IQuoteProvider interface declarations.

Listing 10-3 illustrates the final IQuoteProvider interface. CProviderYahoo and all other quote provider components implement this standard quote provider interface. After we're done walking through the rest of CProviderYahoo's design and implementation, I'll quickly show you how to implement two other quote provider components (CProviderDatek and CProviderFastQuote), which also implement the IQuoteProvider interface and are used by the Stock Watcher application.

Listing 10-3   QuoteProviders.idl

```
// QuoteProviders.idl : IDL source for QuoteProviders.dll
//

// This file will be processed by the MIDL tool to
// produce the type library (QuoteProviders.tlb) and marshalling code.

import "oaidl.idl";
import "ocidl.idl";
    [

        uuid(F02EAD3F-9F0C-11D1-B2B2-006008ACADF7),

        helpstring("IQuoteProvider Interface"),
        pointer_default(unique)
    ]
    interface IQuoteProvider : IUnknown
    {
        [helpstring("method GetHost")] HRESULT GetHost(LPSTR lpszHost, DWORD
                dwLen);
        [helpstring("method GetPort")] HRESULT GetPort(USHORT* pnPort);
        [helpstring("method LoginIsRequired")] HRESULT LoginIsRequired(BOOL*
                pbResult);
        [helpstring("method GetMethod")] HRESULT GetMethod(LPSTR lpszMethod,
                DWORD dwLen);
```

```
    [helpstring("method GetURL")] HRESULT GetURL(LPSTR lpszURL, DWORD
            dwLen);
    [helpstring("method GetAcceptTypes")] HRESULT GetAcceptTypes(LPSTR
            lpszAcceptTypes, DWORD dwLen);
    [helpstring("method GetHttpVersion")] HRESULT GetHttpVersion(LPSTR
            lpszHttpVersion, DWORD dwLen);
    [helpstring("method GetFlags")] HRESULT GetFlags(DWORD* pdwFlags);
    [helpstring("method GetHeaders")] HRESULT GetHeaders(LPSTR lpszHeaders,
            DWORD dwLen);
    [helpstring("method GetData")] HRESULT GetData(LPSTR lpszData, DWORD
            dwLen);
    [helpstring("method ParseResult")] HRESULT ParseResult(LPSTR
            lpszResult);
    [helpstring("method InitializeData")] HRESULT InitializeData(LPSTR
            lpszData);
};
```

Connection Points

The ProviderYahoo component needs a mechanism for notifying its clients when it finishes parsing the HTTP response data. COM provides the IConnectionPoint and IConnectoinPointContainer interfaces for supporting events. If you've ever tried implementing a connection point by hand, you'll appreciate the shortcuts offered by ATL.

Remember, when we created the ProviderYahoo component, we selected the Support Connection Points option. This option adds a few extra lines of code to the ATL object class declaration. For example, if you take a look at provideryahoo.h, you'll notice that CProviderYahoo inherits from IConnectionPointContainerImpl (among other interfaces):

```
CProviderYahoo : public IConnectionPointContainerImpl<CProviderYahoo>,
```

Additionally, the wizard adds COM_INTERFACE_ENTRY_IMPL for IConnectionPointContainer to the CProviderYahoo COM map:

```
BEGIN_COM_MAP(CProviderYahoo)
    COM_INTERFACE_ENTRY(IQuoteProvider)
```

```
        COM_INTERFACE_ENTRY_IMPL(IConnectionPointContainer)
END_COM_MAP()
```

And finally, the wizard adds a connection point map without any initial entries:

```
BEGIN_CONNECTION_POINT_MAP(CProviderYahoo)
END_CONNECTION_POINT_MAP()
```

This wizard-generated code fully implements the IConnectionPointContainer interface. Now we simply need to implement our own connection point interface.

IQuoteProviderEvent

The connection point interface that I implemented for CProviderYahoo is called IQuoteProviderEvent. IQuoteProviderEvent consists of one method called UpdateSymbol, which passes the information gathered from the Internet back to the client.

To implement a connection point using ATL, the first step is to describe the interface in quoteproviders.idl. To do so you'll need to generate a new GUID using guidgen.exe found in the \Devstudio\VC\bin directory. Then you can add the new interface to the interface section of the IDL file. Here is what IQuoteProviderEvent looks like:

```
[
    uuid(BFD86BC0-A004-11d1-9912-004033D06B6E),
    helpstring("IQuoteProviderEvent Interface"),
    pointer_default(unique)
]
interface IQuoteProviderEvent : IUnknown
{
    import "oaidl.idl";
    HRESULT UpdateSymbol(LPCTSTR lpszSymbol, LPCTSTR lpszPrice,
            LPCTSTR lpszChange, LPCTSTR lpszOpen, LPCTSTR
            lpszVolume);
};
```

At this point you must recompile the QuoteProviders project to generate a new type library containing the IQuoteProviderEvent interface information. After you've generated a new type library, you're ready to use the ATL Proxy Generator component.

You can access the ATL Proxy Generator by going to the Components and Controls Gallery (go to the Project | Add To Project | Components and Controls menu item).

Double click on the Develop Studio Components directory and you should see the dialog shown in Figure 10-9. Select the ATL Proxy Generator component and press Insert. After confirming, the ATL Proxy Generator dialog appears as illustrated in Figure 10-10.

Type in the path to the QuoteProvider type library (quoteprovider.tlb), and both the IQuoteProvider and IQuoteProviderEvent interfaces should appear on the left. Select the IQuoteProviderEvent interface and make sure the Proxy Type is set to Connection Point before pressing Insert.

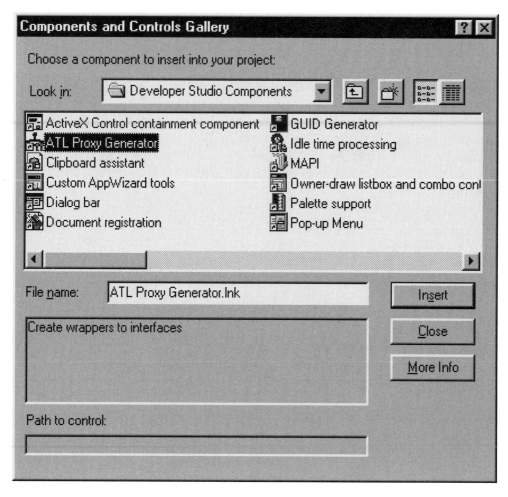

Figure 10-9 Components and Controls Gallery

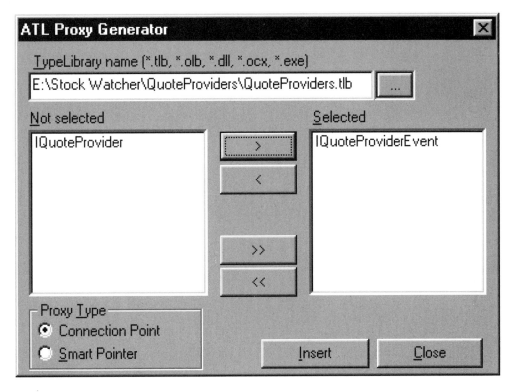

Figure 10-10   ATL Proxy Generator dialog

The ATL Proxy Generator generates a new file named cpquoteproviders.h (see Listing 10-4), which contains the declaration of CProxyIQuoteProviderEvent. CProxyIQuoteProviderEvent implements the IConnetionPoint interface and is capable of calling UpdateSymbol on all clients of this connection point through its Fire_UpdateSymbol method.

Listing 10-4   CProxyIQuoteProviderEvent

```
#ifndef __CPROXYIQUOTEPROVIDEREVENT_H__
#define __CPROXYIQUOTEPROVIDEREVENT_H__


/////////////////////////////////////////////////////////////////////////////
// CProxyIQuoteProviderEvent
template <class T>
class CProxyIQuoteProviderEvent : public IConnectionPointImpl<T,
&IID_IQuoteProviderEvent, CComDynamicUnkArray>
{
```

```
public:

//IQuoteProviderEvent : IUnknown
public:
    HRESULT Fire_UpdateSymbol(
        LPCTSTR lpszSymbol,
        LPCTSTR lpszPrice,
        LPCTSTR lpszChange,
        LPCTSTR lpszOpen,
        LPCTSTR lpszVolume)
    {
        T* pT = (T*)this;
        pT->Lock();
        HRESULT ret;
        IUnknown** pp = m_vec.begin();

        // fires UpdateSymbol on all connected objects

        while (pp < m_vec.end())
        {
            if (*pp != NULL)
            {
                IQuoteProviderEvent* pIQuoteProviderEvent =
                        reinterpret_cast<IQuoteProviderEvent*>(*pp);
                ret = pIQuoteProviderEvent->UpdateSymbol(lpszSymbol, lpszPrice,
                        lpszChange, lpszOpen, lpszVolume);
            }
            pp++;
        }
        pT->Unlock();
        return ret;
    }
};
#endif
```

To add this functionality to the CProviderYahoo component, CProviderYahoo also needs to inherit from the CProxyIQuoteProviderEvent template. Add the following line of code to the list of CProviderYahoo base classes:

```
public CProxyIQuoteProviderEvent<CProviderYahoo>
```

Finally, add a connection point entry for the IQuoteProviderEvent interface to the CProviderYahoo connection point map:

```
BEGIN_CONNECTION_POINT_MAP(CProviderYahoo)
    CONNECTION_POINT_ENTRY(IID_IQuoteProviderEvent)
END_CONNECTION_POINT_MAP()
```

Listing 10-5 illustrates what the CProviderYahoo class declaration looks like with connection point support and the methods we added earlier. This approach to adding connection point functionality to your ATL COM components greatly reduces the amount of code that you must write.

Listing 10-5   CProviderYahoo.h (complete)

```
#ifndef __PROVIDERYAHOO_H_
#define __PROVIDERYAHOO_H_

#include "resource.h"       // main symbols
#include "CPQuoteProviders.h"

/////////////////////////////////////////////////////////////////////////////
// CProviderYahoo
class ATL_NO_VTABLE CProviderYahoo :
    public CComObjectRootEx<CComSingleThreadModel>,
    public CComCoClass<CProviderYahoo, &CLSID_ProviderYahoo>,
    public IConnectionPointContainerImpl<CProviderYahoo>,
    public CProxyIQuoteProviderEvent<CProviderYahoo>,
    public IQuoteProvider
{
public:
    CProviderYahoo()
    {
    }
    ~CProviderYahoo()
    {
    }

DECLARE_REGISTRY_RESOURCEID(IDR_PROVIDERYAHOO)

BEGIN_COM_MAP(CProviderYahoo)
    COM_INTERFACE_ENTRY(IQuoteProvider)
```

```
        COM_INTERFACE_ENTRY_IMPL(IConnectionPointContainer)
END_COM_MAP()

BEGIN_CONNECTION_POINT_MAP(CProviderYahoo)
    CONNECTION_POINT_ENTRY(IID_IQuoteProviderEvent)
END_CONNECTION_POINT_MAP()

// IProviderYahoo
public:
    STDMETHOD(InitializeData)(LPSTR lpszData);
    STDMETHOD(ParseResult)(LPSTR lpszResult);
    STDMETHOD(GetData)(LPSTR lpszData, DWORD dwLen);
    STDMETHOD(GetHeaders)(LPSTR lpszHeaders, DWORD dwLen);
    STDMETHOD(GetFlags)(DWORD* pdwFlags);
    STDMETHOD(GetHttpVersion)(LPSTR lpszHttpVersion, DWORD dwLen);
    STDMETHOD(GetAcceptTypes)(LPSTR lpszAcceptTypes, DWORD dwLen);
    STDMETHOD(GetURL)(LPSTR lpszURL, DWORD dwLen);
    STDMETHOD(GetMethod)(LPSTR lpszMethod, DWORD dwLen);
    STDMETHOD(LoginIsRequired)(BOOL* pbResult);
    STDMETHOD(GetPort)(USHORT* pnPort);
    STDMETHOD(GetHost)(LPSTR lpszHost, DWORD dwLen);
};
#endif //__PROVIDERYAHOO_H_
```

Before moving on, let's take a look at the final implementation of CProviderYahoo (see Listing 10-6). Notice that most of the methods simply return a value that is specified with a #define preprocessor directive. This simply makes it easier to know what data needs to be modified by each new quote provider that is implemented.

 I could have taken it a step further by saving all of the #define values in the registry. Using the registry would allow most quote providers to share the same code for most of the Get routines—all they would need to do is configure the registry properly on installation. Although this gets us closer to reusable code, the data initialization and parsing logic are unique enough that all quote provider components need their own implementation.

Don't get scared off by InitializeData and ParseResult. InitializeData is simply responsible for formatting the data string that is passed to the quote provider. For example, the Yahoo! quote server expects to receive all the stock symbols separated by a +. Hence the URL might look like this:

```
/q?d=v2&s=MSFT+INTC+NOVL
```

Other quote servers might expect the symbols to be separated by commas or colons, for example. InitializeData does nothing more than format the data properly before sending it.

ParseResult simply searches through the HTML received in the response, looking for the symbols the user requested. Most quote providers show this information in an HTML table. Thus, the ParseResult function provided with CProviderYahoo looks for certain table tags and parses out the information of interest. These functions can be extended to provide more functionality and to fit your needs exactly.

Listing 10-6   CProviderYahoo.cpp (complete)

```cpp
// ProviderYahoo.cpp : Implementation of CProviderYahoo
//

#include "stdafx.h"
#include "QuoteProviders.h"
#include "ProviderYahoo.h"
#include "QPGlobal.h"


/////////////////////////////////////////////////////////////////////////////
// CProviderYahoo

#define PROVIDER_HOST                   "quote.yahoo.com"
#define PROVIDER_PORT                   80
#define PROVIDER_LOGIN_REQUIRED         FALSE
#define PROVIDER_METHOD                 "GET"
#define PROVIDER_URL                    "/q?d=v2&s="
#define PROVIDER_ACCEPT_TYPES           ""
#define PROVIDER_HTTP_VERSION           "HTTP/1.0"
#define PROVIDER_FLAGS                  0
#define TAG_COL_BEGIN                   "<td"
#define SYMBOL_FORMAT                   ">%s<"
#define PROVIDER_HEADERS "Content-type: application/html-form-urlencoded\r\n"

STDMETHODIMP CProviderYahoo::GetHost(LPSTR lpszHost, DWORD dwLen)
```

```
{
    AFX_MANAGE_STATE(AfxGetStaticModuleState())
    if (strlen(PROVIDER_HOST) >= dwLen)
        return E_FAIL;
    strcpy(lpszHost, PROVIDER_HOST);
    return S_OK;
}


STDMETHODIMP CProviderYahoo::GetPort(USHORT* pnPort)
{
    AFX_MANAGE_STATE(AfxGetStaticModuleState())
    *pnPort = PROVIDER_PORT;
    return S_OK;
}


STDMETHODIMP CProviderYahoo::LoginIsRequired(BOOL * pbResult)
{
    AFX_MANAGE_STATE(AfxGetStaticModuleState())
    *pbResult = PROVIDER_LOGIN_REQUIRED;
    return S_OK;
}


STDMETHODIMP CProviderYahoo::GetMethod(LPSTR lpszMethod, DWORD dwLen)
{
    AFX_MANAGE_STATE(AfxGetStaticModuleState())
    if (strlen(PROVIDER_METHOD) >= dwLen)
        return E_FAIL;
    strcpy(lpszMethod, PROVIDER_METHOD);
    return S_OK;
}


STDMETHODIMP CProviderYahoo::GetURL(LPSTR lpszURL, DWORD dwLen)
{
    AFX_MANAGE_STATE(AfxGetStaticModuleState())
    if (strlen(m_strURL) >= dwLen)
        return E_FAIL;
    strcpy(lpszURL, m_strURL);
    return S_OK;
}


STDMETHODIMP CProviderYahoo::GetAcceptTypes(LPSTR lpszAcceptTypes, DWORD dwLen)
{
```

```
    AFX_MANAGE_STATE(AfxGetStaticModuleState())
    if (strlen(PROVIDER_ACCEPT_TYPES) >= dwLen)
        return E_FAIL;
    strcpy(lpszAcceptTypes, PROVIDER_ACCEPT_TYPES);
    return S_OK;
}


STDMETHODIMP CProviderYahoo::GetHttpVersion(LPSTR lpszHttpVersion, DWORD dwLen)
{
    AFX_MANAGE_STATE(AfxGetStaticModuleState())
    if (strlen(PROVIDER_HTTP_VERSION) >= dwLen)
        return E_FAIL;
    strcpy(lpszHttpVersion, PROVIDER_HTTP_VERSION);
    return S_OK;
}


STDMETHODIMP CProviderYahoo::GetFlags(DWORD * pdwFlags)
{
    AFX_MANAGE_STATE(AfxGetStaticModuleState())
    *pdwFlags = PROVIDER_FLAGS;
    return S_OK;
}


STDMETHODIMP CProviderYahoo::GetHeaders(LPSTR lpszHeaders, DWORD dwLen)
{
    AFX_MANAGE_STATE(AfxGetStaticModuleState())
    if (strlen(PROVIDER_HEADERS) >= dwLen)
        return E_FAIL;
    strcpy(lpszHeaders, PROVIDER_HEADERS);
    return S_OK;
}


STDMETHODIMP CProviderYahoo::GetData(LPSTR lpszData, DWORD dwLen)
{
    AFX_MANAGE_STATE(AfxGetStaticModuleState())
    if (strlen(m_strDataLine) >= dwLen)
        return E_FAIL;
    strcpy(lpszData, m_strDataLine);
    return S_OK;
}
```

```
STDMETHODIMP CProviderYahoo::InitializeData(LPSTR lpszData)
{
    AFX_MANAGE_STATE(AfxGetStaticModuleState())
    LPSTR lpsz1, lpsz2;
    CString strSymbol, strSymbolFormat(SYMBOL_FORMAT);

    // build the data string that will be sent to the server

    m_strURL = PROVIDER_URL;
    lpsz1 = lpszData;
    while (lpsz2 = strchr(lpsz1, ' '))
    {
        *lpsz2=0;
        m_strURL += lpsz1;
        m_arrSymbols.Add(lpsz1);
        m_strURL += "+";
        strSymbol.Format(strSymbolFormat, lpsz1);
        //this array will be used later for parsing
        m_arrSearchKeys.Add(strSymbol);
        *lpsz2= ' ';
        lpsz2++;
        lpsz1 = lpsz2;
    }
    m_strURL += lpsz1;
    m_arrSymbols.Add(lpsz1);
    strSymbol.Format(strSymbolFormat, lpsz1);
    m_arrSearchKeys.Add(strSymbol);
    return S_OK;
}


STDMETHODIMP CProviderYahoo::ParseResult(LPSTR lpszResult)
{
    AFX_MANAGE_STATE(AfxGetStaticModuleState())
    HRESULT hr;
    long lNumSymbols = m_arrSearchKeys.GetSize(), i;

    // find each symbol in the text and call ParseSymbol

    for (i=0; i<lNumSymbols; i++)
    {
        hr = ParseSymbol(i, lpszResult);
```

```
        if (FAILED(hr))
            return hr;
    }
    return S_OK;
}


HRESULT CProviderYahoo::ParseSymbol(long lIndex, LPSTR lpszResult)
{
    LPSTR lpszBegin=NULL, lpszEnd=NULL;
    CString strPrice, strChange, strVolume, strOpen;
    HRESULT hr;
    LPCTSTR lpszSymbol = m_arrSearchKeys.GetAt(lIndex);

    //find table row for symbol
    lpszBegin = strstr(lpszResult, lpszSymbol);
    CHECK_POINTER(lpszBegin);

    //pass time column
    lpszEnd = strstr(lpszBegin, TAG_COL_BEGIN);
    CHECK_POINTER(lpszEnd);
    lpszBegin = strstr(lpszEnd+1, TAG_COL_BEGIN);
    CHECK_POINTER(lpszBegin);

    //price column
    lpszEnd = strstr(lpszBegin+1, TAG_COL_BEGIN);
    CHECK_POINTER(lpszEnd);
    hr = ParseData(strPrice, lpszBegin, lpszEnd);
    if (FAILED(hr))
        return hr;

    //change
    lpszBegin = lpszEnd;
    CHECK_POINTER(lpszBegin);
    lpszEnd = strstr(lpszBegin+1, TAG_COL_BEGIN);
    CHECK_POINTER(lpszEnd);
    hr = ParseData(strChange, lpszBegin, lpszEnd);
    if (FAILED(hr))
        return hr;

    //pass change percent
    lpszBegin = strstr(lpszEnd+1, TAG_COL_BEGIN);
```

```
CHECK_POINTER(lpszBegin);

//volume
lpszEnd = strstr(lpszBegin+1, TAG_COL_BEGIN);
CHECK_POINTER(lpszEnd);
hr = ParseData(strVolume, lpszBegin, lpszEnd);
if (FAILED(hr))
    return hr;

//pass avg volume
lpszBegin = strstr(lpszEnd+1, TAG_COL_BEGIN);
CHECK_POINTER(lpszBegin);

//open
lpszEnd = strstr(lpszBegin+1, TAG_COL_BEGIN);
CHECK_POINTER(lpszEnd);
hr = ParseData(strOpen, lpszBegin, lpszEnd);
if (FAILED(hr))
    return hr;
//notify mainframe to update
Fire_UpdateSymbol(m_arrSymbols.GetAt(lIndex), strPrice, strChange, strOpen,
        strVolume);

return S_OK;
}
```

Creating Additional IQuoteProvider Components

Now that we've created the IQuoteProvider interface and the CProviderYahoo component, creating additional IQuoteProvider components is a breeze. The Stock Watcher sample contains a total of three IQuoteProvider components: CProviderYahoo, CProviderDatek, and CProviderFastQuote. They provide functionality for communicating with the Yahoo!, Datek, and Quote.com quote servers.

To create CProviderDatek and CProviderFastQuote, I simply ran the ATL Object Wizard for each new component. Because we've already defined the IQuoteProvider interface, there is no need to use the Add Method to Interface dialog. Instead, you can simply cut and paste the declaration of CProviderYahoo to each of these new component header files. The new component needs to inherit from the IQuoteProvider interface along with the other wizard-generated base classes. Then you can cut and paste the implementation of CProviderYahoo to each of the new component implementation files. At this point you can start making the changes required by the new component.

Listing 10-7 shows the CProviderDatek declaration. Notice how much it looks like the CProviderYahoo declaration. As you can see, it takes very little time to create the structure of these new components. The difference, however, lies in the implementation of the components. For example, the CProviderYahoo component doesn't require any form of authentication, and it transmits clear text. CProviderDatek, on the other hand, requires authentication (user name and password) and transmits encrypted data via SSL. The knowledge of how each quote provider behaves is built into the implementation of each quote provider component. For more details on how their implementations differ, see each quote provider component implementation file (ProviderYahoo.cpp, ProviderDatek.cpp, and ProviderFastQuote.cpp).

Listing 10-7 ProviderDatek.h

```
// ProviderDatek.h : Declaration of CProviderDatek

#ifndef __PROVIDERDATEK_H_
#define __PROVIDERDATEK_H_

#include "resource.h"       // main symbols
#include "CPQuoteProviders.h"

/////////////////////////////////////////////////////////////////////////////
// CProviderDatek
class ATL_NO_VTABLE CProviderDatek :
    public CComObjectRootEx<CComSingleThreadModel>,
    public CComCoClass<CProviderDatek, &CLSID_ProviderDatek>,
    public IConnectionPointContainerImpl<CProviderDatek>,
    public CProxyIQuoteProviderEvent<CProviderDatek>,
    public IQuoteProvider
{
public:
    CProviderDatek()
    {
    }
    CStringArray m_arrSymbols;
    CStringArray m_arrSearchKeys;
    CString m_strDataLine;
    CString m_strURL;
```

```
DECLARE_REGISTRY_RESOURCEID(IDR_PROVIDERDATEK)

BEGIN_COM_MAP(CProviderDatek)
    COM_INTERFACE_ENTRY(IQuoteProvider)
    COM_INTERFACE_ENTRY_IMPL(IConnectionPointContainer)
END_COM_MAP()


BEGIN_CONNECTION_POINT_MAP(CProviderDatek)
    CONNECTION_POINT_ENTRY(IID_IQuoteProviderEvent)
END_CONNECTION_POINT_MAP()

// IProviderDatek
public:
    STDMETHOD(InitializeData)(LPSTR lpszData);
    STDMETHOD(ParseResult)(LPSTR lpszResult);
    STDMETHOD(GetData)(LPSTR lpszData, DWORD dwLen);
    STDMETHOD(GetHeaders)(LPSTR lpszHeaders, DWORD dwLen);
    STDMETHOD(GetFlags)(DWORD* pdwFlags);
    STDMETHOD(GetHttpVersion)(LPSTR lpszHttpVersion, DWORD dwLen);
    STDMETHOD(GetAcceptTypes)(LPSTR lpszAcceptTypes, DWORD dwLen);
    STDMETHOD(GetURL)(LPSTR lpszURL, DWORD dwLen);
    STDMETHOD(GetMethod)(LPSTR lpszMethod, DWORD dwLen);
    STDMETHOD(LoginIsRequired)(BOOL* pbResult);
    STDMETHOD(GetPort)(USHORT* pnPort);
    STDMETHOD(GetHost)(LPSTR lpszHost, DWORD dwLen);
protected:
    HRESULT ParseFraction(CString& strPrice, LPSTR lpszPriceBegin, LPSTR
lpszPriceEnd);
    HRESULT ParseSymbol(long lIndex, LPSTR lpszResult);
};
#endif //__PROVIDERDATEK_H_
```

The QuoteProvider Component Category

The main goal behind this design is to allow additional IQuoteProvider components to be added at runtime. For example, the rest of the stock quote providers on the Internet could implement their own components that adhere to the IQuoteProvider interface. After they're installed on the user's machine, the Stock Watcher application needs to detect these new components and provide a way for them to be used.

A simple way for the Stock Watcher application to detect newly added components is through COM component categories. A component category is simply a registry convention that tells you if a given component implements certain interfaces.

To take advantage of component categories, you can use the Component Category Manager system component. The Component Category Manager implements two interfaces: ICatRegister and ICatInformation. As their names suggest, these interfaces are used for registering component categories, registering components with component categories, and retrieving information on a component category.

To create the quote provider component category, I generated a new GUID and called it CATID_QuoteProviders:

```
// {32014981-9CD4-11d1-9912-004033D06B6E}
DEFINE_GUID(CATID_QuoteProviders,
0x32014981, 0x9cd4, 0x11d1, 0x99, 0x12, 0x0, 0x40, 0x33, 0xd0, 0x6b, 0x6e);
```

Then, in QuoteProviders.cpp, I add some component category helper functions to make it easier to create the component category and to register/unregister components with the category (see Listing 10-8).

Listing 10-8   QuoteProviders.cpp

```
// QuoteProviders.cpp : Implementation of DLL Exports.
//

#include "stdafx.h"
#include "resource.h"
#include "CategoryGuid.h"
#include "initguid.h"
#include "QuoteProviders.h"
#include "QuoteProviders_i.c"
#include "ProviderYahoo.h"
#include "ProviderFastQuote.h"
#include "comcat.h"

//Component Category Helper Functions
HRESULT CreateComponentCategory(CATID catid, WCHAR* catDescription);
HRESULT RegisterCLSIDInCategory(REFCLSID clsid, CATID catid);
HRESULT UnRegisterCLSIDInCategory(REFCLSID clsid, CATID catid);

CRITICAL_SECTION g_CS;

CComModule _Module;
```

```
BEGIN_OBJECT_MAP(ObjectMap)
    OBJECT_ENTRY(CLSID_ProviderYahoo, CProviderYahoo)
    OBJECT_ENTRY(CLSID_ProviderFastQuote, CProviderFastQuote)
END_OBJECT_MAP()

class CQuoteProvidersApp : public CWinApp
{
public:
    virtual BOOL InitInstance();
    virtual int ExitInstance();
};

CQuoteProvidersApp theApp;

BOOL CQuoteProvidersApp::InitInstance()
{
    _Module.Init(ObjectMap, m_hInstance);
    return CWinApp::InitInstance();
}

int CQuoteProvidersApp::ExitInstance()
{
    _Module.Term();
    return CWinApp::ExitInstance();
}

/////////////////////////////////////////////////////////////////////////////
// Used to determine whether the DLL can be unloaded by OLE

STDAPI DllCanUnloadNow(void)
{
    AFX_MANAGE_STATE(AfxGetStaticModuleState());
    return (AfxDllCanUnloadNow()==S_OK && _Module.GetLockCount()==0) ? S_OK :
        S_FALSE;
}

/////////////////////////////////////////////////////////////////////////////
// Returns a class factory to create an object of the requested type

STDAPI DllGetClassObject(REFCLSID rclsid, REFIID riid, LPVOID* ppv)
{
```

```
        return _Module.GetClassObject(rclsid, riid, ppv);
}


//////////////////////////////////////////////////////////////////////
// DllRegisterServer - Adds entries to the system registry

STDAPI DllRegisterServer(void)
{
    HRESULT hr;
    // registers object, typelib and all interfaces in typelib
    hr = _Module.RegisterServer(TRUE);
    if (FAILED(hr))
        return hr;

    // create the IQuoteProvider component category
    hr = CreateComponentCategory(CATID_QuoteProviders, L"Stock Watcher Quote
            Providers");
    if (FAILED(hr))
        return hr;

    // register the CProviderYahoo component
    hr = RegisterCLSIDInCategory(CLSID_ProviderYahoo, CATID_QuoteProviders);
    if (FAILED(hr))
        return hr;

    // register the CProviderFastQuote component
    hr = RegisterCLSIDInCategory(CLSID_ProviderFastQuote,
                CATID_QuoteProviders);
    if (FAILED(hr))
        return hr;

    // register the CProviderDatek component
    hr = RegisterCLSIDInCategory(CLSID_ProviderDatek, CATID_QuoteProviders);
    if (FAILED(hr))
        return hr;
    return S_OK;
}


//////////////////////////////////////////////////////////////////////
// DllUnregisterServer - Removes entries from the system registry
```

```
STDAPI DllUnregisterServer(void)
{
    HRESULT hr;
    _Module.UnregisterServer();

    // unregister the CProviderYahoo component
    hr=UnRegisterCLSIDInCategory(CLSID_ProviderYahoo, CATID_QuoteProviders);
    if (FAILED(hr))
        return hr;

    // unregister the CProviderFastQuote component
    hr=UnRegisterCLSIDInCategory(CLSID_ProviderFastQuote,CATID_QuoteProviders);
    if (FAILED(hr))
        return hr;

    // unregister the CProviderDatek component
    hr=UnRegisterCLSIDInCategory(CLSID_ProviderDatek, CATID_QuoteProviders);
    if (FAILED(hr))
        return hr;
    return S_OK;
}

HRESULT CreateComponentCategory(CATID catid, WCHAR* catDescription)
{

    ICatRegister* pcr = NULL ;
    HRESULT hr = S_OK ;
    hr = CoCreateInstance(CLSID_StdComponentCategoriesMgr,
            NULL, CLSCTX_INPROC_SERVER, IID_ICatRegister, (void**)&pcr);
    if (FAILED(hr))
        return hr;

    // Make sure the HKCR\Component Categories\{..catid...}
    // key is registered.
    CATEGORYINFO catinfo;
    catinfo.catid = catid;
    catinfo.lcid = 0x0409 ; // english
```

```
        // Make sure the provided description is not too long.
        // Only copy the first 127 characters if it is.
        int len = wcslen(catDescription);
        if (len>127)
            len = 127;
        wcsncpy(catinfo.szDescription, catDescription, len);
        // Make sure the description is null terminated.
        catinfo.szDescription[len] = _T('\0');

        hr = pcr->RegisterCategories(1, &catinfo);
        pcr->Release();

        return hr;
    }


HRESULT RegisterCLSIDInCategory(REFCLSID clsid, CATID catid)
{
        // Register your component categories information.
        ICatRegister* pcr = NULL ;
        HRESULT hr = S_OK ;

        // create the COM Component Category Manager
        hr = CoCreateInstance(CLSID_StdComponentCategoriesMgr,
              NULL, CLSCTX_INPROC_SERVER, IID_ICatRegister, (void**)&pcr);

        if (SUCCEEDED(hr))
        {
           // Register this category as being "implemented" by the class.
           CATID rgcatid[1] ;
           rgcatid[0] = catid;
           hr = pcr->RegisterClassImplCategories(clsid, 1, rgcatid);
        }
        if (pcr != NULL)
            pcr->Release();
        return hr;
    }


HRESULT UnRegisterCLSIDInCategory(REFCLSID clsid, CATID catid)
{
```

```
    ICatRegister* pcr = NULL ;
    HRESULT hr = S_OK ;

    // create the COM Component Category Manager
    hr = CoCreateInstance(CLSID_StdComponentCategoriesMgr,
          NULL, CLSCTX_INPROC_SERVER, IID_ICatRegister, (void**)&pcr);

    if (SUCCEEDED(hr))
    {
       // Unregister this category as being "implemented" by the class.
       CATID rgcatid[1] ;
       rgcatid[0] = catid;
       hr = pcr->UnRegisterClassImplCategories(clsid, 1, rgcatid);
    }
    if (pcr != NULL)
    pcr->Release();
    return hr;
}
```

The following code is required in DllRegisterServer to register the quote provider component category and the CProviderYahoo component:

```
hr = CreateComponentCategory(CATID_QuoteProviders,
       L"Stock Watcher Quote Providers");
if (FAILED(hr))
    return hr;
hr = RegisterCLSIDInCategory(CLSID_ProviderYahoo, CATID_QuoteProviders);
if (FAILED(hr))
    return hr;
```

Conversely, the following code is required to unregister the CProviderYahoo component:

```
hr=UnRegisterCLSIDInCategory(CLSID_ProviderYahoo, CATID_QuoteProviders);
if (FAILED(hr))
    return hr;
```

The Stock Watcher application uses the Component Category Manager to query the CATID_QuoteProviders component category for all available quote provider components (I'll cover how to do this when we look at the CQuoteProviderDlg implementation). After Stock Watcher has been installed, additional quote provider components may be added to the user's system by simply registering them with the CATID_ QuoteProviders component category.

The HTTP Component

The HTTP component is only responsible for the HTTP transaction functionality. The HTTP transaction functionality consists primarily of sending and receiving data. To make the HTTP component abstract and reusable, the HTTP component relies on the IQuoteProvider component to provide the HTTP transaction details.

I created a separate project for the HTTP component called HttpObjectServer. It contains a single COM server for the CHttpRequest component. The CHttpRequest component implements the IHttpRequest interface. I created the ATL project and objects in the same manner as described for the QuoteProviders project.

IHttpRequest Interface

The IHttpRequest interface is defined in httpobjectserver.idl (see Listing 10-9), and the class declaration is found in httprequest.h (see Listing 10-10).

Listing 10-9   HttpObjectServer.idl

```
// HttpObjectServer.idl : IDL source for HttpObjectServer.dll
// This file will be processed by the MIDL tool to
// produce the type library (HttpObjectServer.tlb) and marshalling code.

import "oaidl.idl";
import "ocidl.idl";
    [
        uuid(10BE7FE8-9CC7-11D1-9912-004033D06B6E),
        helpstring("IHttpRequest Interface"),
        pointer_default(unique)
    ]
    interface IHttpRequest : IUnknown //IDispatch
    {
        [helpstring("method ProcessRequest")] HRESULT ProcessRequest(IUnknown*
                pQuoteProvider, long lMainHwnd);
        [helpstring("method GetProviderInterface")]
                HRESULT GetProviderInterface(IUnknown** ppUnk);
    };
```

```
[
    uuid(10BE7FDB-9CC7-11D1-9912-004033D06B6E),
    version(1.0),
    helpstring("HttpObjectServer 1.0 Type Library")
]
library HTTPOBJECTSERVERLib
{
    importlib("stdole32.tlb");
    importlib("stdole2.tlb");

    [
        uuid(10BE7FE9-9CC7-11D1-9912-004033D06B6E),
        helpstring("HttpRequest Class")
    ]
    coclass HttpRequest
    {
        [default] interface IHttpRequest;
    };
};
```

Listing 10-10   CHttpRequest

```
#ifndef __HTTPREQUEST_H_
#define __HTTPREQUEST_H_

#include "resource.h"        // main symbols
#include "..\QuoteProviders\QuoteProviders.h"

////////////////////////////////////////////////////////////////////////////
// CHttpRequest
class ATL_NO_VTABLE CHttpRequest :
    public CComObjectRootEx<CComSingleThreadModel>,
    public CComCoClass<CHttpRequest, &CLSID_HttpRequest>,
    public IHttpRequest
{
public:
    CHttpRequest()
    {
        m_pQuoteProvider = NULL;
    }
    ~CHttpRequest()
    {
```

```
        //release the IQuoteProvider interface
        if (m_pQuoteProvider)
            m_pQuoteProvider->Release();
    }


    //pointer to current quote provider interface
    IQuoteProvider* m_pQuoteProvider;

    //main application HWND
    HWND m_hwndMain;

DECLARE_REGISTRY_RESOURCEID(IDR_HTTPREQUEST)


BEGIN_COM_MAP(CHttpRequest)
    COM_INTERFACE_ENTRY(IHttpRequest)
END_COM_MAP()

// IHttpRequest
public:
    STDMETHOD(GetProviderInterface)(IUnknown** ppUnk);
    STDMETHOD(ProcessRequest)(IUnknown* pQuoteProvider, long lMainHwnd);
};


#endif //__HTTPREQUEST_H_
```

IHttpRequest consists only of the two methods described in Table 10-3.

ProcessRequest encapsulates the entire HTTP transaction process. The following is the implementation of ProcessRequest:

```
STDMETHODIMP CHttpRequest::ProcessRequest(IUnknown* pQuoteProvider,
                                          long lMainHwnd)

{
```

Table 10-3   IHttpRequest methods

Method	Description
ProcessRequest	Encapsulates the HTTP transaction functionality.
GetProviderInterface	Returns the IQuoteProvider interface currently being used by this component.

```
AFX_MANAGE_STATE(AfxGetStaticModuleState())

    // save the IQuoteProvider pointer
    m_pQuoteProvider = static_cast<IQuoteProvider*>(pQuoteProvider);
    // increment ref count
    m_pQuoteProvider->AddRef();
    // save the main application's HWND
    // this will be used later for posting messages
    m_hwndMain = reinterpret_cast<HWND>(lMainHwnd);

    // start the HttpWorkerThread
    AfxBeginThread(HttpWorkerThread, this);
    return S_OK;
}
```

After storing the IQuoteProvider pointer in m_pQuoteProvider, ProcessRequest must call IUnknown::AddRef on the interface pointer. ProcessRequest launches a worker thread, HttpWorkerThread, which takes care of the WinInet functionality from this point.

WinInet and Threads—A Quick Thread Tutorial

In the last chapter I showed you how to use WinInet asynchronously. Another approach that achieves the same user-friendly results is to use 32-bit multithreaded programming techniques. Because WinInet is a set of Win32 functions, it's designed to be used in multithreaded environments.

Using multithreaded programming techniques, you can put each WinInet operation in its own worker thread and make all of your WinInet function calls synchronously. Although this approach requires you to handle thread synchronization, it saves you from worrying about pending asynchronous operations. Here are a few reasons why you might want to use WinInet in threads instead of asynchronous mode:

- Threads ultimately give you more control over asynchronous behavior.
- Threads simplify your WinInet code by allowing you to make simple blocking calls.
- Threads allow you to leverage your multithreaded programming experience.

Although using threads definitely has its advantages, threads are often more costly than the API's built-in asynchronous implementation and are more difficult to implement properly. Study your options thoroughly before making this important design decision.

Most Internet-related functions take a considerable amount of time to complete. A typical request consists of the client computer requesting some data from the server. The server then processes the request and formulates the data. After the server has finished preparing the data, it's sent back over the wire to the waiting client. If the client application displays a busy cursor during that entire process, the user might get frustrated very quickly.

 This section is only meant to server as a high-level overview of Windows multithread programming. For more detailed information on Windows multithreading techniques, refer to the following excellent books:

- *Win32 System Programming* by Johnson M. Hart (Reading, MA: Addison Wesley Longman, 1997).
- *Win32 Programming* by Brent E. Rector and Joseph M. Newcomer (Reading, MA: Addison Wesley Longman, 1997).
- *Multithreading Applications in Win32: The Complete Guide to Threads* by Jim Beveridge and Robert Wiener (Reading, MA: Addison Wesley Longman, 1997).
- *Advanced Windows, Third Edition* by Jeffrey Richter (Redmond, WA: Microsoft Press, 1997).

Whether you're programming in Win32 or in MFC, you can use the threading capabilities built into the tools that you're used to using. One approach is to make each time-consuming WinInet request a separate worker thread. Designing your program this way reduces the need to use the asynchronous WinInet calls. You handle each thread individually and allow the WinInet function calls to block without interrupting the flow of the main program. The user should never get a busy cursor while processing Internet requests.

To accomplish this, you need to set up a worker thread that can be used by each request. In Win32 you can accomplish this using the CreateThread function. Here is the function prototype:

```
HANDLE CreateThread(
    LPSECURITY_ATTRIBUTES lpThreadAttributes,
    DWORD dwStackSize,
    LPTHREAD_START_ROUTINE lpStartAddress,
    LPVOID lpParameter,
    DWORD dwCreationFlags,
    LPDWORD lpThreadID
    );
```

The lpStartAddress parameter is the pointer to the thread function. The thread function must have the following signature, which is described by LPTHREAD_START_ROUTINE:

```
DWORD WINAPI ThreadFunc( LPVOID );
```

See the Win32 documentation for complete information on the rest of the parameters and function behavior. Now let's take a look at an example of how to use CreateThread. Listing 10-11 demonstrates how to use CreateThread to start a thread that could take care of handling a WinInet request. When CreateThread is called, MyThreadProc begins to execute in its own thread, and ProcessRequest continues executing in the primary thread.

Inside of MyThreadProc, you can call WinInet functions synchronously to avoid even more synchronization overhead. This approach helps break down the WinInet requests into more manageable objects.

Listing 10-11:   CreateThread example

```
DWORD WINAPI MyThreadProc(LPVOID lpVoid)
{
    //Call time-consuming WinInet functions
    return 0;
}


void ProcessRequest()
{
    DWORD dwThreadID;
    HANDLE hThread;

    hThread = CreateThread(NULL, 0, MyThreadProc, NULL, 0, &dwThreadID);

    //Continue other processing
}
```

You can achieve the same results in MFC by using AfxBeginThread. Here is the function prototype for AfxBeginThread:

```
CWinThread* AfxBeginThread(
    AFX_THREADPROC pfnThreadProc,
    LPVOID pParam,
    int nPriority = THREAD_PRIORITY_NORMAL,
    UINT nStackSize = 0,
```

```
    DWORD dwCreateFlags = 0,
    LPSECURITY_ATTRIBUTES lpSecurityAttrs = NULL
);
```

One of the nice things about MFC (and C++ in general) is how it takes care of the default parameters for you. The pfnThreadProc parameter is the pointer to the thread function, which must have the following signature:

```
UINT MyControllingFunction( LPVOID pParam );
```

Another difference between CreateThread and AfxBeginThread is that CreateThread returns a HANDLE to the thread whereas AfxBeginThread returns a pointer to the newly created CWinThread object. Let's take a look at an example of how to accomplish this in MFC (see Listing 10-12).

Listing 10-12   AfxBeginThread example

```
UINT MyThreadProc(LPVOID lpVoid)
{
    //Call WinInet functions
    return 0;
}

void ProcessRequest()
{
    CWinThread* pThread=NULL;

    pThread = AfxBeginThread(MyThreadProc, 0);
    //Continue processing
}
```

Again, when AfxBeginThread is called, MyThreadProc begins execution in its own thread, and ProcessRequest continues executing in the primary thread. When inside the thread, you can call the WinInet functions needed to complete the request.

The only drawback to using multithread programming techniques is that it requires thread synchronization. If you have a global resource that all of your WinInet request threads must access (database, file, memory, and so forth), you need to use some type of synchronization technique to manage the global resource. For example, you could use a critical section, mutex, semaphore, or events to manage the global resource. Although synchronizing the global resources adds a little overhead to your program, multithread programming greatly increases the usability of your application.

To help illustrate this, let's look at an example of how to use a critical section in the worker thread used earlier (see Listing 10-13). To use a critical section, you must first initialize it. If it's a global critical section, you should do this in your application's initialization routine (in MFC, that would be the application object's InitInstance method).

Listing 10-13   Synchronization example using critical sections

```
CRITICAL_SECTION g_CriticalSection;

BOOL CMyApp::InitInstance()
{
    //Standard app initialization
    //Initialize global critical section
    IniializeCriticalSection(&g_CriticalSection);
}

UINT MyThreadProc(LPVOID lpVoid)
{
    //Enter the critical section
    EnterCriticalSection(&g_CriticalSection);

    //Access global resources

    //Leave the critical section
    LeaveCriticalSection(&g_CriticalSection);

    return 0;
}

void ProcessRequest()
{
    CWinThread* pThread=NULL;

    pThread = AfxBeginThread(MyThreadProc, 0);
    //Continue processing
}
```

Before you attempt to access the global resource from within the thread, you must call EnterCriticalSection. This only allows one thread at a time to access the global resource. After you're done accessing the global resource, the call to LeaveCriticalSection makes it available to other threads waiting on it. If this approach doesn't fit your needs exactly, you should look into some of the other available synchronization techniques.

In this sample program, I use worker threads and critical sections. If you look at the implementation of CHttpRequest::ProcessRequest, you'll notice the following line of code that spawns the worker thread:

```
AfxBeginThread(HttpWorkerThread, this);
```

An HttpWorkerThread is spawned for each HTTP request made by the application. When the HTTP transaction receives data from the server and is ready to parse the information, a critical section is used to protect the global array of stock symbol objects that are updated in the IQuoteProvider::ParseResult routine. The following code snippet (from Listing 10-15) demonstrates how this happens:

```
//parse the HTTP response
EnterCriticalSection(&g_CS);
pProvider->ParseResult(lpszResult);
LeaveCriticalSection(&g_CS);
```

The use of a critical section prevents two threads from writing to the global array of stock symbol objects at the same time. Without this synchronization, your application may experience strange results, if not GPFs.

 Because each MFC thread has its own MFC state data, calls that manipulate the main application's MFC objects must be synchronized through Window messages. When HttpWorkerThread is finished processing the request, it posts a message to the application's main window telling it to update all of the active document's views:

```
//notify the main application window
if (pRequest->m_hwndMain)
    ::PostMessage(pRequest->m_hwndMain,
        WM_HTTP_THREAD_MESSAGE, UPDATE_ALL_VIEWS, 0);
```

The handler for this message in CMainFrame calls UpdateAllViews on the active document. Why can't you just call CStockWatcherDoc:: UpdateAllViews directly from HttpWorkerThread? If you try it, you'll get an access violation. This goes back to the MFC state issues discussed at the beginning of this chapter.

Although a multithread approach can greatly enhance your WinInet program, it would be impossible for me to cover sufficiently multithread programming techniques in this book. This is better left for another book (see the recommended reading at the beginning of this section and in Appendix E). Hopefully this section has given you enough information to understand how this sample program works. In the following section, I'll cover the implementation of Stock Watcher HttpWorkerThread.

HttpWorkerThread

You'll be able to study the coding details of HttpWorkerThread in the pages that follow. However, before letting you loose, I want to give you a high-level overview of the basic functionality. The following list describes the high-level steps that make up HttpWorkerThread:

1. Create the CInternetSession object.
2. Get authentication information from the user.
3. Call CInternetSession::GetHttpConnection (creates a CHttpConnection).
4. Call CHttpConnection::OpenRequest (creates a CHttpFile).
5. Call CHttpFile::SendRequest (transmits data).
6. Call CHttpFile::Read (reads the HTTP response).
7. Call IQuoteProvider::ParseResult (protects with critical section).
8. Notify main application of request completion (Windows message).

The first step in the worker thread is to create the CInternetSession object. To override the OnStatusCallback method, I declared an instance of CMyInternetSession, which is derived from CInternetSession (see Listing 10-14). Then, to enable the status callback method, you must call CInternetSession::EnableStatusCallback. WinInet calls the OnStatusCallback method as the status of CInternetSession changes.

 Although this example implements one thread per HTTP connection, this is definitely not the most optimized solution. If your application needs to support an unlimited number of connections simultaneously, a thread-per-connection solution is not acceptable. In this case you need to explore the possibilities of thread optimization (such as thread pooling).

Listing 10-14 CMyInternetSession

```
class CMyInternetSession : public CInternetSession
{
public:
    CMyInternetSession(LPCTSTR pstrAgent = NULL, DWORD dwContext = 1, DWORD
```

```
        dwAccessType = INTERNET_OPEN_TYPE_PRECONFIG,
        LPCTSTR pstrProxyName = NULL, LPCTSTR pstrProxyBypass = NULL,
        DWORD dwFlags = 0 )
    : CInternetSession(pstrAgent, dwContext, dwAccessType, pstrProxyName,
            pstrProxyBypass, dwFlags) { m_pRequest=NULL; };

    //override OnStatusCallback
    virtual void OnStatusCallback(DWORD dwContext, DWORD dwInternetStatus,
            LPVOID lpvStatusInformation, DWORD dwStatusInformationLength );

    //pointer to the CHttpRequest object controlling this Internet session
    CHttpRequest* m_pRequest;
};
```

The next step consists of getting the user's authentication information. First, HttpWorkerThread looks in the registry for the user's user name and password. If it doesn't find both values, it displays the authentication dialog as shown in Figure 10-11.

Both the user name and password are passed to GetHttpConnection and are used by WinInet for authentication. The rest of the steps consist of calling the appropriate HTTP function. HttpWorkerThread gathers all of the information it needs to make these WinInet HTTP calls by querying the appropriate IQuoteProvider methods. For example, CInternetSession::GetHttpConnection requires a host name and a port number. Thus, before calling this method, HttpWorkerThread calls IQuoteProvider:: GetHost and IQuoteProvider::GetPort to retrieve the provider-specific information. Furthermore, after HttpWorkerThread finishes receiving the HTTP response, it allows

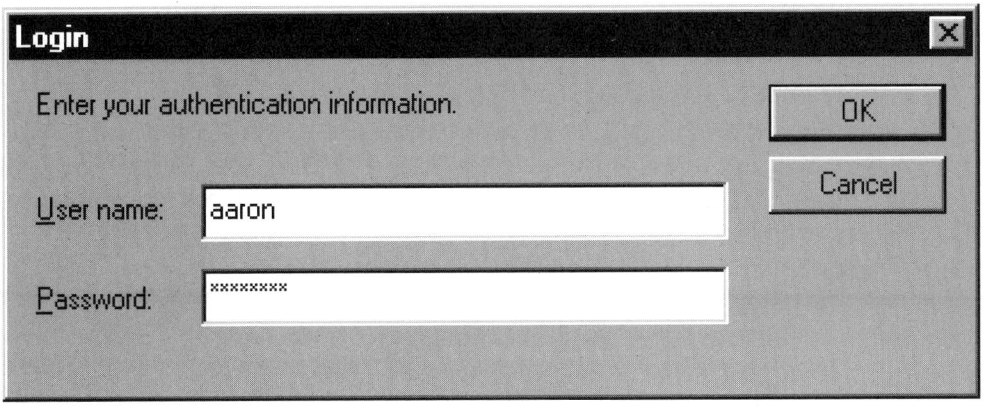

Figure 10-11 User authentication dialog

each quote provider to handle their responses differently by calling IQuoteProvider::
ParseResult. Peruse httprequest.cpp for more details on HttpWorkerThread (see
Listing 10-15).

The CHttpRequest object is generic enough to support all types of Internet stock
quote providers. As additional IQuoteProvider components are implemented and
released, the CHttpRequest component is able to transmit data to and from the new
providers without modifying a single line of code.

Listing 10-15 HttpRequest.cpp

```cpp
// HttpRequest.cpp : Implementation of CHttpRequest
//

#include "stdafx.h"
#include "HttpObjectServer.h"
#include "HttpRequest.h"
#include "MyInternetSession.h"
#include "LoginDlg.h"
#include "profile.h"
#include "..\QuoteProviders\QuoteProviders.h"
#include "..\Stock Watcher\globals.h"

#define HTTPFILE_BUFFLEN    4096
#define BUFFLEN             255

extern CRITICAL_SECTION g_CS;

UINT HttpWorkerThread(LPVOID lpVoid);

//////////////////////////////////////////////////////////////////////
// CMyInternetSession

void CMyInternetSession::OnStatusCallback(DWORD dwContext, DWORD
dwInternetStatus, LPVOID lpvStatusInformation, DWORD dwStatusInformationLength
)
{
    if (m_pRequest)
    {
        if (m_pRequest->m_hwndMain)
            ::PostMessage(m_pRequest->m_hwndMain, WM_HTTP_THREAD_MESSAGE,
                UPDATE_STATUS, dwInternetStatus);
    }
}
```

```
////////////////////////////////////////////////////////////////////////////
// CHttpRequest

STDMETHODIMP CHttpRequest::ProcessRequest(IUnknown* pQuoteProvider, long
lMainHwnd)
{
    AFX_MANAGE_STATE(AfxGetStaticModuleState())

    // save the IQuoteProvider pointer
    m_pQuoteProvider = static_cast<IQuoteProvider*>(pQuoteProvider);
    // increment ref count
    m_pQuoteProvider->AddRef();
    // save the main application's HWND
    // this will be used later for posting messages
    m_hwndMain = reinterpret_cast<HWND>(lMainHwnd);

    // start the HttpWorkerThread
    AfxBeginThread(HttpWorkerThread, this);
    return S_OK;
}

STDMETHODIMP CHttpRequest::GetProviderInterface(IUnknown * * ppUnk)
{
    AFX_MANAGE_STATE(AfxGetStaticModuleState())
    *ppUnk = m_pQuoteProvider;
    return S_OK;
}


////////////////////////////////////////////////////////////////////////////
// HttpWorkerThread

UINT HttpWorkerThread(LPVOID lpVoid)
{
    // we passed in a pointer to the CHttpRequest object
    CHttpRequest* pRequest = reinterpret_cast<CHttpRequest*>(lpVoid);
    // get the IQuoteProvider pointer
    IQuoteProvider* pProvider = pRequest->m_pQuoteProvider;

    // local variables
    CHttpConnection* pHttpConnection = NULL;
    CHttpFile* pHttpFile = NULL;
```

```
LPVOID lpvoid = NULL;
char lpszHost[BUFFLEN], lpszUserName[BUFFLEN], lpszPassword[BUFFLEN];
char lpszMethod[BUFFLEN], char lpszURL[BUFFLEN], lpszAcceptTypes[BUFFLEN];
char lpszHttpVersion[BUFFLEN], char lpszHeaders[BUFFLEN];
char lpszData[BUFFLEN];
DWORD dwFlags;
LPCTSTR pstrAcceptTypes[2];
INTERNET_PORT nPort;
BOOL bResult;

// declare CMyInternetSession object
CMyInternetSession InternetSession(NULL, 1, INTERNET_OPEN_TYPE_PRECONFIG);

try
{
    // enable the status callback
    InternetSession.EnableStatusCallback(TRUE);
    InternetSession.m_pRequest = pRequest;

    // get connection information
    pProvider->GetHost(lpszHost, BUFFLEN);
    pProvider->GetPort(&nPort);

    // find out if authentication is required—if so, get information
    pProvider->LoginIsRequired(&bResult);
    if (bResult)
    {
        Cstring strUserName, strPassword;

        // get user name and password from registry
        strUserName = GetMyProfileString("Settings", "username", "");
        strPassword = GetMyProfileString("Settings", "password", "");

        // if either is empty, show authentication dialog
        if (strUserName.IsEmpty() || strPassword.IsEmpty())
        {
            // get user name and password information
            CLoginDlg dlg;
            if (IDCANCEL == dlg.DoModal())
                return 0;
            // save user name and password to registry
```

```
                WriteMyProfileString("Settings", "username",
                        dlg.m_strUserName);
                WriteMyProfileString("Settings", "password",
                        dlg.m_strPassword);
                strcpy(lpszUserName, dlg.m_strUserName);
                strcpy(lpszPassword, dlg.m_strPassword);
            }
            else
            {
                strcpy(lpszUserName, strUserName);
                strcpy(lpszPassword, strPassword);
            }
        }


        // establish the HTTP connection
        pHttpConnection = InternetSession.GetHttpConnection( lpszHost, nPort,
                lpszUserName, lpszPassword);


        // get request-specific information
        pProvider->GetMethod(lpszMethod, BUFFLEN);
        pProvider->GetURL(lpszURL, BUFFLEN);
        pProvider->GetAcceptTypes(lpszAcceptTypes, BUFFLEN);
        pstrAcceptTypes[0] = lpszAcceptTypes;
        pstrAcceptTypes[1] = NULL;
        pProvider->GetHttpVersion(lpszHttpVersion, BUFFLEN);
        pProvider->GetFlags(&dwFlags);


        // open the HTTP request
        pHttpFile = pHttpConnection->OpenRequest(lpszMethod, lpszURL, "", 1,
                pstrAcceptTypes, lpszHttpVersion, dwFlags);


        // get the request data
        pProvider->GetHeaders(lpszHeaders, BUFFLEN);
        pProvider->GetData(lpszData, BUFFLEN);


        // send the HTTP request
        if (pHttpFile->SendRequest(lpszHeaders, strlen(lpszHeaders),
                static_cast<void*>(lpszData), strlen(lpszData)))
        {
            DWORD dwRet;
            // query the HTTP status code
```

```
pHttpFile->QueryInfoStatusCode(dwRet);

// if authentication failed, ask user to authenticate again
// then resend the request with new information
while (dwRet == HTTP_STATUS_DENIED)
{
    CLoginDlg dlg;
    dlg.m_strUserName = GetMyProfileString("Settings", "username",
            "");
    dlg.m_strPassword = GetMyProfileString("Settings", "password",
            "");
    if (IDCANCEL == dlg.DoModal())
    {
        if (pHttpConnection)
        {
            pHttpConnection->Close();
            delete pHttpConnection;
        }
        if (pHttpFile)
        {
            pHttpFile->Close();
            delete pHttpFile;
        }
        return 0;
    }

    WriteMyProfileString("Settings", "username",
            dlg.m_strUserName);
    WriteMyProfileString("Settings", "password",
            dlg.m_strPassword);
    strcpy(lpszUserName, dlg.m_strUserName);
    strcpy(lpszPassword, dlg.m_strPassword);

    InternetSetOption((HINTERNET)(*pHttpFile),
            INTERNET_OPTION_USERNAME, lpszUserName,
            strlen(lpszUserName));

    InternetSetOption((HINTERNET)(*pHttpFile),
            INTERNET_OPTION_PASSWORD, lpszPassword,
            strlen(lpszPassword));
```

```
        pHttpFile->SendRequest(lpszHeaders, strlen(lpszHeaders),
            static_cast<void*>(lpszData), strlen(lpszData));

        pHttpFile->QueryInfoStatusCode(dwRet);
}

if (dwRet == HTTP_STATUS_OK)
{
    CString strContentLen;
    LPSTR lpszResult=NULL;
    UINT nRead=0, nTotalRead=0;

    lpvoid = malloc(HTTPFILE_BUFFLEN);
    //memory error
    if (!lpvoid)
        return 0;

    //read the HTTP response
    nRead = pHttpFile->Read(lpvoid, HTTPFILE_BUFFLEN);
    nTotalRead += nRead;
    while (nRead == HTTPFILE_BUFFLEN)
    {
        lpvoid = realloc(lpvoid, nTotalRead+HTTPFILE_BUFFLEN);
        nRead = pHttpFile->Read((byte*)lpvoid+nTotalRead,
            HTTPFILE_BUFFLEN);
        nTotalRead += nRead;
    }

    lpszResult = (LPSTR)lpvoid;
    *(lpszResult + nTotalRead) = NULL;

    //parse the HTTP response
    EnterCriticalSection(&g_CS);
    pProvider->ParseResult(lpszResult);
    LeaveCriticalSection(&g_CS);

    //notify the main application window
    if (pRequest->m_hwndMain)
        ::PostMessage(pRequest->m_hwndMain, WM_HTTP_THREAD_MESSAGE,
            UPDATE_ALL_VIEWS, 0);
}
```

```
        }
    }
    catch(CInternetException *e)
    {
        e->ReportError();
        e->Delete();
    }

    // clean up
    if (lpvoid)
        free(lpvoid);

    if (pHttpFile)
    {
        pHttpFile->Close();
        delete pHttpFile;
    }
    if (pHttpConnection)
    {
        pHttpConnection->Close();
        delete pHttpConnection;
    }
    return 0;
}
```

The Stock Watcher Application

Although there isn't enough space to cover the details of the Stock Watcher application, there are a few aspects of the application that I want to discuss briefly, including the CQuoteProviderDlg, CQuoteProviderEventSink, and Refresh All functionality.

CQuoteProviderDlg

Figure 10-12 illustrates CQuoteProviderDlg. I've provided three quote provider components with the Stock Watcher sample application (Yahoo!, Quote.com, and Datek). CQuoteProviderDlg enumerates all of the components that belong to the CATID_ QuoteProviders component category and allows the user to select one of them in the quote provider combo box (see Listing 10-16). Hence, if you implement your own

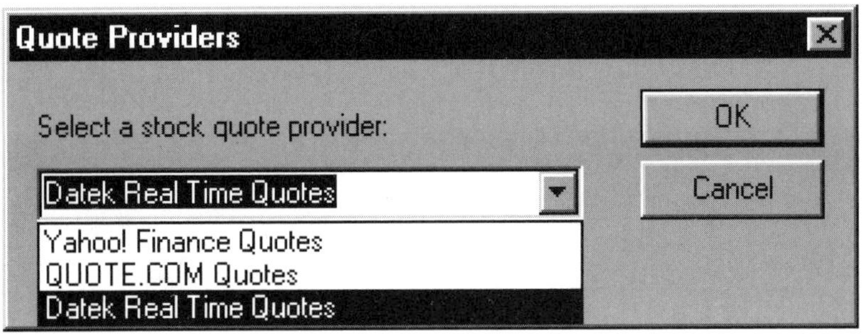

Figure 10-12   Quote Providers dialog

quote provider component and register it with the quote provider component category, it *magically* appears in the dialog's list of providers.

After the user selects a stock provider and presses OK, CQuoteProviderDlg saves the class identifier (CLSID) of the component to an application-specific registry key named ProviderCLSID (see Listing 10-16). From this point on, the application uses the selected quote provider component.

Listing 10-16   **QuoteProviderDlg.cpp**

```cpp
BOOL CQuoteProviderDlg::OnInitDialog()
{
    CString strCLSID;
    CDialog::OnInitDialog();

    // query system for all IQuoteProvider components
    HRESULT hr = EnumQuoteProviders(&m_cbQuoteProviders);
    if (FAILED(hr))
        AfxMessageBox("Error enumerating component category");
    // read the currently selected IQuoteProvider component from registry
    // and reselect if one is found, otherwise just select the first one

    strCLSID = AfxGetApp()->GetProfileString("Settings", "ProviderCLSID", "");
    if (!strCLSID.IsEmpty())
    {
        long lCount = m_cbQuoteProviders.GetCount();
        for (long i=0; i<lCount; i++)
        {
            if ( (m_CLSIDs.GetAt(i)) == strCLSID )
                break;
        }
    }
```

```
        if (i == lCount) i = 0;
        m_cbQuoteProviders.SetCurSel(i);
    }
    else m_cbQuoteProviders.SetCurSel(0);
    return TRUE;
}


HRESULT CQuoteProviderDlg::EnumQuoteProviders(CComboBox* pBox)
{
    ICatInformation* pci = NULL ;
    HRESULT hr = S_OK ;

    // create the COM component manager
    hr = CoCreateInstance(CLSID_StdComponentCategoriesMgr,
            NULL, CLSCTX_INPROC_SERVER, IID_ICatInformation, (void**)&pci);
    if (FAILED(hr))
      return hr;

    CATID arrCATID[1];
    arrCATID[0] = CATID_QuoteProviders;

    // enumerate the components in category
    IEnumCLSID* penumCLSID = NULL;
    pci->EnumClassesOfCategories(1, arrCATID, 0, 0, &penumCLSID);
    if (FAILED(hr))
    {
        pci->Release();
        return hr;
    }

    // add each component to the drop-down combo box
    ULONG lItems=1, lIndex=0;
    hr = penumCLSID->Next(1, arrCATID, NULL);
    while (S_OK == SUCCEEDED(hr))
    {
        USES_CONVERSION;
        LPOLESTR lpszDisplay, lpszCLSIDString;
        char* lpszAnsiDisplay, *lpszAnsiClassString;
        CString strGUID;

        OleRegGetUserType(arrCATID[0], USERCLASSTYPE_FULL, &lpszDisplay);
```

```
        lpszAnsiDisplay = W2A(lpszDisplay);
        pBox->AddString(lpszAnsiDisplay);
        StringFromCLSID(arrCATID[0], &lpszCLSIDString);
        lpszAnsiClassString = W2A(lpszCLSIDString);
        m_CLSIDs.Add(lpszAnsiClassString);
        hr = penumCLSID->Next(1, arrCATID, NULL);
        lIndex++;
    }
    pci->Release();
    penumCLSID->Release();
    return S_OK;
}


void CQuoteProviderDlg::OnOK()
{
    CString strCLSID;

    long lCurSel = m_cbQuoteProviders.GetCurSel();
    if (CB_ERR == lCurSel)
        return;

    ASSERT( (lCurSel >= 0) && (lCurSel <= m_CLSIDs.GetUpperBound()) );
    strCLSID = AfxGetApp()->GetProfileString("Settings","ProviderCLSID","");

    // if the user changed the selected IQuoteProvider component,
    // clear the user name and password saved in the registry
    // (they won't apply to the new stock quote provider)

    if (strCLSID != m_CLSIDs.GetAt(lCurSel))
    {
        AfxGetApp()->WriteProfileString("Settings", "username", "");
        AfxGetApp()->WriteProfileString("Settings", "password", "");
    }

    // save the selected IQuoteProvider component CLSID to registry

    AfxGetApp()->WriteProfileString("Settings", "ProviderCLSID", ]
            m_CLSIDs.GetAt(lCurSel));

    CDialog::OnOK();
}
```

CQuoteProviderEventSink

In order for Stock Watcher to receive events fired by the IQuoteProvider components, it must implement a sink object and establish a connection with the IQuoteProvider connection point. I called the sink object used by the application CQuoteProviderEventSink. The following is the CQuoteProviderEventSink class declaration:

```
class CQuoteProviderEventSink :
    public CComObjectRoot,
    public IQuoteProviderEvent
{
public:
    CStockWatcherDoc* m_pDoc;
    CQuoteProviderEventSink() {}

BEGIN_COM_MAP(CQuoteProviderEventSink)
    COM_INTERFACE_ENTRY(IQuoteProviderEvent)
END_COM_MAP()
// IHttpEvent Methods
    STDMETHOD(UpdateSymbol)(LPCTSTR lpszSymbol, LPCTSTR lpszPrice,
        LPCTSTR lpszChange, LPCTSTR lpszOpen, LPCTSTR lpszVolume);
};
```

CStockWatcherDoc creates an instance of this object in its constructor. Then, each time it creates an IHttpRequest component, it calls AtlAdvise to establish the connection point with IQuoteProvider. When CProviderYahoo::ParseResult calls Fire_UpdateSymbol, the CQuoteProviderEventSink::UpdateSymbol method is called.

Refresh All

The Stock Watcher application allows the user to decide when to update the stock quote information by choosing Refresh All from the Symbol menu. The CStockWatcherDoc::OnRefreshAllSymbols handler creates an instance of the currently selected quote provider component along with an IHttpRequest component. Then it passes the stock symbol information to the quote provider component using the IQuoteProvider::InitializeData method. Finally, after establishing the connection point with IQuoteProvider, it calls IHttpRequest::ProcessRequest (see Listing 10-17), which encapsulates the entire HTTP transaction functionality.

Listing 10-17 CStockWatcherDoc.cpp

```
// Stock WatcherDoc.cpp : implementation of the CStockWatcherDoc class
//

#include "stdafx.h"
#include "Stock Watcher.h"
#include "Stock WatcherDoc.h"
#include "Mainfrm.h"
#include "AddSymbolDlg.h"
#include "QuoteProviderDlg.h"
#include "..\QuoteProviders\QuoteProviders.h"

#ifdef _DEBUG
#define new DEBUG_NEW
#undef THIS_FILE
static char THIS_FILE[] = __FILE__;
#endif

IMPLEMENT_SERIAL(CStockSymbol, CObject, 1);

/////////////////////////////////////////////////////////////////////////
// CStockWatcherDoc

IMPLEMENT_DYNCREATE(CStockWatcherDoc, CDocument)

BEGIN_MESSAGE_MAP(CStockWatcherDoc, CDocument)
    //{{AFX_MSG_MAP(CStockWatcherDoc)
    ON_COMMAND(ID_SYMBOL_NEW, OnSymbolNew)
    ON_COMMAND(ID_REFRESH_ALL_SYMBOLS, OnRefreshAllSymbols)
    ON_COMMAND(ID_QUOTE_PROVIDER, OnQuoteProvider)
    //}}AFX_MSG_MAP
END_MESSAGE_MAP()

/////////////////////////////////////////////////////////////////////////
// CStockWatcherDoc construction/destruction

CStockWatcherDoc::CStockWatcherDoc()
{
    //create and initialize the CQuoteProviderEventSink object

    CComObject<CQuoteProviderEventSink>::CreateInstance(&m_pQuoteProviderEventSink);
```

```
    m_pQuoteProviderEventSink->AddRef();
    m_pQuoteProviderEventSink->m_pDoc = this;
}

CStockWatcherDoc::~CStockWatcherDoc()
{
    EmptySymbolList();

    //release all IHttpRequest interfaces
    long lSize = m_arrConnections.GetSize(), i;
    for (i=0; i<lSize; i++)
    {
        IHttpRequest* pRequest =
                static_cast<IHttpRequest*>(m_arrIHttpRequests.GetAt(i));
        IQuoteProvider* pProvider = NULL;

        pRequest->GetProviderInterface(
                reinterpret_cast<IUnknown**>(&pProvider));

        // disconnect the event sink
        if (pProvider)
            AtlUnadvise(pProvider, IID_IQuoteProviderEvent,
                    m_arrConnections.GetAt(i));

        // decrement ref count
        pRequest->Release();
    }
    //release the CQuoteProviderEventSink
    m_pQuoteProviderEventSink->Release();
}

void CStockWatcherDoc::OnRefreshAllSymbols()
{
    long lSize = m_Objects.GetSize(), i;
    CStockSymbol* pSymbol;
    CString strSymbols, strCLSID;
    DWORD dwConnection;

    if (lSize == 0)
        return;

    //get the currently selected quote provider's CLSID
    strCLSID = AfxGetApp()->GetProfileString("Settings", "ProviderCLSID", "");
```

```
if (strCLSID.IsEmpty())
    return;

LPOLESTR lpszCLSID;
USES_CONVERSION;
lpszCLSID = A2W(strCLSID.GetBuffer(255));
CLSID clsid;

//convert from string to CLSID
CLSIDFromString(lpszCLSID, &clsid);

for (i=0; i<lSize; i++)
{
    pSymbol = static_cast<CStockSymbol*>(m_Objects.GetAt(i));
    if (i == 0)
        strSymbols += pSymbol->m_strSymbol;
    else strSymbols += ' ' + pSymbol->m_strSymbol;
}

//create the IHttpRequest component
IHttpRequest* pRequest = NULL;
CoCreateInstance(CLSID_HttpRequest, NULL, CLSCTX_ALL, IID_IHttpRequest,
        (void**)&pRequest);
_ASSERTE(pRequest != NULL);
m_arrIHttpRequests.Add(pRequest);

//create the IQuoteProvider component
IQuoteProvider *pQuoteProvider = NULL;
CoCreateInstance(clsid, NULL, CLSCTX_ALL, IID_IQuoteProvider,
        (void**)&pQuoteProvider);
_ASSERTE(pQuoteProvider != NULL);

//establish the connection point
AtlAdvise(pQuoteProvider, m_pQuoteProviderEventSink->GetUnknown(),
        IID_IQuoteProviderEvent, &dwConnection);
m_arrConnections.Add(dwConnection);

//initialize the data (strSymbols)
pQuoteProvider->InitializeData(strSymbols.GetBuffer(255));

//call ProcessRequest
pRequest->ProcessRequest(pQuoteProvider,
        reinterpret_cast<long>(AfxGetMainWnd()->GetSafeHwnd()));
```

```
        //release IQuoteProvider, let the IHttpRequest object manage lifetime
        pQuoteProvider->Release();
}


void CStockWatcherDoc::UpdateSymbol(LPCTSTR lpszSymbol, LPCTSTR lpszPrice,
        LPCTSTR lpszChange, LPCTSTR lpszOpen, LPCTSTR lpszVolume)
{
        CStockSymbol* pSymbol = FindObjectBySymbol(lpszSymbol);
        pSymbol->m_strPrice = lpszPrice;
        pSymbol->m_strChange = lpszChange;
        pSymbol->m_strOpen = lpszOpen;
        pSymbol->m_strVolume = lpszVolume;
        pSymbol->m_dtLastUpdate = COleDateTime::GetCurrentTime();
        SetModifiedFlag();
}


CStockSymbol* CStockWatcherDoc::FindObjectBySymbol(LPCTSTR lpszSymbol)
{
        long lSize = m_Objects.GetSize(), i;
        CStockSymbol* pSymbol=NULL;

        for (i=0; i<lSize; i++)
        {
            pSymbol = static_cast<CStockSymbol*>(m_Objects.GetAt(i));
            if (pSymbol->m_strSymbol.CompareNoCase(lpszSymbol) == 0)
                return pSymbol;
        }
        return pSymbol;
}


STDMETHODIMP CQuoteProviderEventSink::UpdateSymbol(LPCTSTR lpszSymbol,
        LPCTSTR lpszPrice, LPCTSTR lpszChange, LPCTSTR lpszOpen,
        LPCTSTR lpszVolume)
{
        m_pDoc->UpdateSymbol(lpszSymbol, lpszPrice, lpszChange, lpszOpen,
                lpszVolume);
        return S_OK;
}
```

Conclusion

I've shown you how to use COM to write reusable WinInet components. Even though WinInet is already a high-level interface that encapsulates a great deal of Internet protocol code, why not make your code even more reusable through COM? Furthermore, with the easy-to-use wizards and templates provided by ATL, it makes sense to leverage this powerful architecture.

The Stock Watcher sample application associated with this chapter illustrates how a simple IHttpRequest interface can encapsulate the entire HTTP transaction functionality. Furthermore, it demonstrates how new quote provider components (IQuoteProvider) can be added to the user's system at runtime to provide additional functionality. As an additional exercise you might want to try implementing your own custom quote provider component and registering it with the component category.

Feel free to reuse the components provided with the Stock Watcher application. Although the name IQuoteProvider is appropriate for this application, the interface can be used for all types of HTTP requests (not only stock quote providers). You can change the name of the interface to something more generic like IHttpRequestInformation.

Hopefully I've helped you appreciate the power of COM/ATL and how well it fits into the WinInet design model. Because everything tied to the Internet changes so quickly, it makes sense to use the easily extensible COM architecture. As things change, COM allows you simply to update the affected component as opposed to the entire application. Incidentally, if any of the quote providers included in the sample application happens to change its HTML formats before this book is published, you may have to tweak the corresponding ParseResult routines.

11
Chapter

Establishing a Dial-up

Connection

So far I've covered how to use WinInet to leverage HTTP, FTP, and Gopher in your Windows applications. Up to this point I've made the big assumption that the user is connected to the Internet while running the application. As with any Internet-enabled application, the developer must decide who is responsible for establishing a dial-up connection with the user's ISP before attempting to use any TCP/IP-based protocol.

The easiest solution (for the developer anyway) is to let the user worry about it. Users are smart enough to know when they need to connect to the Internet . . . aren't they? While this thought frequently crosses my mind, it usually leads to less user-friendly software. The truth is most users don't have a clue. A well-written Internet-enabled application establishes a connection with the user's ISP automatically as needed.

If there is one common complaint among Windows Internet developers, it's that there isn't enough documentation on establishing dial-up connections from their application. Although most developers are required to add this functionality to their applications, the amount of information available is limited to the brief API specifications in the Visual C++ online help system. I couldn't let this book come to an end without providing a chapter to answer this cry for help. This chapter helps you to become completely familiar with the dial-up interfaces available to you as a Windows Internet developer.

Currently there are two dial-up development interfaces: the WinInet dial-up functions and the RAS API. The former is a newer high-level interface to the latter. In this chapter, I'll cover the WinInet dial-up functions and discuss some of their advantages and disadvantages. Then I'll dive deep into the RAS API. In particular, I'll show you how to take advantage of the RAS common dialogs as well as the low-level dialing functions. Not only will you learn how to begin and end a RAS connection programmatically, you'll also learn how to manipulate the system phonebook entries. Furthermore, I'll cover a few advanced RAS issues like AutoDial and connection notifications. By the time you're done with this chapter, you'll understand the ins and outs of establishing a dial-up connection from your Windows application.

Prerequisites

Before WinInet came into existence, developers only had one interface to dial-up functionality—the RAS API. So why haven't you heard of RAS before? If you're a Windows 95 user, you're probably more familiar with the term dial-up networking. Both dial-up networking and RAS refer to the same underlying dial-up functionality. The system dial-up functions available to you as a developer make up what is known as the RAS API.

The general RAS functionality is contained in rasapi32.dll. To use the general RAS functions you must link against rasapi32.lib and include ras.h. The RAS common dialogs, which are only supported on Windows NT 4.0, are implemented in rasdlg.dll. To use this functionality, you must link against rasdlg.lib and include rasdlg.h. Many of the RAS APIs are only supported on Windows NT (and not on Windows 95). Throughout the chapter I'll try to make it clear which functions are available on Windows 95, Windows NT 4.0, or both. Nevertheless, the best source of documentation on RAS compatibility is found in the Visual C++ 5.0 help system.

The WinInet dial-up functions are contained in wininet.dll. You can take advantage of the WinInet dial-up functions in the same manner as the other WinInet functions I've already covered.

When you've got the development tools described earlier, you're ready to start leveraging the powerful dial-up capabilities made available by the Windows operating system. Now it's just a matter of deciding exactly what you want to accomplish and the best strategy to make it happen.

WinInet Dial-up Functions

WinInet offers a high-level interface to certain aspects of the RAS API. Table 11-1 describes the dial-up functions offered by WinInet. Although the WinInet functions have their problems, at times they can offer sufficient and pragmatic solutions.

As you'll see shortly, using the WinInet dial-up functions greatly reduces the amount of code you need to write to establish a dial-up connection. Plus, because WinInet is part of the IE update to Windows, these functions are supported on both Windows 95 and Windows NT 4.0. Unlike WinInet, RAS presents many compatibility challenges because much of the functionality is only supported on Windows NT. Now let's look at the WinInet functions in more detail.

InternetAutodial and InternetAutodialHangup

InternetAutodial causes the modem to dial the default Internet connection (or phonebook entry) automatically. InternetAutodialHangup closes a connection initiated by InternetAutodial. First, let's take a look at InternetAutodial's declaration:

```
BOOL InternetAutodial(
    IN DWORD dwFlags,
    IN DWORD dwReserved
);
```

dwFlags is a double-word value that contains the flags controlling the dialing operation. It can contain one of the values described in Table 11-2.

Table 11-1   **WinInet dial-up functions**

Name	Description
InternetAutodial	Initiates an unattended dial-up connection using the default phonebook entry.
InternetAutodialHangup	Disconnects a modem connection initiated by InternetAutodial.
InternetDial	Initiates a dial-up connection with a specific phonebook entry.
InternetHangUp	Disconnects a modem connection initiated by InternetDial.
InternetGoOnline	Prompts the user for permission to initiate a dial-up connection to the given URL.
InternetGetConnectedState	Retrieves the current state of the Internet connection.
InternetSetDialState	Sets the current state of the Internet connection.

Table 11-2   InternetAutodial flags

Flag	Description
INTERNET_AUTODIAL_FORCE_ONLINE	Forces an online Internet connection.
INTERNET_AUTODIAL_FORCE_UNATTENDED	Forces an unattended Internet dial-up.

If you want to initiate the user's default phonebook entry without any user intervention, you can use InternetAutodial in the following manner:

```
InternetAutodial(INTERNET_AUTODIAL_FORCE_UNATTENDED, 0);
```

A return value of TRUE indicates success. When this function is called, the dialog shown in Figure 11-1 appears and the system begins calling your default phonebook entry. If you press Cancel, the dialog shown in Figure 11-2 appears, allowing you to modify your user name, password, and phonebook entry settings.

Use InternetAutodialHangup to disconnect the connection initiated by InternetAutodial in the following manner:

```
InternetAutodialHangup(0);
```

Figure 11-1   InternetAutodial Dialing
Progress dialog

Figure 11-2 InternetAutodial Dial-up
Connection dialog

So how does InternetAutodial know which phonebook entry is the default? The
default phonebook entry is specified in the Internet Properties dialog (right click on
the Internet Explorer icon and select Properties). From the Connection tab the user
can either walk through a Connection wizard or specify the desired Internet connection settings directly (see Figure 11-3).

If the user selects the LAN option, InternetAutodial assumes that the user's
machine has a direct connection to the Internet and does nothing. If the user selects
the modem option, InternetAutodial uses the phonebook entry settings specified in the
Dial-Up Settings dialog (see Figure 11-4) to establish the dial-up connection.

As you can see, the WinInet dial-up functions are tightly coupled with the IE 4.x
system properties. Although at first this may seem like a convenience, it's more often
problematic. For example, if you want to use InternetAutodial to force an unattended
dial-up connection, all the user information (user name, password, and so forth) must
be configured properly in the Dial-Up Settings dialog before attempting the call. If
user information is missing, either the call fails or the user is prompted to enter it
(depending on the flag passed to InternetAutodial). Either way, this defeats the goal of
establishing an unattended connection. Unfortunately, WinInet doesn't offer a method
to determine whether any information is missing before attempting the call.

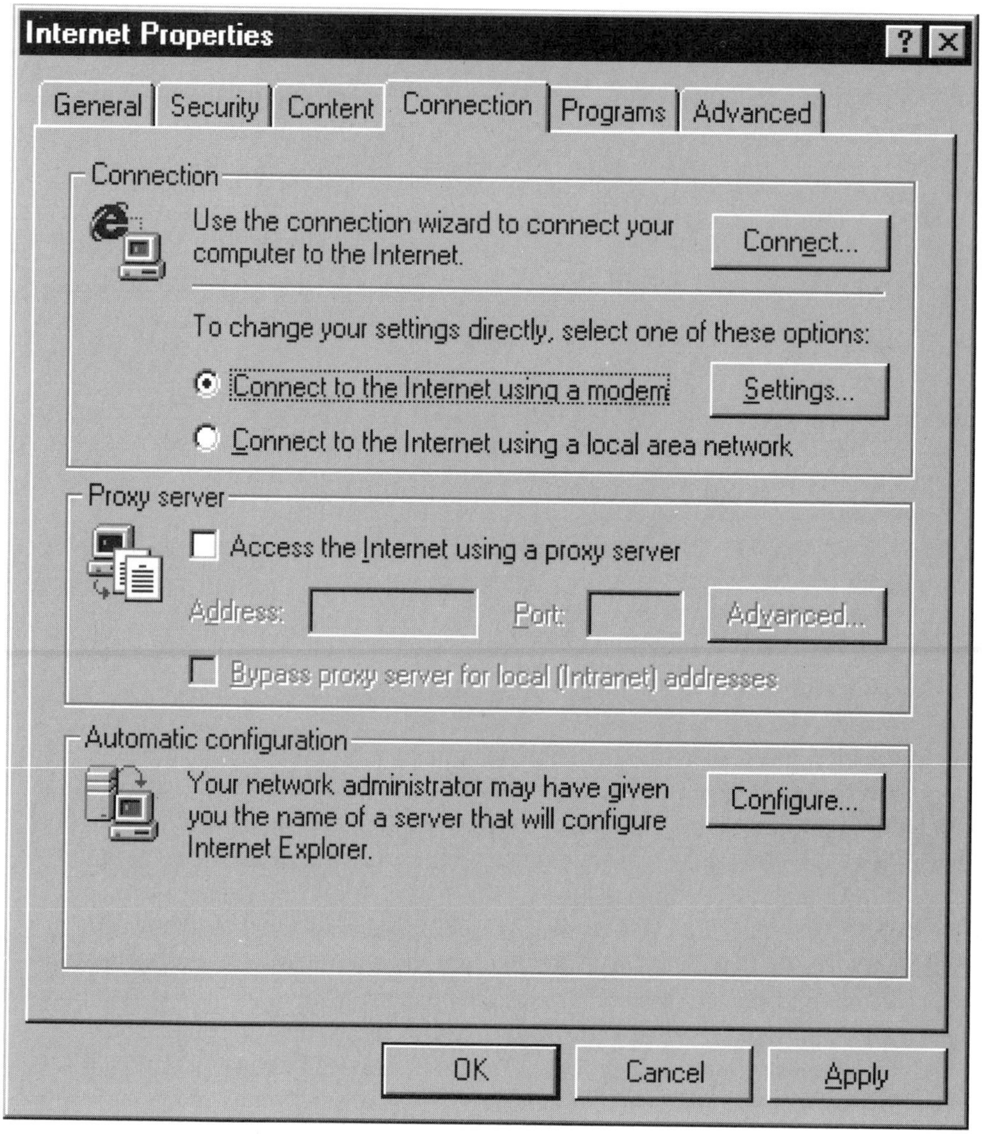

Figure 11-3   Internet Properties dialog

InternetDial and InternetHangUp

InternetDial and InternetHangUp are very similar to InternetAutodial and
InternetAutodialHangup. InternetDial displays the same UI as InternetAutodial.
There are, however, a few subtle differences. First, take a look at InternetDial's
declaration:

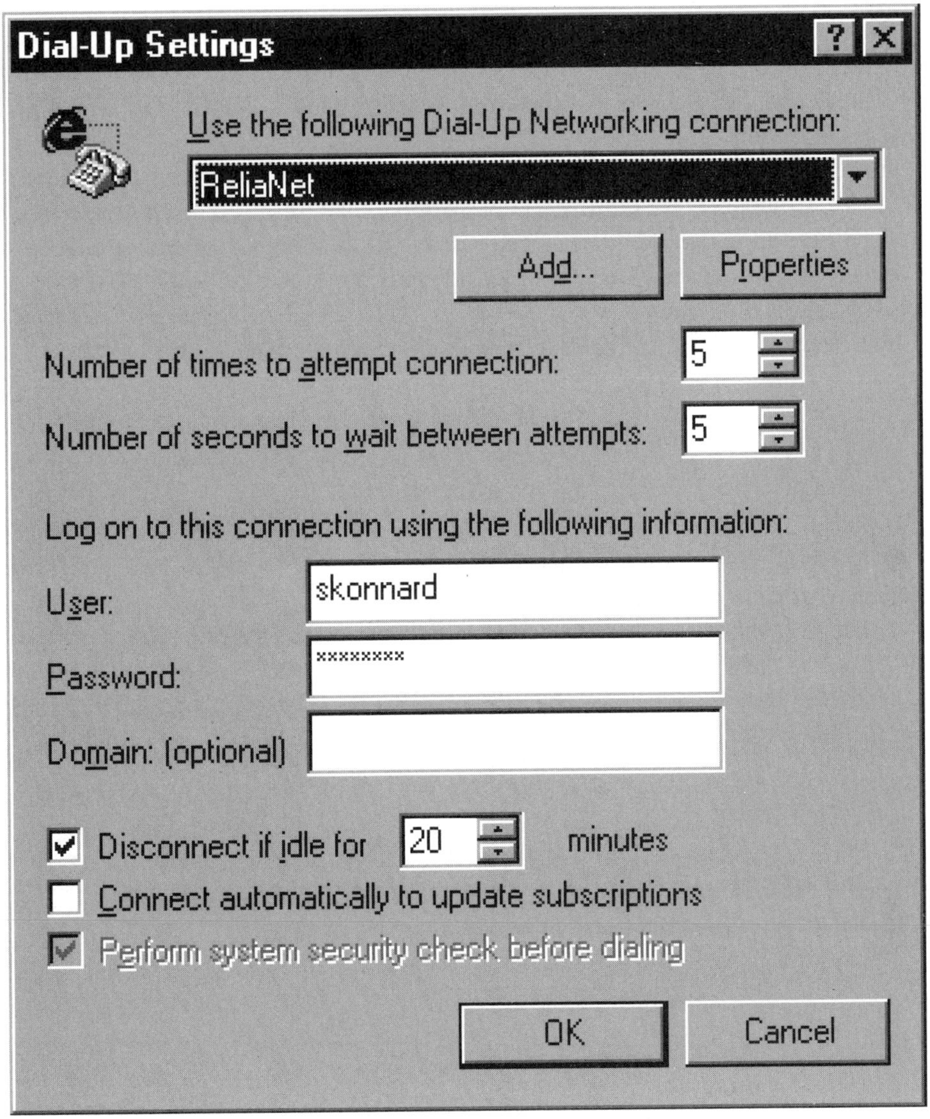

Figure 11-4   Dial-Up Settings dialog

```
DWORD InternetDial(
    IN HWND hwndParent,
    IN LPTSTR lpszConnectoid,
    IN DWORD dwFlags,
    OUT LPDWORD lpdwConnection,
    IN DWORD dwReserved
);
```

The first apparent difference is that InternetDial allows you to specify the phonebook entry. lpszConnectoid is the name of the phonebook entry to use for the connection. The second difference is that there is another possible value for dwFlags. dwFlags can be one of the values described in Table 11-3.

INTERNET_DIAL_UNATTENDED, which is not supported by InternetAutodial, can be used to suppress the dialing UI completely. The last difference between InternetDial and InternetAutodial is the return value. Although InternetAutodial returns a BOOL (indicating success or failure), InternetDial returns a DWORD (identifying the connection).

InternetHangUp is also slightly different than InternetAutodialHangup. Take a look:

```
DWORD InternetHangUp(
    IN DWORD dwConnection,
    IN DWORD dwReserved
);
```

InternetHangUp takes a DWORD, dwConnection, and specifies the connection identifier returned by InternetDial.

Although InternetDial requires you to have knowledge about the system phonebook entries to make the call (lspzConnectoid), WinInet doesn't offer a mechanism to enumerate the system phonebook. Later in this chapter I'll demonstrate how to do this using the RAS API.

InternetGoOnline

InternetGoOnline prompts the user for permission to initiate a connection to a specific URL. Take a look at the function declaration:

```
BOOL InternetGoOnline(
    IN LPTSTR lpszURL,
    IN HWND hwndParent,
    IN DWORD dwReserved
);
```

Table 11-3   InternetDial flags

Flag	Description
INTERNET_AUTODIAL_FORCE_ONLINE	Forces an online connection.
INTERNET_AUTODIAL_FORCE_UNATTENDED	Forces an unattended Internet dial-up.
INTERNET_DIAL_UNATTENDED	Connects to the Internet through a modem, without displaying a UI.

This function deals with the online/offline functionality of IE. For example, open the IE File menu and you'll see a menu item labeled Work Offline. If this menu item is checked, you're working in offline mode. If you type `http://www.microsoft.com` while working in offline mode, IE prompts the user for permission to go online.

InternetGoOnline displays the dialog shown in Figure 11-5. However, this dialog is shown only if the user is currently working in offline mode. If the user is working in online mode, InternetGoOnline always returns TRUE without prompting the user. If InternetGoOnline returns FALSE, the user chooses Stay Offline, and the application should behave accordingly.

InternetGetConnectedState

InternetGetConnectedState retrieves the connected state of the local system. Simply put, it returns TRUE if there is an Internet connection and FALSE if there isn't. Take a look at its function prototype:

```
BOOL InternetGetConnectedState(
    OUT LPDWORD lpdwFlags,
    IN DWORD dwReserved
);
```

You pass in a pointer to a DWORD, lpdwFlags, where the connection description is returned. You can determine the type of connection by testing the returned DWORD value against the values described in Table 11-4.

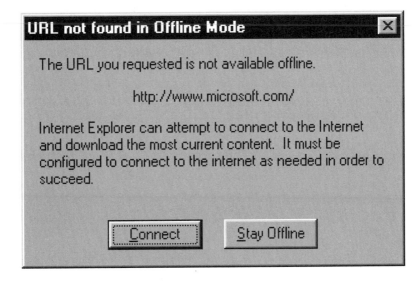

Figure 11-5   InternetGoOnline dialog

Table 11-4   InternetGetConnectedState flags

Flag	Description
INTERNET_CONNECTION_MODEM	Local system uses a modem to connect to the Internet.
INTERNET_CONNECTION_LAN	Local system uses a LAN to connect to the Internet.
INTERNET_CONNECTION_PROXY	Local system uses a proxy server to connect to the Internet.
INTERNET_CONNECTION_MODEM_BUSY	Local system's modem is busy with a non-Internet connection.

When most developers first see InternetGetConnectedState, they are amazed that it can figure out if the user's Internet connection is over a modem, LAN, or even a proxy. I hate to spoil the fun, but there is nothing amazing about InternetGetConnectedState. In fact, InternetGetConnectedState does nothing more than return the connection information stored in the registry and configured by the user in the Internet system properties dialog Connection tab (see Figure 11-3). For example, if the user has selected "Connect to the Internet using a modem," InternetGetConnectedState makes sure the INTERNET_CONNECTION_MODEM bit is set in lpdwFlags.

To help you understand how you might use this function, I wrote a simple function that calls InternetGetConnectedState and then checks to see which of the bits are set (see Listing 11-1).

Listing 11-1   InternetGetConnectedState

```
void GetConnectionInformation()
{
    DWORD dwState;
    BOOL bRet = InternetGetConnectedState(&dwState, 0);

    if (dwState & INTERNET_CONNECTION_MODEM)
        AfxMessageBox("INTERNET_CONNECTION_MODEM");
    if (dwState & INTERNET_CONNECTION_LAN)
        AfxMessageBox("INTERNET_CONNECTION_LAN");
```

```
    if (dwState & INTERNET_CONNECTION_PROXY)
        AfxMessageBox("INTERNET_CONNECTION_PROXY");
    if (dwState & INTERNET_CONNECTION_MODEM_BUSY)
        AfxMessageBox("INTERNET_CONNECTION_MODEM_BUSY");
}
```

InternetSetDialState

The last WinInet dial-up function is InternetSetDialState. InternetSetDialState sets the modem dialing state.

```
BOOL InternetSetDialState(
    IN LPCSTR lpszConnectoid,
    IN DWORD dwState,
    IN DWORD dwReserved
);
```

Currently, INTERNET_DIALSTATE_DISCONNECTED is the only supported dialing state value that can be used in dwState.

To Use or Not to Use . . . That Is the Question!

At this point I'm not too keen on using the WinInet dial-up functions in production code. The bottom line is that they need some improvement. When we start looking at the RAS API, however, you'll appreciate how much these functions encapsulate, and you'll be tempted to use them anyway. I'm convinced that using the WinInet dial-up functions will soon be a better solution than using the RAS API in many situations.

For the time being, the WinInet dial-up functions are limited in terms of flexibility. If you need absolute control over the RAS phonebook entries and how a dial-up connection is established, the WinInet functions have little to offer. Plus, if there is one common complaint on the WinInet newsgroup, it's that the new WinInet dial-up functions don't behave as documented. Although these issues will surely be worked out with time, if you need a reliable dial-up solution today, the RAS API is probably the best choice.

 Be careful using the WinInet dial-up functions in production code (at least for now). They are limited in terms of flexibility. The RAS API offers a more fail-safe solution to your dial-up needs.

Remote Access Service

The RAS API offers a wide range of flexibility. You can either take advantage of the RAS common system dialogs (used by dial-up networking) or use the lower level RAS functions and provide your own UI. Either way, RAS gives you a high degree of control over the process of establishing a dial-up connection with another computer.

I wrote a sample application for this chapter called RasJazz. I wrote RasJazz on Windows NT 4.0 using Visual C++ 5.0. Most of the functionality covered in the sample application deals with RAS features offered only by Windows NT 4.0. Thus, you must be running Windows NT 4.0 for RasJazz to function properly. You may use the sample code in Windows 95 applications as long as the specific function is Windows 95 compatible. Table 11-5 describes the compatibility of the most commonly used RAS functions.

RasJazz displays a dialog box (see Figure 11-6) that gives you a menu to various RAS features. Throughout this chapter I'll cover these features in detail using RasJazz as a reference. Let's begin by looking at the RAS common dialog functions.

Using the RAS Common Dialogs

The RAS common dialogs are contained in rasdlg.dll (you need to include rasdlg.h and link against rasdlg.lib). If you're developing on Windows 95, you won't find these

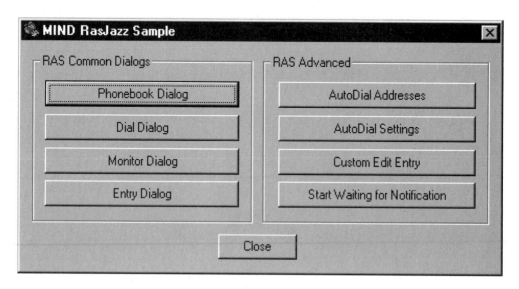

Figure 11-6   RasJazz dialog

Table 11-5   RAS compatibility Windows 95/Windows NT

RAS Function	Windows 95	Windows NT
RasPhonebookDlg	No	Yes
RasDialDlg	No	Yes
RasMonitorDlg	No	Yes
RasEntryDlg	No	Yes
RasDial	Yes	Yes
RasHangUp	Yes	Yes
RasGetConnectStatus	Yes	Yes
RasGetErrorString	Yes	Yes
RasCreatePhonebookEntry	Yes	Yes
RasEditPhonebookEntry	Yes	Yes
RasEnumEntries	Yes	Yes
RasRenameEntry	No	Yes
RasDeleteEntry	No	Yes
RasValidateEntryName	No	Yes
RasGetEntryDialParams	Yes	Yes
RasSetEntryDialParams	Yes	Yes
RasGetEntryProperties	No	Yes
RasSetEntryProperties	No	Yes
RasEnumAutodialAddresses	No	Yes
RasGetAutodialAddress	No	Yes
RasSetAutodialAddress	No	Yes
RasEnumConnections	Yes	Yes
RasEnumDevices	No	Yes
RasConnectionNotification	No	Yes

files. Unfortunately, the RAS common dialogs are only supported on Windows NT 4.0. Hopefully sometime soon the Windows 9x RAS functionality will mirror that of Windows NT. For the time being, however, you should be aware of this limitation when designing a solution.

 The RAS common dialog functions are only supported on Windows NT 4.0 and greater.

Table 11-6 describes the RAS common dialog functions provided by rasdlg.dll.

Table 11-6 RAS common dialog functions

API Name	Description
RasPhonebookDlg	Displays the main Dial-Up Networking dialog. From this modal dialog, the user can dial, edit, or delete a selected phonebook entry, create a new phonebook entry, or specify user preferences.
RasDialDlg	Attempts to establish a RAS connection using a specified phonebook entry and the credentials of the logged-on user. The function displays a stream of dialogs that indicate the state of the connection operation.
RasMonitorDlg	Displays the Dial-Up Networking Monitor property sheet that describes the status of RAS connections.
RasEntryDlg	Displays modal property sheets that allow a user to manipulate phonebook entries. If editing or copying an existing phonebook entry, the function displays a phonebook entry property sheet.

These functions allow you to take advantage of the dial-up networking dialogs offered by Windows NT 4.0. One advantage of this approach is that users familiar with dial-up networking benefit from your application's consistent look and feel. Let's look at each of these functions in more detail.

RasPhonebookDlg

The RasPhonebookDlg function displays the main dial-up networking dialog. Double clicking on the dial-up networking icon (found in My Computer) also displays this dialog (see Figure 11-7).

The following is the prototype for RasPhonebookDlg:

```
BOOL RasPhonebookDlg(
    LPTSTR lpszPhonebook,
    LPTSTR lpszEntry,
    LPRASPBDLG lpInfo,
);
```

The first parameter allows you to supply a path to the phonebook file that you want to use. On Windows NT 4.0, a phonebook is stored as a text file with a .pbk extension. In the User Preferences dialog, you can specify which phonebook file you want dial-up networking to use (see Figure 11-8). This has the same effect as passing in a different phonebook file to RasPhonebookDlg.

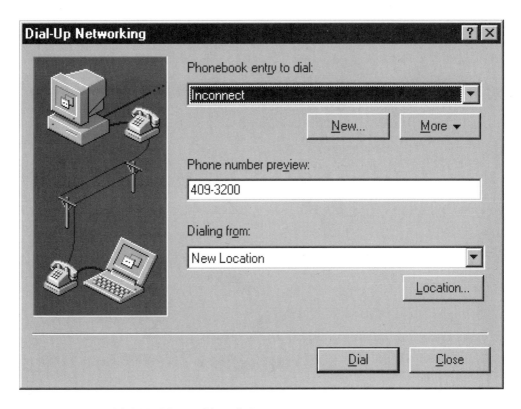

Figure 11-7   Dial-Up Networking dialog

The second parameter, lpszEntry, specifies the phonebook entry you want selected by default in the dial-up networking dialog. lpszEntry should contain the user-defined description of the phonebook entry.

The last parameter, lpInfo, is a pointer to a RASPBDLG structure that contains additional parameters associated with the dialog. The following is the declaration of RASPBDLG:

```
typedef struct tagRASPBDLG {
    IN  DWORD          dwSize;
    IN  HWND           hwndOwner;
    IN  DWORD          dwFlags;
    IN  LONG           xDlg;
    IN  LONG           yDlg;
    IN  DWORD          dwCallbackId;
    IN  RASPBDLGFUNC   pCallback;
    OUT DWORD          dwError;
```

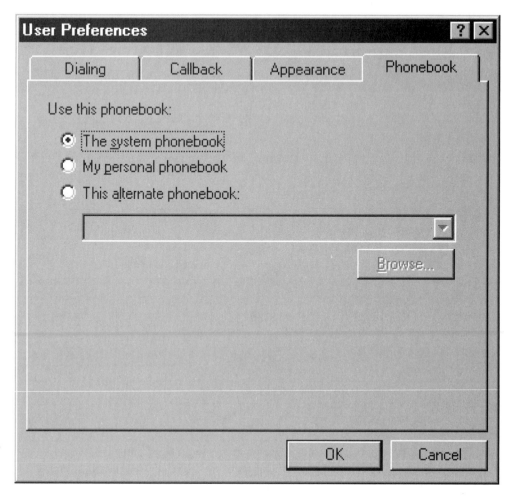

Figure 11-8 Dial-up networking User Preferences dialog

```
    IN   DWORD        reserved;
    IN   DWORD        reserved2;
} RASPBDLG;
```

Before using an instance of this structure you must set dwSize to the size of the structure for version information. Now let's look at some sample code. The RasJazz dialog contains a button labeled Phonebook Dialog, which invokes the following handler:

```
void CRasJazzDlg::OnPhonebookDlg()
{
```

```
    RASPBDLG raspbdlg;
    raspbdlg.dwSize = sizeof(RASPBDLG);
    raspbdlg.hwndOwner = GetSafeHwnd();
    //continue initializing structure

    RasPhonebookDlg(NULL, NULL, &raspbdlg);
}
```

Notice that I pass in NULL for the first two parameters of RasPhonebookDlg. This means that it will use the system phonebook and select the first phonebook entry (alphabetically).

With a few lines of code, you have an interface to the powerful functionality of dial-up networking. Because RasPhonebookDlg doesn't return until the dialog closes, the user can perform any of the following tasks before continuing: dial an entry, edit an entry, create a new entry, delete an entry, clone an entry, modify modem properties, display the dial-up monitor, and even modify dial-up preferences. Although this dialog is the most general and provides an interface to all the other common dialogs, in certain situations you may want to bypass it all together.

RasDialDlg

The RasDialDlg function gives you a direct interface to dialing a phonebook entry. Take a look at the following declaration:

```
BOOL RasDialDlg(
    LPTSTR lpszPhonebook,
    LPTSTR lpszEntry,
    LPTSTR lpszPhoneNumber,
    LPRASDIALDLG lpInfo
);
```

As you'll notice, the first two parameters are identical to those of RasPhonebookDlg. Refer to the previous section for more details on those parameters. The last parameter, lpInfo, is a pointer to a RASDIALDLG structure. Although it has a different name, it's almost structurally identical to RASPBDLG.

The parameter of interest here is lpszPhoneNumber. Each phonebook entry already has an associated phone number, and this parameter allows you to provide a replacement phone number (to be used instead of the associated phone number). If you pass NULL for this parameter, RasDialDlg uses the associated number.

The following is the handler for the RasJazz button labeled Dial Dialog:

```
void CRasJazzDlg::OnDialDlg()
{
    RASDIALDLG rasdialdlg;
    rasdialdlg.dwSize = sizeof(RASDIALDLG);
    rasdialdlg.hwndOwner = GetSafeHwnd();
    //continue initializing structure

    RasDialDlg(NULL, "ReliaNet", "", &rasdialdlg);
}
```

ReliaNet is the phonebook entry name for one of my local ISPs. If you download RasJazz, you'll want to replace this with your own phonebook entry name. Shortly I'll demonstrate how to enumerate the phonebook entries at runtime. This approach would obviously be a much better solution than hard coding the entry name.

RasDialDlg displays a stream of dialogs that provide the status of the dialing operation (see Figure 11-9). The same stream of dialogs appears if you press Dial on the main Dial-Up Networking dialog.

RasMonitorDlg

RasMonitorDlg displays the Dial-Up Networking Monitor dialog (see Figure 11-10). This function is even simpler than the previous two. Take a look at its declaration:

```
BOOL RasMonitorDlg(
    LPTSTR lpszDeviceName,
    LPRASMONITORDLG lpInfo
);
```

Because the Dial-Up Networking Monitor dialog monitors the status of different devices, you can specify the device name of interest in the first parameter. The second parameter, once again, is the additional parameter structure. RasJazz has a button labeled Monitor Dialog, which invokes the following handler:

```
void CRasJazzDlg::OnMonitorDlg()
{
    RASMONITORDLG rasmonitordlg;
    rasmonitordlg.dwSize = sizeof(RASMONITORDLG);
    rasmonitordlg.hwndOwner = GetSafeHwnd();
    //continue initializing structure

    RasMonitorDlg(NULL, &rasmonitordlg);
}
```

If you pass NULL for the first parameter, RasMonitorDlg uses the first enumerated device.

Figure 11-9 RasDial dialog

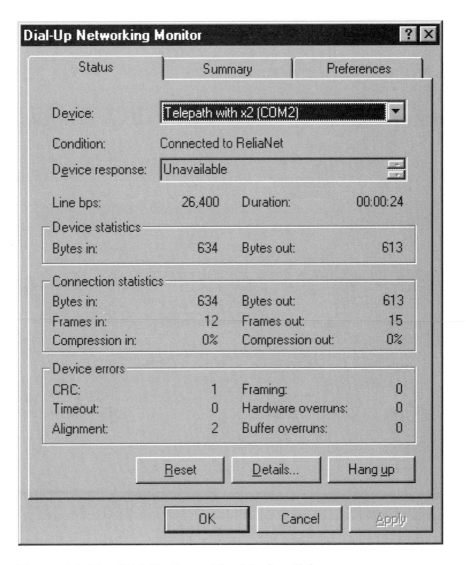

Figure 11-10 Dial-Up Networking Monitor dialog

RasEntryDlg

The RasEntryDlg displays the phonebook entry property sheet (see Figure 11-11). Using this dialog, users can edit all properties associated with a phonebook entry including basic, server, and security settings. The following is RasEntryDlg's function declaration:

```
BOOL RasEntryDlg(
    LPTSTR lpszPhonebook,
    LPTSTR lpszEntry,
    LPRASENTRYDLG lpInfo
);
```

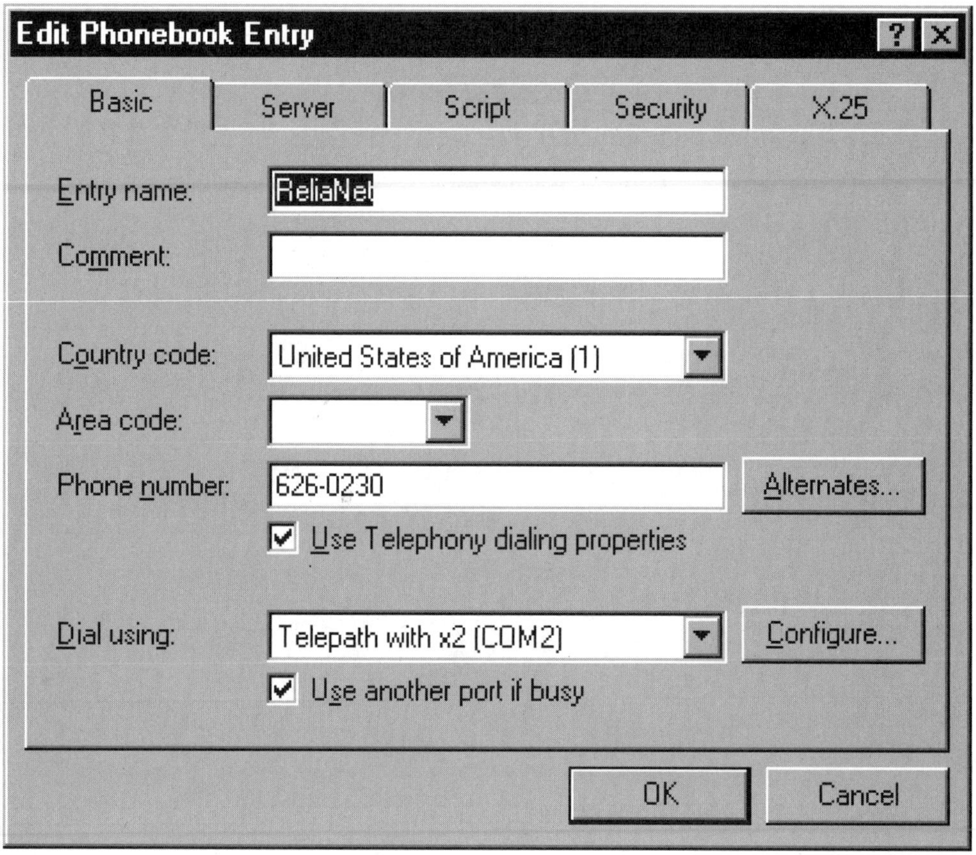

Figure 11-11   Edit Phonebook Entry dialog

By now you should feel comfortable with the various parameters. Using this function is just like using the previous dialog functions. The RasJazz dialog contains a button labeled Entry Dialog, which invokes the following handler:

```
void CRasJazzDlg::OnEntryDlg()
{
    RASENTRYDLG rasentrydlg;
    rasentrydlg.dwSize = sizeof(RASENTRYDLG);
    rasentrydlg.hwndOwner = GetSafeHwnd();
    //continue initializing structure

    RasEntryDlg(NULL, "ReliaNet", &rasentrydlg);
}
```

The RAS common dialog functions offer an easy-to-use interface and provide a consistent dial-up networking look and feel. Although these functions do offer more flexibility than the WinInet dial-up functions, you're still restricted to the UI and functionality provided by the dialogs. In most cases this may be sufficient, but you may be required to provide a custom UI or to tweak the standard functionality to fit your needs.

Begin and End a RAS Connection with RasDial and RasHangUp

We've already looked at how to begin and end a RAS connection using the RAS common dialog functions. Now we're going to look at the RasDial and RasHangUp functions—the lower level dial-up functions that give you total control over the RAS dial-up behavior and let you provide your own UI or none at all.

RasDial

RasDial simply takes care of establishing a connection between two computers without displaying any UI. RasDial is supported on both Windows NT 4.0 and Windows 95, but some of the parameters are ignored on Windows 95. Take a look at the RasDial function declaration:

```
DWORD RasDial(
    LPRASDIALEXTENSIONS lpRasDialExtensions,
    LPTSTR lpszPhonebook,
    LPRASDIALPARAMS lpRasDialParams,
    DWORD dwNotifierType,
    LPVOID lpvNotifier,
    LPHRASCONN lphRasConn
);
```

The first parameter, lpRasDialExtensions, allows you to take advantage of dial-up networking's extended dialing features like using a dialing prefix, enabling software compression, ignoring the modem speaker, and pausing for a script. lpRasDialExtensions is ignored on Windows 95. The second parameter (also ignored on Windows 95) allows you to specify the full path and file name of the phonebook file to be used.

The next parameter, lpRasDialParams, is a pointer to a RASDIALPARAMS structure that contains most of the phonebook entry and user credential information:

```
typedef struct _RASDIALPARAMS {
    DWORD dwSize;
    TCHAR szEntryName[RAS_MaxEntryName + 1];
    TCHAR szPhoneNumber[RAS_MaxPhoneNumber + 1];
    TCHAR szCallbackNumber[RAS_MaxCallbackNumber + 1];
    TCHAR szUserName[UNLEN + 1];
    TCHAR szPassword[PWLEN + 1];
    TCHAR szDomain[DNLEN + 1] ;
    #if (WINVER >= 0x401)
    DWORD dwSubEntry;
    DWORD dwCallbackId;#endif
} RASDIALPARAMS;
```

As with all other parameter structures, you must be sure to set dwSize to sizeof(RASDIALPARAMS) before passing it to RasDial. This structure is pretty self-explanatory. However, there are a few things to note. First, if you leave szEntryName empty, RasDial performs a simple modem connection that requires you to provide a phone number in szPhoneNumber. Second, if you leave szUserName and szPassword empty, RAS uses the user name and password of the current log-on session.

The next two RasDial parameters, dwNotifierType and lpvNotifier, give you control over the blocking behavior of RasDial. Because RasDial typically takes a while to complete, it's usually better to make the call asynchronously. Otherwise, your application is tied up waiting for the synchronous call to return. To take advantage of RasDial's asynchronous support you must specify which callback mechanism you wish to use (dwNotifierType) and provide a pointer to the callback mechanism (lpvNotifier). Table 11-7 describes the callback mechanism used by each dwNotifierType value.

As you can see, there are three RasDial callback functions: RasDial, RasDial1, and RasDial2. Choose the one that best fits your needs (see the RAS documentation for more information on each callback). If you pass 0xFFFFFFFF in dwNotifierType, lpvNotifier must point to a valid Window handle. In this case, instead of calling a callback function, RAS sends the specified Window handle progress notification messages. Any one of these mechanisms allows you to provide the user with valuable status information while dialing is taking place.

Table 11-7   RasDial dwNotifierType values

dwNotifierType	Callback Mechanism
0xFFFFFFFF	Windows message
0	RasDialFunc
1	RasDialFunc1
2	RasDialFunc2 (Windows NT 4.0)

The final RasDial parameter, lphRasConn, is a pointer to the handle of the established RAS connection. You need this handle to call RasHangUp.

 Because RasDial doesn't set lphRasConn to NULL when the call fails, you should set it to NULL before calling RasDial. You need this handle to call RasHangUp.

Listing 11-2 provides an example of how to use RasDial.

Listing 11-2   RasDial example

```
void MyDial(CString& strEntry)
{
    RASDIALPARAMS RasDialParams;
    BOOL bPassword;
    HRASCONN hRasConn;
    DWORD dwRet;

    RasDialParams.dwSize = sizeof(RASDIALPARAMS);
    strcpy(RasDialParams.szEntryName, strEntry);

    dwRet = RasGetEntryDialParams( NULL, &RasDialParams, &bPassword);

    dlg.m_strEntry = RasDialParams.szEntryName;
    dlg.m_strUserName = RasDialParams.szUserName;
    dlg.m_strPassword = RasDialParams.szPassword;

    dwRet = RasDial(NULL, NULL, &RasDialParams, 0, NULL, &hRasConn);
}
```

One common question on newsgroups is how to perform a dial-up connection behind the scenes without any user interface or user intervention. As you now know, RasDial is the key to that solution.

RasHangUp

Fortunately, ending a RAS connection is much simpler then beginning one. In fact, to end a RAS connection you simply call RasHangUp with the handle to the active RAS connection that you wish to disconnect. For example, assuming hConnection contains a handle to an active RAS connection, the following line of code would suffice:

```
DWORD dwRet = RasHangUp(hConnection);
```

Although at first this appears very simple, there is one common pitfall that deceives most developers. After calling RasHangUp, the connection state machine needs time to shut down properly. This shutdown time can take as long as one or two seconds. If the system shuts down the state machine prematurely, the modem can be left in a bad state (leaving the port open and so on). A bad state can cause future RasDial calls to fail. Therefore, after calling RasHangUp, your code shouldn't exit immediately. Instead, you should give RAS time to reset the connection state.

A simple solution is to call Sleep(3000) after returning from RasHangUp. However, a more fail-safe solution is to use the loop shown in Listing 11-3, which doesn't break until the connection state has been reset properly.

Listing 11-3   Safe RasHangUp example

```
RASCONNSTATUS RasConnStatus;
RasConnStatus.dwSize = sizeof(RASCONNSTATUS);
RasConnStatus.dwError = 0;
while (ERROR_INVALID_HANDLE != RasConnStatus.dwError)
{
    Sleep(0);
    RasGetConnectStatus(hConnection, &RasConnStatus);
}
```

 A thread can relinquish the remainder of its time slice by calling Sleep with a value of zero milliseconds.

Working with Phonebook Entries

There is a big difference between the storage of Windows 95 and Windows NT 4.0 phonebooks. Windows 95 stores all phonebook information in the system registry whereas Windows NT 4.0 uses .pbk files. With Windows 95 you only have one system phonebook. With Windows NT 4.0 you can have as many phonebooks as your heart desires.

We also already talked about how you can control phonebook entries through the RasPhonebookDlg and RasEntryDlg common dialog functions (refer to Using the RAS Common Dialogs). Although these functions are very useful (with Windows NT 4.0), there are a handful of other phonebook-specific functions that can be used with both Windows 95 and Windows NT 4.0 (see Table 11-8).

Table 11-8   RAS phonebook entry functions

Phonebook Entry Function	Description
RasCreatePhonebookEntry	Creates a new phonebook entry. The function displays a dialog in which the user types information about the phonebook entry. (Applications written for Windows NT 4.0 should use RasEntry.)
RasEditPhonebookEntry	Edits an existing phonebook entry. The function displays a dialog in which the user can modify the existing information. (Applications written for Windows NT 4.0 should use RasEntry.)
RasEnumEntries	Lists all entry names in a RAS phonebook.
RasRenameEntry	Changes the name of an entry in a phonebook.
RasDeleteEntry	Deletes an entry from a phonebook.
RasValidateEntryName	Validates the format of an entry name. The name must contain at least one nonwhite space alphanumeric character.
RasGetEntryDialParams	Retrieves the connection information saved by the last successful call to the RasDial or RasSetEntryDialParams function for a specified phonebook entry.
RasSetEntryDialParams	Changes the connection information saved by the last successful call to the RasDial or RasSetEntryDialParams function for a specified phonebook entry.
RasGetEntryProperties	Retrieves the properties of a phonebook entry.
RasSetEntryProperties	Changes the connection information for an entry in the phonebook or creates a new phonebook entry.

I probably should have included the first two functions, RasCreatePhonebookEntry and RasEditPhonebookEntry, in the RAS common dialogs section because they also provide a dialog interface. These two functions simply provide the system dialogs for creating and editing a phonebook entry. Applications written for Windows NT 4.0, should use RasEntry instead.

One phonebook entry function that often causes developers grief is RasEnumEntries. Listing 11-4 illustrates how to use RasEnumEntries to populate a combo box (m_Phonebook) with all the system phonebook entries.

Listing 11-4   RasEnumEntries example

```
BOOL CAddAutoDialAddressDlg::OnInitDialog()
{
    CDialog::OnInitDialog();
    LPRASENTRYNAME lpRasEntry;
    DWORD dwBuf, dwEntry, dwRet;
    CString strRet;

    // malloc initial buffer
    dwBuf = sizeof(RASENTRYNAME);
    if ((lpRasEntry = (LPRASENTRYNAME)malloc((UINT)dwBuf)) != NULL)
    {
        // set size for version tracking
        lpRasEntry->dwSize = sizeof(RASENTRYNAME);

        // call RasEnumEntries
        dwRet = RasEnumEntries(NULL, NULL, lpRasEntry, &dwBuf, &dwEntry);

        if (dwRet == ERROR_BUFFER_TOO_SMALL)
        {
            // buffer too small - realloc size in dwBuf
            if ((lpRasEntry = (LPRASENTRYNAME)realloc(lpRasEntry, (UINT)dwBuf))
                    != NULL)
                dwRet = RasEnumEntries(NULL, NULL, lpRasEntry, &dwBuf,
                    &dwEntry);
            else
            {
              //handle error
            }
        }
        else if (dwRet != 0) // other error
```

```
    {
        //handle error
    }
    //succeeded
    if (dwRet == 0)
    {
        //fill in combo box
        for(DWORD nIndex = 0; nIndex < dwEntry; nIndex++)
        {
            CString strEntry;

            strEntry.Format("%s", lpRasEntry[nIndex].szEntryName);
            m_Phonebook.AddString(strEntry);
        }
        if (m_Phonebook.GetCount() > 0)
            m_Phonebook.SetCurSel(0);
    }
    free(lpRasEntry);
    }
    return TRUE;
}
```

The rest of the RAS phonebook entry functions are fairly straightforward. I'll let you peruse the details of this group on your own (see the Visual C++ online help).

Windows NT 4.0 RAS AutoDial

Windows NT 4.0 supports a new feature called AutoDial. When an application attempts to establish a connection with a network address, AutoDial establishes a dial-up networking connection automatically, using a specific phonebook entry (assuming the computer doesn't have a persistent connection to the Internet). You can test AutoDial by simply opening a command prompt and typing ping www. microsoft.com. If AutoDial is enabled and your machine is configured properly, AutoDial should prompt you to establish a dial-up networking connection.

AutoDial Mapping Database

The key to AutoDial is the AutoDial mapping database. The AutoDial mapping database maps a network address to a RASAUTODIALENTRY structure, which contains a phonebook entry and a dialing location. Network addresses can include IP addresses

(127.95.1.4), Internet host names (*www.microsoft.com*), and even NetBIOS names. If AutoDial is enabled, addresses are added automatically to the database whenever the user connects to a network address over a RAS connection. Addresses are added to the database along with the properties of the active RAS connection.

If you want to manipulate the AutoDial mapping database manually, you can use the RasSetAutodialAddress, RasGetAutodialAddress, and RasEnumAutodialAddresses functions. The RasJazz sample has a button labeled AutoDial Addresses, which displays the dialog shown in Figure 11-12. The dialog populates a list box with all the addresses in your system AutoDial mapping database. The code segment in Listing 11-5 illustrates how RasEnumAutodialAddresses is used to populate the list box (m_Addresses).

Listing 11-5   RasEnumAutodialAddresses example

```
LPTSTR *lppAddresses = NULL;
DWORD dwSize=0, dwAddresses=0;
ULONG i;

DWORD dwRet = RasEnumAutodialAddresses(lppAddresses, &dwSize, &dwAddresses);
if (dwSize)
{
    lppAddresses = (LPTSTR*)malloc(dwSize);
    dwRet = RasEnumAutodialAddresses(lppAddresses, &dwSize, &dwAddresses);
}
for (i=0; i<dwAddresses; i++)
    m_Addresses.AddString(lppAddresses[i]);
//clean up and free memory
```

If you press Add in this dialog, you'll see the dialog in Figure 11-13. After you enter an address, select a phonebook entry, and press OK; the following code snippet (see Listing 11-6) inserts the new address into the AutoDial mapping database:

Listing 11-6   RasSetAutodialAddress example

```
RASAUTODIALENTRY lppAutoDialEntry[1];
lppAutoDialEntry[0].dwSize = sizeof(RASAUTODIALENTRY);
lppAutoDialEntry[0].dwFlags = 0;
lppAutoDialEntry[0].dwDialingLocation = 1; //default location
strcpy(lppAutoDialEntry[0].szEntry, m_strPhonebook.GetBuffer(0));

DWORD dwRet = RasSetAutodialAddress(m_strAddress.GetBuffer(0), 0,
        lppAutoDialEntry,  sizeof(RASAUTODIALENTRY), 1);
```

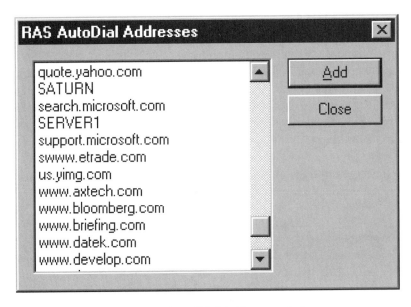

Figure 11-12   RasJazz AutoDial Addresses dialog

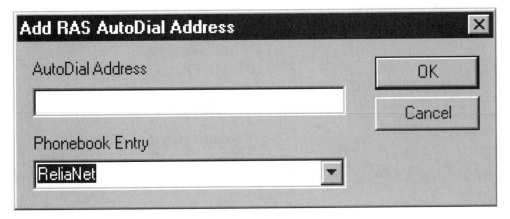

Figure 11-13   Add RAS AutoDial Address dialog

Troubleshooting AutoDial

Before you start banging your head against your computer trying to get AutoDial to work, let me point out some problems that caused me some grief. First of all, you should verify that AutoDial is enabled for the current dialing location. To do so, open the Dial-Up Networking dialog and choose User Preferences. You should see the dialog in Figure 11-14. Make sure that AutoDial is checked for the current location (to change the current location, use the Telephony applet in the Control Panel).

If your machine is on a network, you must disable your network card in order for AutoDial to function properly. Unfortunately, unplugging your network cable doesn't do the trick. To simulate not being on a network you must create a new hardware profile and disable your network card in the new profile. When you reboot your machine, be sure to select the No Network profile that you just created. With your network card disabled (and assuming everything else is configured properly), AutoDial should begin working.

One last thing that threw me for a loop is how the system disables all AutoDial connections automatically for the current log-on session. Each time a new user logs

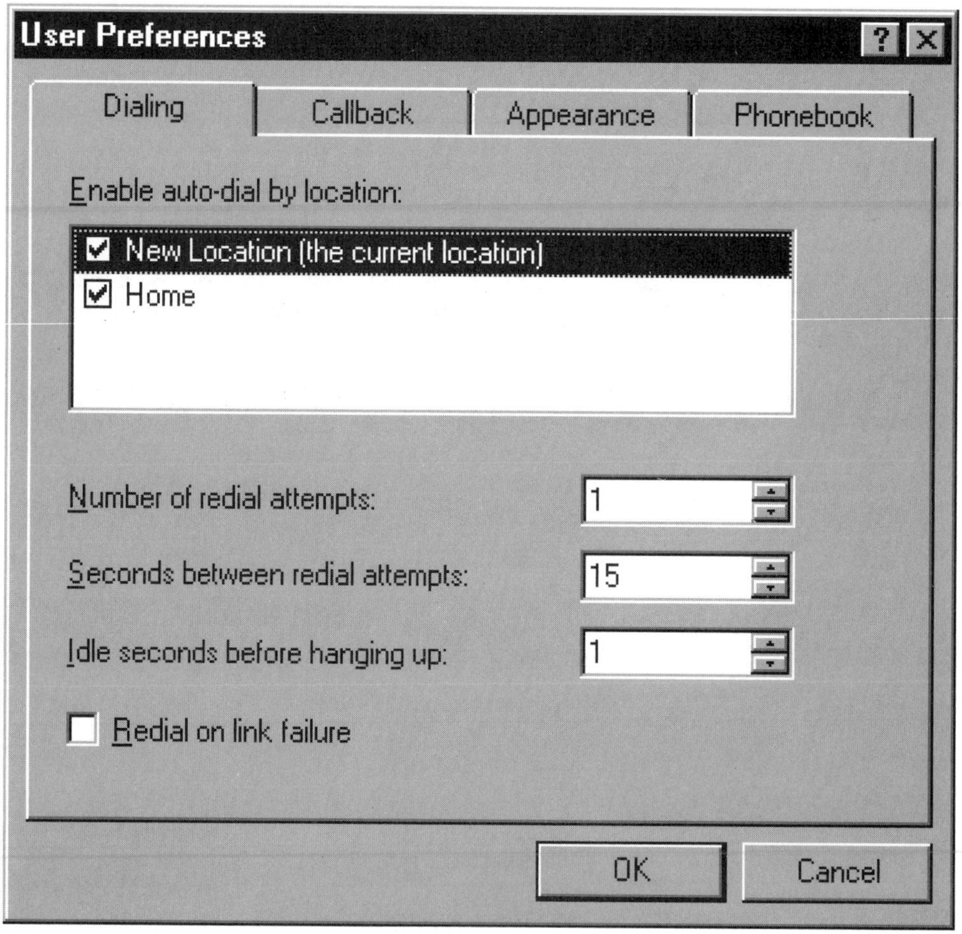

Figure 11-14   Dial-Up Networking User Preferences dialog

on, AutoDial connections are disabled. To see if AutoDial is disabled on your system, look in the registry in the following location:

```
HKEY_CURRENT_USER\Software\Microsoft\RAS Autodial\Control
```

If the value of LoginSessionDisable is set to one, AutoDial connections are disabled for the current log-on session. Change this value to zero, and things should start working. The DisableConnectionQuery value controls whether AutoDial prompts the user before dialing the entry found in the AutoDial mapping database, as shown in Figure 11-15. This is the same dialog that is used if no entry is found in the AutoDial database.

To control these registry settings programmatically, you can use RasGetAutodialParam and RasSetAutodialParam. I added a dialog to RasJazz that allows you to modify all the AutoDial control registry settings (see Figure 11-16).

Using a Custom UI DLL

One of the coolest features of AutoDial is the ability to provide a custom UI DLL. To take advantage of this, you must implement a DLL with both an ASCII and a Unicode version of the following entry point:

```
BOOL WINAPI RASADFunc(
    LPTSTR lpszPhonebook,
    LPTSTR lpszEntry,
    LPRASADPARAMS lpAutodialParams,
    LPDWORD lpdwRetCode
);
```

RASADFunc should return TRUE to indicate that it took over the dialing, or FALSE to allow the system to continue dialing. The RasJazz sample contains a project called MyAutoDial that implements this entry point (see Listing 11-7) and a custom AutoDial dialog (see Figure 11-17).

Listing 11-7   MyAutoDial.cpp

```
// MyAutoDial.cpp : Defines the initialization routines for the DLL.
//

#include "stdafx.h"
#include "MyAutoDial.h"
#include "CustomAutoDialDlg.h"
```

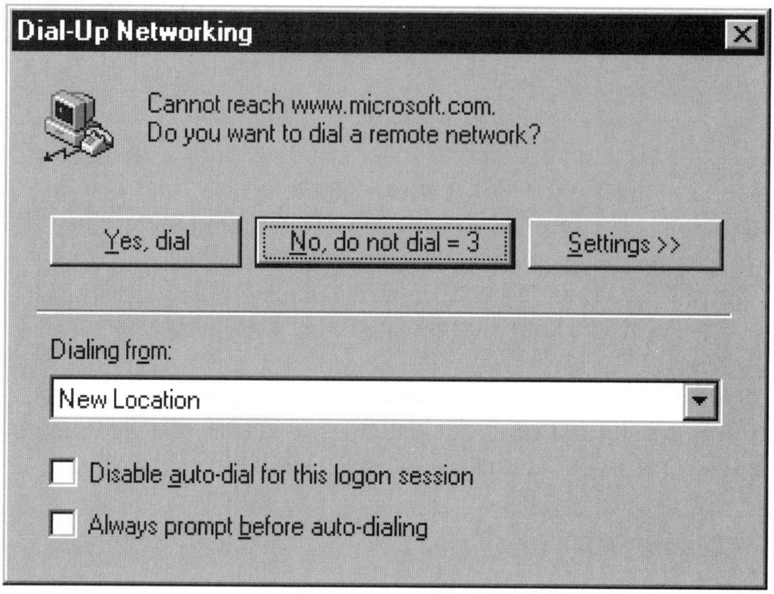

Figure 11-15   AutoDial prompt dialog

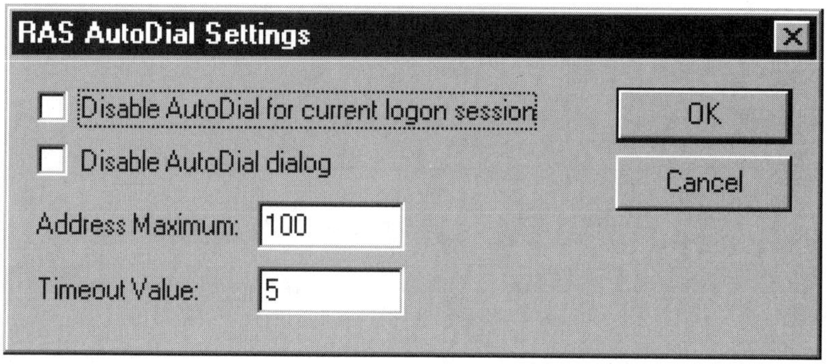

Figure 11-16   RasJazz AutoDial Settings dialog

```
#include <ras.h>

#ifdef _DEBUG
#define new DEBUG_NEW
#undef THIS_FILE
static char THIS_FILE[] = __FILE__;
#endif
```

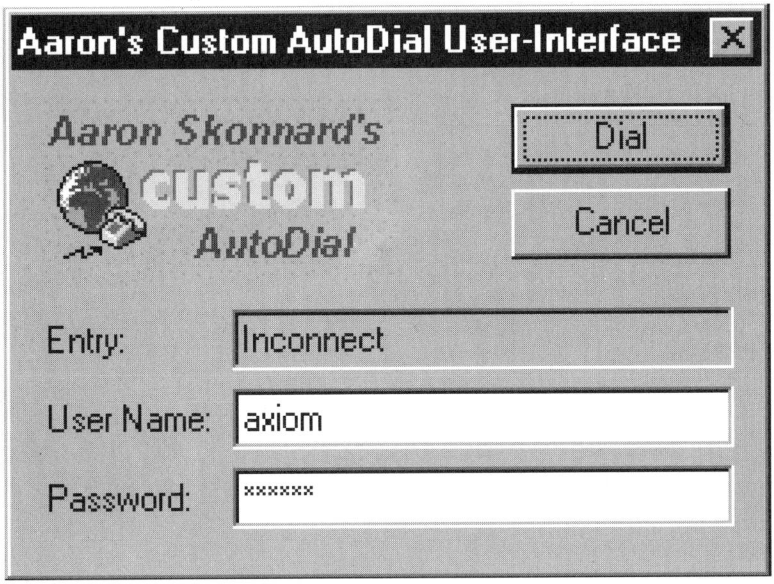

Figure 11-17   Custom AutoDial User Interface sample

```
///////////////////////////////////////////////////////////////////////////
// CMyAutoDialApp

BEGIN_MESSAGE_MAP(CMyAutoDialApp, CWinApp)
    //{{AFX_MSG_MAP(CMyAutoDialApp)
    //}}AFX_MSG_MAP
END_MESSAGE_MAP()

///////////////////////////////////////////////////////////////////////////
// CMyAutoDialApp construction

CMyAutoDialApp::CMyAutoDialApp()
{
}

///////////////////////////////////////////////////////////////////////////
// The one and only CMyAutoDialApp object

CMyAutoDialApp theApp;

void ShowCustomUI(CString& strEntry)
```

```
{
    RASDIALPARAMS RasDialParams;
    BOOL bPassword;
    HRASCONN hRasConn;
    DWORD dwRet;
    CCustomAutoDialDlg dlg;

    RasDialParams.dwSize = sizeof(RASDIALPARAMS);
    strcpy(RasDialParams.szEntryName, strEntry);

    dwRet = RasGetEntryDialParams( NULL, &RasDialParams, &bPassword);

    dlg.m_strEntry = RasDialParams.szEntryName;
    dlg.m_strUserName = RasDialParams.szUserName;
    dlg.m_strPassword = RasDialParams.szPassword;

    // show my custom dialog

    if (IDOK == dlg.DoModal())
        dwRet = RasDial(NULL, NULL, &RasDialParams, 0, NULL, &hRasConn);
}

extern "C" BOOL WINAPI MyAutoDialHandlerA(LPSTR lpszPhonebook, LPSTR lpszEntry,
    LPRASADPARAMS lpAutoDialParams, LPDWORD lpdwRetCode)
{
    AFX_MANAGE_STATE(AfxGetStaticModuleState());
    CString strEntry = lpszEntry;
    ShowCustomUI(strEntry);
    *lpdwRetCode = ERROR_SUCCESS
    return TRUE;
}

extern "C" BOOL WINAPI MyAutoDialHandlerW(LPWSTR lpszPhonebook,
    LPWSTR lpszEntry, LPRASADPARAMS lpAutoDialParams, LPDWORD lpdwRetCode)
{
    AFX_MANAGE_STATE(AfxGetStaticModuleState());
    CString strEntry = lpszEntry;
    ShowCustomUI(strEntry);
    *lpdwRetCode = ERROR_SUCCESS;
    return TRUE;
}
```

So how does AutoDial know which custom UI DLL to call for a specific entry? You can associate a custom AutoDial DLL with each phonebook entry by calling RasSetEntryProperties. I added a dialog to RasJazz that allows you to modify certain properties of a phonebook entry including the AutoDial DLL path and function name (see Figure 11-18). Listing 11-8 illustrates how to use RasSetEntryProperties.

Listing 11-8 RasSetEntryProperties example

```
RASENTRY Entry;
Entry.dwSize = sizeof(RASENTRY);
Entry.dwAlternateOffset = 0;
strcpy(Entry.szAreaCode, m_strArea);
strcpy(Entry.szLocalPhoneNumber, m_strPhone);
strcpy(Entry.szDeviceName, m_strDevice);
strcpy(Entry.szAutodialDll, m_strAutoDialDLL);
strcpy(Entry.szAutodialFunc, m_strAutoDialFunc);
DWORD dwSize = sizeof(Entry);

DWORD dwRet = RasSetEntryProperties( NULL, m_strPhonebook.GetBuffer(0),
        &Entry, dwSize, NULL, 0);
```

After you associate a custom AutoDial DLL with a phonebook entry, you can test the DLL by trying to connect to a network address mapped to that entry. For example, if *www.microsoft.com* is mapped to the phonebook entry Inconnect, typing `ping www.microsoft.com` from a command prompt should cause my custom AutoDial dialog to appear (see Figure 11-17).

RAS Connection Information

In certain situations you may want to enumerate over the current RAS connections or the available RAS devices. To do this, use RasEnumConnections and RasEnumDevices. These functions allow you to determine if the current connection and device are suitable for the task your program performs.

Another hot topic is how to determine when a RAS connection is established. You can probably come up with a slick mechanism to enumerate the connections periodically (using RasEnumConnections) and check the status of each one. Windows NT 4.0, however, offers a much more elegant solution—RasConnectionNotification.

Using RasConnectionNotification, your application can register an event that the system signals when the following RAS events occur:

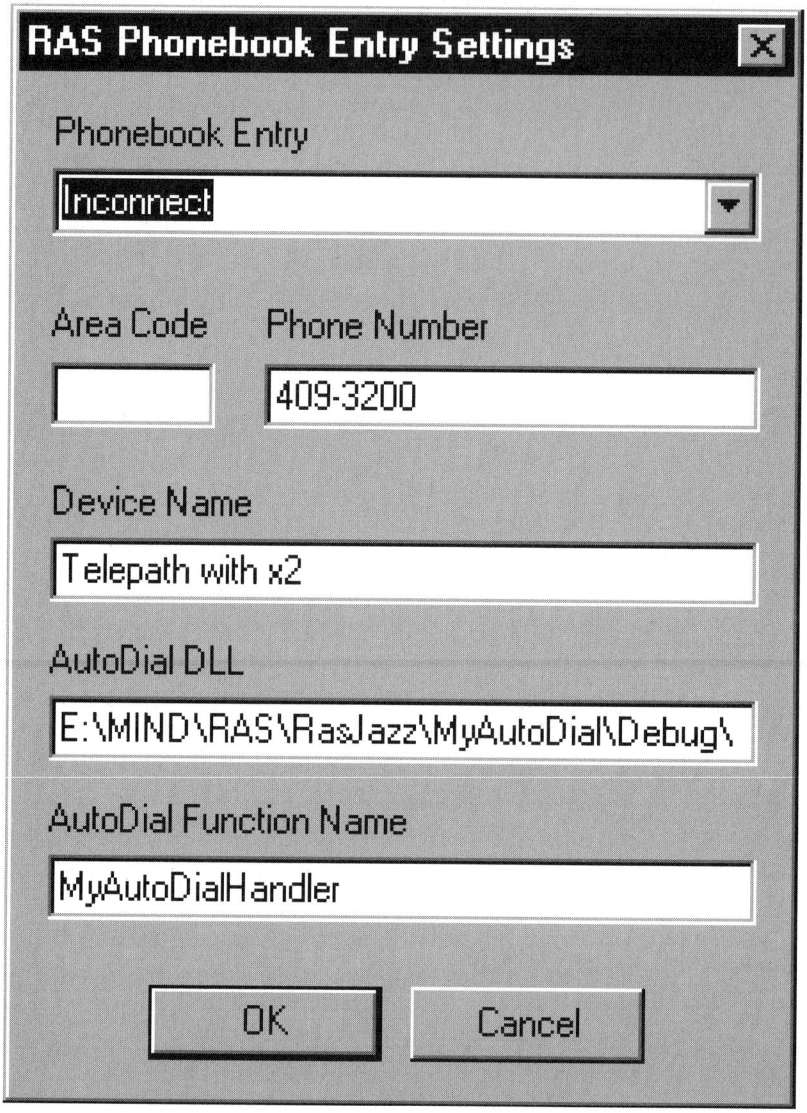

Figure 11-18   RasJazz Phonebook Entry Settings dialog

- A new RAS connection is established
- An existing RAS connection is terminated
- RAS bandwidth is added
- RAS bandwidth is removed

The RasJazz dialog contains a button labeled Start Waiting for Notification, which spawns the thread shown in Listing 11-9.

 What Is RAS Bandwidth?
One of the many Windows NT 4.0 RAS enhancements includes Multi-link PPP. Multi-link PPP is a communications protocol that allows the combination of two or more B channels into a single, faster PPP connection (with more bandwidth). With Multi-link PPP, you can have a 128-Kb/sec PPP connection over a basic rate ISDN line.

Listing 11-9   WaitForRasNotificationThread

```
UINT WaitForRasNotificationsThread(LPVOID lpvoid)
{
    HANDLE hEvent = CreateEvent(NULL, FALSE, FALSE,"RasNotification");

    if (hEvent)
        RasConnectionNotification((HRASCONN)INVALID_HANDLE_VALUE,
                hEvent, RASCN_Connection | RASCN_Disconnection |
                RASCN_BandwidthAdded | RASCN_BandwidthRemoved);

    if (WAIT_OBJECT_0 == WaitForSingleObject(hEvent, INFINITE))
    {
        ::MessageBox(NULL, "Ras notification received", "RAS Notification",
                MB_OK | MB_SETFOREGROUND );

        CloseHandle(hEvent);
    }
    return 0;
}
```

If you press the Start Waiting for Notification button and then, manually, begin a dial-up connection (through dial-up networking), RasJazz displays a message box when the RAS connection is established.

Conclusion

In this chapter I covered how to use the WinInet dialing functions along with the RAS API. In particular, I've shown you how to use the RAS common dialog functions, the RasDial/RasHangUp functions, and the RAS phonebook entry functions. Furthermore I tried to expose you to some of the advanced RAS features like RAS AutoDial and RAS connection notifications.

By now, you should be familiar enough with the dial-up services offered by Windows to take advantage of them in your applications. Hopefully, the problems and pitfalls I've covered will save you some time and energy.

Part

V

Internet Client/Server Applications

12
Chapter

Internet Client/Server Applications with WinInet, ISAPI, and ASP

Throughout this book I've discussed how to use WinInet to communicate via the HTTP, FTP, and Gopher protocols. The discussion has focused entirely on the client-side WinInet code. For example, the Stock Watcher application presented in the advanced section shows how to communicate with various stock quote providers on the Internet, but it doesn't show anything about how the stock quote providers were implemented on the server. You really need to understand what's happening on the server to create powerful and robust Internet solutions. Hence, the purpose of this chapter is to introduce the concept of client/server Internet programming.

First let me explain what I mean by Internet client/server applications. An Internet client/server application consists of one or more Internet server components and a client application that understands how to communicate with them. For example, an Internet banking system would be considered an Internet client/server application. A banking system would consist of various server components (CGI, ASP, ISAPI, and so forth) and a Windows application (Microsoft Money and so on). Also, by this definition, the Stock Watcher sample introduced in Chapter 10 would be considered an Internet client/server application.

When I implemented the Stock Watcher application, I simply tapped into the various stock quote provider components that already exist on the Internet. Typically when implementing an Internet client/server solution you develop both the client and server components together. This gives you much more control and flexibility. Having control over the server-side components as well as the client-side code allows you to develop more powerful and flexible solutions.

In this chapter I'll introduce you to the common client/server development decisions. Then I'll dive into a sample application called BugTracker that illustrates how to develop a complete Internet client/server application using WinInet, ISAPI, and ASP. The BugTracker sample should help you understand how to develop client/server applications using any type of Internet server component (not only ISAPI and ASP).

By the time you're done reading this chapter, you should feel comfortable with the concept of Internet client/server programming. You'll be familiar with not only the available server technologies, but also with some of the most common client/server design decisions. And most important (as far as this book is concerned), you should understand completely the role of WinInet in a complete Windows Internet client/server solution.

Internet Client/Server Development Decisions

When you start developing Internet client/server applications, you run across a plethora of design decisions. Although there are some general design decisions (such as whether the application will run on your local intranet or on the Internet), most decisions are related directly either to the client or to the server solution (see Figure 12-1).

Client Decisions

When developing a Windows Internet client/server application you must decide what technology you want to use on the client side. If your solution is going to leverage HTTP, FTP, or Gopher, WinInet is the best choice. However if you need to take advantage of another Internet protocol that isn't supported by WinInet, Winsock is your only choice unless you want to purchase a third-party component.

There are plenty of third-party components that implement most of the application-level Internet protocols. The only problem with these utilities is that you're restricted to their implementation and have very little control over the underlying behavior. It's the common dilemma that you run across when purchasing any ActiveX control. Unless you buy the source code, you must conform to the functionality provided by

Figure 12-1   Internet client/server model

the control. In most cases it's better just to bite the bullet and implement the functionality yourself with Winsock.

Table 12-1 describes the pros and cons for each Windows client-side technology.

One thing that you'll find is that HTTP is being used more and more by sophisticated client/server applications. Because HTTP is so widespread and flexible, it's the perfect protocol for many situations. I recently finished a distributer management system that was completely implemented using the HTTP protocol. One of the major benefits of using the HTTP protocol is the ability to use SSL.

As you sit down to decide what protocol to use in your Internet client/server application, don't underestimate the power of HTTP. It appears that HTTP, or some extension of HTTP, will continue to be the protocol of the future. Both the Stock Watcher sample in Chapter 10 and the BugTracker sample in this chapter illustrate how HTTP can be used to develop practical client/server applications.

If you decide to use HTTP, it's wise to use WinInet. Because Microsoft is dedicated to maintaining the WinInet API amid protocol evolution, you won't have to worry about modifying your code as the HTTP protocol changes. This is a major

Table 12-1   **Client technology comparison**

Technology	Protocols	Pros	Cons
WinInet	HTTP, FTP, and Gopher	Very simple, high-level protocol	Only supports HTTP, FTP, and Gopher
Winsock	Any TCP/IP-based protocol	Supports any TCP/IP-based protocol	Complex and time-consuming
Third-party component	Depends on the component (you can find components for most protocols)	Simple; available for most protocols	You get what you pay for; very inflexible

benefit to say the least. Furthermore, WinInet allows you to concentrate on the powerful (and higher level) HTTP features instead of getting bogged down by the pesky and annoying HTTP protocol details.

Server Decisions

Deciding how to implement the server side of your Internet client/server application turns out to be much more complicated than the client side. Because this book is about *Windows* Internet application development, I isolated the client application to the Windows operating system. The Internet server-side components, however, rely on the operating system and Web server that will be used by your application. Even though the number of Windows NT servers on the Internet is increasing, there are still many more Unix-based systems.

Depending on your situation, you'll have to figure out which server-side solution works for you. Sometimes this is not an easy task; there are probably more than a hundred books on the various different server-side technologies that can be used on the Web (HTTP). In this section I'll give you a high-level introduction to today's most common Windows Internet server technologies.

Internet Server Technologies

The three most commonly used Windows Internet server technologies are CGI, ISAPI, and ASP. Let's look at how each of these technologies works.

CGI applications are usually implemented as a C/C++ executable or with a scripting language like Perl. CGI requires a separate name and URL mapping for each request. For example, to provide two requests called getnames and getnumbers, you need two CGI applications (such as getnames.exe and getnumbers.exe).

The server creates a separate process for each request of the CGI application and communicates with the new process through environment variables and stdin/stdout. If 1,000 clients access a CGI application at the same time, the server creates 1,000 processes to handle the requests. As you'll see shortly, the process creation and interprocess communication required by CGI requires more overhead than some of the newer models.

ISAPI extension DLLs, as their name suggests, extend the functionality of the Web server on which they run. Unlike CGI applications, ISAPI components are implemented as DLLs. ISAPI allows multiple commands in a single DLL; a single ISAPI DLL can contain both a getnames and a getnumbers request.

The ISAPI model reduces the overhead required by multiple requests. The first time an ISAPI DLL is requested, the server loads it into memory. From that point on, the ISAPI DLL remains in memory until the server shuts down. Because all client

Table 12-2   **Internet server technologies comparison**

Technology	Pros	Cons
CGI	Commonly used; can be implemented in either C or C++ or in scripting languages like Perl	Poorer performance than newer technologies; one process per request
ISAPI	Good performance; a single DLL processes all requests	Must be implemented using C++/MFC
ASP	Good performance; benefits from the ISAPI model; simple to implement with scripting languages like VBScript and JScript	You lose some of the control that you have with ISAPI

requests access the loaded DLL, there is no overhead for process creation. Furthermore, ISAPI DLLs run in the same address space as the Web server and have access to all the same resources. There is no need for interprocess communication. ISAPI DLLs must be threadsafe, however, because they receive multiple requests simultaneously.

The ASP model combines the flexibility of both ISAPI and scripting languages. ASP pages can be written in today's most common scripting languages like VBScript or JScript. The ASP runtime ISAPI DLL processes ASP pages on the server and returns the result to the client. Because ASP is built on ISAPI technology, it benefits from all the same performance gains.

Table 12-2 describes the pros and cons for each of the three server technologies just described.

The Future

ASP is definitely the current hype. It gives you the performance gains of ISAPI and still allows you to benefit from the simplicity of scripting languages. Although it seems obvious that ASP will continue to dominate in the Microsoft arena for the short term, you never know what's coming next. Because most of these technologies are so new, and newer ones are being introduced all the time, you probably need to gather more information than I'm providing here to make a decision. Like I said, there is definitely not a shortage of books on Internet server technologies.

BugTracker: A Client/Server Bug-Tracking System

I could write all day about Internet client/server design and implementation, but until you see a clear example of how it works, it probably won't mean much to you. In the following sections I'll show you how to implement a bug-tracking client/server application. The client side of the application looks a lot like the other examples that I've presented throughout this book. The server side, on the other hand, is implemented using an ISAPI extension DLL along with ASP scripts.

BugTracker Overview

Before getting into the details, let me give you an overview of how this application should work. As its name suggests, BugTracker keeps track of bugs in a development environment. The client application (see Figure 12-2) shows you a list of all bugs found in the server's bug database.

If you double click on a bug, you can modify the bug properties and update the bug on the server (see Figure 12-3).

You can add a new bug to the system by selecting the File | New Bug menu option (or by pressing the New button on the toolbar) and filling out the ensuing dialog (see Figure 12-4).

The client refreshes its view of the database every minute, or you can do a refresh manually by selecting the File | Refresh Bugs menu option (or by pressing the Refresh button on the toolbar as shown in Figure 12-5).

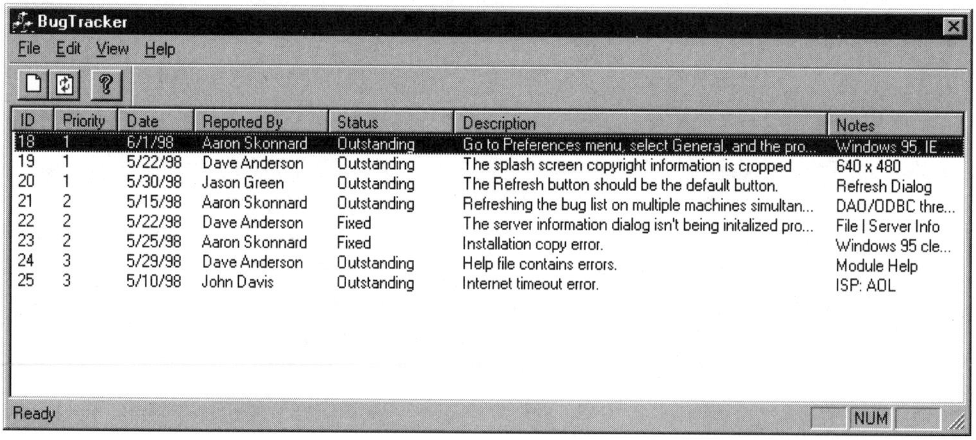

ID	Priority	Date	Reported By	Status	Description	Notes
18	1	6/1/98	Aaron Skonnard	Outstanding	Go to Preferences menu, select General, and the pro...	Windows 95, IE ...
19	1	5/22/98	Dave Anderson	Outstanding	The splash screen copyright information is cropped	640 x 480
20	1	5/30/98	Jason Green	Outstanding	The Refresh button should be the default button.	Refresh Dialog
21	2	5/15/98	Aaron Skonnard	Outstanding	Refreshing the bug list on multiple machines simultan...	DAO/ODBC thre...
22	2	5/22/98	Dave Anderson	Fixed	The server information dialog isn't being initalized pro...	File	Server Info
23	2	5/25/98	Aaron Skonnard	Fixed	Installation copy error.	Windows 95 cle...
24	3	5/29/98	Dave Anderson	Outstanding	Help file contains errors.	Module Help
25	3	5/10/98	John Davis	Outstanding	Internet timeout error.	ISP: AOL

Figure 12-2   BugTracker screen shot

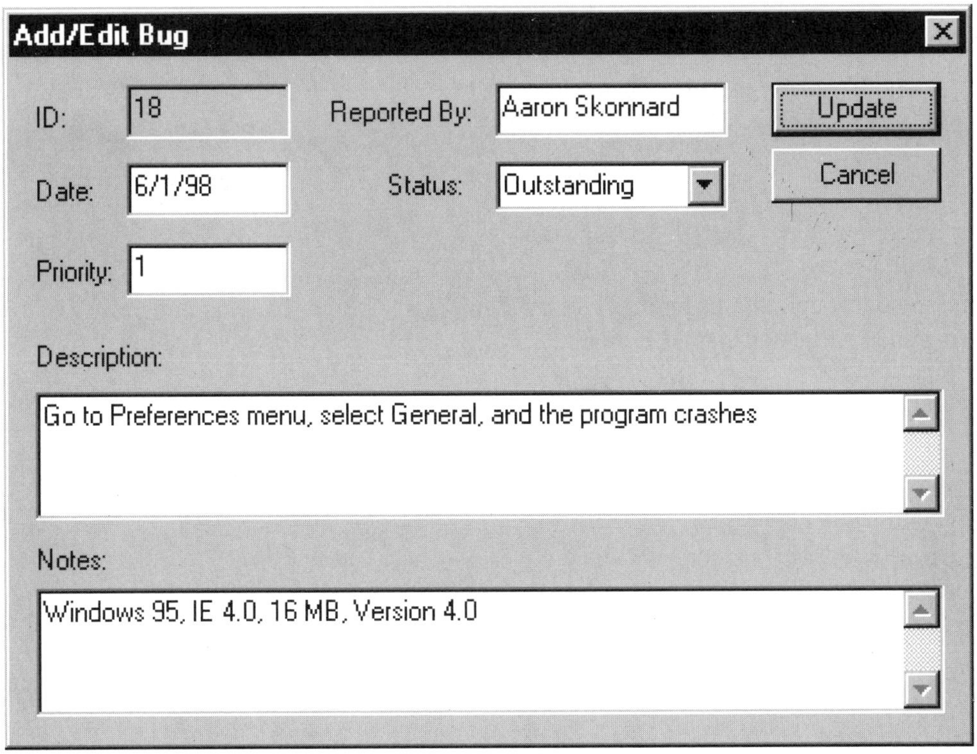

Figure 12-3   Edit bug dialog

The client application also allows you to change the server configuration. You can specify the server, port, and path to the scripts by using the Server Information dialog (see Figure 12-6). This allows you to use this client with different BugTracker servers. This dialog also allows you to specify whether you want to use the ISAPI DLL or the ASP scripts. As you'll see, both behave identically.

Most of you have probably used a bug-tracking system before. The idea here is that various developers and testers can use this application to add, modify, and review bugs interactively. Because the bug database is stored on the Web server, any beta tester or programmer—regardless of physical location—can access the system (they only need a connection to the Internet). If I add a bug to the system, all other users of the application see my new bug within the next minute.

Sample ISAPI Extension DLL

I implemented all of BugTracker's server-side functionality using an ISAPI extension DLL. To keep things simple, the ISAPI DLL only contains two requests: refresh and

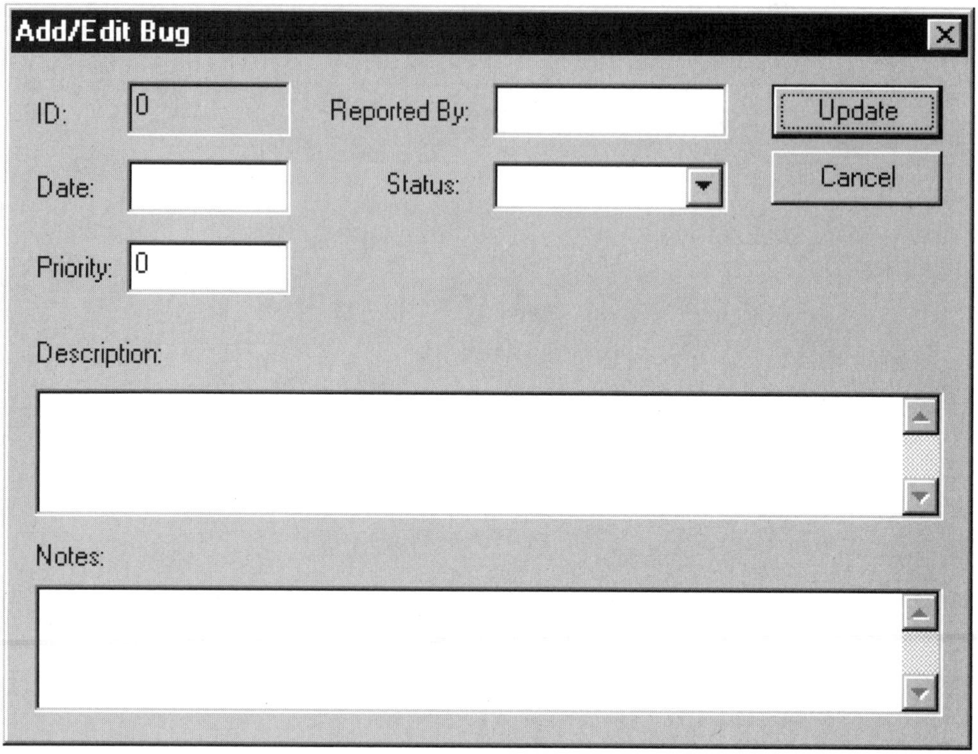

Figure 12-4 Add bug dialog

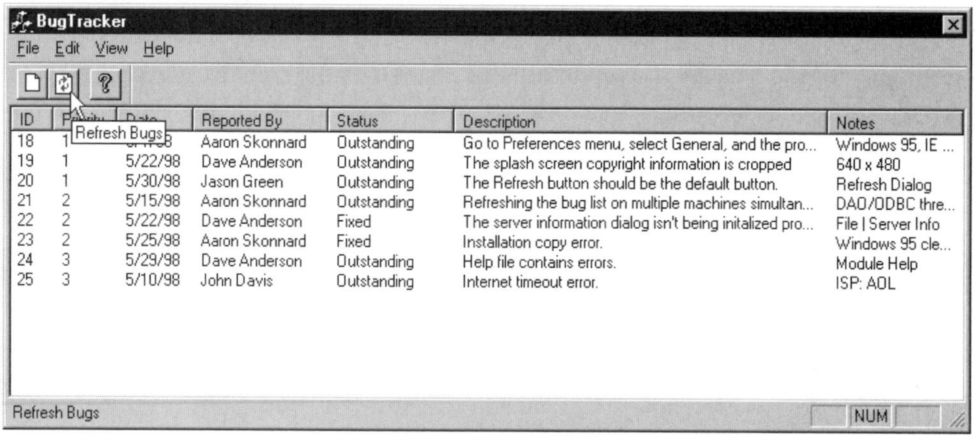

Figure 12-5 Refresh bugs toolbar button

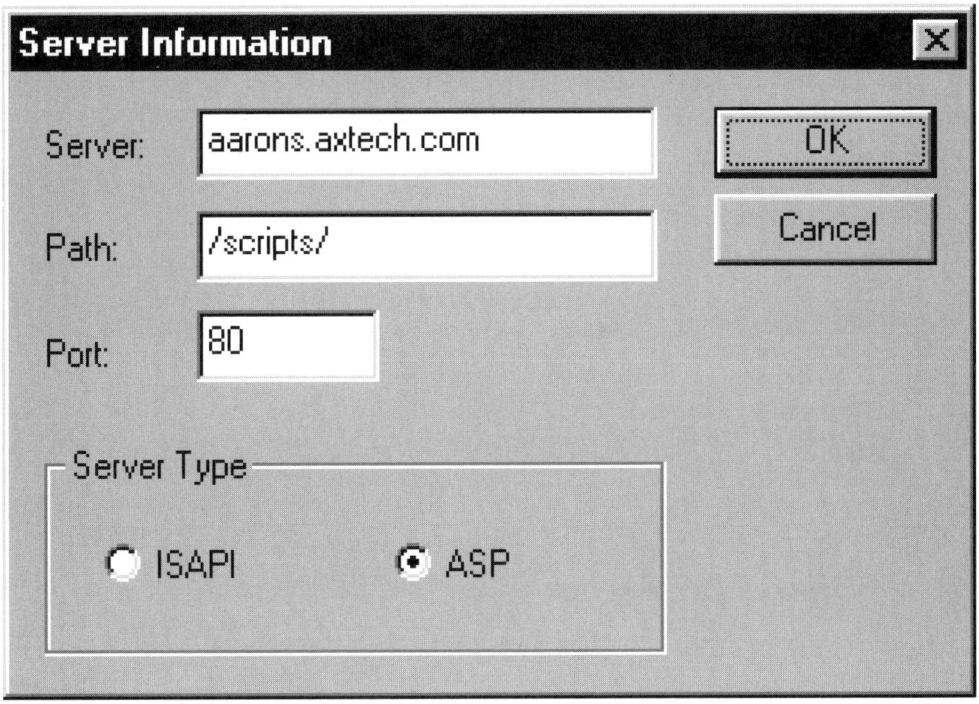

Figure 12-6   Server Information dialog

addeditbug. The refresh request returns a list of all bugs found in the server's bug database. The addeditbug request either adds a new bug to the database or updates an existing bug. The WinInet client uses these two methods to interact with the server's bug database. Like all the other examples in this book, I used Visual C++ 5.0 to implement the ISAPI extension DLL.

Creating the Project

Create a new project by going to the File | New menu. Go to the Projects tab and select the ISAPI Extension Wizard (see Figure 12-7). I used Bugs in the Project name field and decided to create a new workspace for this project. After you press OK, the ISAPI Wizard dialog appears (see Figure 12-8).

You can accept all of the default settings in the ISAPI Extension Wizard and press Finish. At this point, the wizard generates the project files for you. After it finishes, take a look at the generated files. The files that we'll be dealing with the most are Bugs.h and Bugs.cpp, which contain the declaration and the implementation of our CBugsExtension class.

You should be able to compile the ISAPI DLL successfully at this point. If you called your project Bugs and didn't change any of the default settings, the resulting

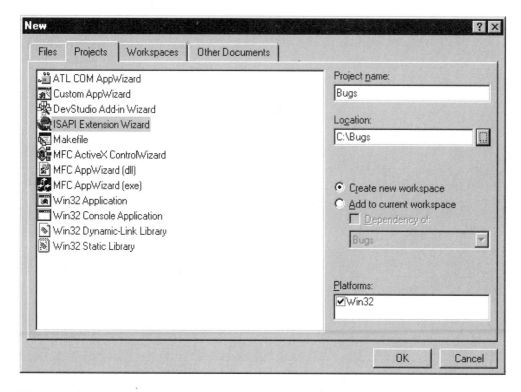

Figure 12-7   Visual C++ 5.0 new project dialog

DLL is called Bugs.dll. When you configure your Web server properly, you should be able to access the default method of Bugs.dll.

I'm not going to cover the details of the ISAPI MFC classes. Instead, I'll show you how to implement this simple example and let you dive in deeper on your own. Now that we have the basic ISAPI DLL framework, let's look at how to implement the refresh and addeditbug requests.

Adding Methods to CBugsExtension

To add methods to CBugsExtension, you must follow three steps:

1. Add the method to the CBugsExtension class declaration.
2. Add ON_PARSE_COMMAND and ON_PARSE_COMMAND_ PARAMS macros.
3. Provide the method implementation.

If you look at the Bugs.h and Bugs.cpp files that were generated by the wizard, you'll notice a default method called Default. It follows all three of these steps. You should be able to find the method declaration in Bugs.h. The ON_PARSE_

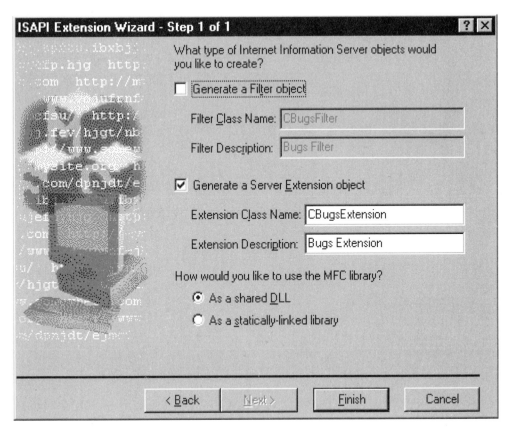

Figure 12-8 ISAPI Extension Wizard Step 1 of 1

COMMAND and ON_PARSE_COMMAND_PARAMS macros are part of the PARSE map in Bugs.cpp. And finally, the implementation of Default is also in Bugs.cpp.

Let's add the refresh and addeditbug methods following the three steps outlined earlier. First let's add the method declarations to the CBugsExtension class. The refresh method doesn't need to accept any parameters besides the required CHttpServerContext pointer. The addeditbug method, on the other hand, needs to accept information about the bug to be added or updated. Listing 12-1 shows what the CBugsExtension declaration looks like after adding these two methods.

Listing 12-1 **CBugsExtension class declaration**

```
class CBugsExtension : public CHttpServer
{
public:
    CBugsExtension();
    ~CBugsExtension();
```

```
// Overrides
    // ClassWizard-generated virtual function overrides
        // NOTE - the ClassWizard will add and remove member functions here.
        //    DO NOT EDIT what you see in these blocks of generated code!
    //{{AFX_VIRTUAL(CBugsExtension)
    public:
    virtual BOOL GetExtensionVersion(HSE_VERSION_INFO* pVer);
    //}}AFX_VIRTUAL

    void Default(CHttpServerContext* pCtxt);
    void refresh(CHttpServerContext* pCtxt);
    void addeditbug(CHttpServerContext* pCtxt, long lID, LPCTSTR lpszDate,
        LPCTSTR lpszReportedBy, long lStatus,
        LPCTSTR lpszDescription, LPCTSTR lpszNotes,
        long lPriority);

    DECLARE_PARSE_MAP()

    //{{AFX_MSG(CBugsExtension)
    //}}AFX_MSG
};
```

Now we need to add the ON_PARSE_COMMAND macros to the PARSE map found in Bugs.cpp. The PARSE map begins with the BEGIN_PARSE_MAP macro and ends with the END_PARSE_MAP macro. The ON_PARSE_COMMAND and ON_PARSE_COMMAND_PARAMS macros are placed in between. These macros control how the class parses the information received by the Web server (see Listing 12-2).

Listing 12-2   CBugsExtension parse map

```
BEGIN_PARSE_MAP(CBugsExtension, CHttpServer)
    ON_PARSE_COMMAND(Default, CBugsExtension, ITS_EMPTY)
    DEFAULT_PARSE_COMMAND(Default, CBugsExtension)
    ON_PARSE_COMMAND(refresh, CBugsExtension, ITS_EMPTY)
    ON_PARSE_COMMAND(addeditbug, CBugsExtension, ITS_I4 ITS_PSTR ITS_PSTR
            ITS_I4 ITS_PSTR ITS_PSTR ITS_I4)
    ON_PARSE_COMMAND_PARAMS("id=0 date=Unavailable reportedby=Unavailable "
            "status=0 description=Unavailable "
            "notes=Unavailable priority=0")
END_PARSE_MAP(CBugsExtension)
```

For example, the ON_PARSE_COMMAND macro for addeditbug specifies that the class should parse an integer, two strings, an integer, two strings, and an integer. When parsed, these values are passed to the addeditbug method. The ON_PARSE_COMMAND_PARAMS macro specifies what the default values should be for each of the possible parameters. Thus, if the client doesn't send a particular parameter, the class sends the default value to the associated method.

Finally, to make this all work we still need to implement the refresh and addeditbug methods (see Listing 12-3).

Listing 12-3   CBugsExtension implementation

```
void CBugsExtension::refresh(CHttpServerContext* pCtxt)
{
    CBSet bugs;
    int i=0;
    CString strBugTag;

    //open DB and make sure it's not empty
    bugs.Open();
    if (bugs.IsEOF() && bugs.IsBOF())
        return;

    //send all bugs to CHttpServerContext
    while (!bugs.IsEOF())
    {
        strBugTag.Format("Bug%d=", i++);
        *pCtxt << strBugTag << bugs.m_ID << SEP << bugs.m_Date << SEP
                << bugs.m_ReportedBy << SEP << bugs.m_Status << SEP
                << bugs.m_Description << SEP << bugs.m_Notes << SEP
                << bugs.m_Priority << SEP << "<eor>";
        //move to next bug
        bugs.MoveNext();
    }
    bugs.Close();
}


void CBugsExtension::addeditbug(CHttpServerContext* pCtxt, long lID,
    LPCTSTR lpszDate, LPCTSTR lpszReportedBy, long lStatus,
    LPCTSTR lpszDescription, LPCTSTR lpszNotes, long lPriority)
{
    CBSet bugs;
```

```
    bugs.Open();

    if (lID == 0)
    {
        //adding a new bug
        bugs.AddNew();
    }
    else
    {
        //updating an existing bug
        while (!bugs.IsEOF())
        {
            //try to find bug
            if (bugs.m_ID == lID)
                break;
            bugs.MoveNext();
        }
        //if bug was found, edit; otherwise, add
        if (bugs.m_ID == lID)
            bugs.Edit();
        else
            bugs.AddNew();
    }

    bugs.m_Date = lpszDate;
    bugs.m_ReportedBy = lpszReportedBy;
    bugs.m_Status = lStatus;
    bugs.m_Description = lpszDescription;
    bugs.m_Notes = lpszNotes;
    bugs.m_Priority = lPriority;
    bugs.Update();
    bugs.Close();

    //fresh the client list
    refresh(pCtxt);
}
```

These methods interact with a Microsoft Access database found on the same server. Take a look at the CBSet implementation in Listing 12-4. The database contains only one table called Bugs, which consists of seven fields. Notice that the GetDefaultConnect method returns the following string: "ODBC;DSN=Bugs". Thus you must have an ODBC data source named Bugs on the Web server. I'll cover how to do this shortly.

Listing 12-4   CBSet class implementation

```
/////////////////////////////////////////////////////////////////////////
// CBSet

IMPLEMENT_DYNAMIC(CBSet, CRecordset)

CBSet::CBSet(CDatabase* pdb)
    : CRecordset(pdb)
{
    //{{AFX_FIELD_INIT(CBSet)
    m_ID = 0;
    m_Date = _T("");
    m_ReportedBy = _T("");
    m_Status = 0;
    m_Description = _T("");
    m_Notes = _T("");
    m_Priority = 0;
    m_nFields = 7;
    //}}AFX_FIELD_INIT
    m_nDefaultType = dynaset;
}


CString CBSet::GetDefaultConnect()
{
    return _T("ODBC;DSN=Bugs");
}


CString CBSet::GetDefaultSQL()
{
    return _T("[Bugs]");
}


void CBSet::DoFieldExchange(CFieldExchange* pFX)
{
    //{{AFX_FIELD_MAP(CBSet)
    pFX->SetFieldType(CFieldExchange::outputColumn);
    RFX_Long(pFX, _T("[ID]"), m_ID);
```

```
    RFX_Text(pFX, _T("[Date]"), m_Date);
    RFX_Text(pFX, _T("[ReportedBy]"), m_ReportedBy);
    RFX_Long(pFX, _T("[Status]"), m_Status);
    RFX_Text(pFX, _T("[Description]"), m_Description);
    RFX_Text(pFX, _T("[Notes]"), m_Notes);
    RFX_Long(pFX, _T("[Priority]"), m_Priority);
    //}}}AFX_FIELD_MAP
}
```

There are a few things that I want to point out about the refresh and addeditbug methods. The refresh method writes each bug record to the CHttpServerContext object and is ultimately returned to the client of the request. Take a look at the `while` loop again that is responsible for writing each bug record to the stream:

```
//send all bugs to CHttpServerContext
while (!bugs.IsEOF())
{
    strBugTag.Format("Bug%d=", i++);
    *pCtxt << strBugTag << bugs.m_ID << SEP << bugs.m_Date << SEP
            << bugs.m_ReportedBy << SEP << bugs.m_Status << SEP
            << bugs.m_Description << SEP << bugs.m_Notes << SEP
            << bugs.m_Priority << SEP << "<eor>";
    //move to next bug
    bugs.MoveNext();
}
```

Notice the format of each record. SEP represents a separator character. Depending on the contents of the database, the client might receive the following text stream back from the refresh request (in this case SEP is a colon):

```
Bug0=100:5/30/98:Aaron:1:Bug Description:Notes:3<eor>
Bug1=101:6/1/98:Monica:1:Bug Description:Notes:2<eor>
Bug2=102:6/1/98:Michelle:1:Bug Description:Notes:1<eor>
Bug3=103:6/2/98:Michael:1:Bug Description:Notes:4<eor>
```

The BugTracker WinInet client is written to understand this bug record format, which makes things much simpler. In the Stock Watcher sample we communicated with preexisting server components and were forced to deal with many different formats (such as raw HTML). Because we're developing this server component along with the client, we can choose a format that is easy to use for both sides.

At this point the ISAPI DLL could look at the User-Agent HTTP header to determine whether the request came from a Web browser or the BugTracker client application. If BugTracker made the request, the DLL could return the application-specific format described earlier. Otherwise, if a Web browser made the request, the DLL could return the information in HTML. Using this methodology you can implement one ISAPI DLL to service both Web browsers and the proprietary BugTracker application.

The addeditbug method simply adds a new record to the database and then calls refresh to send all bug records, including the new one, back to the client. Because I wanted to keep this example simple, I didn't make this ISAPI DLL thread safe. This could cause big problems if the DLL is used heavily by many different users simultaneously. These methods should use standard thread synchronization techniques to ensure that the database isn't corrupted. For example, you could use a global critical section object to synchronize access to the problematic areas.

 Microsoft Access isn't the best choice for an Internet client/server database. In fact, because the Microsoft Jet engine isn't thread safe, anything that uses the Jet engine shouldn't be used in a multithread environment. Because ISAPI does use threads, you should use a more sophisticated database like Microsoft SQL Server in production code.

When you've got the previous code incorporated into your project, you're ready to configure the Web server to use the new DLL.

Configuring the DLL on Internet Information Server (IIS)

The first thing you need to do is to set up the Bug database on the Web server. This consists of adding an ODBC data source to the Web server. You want to place the Access database somewhere on the Web server (the location doesn't matter). Then, go to the Control Panel and double click on the ODBC32 icon (see Figure 12-9).

Then, go to the System DSN tab as shown in Figure 12-10.

Press Add, select the Microsoft Access Driver, and press Finish. At this point, you should see the dialog shown in Figure 12-11.

Because the record set class—CBSet—looks for a Domain Name System (DNS) called Bugs, you need to name the data source Bugs. Choose the path to the Access

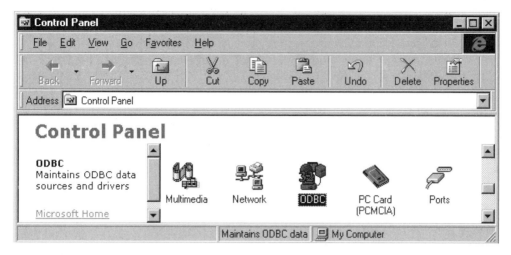

Figure 12-9   Control Panel dialog

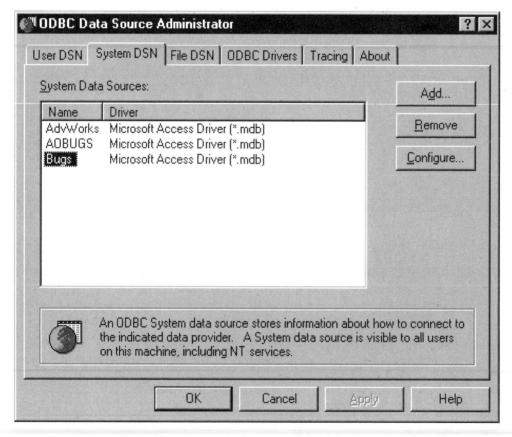

Figure 12-10   ODBC Data Source Administrator dialog

database on the Web server and press OK. After completing these steps, your database is ready to be used via the ISAPI DLL.

Configuring the ISAPI DLL is much simpler. You need to place the DLL in the InetPub\Scripts directory or any other directory with Execute rights. You can manage this from the Microsoft Internet Service Manager. When you've copied the DLL to the appropriate directory, you're ready to give it a try.

Test DLL with IE

You can test the ISAPI DLL with IE or any other Web browser. Assuming that the Bugs ISAPI DLL is in the \Inetpub\scripts directory, the following URL executes the refresh method:

```
http://www.server.com/scripts/bugs.dll?refresh
```

Calling an ISAPI DLL is a lot like calling a CGI script. The first parameter for an ISAPI DLL is the command (or request) name. If no name is provided, the

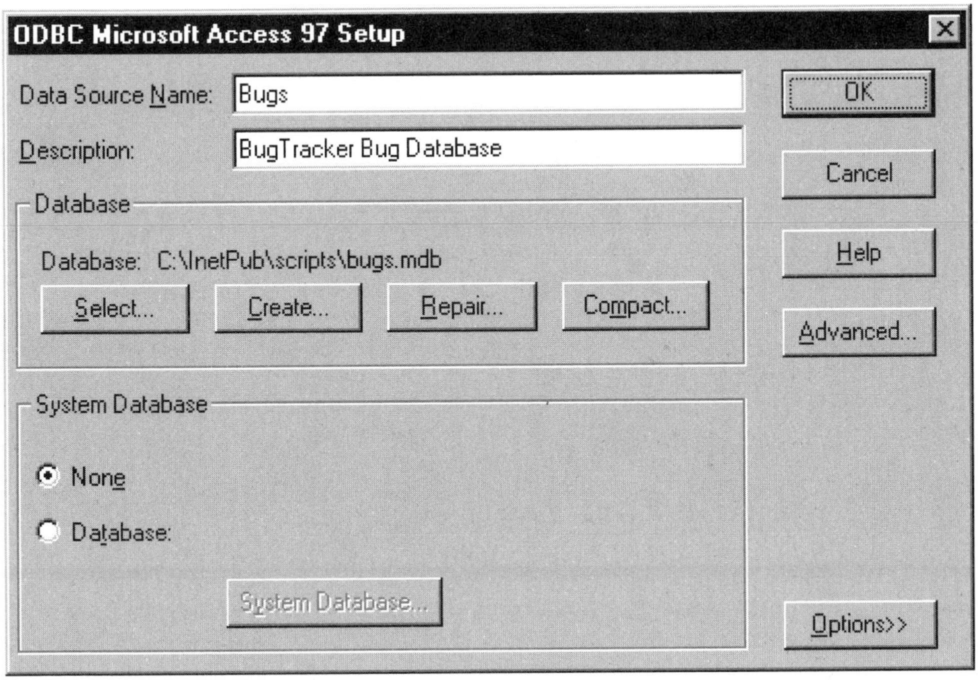

Figure 12-11   ODBC Microsoft Access 97 Setup

default ISAPI command is processed. This is specified by the DEFAULT_PARSE_
COMMAND macro.

Figure 12-12 shows the response received by IE.

Active Server Pages

Now that we've covered ISAPI, let's look at how you could accomplish the same
functionality using ASP. Listing 12-5 contains the contents of refreshbugs.asp, which
produces the same functionality as the ISAPI DLL refresh method. Using ActiveX
Data Objects (ADO), refreshbugs.asp accesses the Bugs database, traverses the
records, and sends them back to the client using the same format as the ISAPI DLL.

Listing 12-5   refreshbugs.asp

```
<%

Session.timeout = 60
If IsObject(Session("Bugs_conn")) Then
    Set conn = Session("Bugs_conn")
Else
```

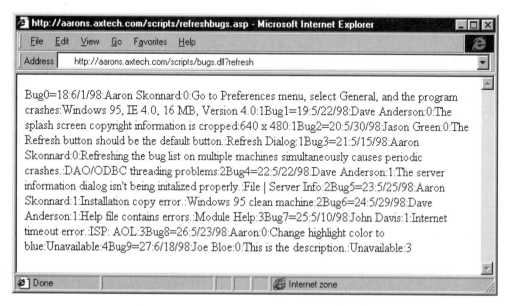

Figure 12-12   Testing Bugs.dll with Internet Explorer

```
    Set conn = Server.CreateObject("ADODB.Connection")
    conn.open "Bugs","",""
    Set Session("Bugs_conn") = conn
End If

sql = "SELECT * FROM [Bugs]"
Set rs = Server.CreateObject("ADODB.Recordset")
rs.Open sql, conn, 3, 3

On Error Resume Next
rs.MoveFirst
recnum = 0

do while Not rs.eof

Response.Write "Bug" & "CStr (recnum) & "="
recnum = recnum + 1

Response.Write Server.HTMLEncode(rs.Fields("ID").Value) & ":"
Response.Write Server.HTMLEncode(rs.Fields("Date").Value) & ":"
Response.Write Server.HTMLEncode(rs.Fields("ReportedBy").Value) & ":"
Response.Write Server.HTMLEncode(rs.Fields("Status").Value) & ":"
Response.Write Server.HTMLEncode(rs.Fields("Description").Value) & ":"
Response.Write Server.HTMLEncode(rs.Fields("Notes").Value) & ":"
Response.Write Server.HTMLEncode(rs.Fields("Priority").Value) & "<eor>"

rs.MoveNext
loop
%>
```

You can test refreshbugs.asp using IE just like you did with the ISAPI DLL. If you point your browser to *http://www.server.com/scripts.refreshbugs.asp,* you should see something like the results shown in Figure 12-13.

As you can see, the response is exactly the same as the response from the ISAPI DLL refresh method (*http://www.server.com/scripts/bugs.dll?refresh*). Because of this, it really doesn't matter which server component we decide to use from the WinInet client. In the following section on developing the WinInet client, you'll notice that either request can use the same parsing code.

ASP leverages scripting languages like VBScript and JavaScript. For many developers this makes the process of developing server components simple and straightforward. There is no doubt that the ASP version of the refresh functionality is much easier to deal with.

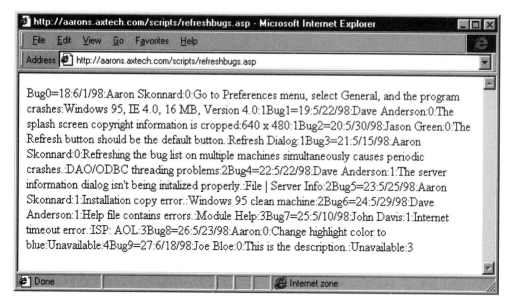

Figure 12-13 Testing Bugs.asp via IE

The ISAPI DLL addeditbug method can also be implemented quite easily using ASP. Listing 12-6 contains addeditbug.asp.

Listing 12-6 **addeditbug.asp**

```
<%
Session.timeout = 60
If IsObject(Session("Bugs_conn")) Then
    Set conn = Session("Bugs_conn")
Else
    Set conn = Server.CreateObject("ADODB.Connection")
    conn.open "Bugs","",""
    Set Session("Bugs_conn") = conn
End If

sql = "SELECT * FROM [Bugs]"
Set rs = Server.CreateObject("ADODB.Recordset")
rs.Open sql, conn, 3, 3

On Error Resume Next
rs.MoveFirst
```

```
recnum = 0
bugid = CLng(Request.QueryString("id"))
addnew = True

' find the bug if editing
do while Not rs.eof
If rs.Fields("ID").Value = bugid Then
    addnew = False
    Exit Do
End If
rs.MoveNext
loop

If addnew Then
    rs.AddNew
End If

rs.Fields("Date").Value = Request.QueryString("date")
rs.Fields("ReportedBy").Value = Request.QueryString("reportedby")
rs.Fields("Status").Value = Request.QueryString("status")
rs.Fields("Description").Value = Request.QueryString("description")
rs.Fields("Notes").Value = Request.QueryString("notes")
rs.Fields("Priority").Value = Request.QueryString("priority")

rs.Update
rs.MoveFirst

do while Not rs.eof
Response.Write "Bug" & CStr (recnum) & "="
recnum = recnum + 1
Response.Write Server.HTMLEncode(rs.Fields("ID").Value) & ":"
Response.Write Server.HTMLEncode(rs.Fields("Date").Value) & ":"
Response.Write Server.HTMLEncode(rs.Fields("ReportedBy").Value) & ":"
Response.Write Server.HTMLEncode(rs.Fields("Status").Value) & ":"
Response.Write Server.HTMLEncode(rs.Fields("Description").Value) & ":"
Response.Write Server.HTMLEncode(rs.Fields("Notes").Value) & ":"
Response.Write Server.HTMLEncode(rs.Fields("Priority").Value) & "<eor>"
rs.MoveNext
loop
%>
```

You can play around with this script from your Web browser as well. For example, the following URL should add (or edit if it already exists) a bug in the server's bug database:

```
http://aarons.axtech.com/scripts/addeditbug.asp?id=3&date=7/30/98&reportedby=Joe
Smith&status=1&description=This is a bug&notes=These are notes&priority=2
```

addeditbug.asp returns a snapshot of the bug database the same as refresh.asp.

Generating an HTML View

While we're on the subject of ASP, I want to show you how easy it is to extend your ASP scripts to generate HTML instead of our proprietary data format. Most client/server applications have some sort of Web interface that provides another way of accessing the data. Users of this BugTracker application might want to check the bug database while at a friend's house. Instead of having to install the BugTracker application, the user could simply pull up an HTML view of the same data. Listing 12-7 shows the source for bugs.asp, which displays the bug records in an HTML table (see Figure 12-14).

Listing 12-7   bugs.asp

```
<HTML>
<HEAD>
<META HTTP-EQUIV="Content-Type" CONTENT="text/html;charset=windows-1252">
<TITLE>Bugs</TITLE>
</HEAD>
<BODY>
<%
If IsObject(Session("Bugs_conn")) Then
    Set conn = Session("Bugs_conn")
Else
    Set conn = Server.CreateObject("ADODB.Connection")
    conn.open "Bugs","",""
    Set Session("Bugs_conn") = conn
End If
%>
<%
    sql = "SELECT * FROM [Bugs]"
    Set rs = Server.CreateObject("ADODB.Recordset")
    rs.Open sql, conn, 3, 3
```

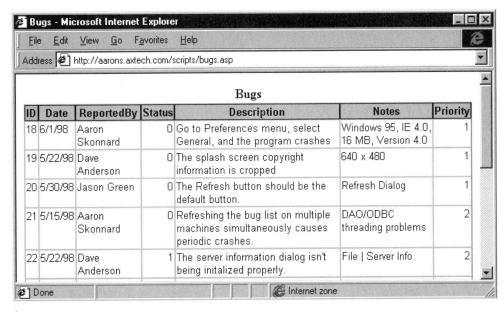

Figure 12-14   bugs.asp in IE

```
%>
<TABLE BORDER=1 BGCOLOR=#ffffff CELLSPACING=0><FONT FACE="Arial"
COLOR=#000000><CAPTION>Bugs</B></CAPTION>

<THEAD>
<TR>
<TH BGCOLOR=#c0c0c0 BORDERCOLOR=#000000 >
<FONT SIZE=2 FACE="Arial" COLOR=#000000>ID</FONT></TH>
<TH BGCOLOR=#c0c0c0 BORDERCOLOR=#000000 >
<FONT SIZE=2 FACE="Arial" COLOR=#000000>Date</FONT></TH>
<TH BGCOLOR=#c0c0c0 BORDERCOLOR=#000000 >
<FONT SIZE=2 FACE="Arial" COLOR=#000000>ReportedBy</FONT></TH>
<TH BGCOLOR=#c0c0c0 BORDERCOLOR=#000000 >
<FONT SIZE=2 FACE="Arial" COLOR=#000000>Status</FONT></TH>
<TH BGCOLOR=#c0c0c0 BORDERCOLOR=#000000 >
<FONT SIZE=2 FACE="Arial" COLOR=#000000>Description</FONT></TH>
<TH BGCOLOR=#c0c0c0 BORDERCOLOR=#000000 >
<FONT SIZE=2 FACE="Arial" COLOR=#000000>Notes</FONT></TH>
<TH BGCOLOR=#c0c0c0 BORDERCOLOR=#000000 >
<FONT SIZE=2 FACE="Arial" COLOR=#000000>Priority</FONT></TH>
```

```
</TR>
</THEAD>
<TBODY>
<%
On Error Resume Next
rs.MoveFirst
do while Not rs.eof
 %>
<TR VALIGN=TOP>
<TD BORDERCOLOR=#c0c0c0  ALIGN=RIGHT>
<FONT SIZE=2 FACE="Arial" COLOR=#000000>
<%=Server.HTMLEncode(rs.Fields("ID").Value)%><BR></FONT></TD>
<TD BORDERCOLOR=#c0c0c0 >
<FONT SIZE=2 FACE="Arial" COLOR=#000000>
<%=Server.HTMLEncode(rs.Fields("Date").Value)%><BR></FONT></TD>
<TD BORDERCOLOR=#c0c0c0 >
<FONT SIZE=2 FACE="Arial" COLOR=#000000>
<%=Server.HTMLEncode(rs.Fields("ReportedBy").Value)%><BR></FONT></TD>
<TD BORDERCOLOR=#c0c0c0  ALIGN=RIGHT>
<FONT SIZE=2 FACE="Arial" COLOR=#000000>
<%=Server.HTMLEncode(rs.Fields("Status").Value)%><BR></FONT></TD>
<TD BORDERCOLOR=#c0c0c0 >
<FONT SIZE=2 FACE="Arial" COLOR=#000000>
<%=Server.HTMLEncode(rs.Fields("Description").Value)%><BR></FONT></TD>
<TD BORDERCOLOR=#c0c0c0 >
<FONT SIZE=2 FACE="Arial" COLOR=#000000>
<%=Server.HTMLEncode(rs.Fields("Notes").Value)%><BR></FONT></TD>
<TD BORDERCOLOR=#c0c0c0  ALIGN=RIGHT>
<FONT SIZE=2 FACE="Arial" COLOR=#000000>
<%=Server.HTMLEncode(rs.Fields("Priority").Value)%><BR></FONT></TD>
</TR>
<%
rs.MoveNext
loop%>
</TBODY>
<TFOOT></TFOOT>
</TABLE>
</BODY>
</HTML>
```

Sample WinInet Client

By now things should start falling into place. The WinInet portion of this client/server application is very simple. The user interface is very similar to that of the Stock Watcher application. It's an SDI application with a simple list view that shows all of the bugs, as shown in Figure 12-2.

The main thing to keep in mind while reviewing this code is that the client also maintains a local Access database, which it synchronizes with the server. This is valuable because it allows users to review bugs without being connected to the Internet (like offline mode). So when you see code accessing the database, remember that this is a local database and not the database found on the Web server.

Remember that you can control which server type (ISAPI DLL or ASP scripts) you want to use in the File | Server Information dialog. Once you choose a server type, it's saved to the registry and all future requests use the specified type until it's modified again.

Because you're now all WinInet experts, the following client code should be easy to understand (see Listing 12-8).

Listing 12-8   CBugTrackerView implementation

```
/////////////////////////////////////////////////////////////////////////
// CBugTrackerView message handlers

void CBugTrackerView::OnUpdate(CView* pSender, LPARAM lHint, CObject* pHint)
{
    //empty list control
    m_ListCtrl.DeleteAllItems();

    //open local bug DB
    CBugsSet bugs;
    bugs.Open(dbOpenTable);
    if (bugs.IsEOF() && bugs.IsBOF())
        return;

    int i=0;
    CString strValue;

    //fill list control with all bugs in local DB
    bugs.MoveFirst();
    while (!bugs.IsEOF())
    {
```

```
            LV_ITEM item;
            item.iItem = i++;
            item.mask = LVIF_TEXT;
            item.iSubItem = 0;
            item.cchTextMax = 50;

            strValue.Format("%d", bugs.m_ID);
            item.pszText = strValue.GetBuffer(50);

            // insert item in list control and set column text info
            m_ListCtrl.InsertItem(&item);
            m_ListCtrl.SetItemText(item.iItem, 1, bugs.m_Date.GetBuffer(50));
            m_ListCtrl.SetItemText(item.iItem, 2, bugs.m_ReportedBy.GetBuffer(50));
            m_ListCtrl.SetItemText(item.iItem, 3, arrStatus[bugs.m_Status]);
            m_ListCtrl.SetItemText(item.iItem, 4, bugs.m_Description.GetBuffer(0));
            m_ListCtrl.SetItemText(item.iItem, 5, bugs.m_Notes.GetBuffer(0));
            strValue.Format("%d", bugs.m_Priority);
            m_ListCtrl.SetItemText(item.iItem, 6, strValue.GetBuffer(0));
            m_ListCtrl.EnsureVisible( item.iItem, TRUE );

            //move to next record and continue
            bugs.MoveNext();
        }
        bugs.Close();
}


void CBugTrackerView::OnDblclkListResult(NMHDR* pNMHDR, LRESULT* pResult)
{
    // get selected item
    UINT index = m_ListCtrl.GetNextItem(-1 , LVNI_SELECTED);
    if (index == -1)
        return;

    CAddEditBugDlg dlg;
    //initialize add/edit dialog
    dlg.m_nID = atol(m_ListCtrl.GetItemText(index, 0));
    dlg.m_strDate = m_ListCtrl.GetItemText(index, 1);
    dlg.m_strReportedBy = m_ListCtrl.GetItemText(index, 2);
    dlg.m_strStatus = m_ListCtrl.GetItemText(index, 3);
    dlg.m_strDesc = m_ListCtrl.GetItemText(index, 4);
    dlg.m_strNotes = m_ListCtrl.GetItemText(index, 5);
```

```
        dlg.m_nPriority = atol(m_ListCtrl.GetItemText(index, 6));

        if (IDCANCEL == dlg.DoModal())
            return;

        //format the request data
        CString strData;

        strData.Format("id=%d&date=%s&reportedby=%s&status=%d"
                "&description=%s&notes=%s&priority=%d",
                dlg.m_nID, dlg.m_strDate, dlg.m_strReportedBy, dlg.m_lStatus,
                dlg.m_strDesc, dlg.m_strNotes, dlg.m_nPriority);

        //send the addeditbug request
        UINT nServerType = AfxGetApp()->GetProfileInt(REG_KEY_SETTINGS, "type", 0);

        if (TYPE_ASP == nServerType)
            SendRequest("addeditbug.asp", strData);
        else
            SendRequest("bugs.dll?addeditbug", strData);

        *pResult = 0;
}


void CBugTrackerView::OnNewBug()
{
        CAddEditBugDlg dlg;
        if (IDCANCEL == dlg.DoModal())
            return;

        CString strData;
        //format the request data
        strData.Format("id=0&date=%s&reportedby=%s&status=%d"
                "&description=%s&notes=%s&priority=%d",
                dlg.m_strDate, dlg.m_strReportedBy, dlg.m_lStatus, dlg.m_strDesc,
                dlg.m_strNotes, dlg.m_nPriority);

        //send the addeditbug request
        UINT nServerType = AfxGetApp()->GetProfileInt(REG_KEY_SETTINGS, "type", 0);
```

```
    if (TYPE_ASP == nServerType)
        SendRequest("addeditbug.asp", strData);
    else
        SendRequest("bugs.dll?addeditbug", strData);
}


void CBugTrackerView::OnRefreshBugs()
{
    CString strData;

    //send the addeditbug request
    UINT nServerType = AfxGetApp()->GetProfileInt(REG_KEY_SETTINGS, "type", 0);

    if (TYPE_ASP == nServerType)
        SendRequest("refreshbugs.asp", strData);
    else
        SendRequest("bugs.dll?refresh", strData);
}


void CBugTrackerView::SendRequest(LPCTSTR lpszObject, CString& strData)
{
    DWORD dwStatus, dwRead;
    CString strResponse;
    CWinApp* pApp = AfxGetApp();

    //get server, port, and path information saved in registry
    CString strServer = pApp->GetProfileString(REG_KEY_SETTINGS, "server",
            "aarons.axtech.com");
    UINT nPort = pApp->GetProfileInt(REG_KEY_SETTINGS, "port", 80);
    CString strPath = pApp->GetProfileString(REG_KEY_SETTINGS, "path",
            "/scripts/");

    //add object passed in lpszObject
    strPath += lpszObject;
    strPath += "?";
    strPath += strData;

    TRY
    {
        //get app Internet session and get HTTP connection
        CInternetSession& session = GetDocument()->m_Session;
```

```
CHttpConnection* pConnection = session.GetHttpConnection(strServer,
        (USHORT)nPort, NULL, NULL);

if (pConnection)
{
    //open the HTTP request
    CHttpFile* pFile = pConnection->OpenRequest("GET", strPath);
    pFile->SendRequest(NULL, 0, NULL, 0); //strData.GetBuffer(0),
            strData.GetLength());

    //check the HTTP status code
    pFile->QueryInfoStatusCode(dwStatus);
    if (dwStatus == HTTP_STATUS_OK)
    {

        //read the response
        char szBuffer[BUFFLEN];
        while(dwRead=pFile->Read(szBuffer, BUFFLEN))
        {
            szBuffer[dwRead]=0;
            strResponse += szBuffer;
        }
        ParseBugs(strResponse.GetBuffer(0));
    }
    //close the HTTP file and connection
    pFile->Close();
    pConnection->Close();

    //delete file and connection objects
    if (pFile)
        delete pFile;
    if (pConnection)
        delete pConnection;
}
}
CATCH(CInternetException,e)
{
    e->ReportError();
}
END_CATCH
}
```

```
void CBugTrackerView::ParseBugs(char *lpszResponse)
{
    CString strBugTag, strBug;
    UINT i=0;

    for (;;)
    {
        strBugTag.Format("Bug%d", i++);
        strBug = GetNameValue(strBugTag.GetBuffer(8), lpszResponse);
        if (strBug.IsEmpty())
            break;
        ParseBug(strBug.GetBuffer(0));
    }
    GetDocument()->UpdateAllViews(NULL);
}


//returns the value associated with pName if one is found,
//otherwise returns an empty CString
CString CBugTrackerView::GetNameValue(char *pName, char *pResponse)
{
    CString strValue;
    char *p1,*p2;
    char *pEOR = "<eor>";

    p1 = pResponse;
    while (p1 = strstr(p1,pName))
    {
        if ( (p1 == pResponse) || ( *(p1-1) == '>' ) )
        {
            p1 += strlen(pName)+1;
            if (p2 = strstr(p1,pEOR))
            {
                char cSave = *p2;
                *p2 = NULL;
                strValue = p1;
                *p2 = cSave;
            }
            break;
        }
        //otherwise move to the next line and search again, skip the fake
        else p1+=strlen(pName)+1;
```

```
        }
        return strValue;
    }


void CBugTrackerView::ParseBug(char* lpszBug)
{
    char *p1, *p2;
    CString strDesc, strDate, strRepBy, strNotes;
    long lID, lStatus, lPriority;

    // parse out information
    lID = atol(strtok(lpszBug, SEP));
    strDate = strtok(NULL, SEP);
    strRepBy = strtok(NULL, SEP);
    lStatus = atol(strtok(NULL, SEP));
    strDesc = strtok(NULL, SEP);
    strNotes = strtok(NULL, SEP);
    lPriority = atol(strtok(NULL, SEP));

    // open local database
    CBugsSet bugs;
    bugs.Open(dbOpenTable);

    //either edit or add new record
    if (bugs.FindBugByID(lID))
        bugs.Edit();
    else
        bugs.AddNew();

    //fill in record set members
    bugs.m_ID = lID;
    bugs.m_Date = strDate;
    bugs.m_ReportedBy = strRepBy;
    bugs.m_Status = lStatus;
    bugs.m_Description = strDesc;
    bugs.m_Notes = strNotes;
    bugs.m_Priority = lPriority;
    bugs.Update();
    bugs.Close();
}
```

```
//automatically synchs w/ bug DB on server
void CBugTrackerView::OnTimer(UINT nIDEvent)
{
    if (nIDEvent == REFRESH_TIMER)
    {
        OnRefreshBugs();
    }
    CView::OnTimer(nIDEvent);
}
```

This code should look very familiar because it's very similar to the other samples presented in this book. The data strings are constructed the same way as before except for the case of the ISAPI DLL, in which the first parameter must be the ISAPI method name. The GetNameValue and ParseBug methods know how to parse the data returned by the server. GetNameValue returns a single record such as Bug1=...<eor> and ParseBug knows how to break the record into its various pieces.

If you play around with BugTracker on a few different machines, you'll notice that they all look at the same data. In fact, you could even call up a friend on the other side of the globe and have him play around with BugTracker at the same time. When he adds a new bug, all the other users, including yourself, see it the next time they refresh. It's really quite exciting when you start thinking about the possibilities.

Conclusion

The purpose of this chapter was to introduce the concept of Internet client/server applications. It would be impossible to cover completely all client/server technologies in this book. However, hopefully this chapter has helped you comprehend what you can accomplish with Internet client/server applications. The ISAPI/ASP/WinInet example is typical of what you can achieve with cooperative Internet client/server components. Writing Internet client/server applications is definitely not a simple task. However, with powerful technologies like WinInet on the client side, they are becoming much easier to master.

A

Appendix

TCP/IP Tutorial

If you've been around the Internet much, you're probably familiar with the term TCP/IP. But what does TCP/IP mean? What does it encompass? Although you can find many definitions for the TCP and IP protocols, the term TCP/IP usually refers to something more encompassing. In fact, most developers use the term TCP/IP to refer to a family of Internet protocols. Three of them—the Transmission Control Protocol, the User Datagram Protocol (UDP), and the Internet Protocol—are low-level protocols on which many of the other application-level Internet protocols are built. However, because all the application-level Internet protocols are built on top of TCP/IP, the term TCP/IP is commonly used to refer to this entire family of Internet protocols.

When you establish a dial-up connection with an ISP, you're essentially opening a channel that is capable of sending and receiving TCP/IP requests. When you're connected to the server, applications can use this channel to communicate via TCP/IP or, in other words, any Internet protocol. For example, your Web browser (Microsoft IE, Netscape, and so forth) uses the HTTP protocol to download Web pages. Behind the scenes, HTTP uses TCP/IP to send the request and transmit the Web page data. When you send an e-mail to someone, TCP/IP is also being used under the hood.

To help you understand how TCP/IP works, it helps to take a look at how the protocols are layered. Then I'll explain the role of each lower level protocol (TCP, UDP, and IP). Although understanding the basics of the Internet protocols is required to develop Internet applications successfully, becoming a TCP/IP protocol expert is unnecessary. WinInet encapsulates all of the confusing details and complexities surrounding TCP/IP. After learning WinInet, you'll find that the information presented in this chapter is more than sufficient to start developing powerful Windows Internet applications.

TCP/IP Protocol Layering

Figure A-1 illustrates how the TCP/IP Internet protocols are layered. Each layer performs specific tasks and plays an important role in the overall functionality of TCP/IP.

The topmost layer is the application protocol layer, which consists of protocols like HTTP, FTP, Gopher, and many others. These are the protocols that we, as developers, deal with most in our applications. The purpose of WinInet is to encapsulate these somewhat complicated protocols into an easy-to-use API.

The application protocol layer is built on top of the transport protocol layer. TCP and UDP are the most commonly used transport layer protocols. The main difference between TCP and UDP lies in protocol reliability. TCP is a reliable, connection-oriented protocol, whereas UDP is an unreliable, connectionless protocol. With TCP there is a one-to-one connection between machines capable of full-duplex communication. UDP, on the other hand, is capable of broadcasting messages to multiple hosts. Unlike TCP, UDP sends packets out but doesn't care if they ever get there. Although UDP has its advantages (especially in games like Quake), TCP is used more commonly by most application-level protocols.

The next layer is the IP. IP is simple in concept because it performs only one basic task: IP finds a path of communication. For example, when you send an e-mail to a buddy, IP is responsible for finding a way for the data to get there. IP isn't concerned with transmission errors; error control is the transport protocol's responsibility.

Like UDP, IP is a connectionless protocol. It simply defines how the packet reaches its destination. Although on smaller networks this may seem trivial, on a larger network it's much more complex, considering the number of hosts through which a given packet may route.

The last and lowest level layer consists of physical protocols such as Ethernet. This layer deals with the protocols that accommodate the physical medium. Because these protocols are medium specific, it is difficult to standardize at this level. With

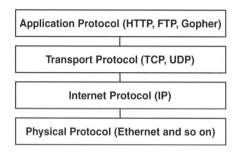

Figure A-1   TCP/IP protocol layering

the high-level tools available today, you'll rarely find the need to work at the physical layer.

TCP

As stated, TCP stands for Transmission Control Protocol. Transmission control deals with guaranteeing error-free data transmissions. This may sound like a complex task considering the size of various data types transmitted over the Internet today, such as graphics, audio, video, and binary executables. So how does TCP make it happen? The answer is simple: TCP divides data into manageable packets that are easier to deal with.

Let's consider a common scenario. Suppose you want to download the latest Windows NT Service Pack (which seems to be getting bigger and bigger each time it's released). Before sending the data, TCP first breaks the binary data into packets (see Figure A-2), which are then transmitted independently. As I'll discuss in the next section, it's IP's role to route the individual packets. However, there is no guarantee the packets will arrive in the same order they were sent or that they will arrive, period. Therefore, TCP is also responsible for reassembling the packets in the correct order on the receiving end. If a packet fails to arrive (because of a transmission error) TCP resends the packet until it has been received at the other end.

Imagine how frustrating it would be if you were 75 MB through a 100-MB file download when an error occurred. Without the flexibility of TCP, you would have to start over again from the beginning because there would be no way to recover from the error. Think of how much bandwidth would be wasted by people trying and retrying to download a big file without encountering an error. Transmission errors are unavoidable. Hence, TCP is necessary.

If an error occurs with TCP, a small packet is all that needs to be retransmitted. It's the flexibility of the low-level protocols (like TCP) that have helped the Internet progress so quickly.

By now you're probably wondering about some of the details. What do these packets look like? How is a TCP connection established? How does TCP know if a packet is transmitted successfully? How do you know when the transmission is complete?

Figure A-2 TCP packets

TCP Header

TCP attaches a header to every packet. The information contained in the header is used primarily for the following reasons:

- To keep multiple TCP connections in order
- To reassemble the packets on the other end
- To detect any transmission errors

Figure A-3 illustrates the header format and how the packets are broken down by TCP. Figure A-4 illustrates what the packets actually look like before TCP passes the packets to the IP layer. The TCP box in the figure represents the TCP header.

If you're like most developers, you're probably used to running your e-mail client, chat client, and multiple browsers all at the same time. Because all these applications use TCP behind the scenes, how does TCP know which packets belong to each application? It needs some way to distinguish between the storm of packets it

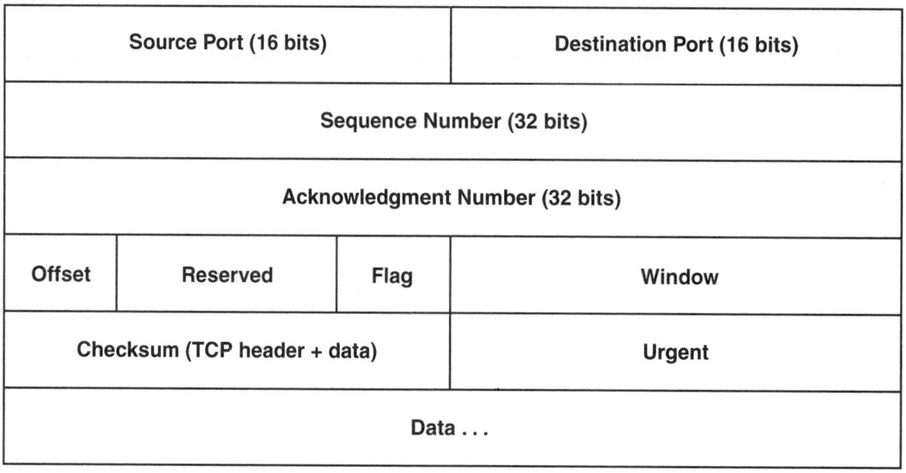

Source Port (16 bits)			Destination Port (16 bits)	
Sequence Number (32 bits)				
Acknowledgment Number (32 bits)				
Offset	Reserved	Flag	Window	
Checksum (TCP header + data)			Urgent	
Data ...				

Figure A-3   TCP header format

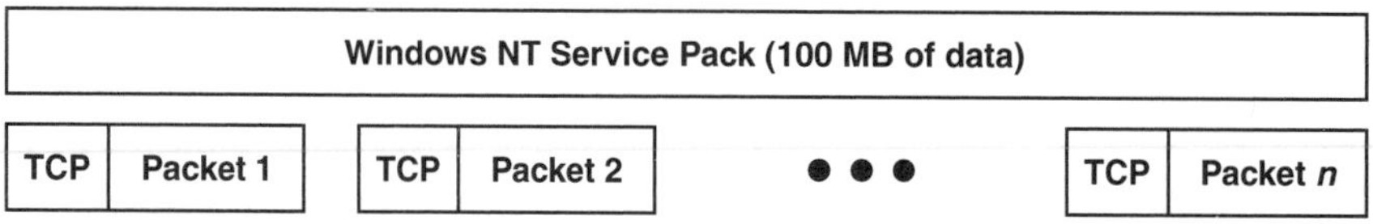

Windows NT Service Pack (100 MB of data)						
TCP	Packet 1	TCP	Packet 2	● ● ●	TCP	Packet *n*

Figure A-4   TCP header and packets

receives while multiple TCP applications are transmitting data simultaneously. The source and destination port fields of the TCP header help keep this straight.

When an application establishes a TCP connection, TCP assigns a port to the sending application as well as the receiving application. These ports are then stored in the source port and destination port fields of each packet header. The port used by the application sending the packet is stored in the source port field whereas the receiving application's port is stored in the destination port field. This makes it possible for various TCP conversations to exist simultaneously. When TCP receives a packet, it looks at the port numbers and knows exactly to which conversation it belongs.

The next field, the sequence number, is used to reassemble the data on the other end. The sequence number keeps track of the order of the packets. Remember that packets can arrive in any order so there must be a way to put them back in the correct order after all the packets have been received successfully. The sequence number tells TCP where the packet fits into the overall data sequence. The sequence number is actually an offset into the byte stream. For example, if a packet has a sequence number of 1,000, TCP knows that this packet belongs at octet 1,000 in the byte stream.

After receiving packets, the receiver responds by sending a packet back to the sender. This packet contains a number in the acknowledgment field. This number tells the sender how many bytes of data have been received successfully. For example, if the sender receives a packet with an acknowledgment number of 1,000, it knows that the other end has received 1,000 bytes of data successfully. If the sender doesn't get an acknowledgment within a certain amount of time, it simply resends the missing packets.

The checksum field is what TCP uses to detect transmission errors. The checksum contains the sum of the TCP header plus all the following data octets. On the other end of the transmission, TCP verifies that this number matches the checksum that it calculates for the packet. If the numbers don't match, a transmission error occurred, in which case TCP throws away the packet and tells the sender to resend it.

So what about the flags, window, and urgent fields? These are used to manage the TCP connection. The flags are used to establish and terminate a connection, which I'll discuss next. The window field is used to tell the sender how fast to send the packets. When the receiver reaches its limit and can't process any more packets, the window is set to zero. When the receiver finishes processing the previous packets and is ready to handle more, it increases the window size. This is how the sender and receiver regulate throughput. Like its name suggests, the urgent field is used to communicate urgent information. If the receiver gets a packet with an urgent value, it evaluates the priority and acts accordingly (for example, it may abort a transmission).

TCP Handshake and Flags

So how does TCP establish a connection to begin with? First, the initiating end sends a packet with the SYN flag set. If the receiving end receives it and can respond, it replies by sending a packet back to the sender with the SYN and ACK flags set. If everything goes well up to this point, the sender sends another packet with the ACK flag set and the connection is considered established. Figure A-5 illustrates how this process works.

When the connection is established, TCP offers a full-duplex (two-way) communication channel for transmitting data. After the sender finishes sending data, it terminates the connection by sending a packet with the FIN flag set. When the other end acknowledges the FIN flag, the TCP connection is considered closed, and no more data can be transmitted via this channel.

That sums up TCP, which is really the heart of most Internet protocols. Once again, a basic understanding of TCP suffices for WinInet programming. WinInet hides all of TCP's complexities and lets you deal with a much higher level interface.

IP

IP is responsible for delivering the packets provided by the TCP layer. Packet delivery is IP's one and only responsibility. IP doesn't care about the data or any of the TCP header information; it tacks on its own header to the TCP header attached to the packet. To understand how IP does its job, we need to look at the IP header in more detail.

IP Header

Figure A-6 illustrates the IP header format. Notice the IP header has its own checksum field. Although the TCP header contains a checksum of the TCP header and the data, the IP header's checksum is simply a checksum of the header. This checksum makes sure that the IP header doesn't get damaged during transmission. Because the IP header tells you where the packet is supposed to go, it wouldn't work very well if that information were corrupted.

The protocol field tells IP on the receiving computer for which protocol this packet is headed. Although the protocol is typically TCP, other protocols (like UDP) can also use IP. The time to live field is used to control the lifetime of a packet. Each time the packet passes through a system, the time-to-live value is decremented. When

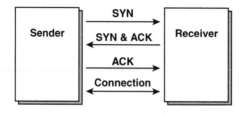

Figure A-5   TCP handshake

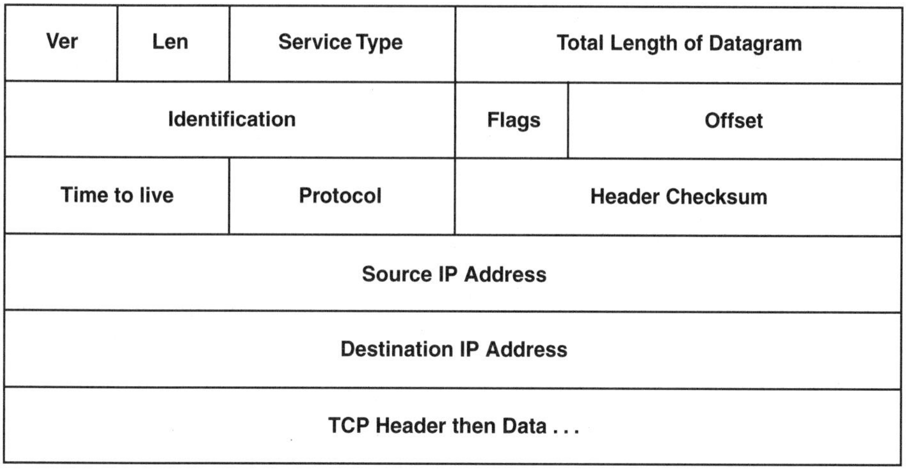

Ver
Len
Service Type
Total Length of Datagram
Identification
Flags
Offset
Time to live
Protocol
Header Checksum
Source IP Address
Destination IP Address
TCP Header then Data . . .

Figure A-6 IP header format

it reaches zero, the packet is destroyed. This helps prevent infinite loop packets from clogging up Internet traffic.

The last two fields that I want to discuss are the source and destination IP address fields. These fields specify IP addresses of the source and destination machines. As the packet jumps from network to network, IP uses this information to decide where the packet should be sent next. IP uses the destination IP address along with the host's route table to determine the IP address of the next location. To learn more about how routing works, you'll want to read up on routing tables along with direct and indirect routine mechanisms.

With the IP header tacked on, Figure A-7 illustrates what the packets look like.

IP Address Basics

Currently, IP addresses are 4-byte, 32-bit numbers that are usually written as four sets of dot-separated octets. Here is the IP address that my computer is using at this very moment:

```
207.173.156.81
```

Windows NT Service Pack (100 MB of data)
IP
TCP
Packet 1
IP
TCP
Packet 2
IP
TCP
Packet n

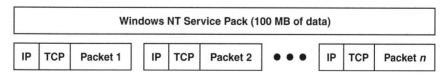

Figure A-7 IP header and packets

If you use an ISP that assigns IP addresses automatically each time you connect, you can see which IP address your machine is using by running the IP configuration utility that comes with Windows. To run the utility on Windows 95, click on the Start menu and press Run. In the Run dialog, type `winipcfg` and press OK. A dialog appears displaying your machine's IP address. On Windows NT 4.0 simply open a command shell and type `ipconfig`.

There are three types of Internet addresses: classes A, B, and C. Every IP address contains both a network ID and a host ID. The difference between the three classes of IP addresses has to do with how many bits are used to describe the network ID and how many bits are used to describe the host ID.

You can determine to which class an IP address belongs by the value of the first octet. Table A-1 describes the ranges for the first octet value of an IP address. For example, because my IP address starts with 207, I know that it's a class C address.

Figure A-8 illustrates the layout of a class A IP address. The first, highest order bit is always zero (a value of one would make the value of the first octet at least 128). The next seven bits are used for the network ID. This means that only 128 ($2^7 = 128$) class A networks are possible. However, because 24 bits are used for the host ID, there can be more than 16 million hosts on a class A network. As you've probably guessed, all the class A addresses have been used up.

Figure A-9 illustrates the layout of a class B IP address. The first two bits must be one and zero. This makes sure that the first octet is in the range of 128 to 191 (127 is reserved for special purposes). The next 14 bits are used for the network ID, and the last 16 bits are used for the host ID. Class B addresses allow for 2^{14} (or 16,384)

Table A-1   IP address first-octet ranges

IP Address Class	First Octet Range
A	1–126
B	128–191
C	192–255

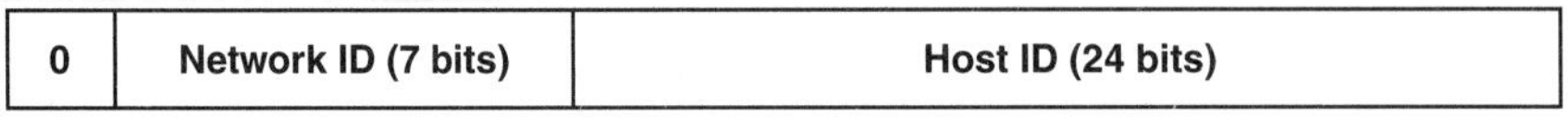

0	Network ID (7 bits)	Host ID (24 bits)

Figure A-8   Class A IP address format

1	0	Network ID (14 bits)	Host ID (16 bits)

Figure A-9   Class B IP address format

networks and 2^{16} (or 65,536) hosts. This is usually enough for most organizations. Unfortunately, all class B addresses are used up as well.

Figure A-10 illustrates the layout of a class C IP address. The first three bits must be 1 1 0. This ensures that the first octet is in the range of 192 to 255 (values between 223 and 255 are reserved for future use). You'll notice that the class C address uses 21 bits for the network ID, which allows for more than 2 million networks with class C addresses. The drawback, however, is that only eight bits are used for the host ID. Eight bits only makes it possible for each network to have 256 hosts on each network.

You're probably wondering how we are going to sustain the constant growth of the Internet if all of the class A and B addresses have been used up and we only have as many as 2 million class C addresses available. At the rate the Internet is growing, we're definitely going to run out of IP addresses soon. Don't worry. I'm not the first genius to figure this out. The shortage of IP addresses has been painfully obvious for quite some time. (Although the designers of the Internet must have never imagined it would become a problem so quickly.)

Currently there is a new IP protocol under development called IPNG (or IPv6) that stands for IP Next Generation. IPNG reformats the IP header and increases the number of bits used for IP addresses from 32 to 128. The 128-bit addresses should be more than sufficient (as least for a while, right?).

Domain Names

When was the last time that you typed in an IP address to navigate to a Web site? The answer is probably never. Most human beings are better with names then numbers. It would be very difficult for average users to keep track of another IP address each time they found a site of interest. To solve this problem, domain names were introduced into the Internet architecture.

A domain name is a textual name mapped to an IP address. For example, the name *www.microsoft.com* might evaluate to 207.68.137.59. So how does this happen?

In the beginning, every machine had a local hosts file (named "hosts"), which it would use to look up the address associated with a name. However, when the Internet

1	1	0	Network ID (21 bits)	Host ID (8 bits)

Figure A-10   Class C IP address format

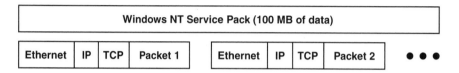

Figure A-11   Ethernet header and packets

started getting bigger, this solution was no longer feasible. Instead, a database was developed that could be accessed universally to look up an IP address. Today this is known as DNS.

Let's look at how DNS makes it possible to retrieve the IP address associated with *www.microsoft.com.* First you would contact a well-known root domain server, which would provide you with a list of servers for specific domains such as edu, com, net, and so forth. Then you would contact one of the com servers and query for Microsoft. If the com server finds Microsoft in its database, the corresponding IP address is returned.

The Physical Layer

When IP is done adding its headers to the packet, it passes them to the physical layer, which is responsible for physically sending the data. The physical layer also adds a header to the packet before it's finally sent. This header varies depending on the type of physical layer being used. For example, on an Ethernet network, the physical layer adds an Ethernet header to the packets, specifying the source and destination Ethernet addresses along with a checksum.

With the Ethernet header included, Figure A-11 illustrates what the packets look like before they are sent.

Conclusion

The information in this appendix is meant to help you grasp the most important TCP/IP concepts. Once again, a basic understanding of the TCP/IP concepts will help you to create better Internet applications.

B
Appendix

API Flags

Many of the Win32 Internet functions accept a double-word array of flags as a parameter. The following is a brief description of the defined flags.

INTERNET_FLAG_ASYNC—Makes only asynchronous requests on handles descended from the handle returned from this function. Only the InternetOpen function uses this flag.

INTERNET_FLAG_CACHE_ASYNC—Allows a lazy cache write.

INTERNET_FLAG_CACHE_IF_NET_FAIL—Returns the resource from the cache if the network request for the resource fails due to an ERROR_INTERNET_CONNECTION_RESET or ERROR_INTERNET_CANNOT_CONNECT. This flag is used by HttpOpenRequest.

INTERNET_FLAG_DONT_CACHE—Does not add the returned entity to the cache. Identical to the preferred value, INTERNET_FLAG_NO_CACHE_WRITE. This flag is used by GopherFindFirstFile, GopherOpenFile, FtpFindFirstFile, FtpGetFile, FtpOpenFile, FtpPutFile, HttpOpenRequest, and InternetOpenUrl.

INTERNET_FLAG_EXISTING_CONNECT—Attempts to use an existing InternetConnect object if one exists with the same attributes required to make the request. This is useful only with FTP operations because FTP is the only protocol that typically performs multiple operations during the same session. The Win32 Internet API caches a single connection handle for each HINTERNET handle generated by InternetOpen. Only the InternetOpenUrl function uses this flag.

INTERNET_FLAG_FORMS_SUBMIT—Indicates that this is a forms submit.

INTERNET_FLAG_FROM_CACHE—Does not make network requests. All entities are returned from the cache. If the requested item is not in the cache, a suitable error such as ERROR_FILE_NOT_FOUND is returned. Only the InternetOpen function uses this flag.

INTERNET_FLAG_HYPERLINK—Forces a reload if there was no Expires time and no Last-Modified time returned from the server when determining whether to reload the item from the network. This flag can be used by GopherFindFirstFile, GopherOpenFile, FtpFindFirstFile, FtpGetFile, FtpOpenFile, FtpPutFile, HttpOpenRequest, and InternetOpenUrl.

INTERNET_FLAG_IGNORE_CERT_CN_INVALID—Disables Win32 Internet function checking of SSL/PCT-based certificates that are returned from the server against the host name given in the request. Win32 Internet functions use a simple check against certificates by comparing for matching host names and simple wildcard rules. This flag can be used by HttpOpenRequest and InternetOpenUrl (for HTTP requests).

INTERNET_FLAG_IGNORE_CERT_DATE_INVALID—Disables Win32 Internet function checking of SSL/PCT-based certificates for proper validity dates. This flag can be used by HttpOpenRequest and InternetOpenUrl (for HTTP requests).

INTERNET_FLAG_IGNORE_REDIRECT_TO_HTTP—Disables the ability of the Win32 Internet functions to detect this special type of redirect. When this flag is used, Win32 Internet functions allow redirects transparently from HTTPS to HTTP URLs. This flag can be used by HttpOpenRequest and InternetOpenUrl (for HTTP requests).

INTERNET_FLAG_IGNORE_REDIRECT_TO_HTTPS—Disables the ability of the Win32 Internet functions to detect this special type of redirect. When this flag is used, Win32 Internet functions allow redirects transparently from HTTP to HTTPS URLs. This flag can be used by HttpOpenRequest and InternetOpenUrl (for HTTP requests).

INTERNET_FLAG_KEEP_CONNECTION—Uses keep-alive semantics, if available, for the connection. This flag is used by HttpOpenRequest and InternetOpenUrl (for HTTP requests). This flag is required for MSN, NTLM, and other types of authentication.

INTERNET_FLAG_MUST_CACHE_REQUEST—Identical to the preferred value, INTERNET_FLAG_NEED_FILE. Causes a temporary file to be created if the file cannot be cached. This flag can be used by GopherFindFirstFile, GopherOpenFile, FtpFindFirstFile, FtpGetFile, FtpOpenFile, FtpPutFile, HttpOpenRequest, and InternetOpenUrl.

INTERNET_FLAG_NEED_FILE—Causes a temporary file to be created if the file cannot be cached. This flag can be used by GopherFindFirstFile, GopherOpenFile, FtpFindFirstFile, FtpGetFile, FtpOpenFile, FtpPutFile, HttpOpenRequest, and InternetOpenUrl.

INTERNET_FLAG_NO_AUTH—Does not attempt authentication automatically. This flag can be used by HttpOpenRequest and InternetOpenUrl (for HTTP requests).

INTERNET_FLAG_NO_AUTO_REDIRECT—Does not handle redirection automatically in HttpSendRequest. This flag can also be used by InternetOpenUrl for HTTP requests.

INTERNET_FLAG_NO_CACHE_WRITE—Does not add the returned entity to the cache. This flag is used by GopherFindFirstFile, GopherOpenFile, FtpFindFirstFile, FtpGetFile, FtpOpenFile, FtpPutFile, HttpOpenRequest, and InternetOpenUrl.

INTERNET_FLAG_NO_COOKIES—Does not add cookie headers automatically to requests, and does not add returned cookies automatically to the cookie database. This flag can be used by HttpOpenRequest and InternetOpenUrl (for HTTP requests).

INTERNET_FLAG_NO_UI—Disables the cookie dialog. This flag can be used by HttpOpenRequest and InternetOpenUrl (HTTP requests only).

INTERNET_FLAG_OFFLINE—Identical to INTERNET_FLAG_FROM_CACHE. Does not make network requests. All entities are returned from the cache. If the requested item is not in the cache, a suitable error such as ERROR_FILE_NOT_FOUND is returned. Only the InternetOpen function uses this flag.

INTERNET_FLAG_PASSIVE—Uses passive FTP semantics. Only InternetConnect and InternetOpenUrl use this flag. InternetConnect uses this flag for FTP requests, and InternetOpenUrl uses this flag for FTP files and directories.

INTERNET_FLAG_PRAGMA_NOCACHE—Forces the request to be resolved by the originating server, even if a cached copy exists on the proxy. The InternetOpenUrl function (on HTTP and HTTPS requests only) and HttpOpenRequest functions use this flag.

INTERNET_FLAG_RAW_DATA—Returns the data as a GOPHER_FIND_DATA structure when retrieving Gopher directory information, or as a WIN32_FIND_DATA structure when retrieving FTP directory information. If this flag is not specified or if the call was made through a CERN proxy, InternetOpenUrl returns an HTML version of the directory. Only the InternetOpenUrl function uses this flag.

INTERNET_FLAG_RELOAD—Forces a download of the requested file, object, or directory listing from the originating server, not from the cache. The GopherFindFirstFile, GopherOpenFile, FtpFindFirstFile, FtpGetFile, FtpOpenFile, FtpPutFile, HttpOpenRequest, and InternetOpenUrl functions utilize this flag.

INTERNET_FLAG_RESYNCHRONIZE—Reloads HTTP resources if the resource has been modified since the last time it was downloaded. All FTP and Gopher resources are reloaded. This flag can be used by GopherFindFirstFile, GopherOpenFile, FtpFindFirstFile, FtpGetFile, FtpOpenFile, FtpPutFile, HttpOpenRequest, and InternetOpenUrl.

INTERNET_FLAG_SECURE—Uses secure transaction semantics. This translates to using SSL/PCT and is only meaningful in HTTP requests. This flag is used by HttpOpenRequest and InternetOpenUrl, but this is made redundant if https:// appears in the URL.

INTERNET_FLAG_TRANSFER_ASCII—Transfers a file as ASCII (FTP only). This flag can be used by FtpOpenFile, FtpGetFile, and FtpPutFile.

INTERNET_FLAG_TRANSFER_BINARY—Transfers a file as Binary (FTP only). This flag can be used by FtpOpenFile, FtpGetFile, and FtpPutFile.

WININET_API_FLAG_ASYNC—Forces asynchronous operations.

WININET_API_FLAG_SYNC—Forces synchronous operations.

WININET_API_FLAG_USE_CONTEXT—Forces the API to use the context value, even if it is set to zero.

C

Appendix

Internet Option Flags

The following list contains the options supported by InternetQueryOption and InternetSetOption.

INTERNET_OPTION_CALLBACK—Returns or sets the address of the callback function defined for this handle. This option can be used on all HINTERNET handles. Used by InternetQueryOption and InternetSetOption.

INTERNET_OPTION_CONNECT_RETRIES—Returns or sets the retry count to use for Internet connection requests. If a connection attempt still fails after the specified number of tries, the request is cancelled. The default is five retries. This option can be used on any HINTERNET handle, including a NULL handle. Used by InternetQueryOption and InternetSetOption.

INTERNET_OPTION_CONNECT_TIMEOUT—Returns or sets the timeout value, in milliseconds, to use for Internet connection requests. If a connection request takes longer than this timeout value, the request is cancelled. This option can be used on any HINTERNET handle, including a NULL handle. Used by InternetQueryOption and InternetSetOption.

INTERNET_OPTION_CONNECTED_STATE—Returns or sets the connected state. Used by InternetQueryOption and InternetSetOption.

INTERNET_OPTION_CONTEXT_VALUE—Returns or sets the context value associated with this Internet handle. This option can be used on any HINTERNET handle. Used by InternetQueryOption and InternetSetOption. Previously, this set the context value to the address stored in the DWORD(lpBuffer) pointer. This has been corrected so that the value stored in the buffer is used and the INTERNET_OPTION_CONTEXT_VALUE flag is reassigned a new value. The old value, 10, has been preserved so that applications written for the old behavior are still supported.

INTERNET_OPTION_CONTROL_RECEIVE_TIMEOUT—Identical to INTERNET_OPTION_RECEIVE_TIMEOUT. Used by InternetQueryOption and InternetSetOption.

INTERNET_OPTION_CONTROL_SEND_TIMEOUT—Identical to INTERNET_OPTION_SEND_TIMEOUT. Used by InternetQueryOption and InternetSetOption.

INTERNET_OPTION_DATA_RECEIVE_TIMEOUT—Returns or sets the timeout value, in milliseconds, to use for Internet data download requests. If a data receive request takes longer than this timeout value, the request is cancelled. Used by InternetQueryOption and InternetSetOption.

INTERNET_OPTION_DATA_SEND_TIMEOUT—Returns or sets the timeout value, in milliseconds, to use for Internet data send requests. If a data send request takes longer than this timeout value, the request is cancelled. Used by InternetQueryOption and InternetSetOption.

INTERNET_OPTION_DATAFILE_NAME—Returns the name of the file backing a downloaded entity. This flag is valid after InternetOpenUrl, FtpOpenFile, GopherOpenFile, or HttpOpenRequest has completed. Used by InternetQueryOption and InternetSetOption.

INTERNET_OPTION_END_BROWSER_SESSION—Flushes entries not in use from the password cache on the hard drive. Also resets the cache time used when the synchronization mode is once per session. Used by InternetSetOption.

INTERNET_OPTION_EXTENDED_ERROR—Returns the Windows Sockets error message that was mapped to the ERROR_INTERNET_ error messages last returned in this thread context. This option is used on a NULL HINTERNET handle by InternetQueryOption.

INTERNET_OPTION_HANDLE_TYPE—Returns the type of the Internet handle passed in. Used by InternetQueryOption on any HINTERNET handle. Possible return values include

- INTERNET_HANDLE_TYPE_CONNECT_FTP
- INTERNET_HANDLE_TYPE_CONNECT_GOPHER
- INTERNET_HANDLE_TYPE_CONNECT_HTTP
- INTERNET_HANDLE_TYPE_FILE_REQUEST
- INTERNET_HANDLE_TYPE_FTP_FILE
- INTERNET_HANDLE_TYPE_FTP_FILE_HTML
- INTERNET_HANDLE_TYPE_FTP_FIND

- INTERNET_HANDLE_TYPE_FTP_FIND_HTML
- INTERNET_HANDLE_TYPE_GOPHER_FILE
- INTERNET_HANDLE_TYPE_GOPHER_FILE_HTML
- INTERNET_HANDLE_TYPE_GOPHER_FIND
- INTERNET_HANDLE_TYPE_GOPHER_FIND_HTML
- INTERNET_HANDLE_TYPE_HTTP_REQUEST
- INTERNET_HANDLE_TYPE_INTERNET

Returns or sets the HTTP version being supported. Must be used on a NULL handle. An HTTP_VERSION_INFO structure is used to set or get the version information. Used by InternetQueryOption and InternetSetOption.

INTERNET_OPTION_PARENT_HANDLE—Returns the parent handle to this handle. This option can be used on any HINTERNET handle by InternetQueryOption.

INTERNET_OPTION_PASSWORD—Returns or sets the password associated with a handle returned by InternetConnect. Used by InternetQueryOption and InternetSetOption.

INTERNET_OPTION_PROXY—Returns or sets the proxy information on an existing InternetOpen handle when the process handle is not NULL. If the process handle is NULL, the function sets or queries the global proxy information. The lpBuffer parameter is an INTERNET_PROXY_INFO structure that contains the proxy information. This option can be used on the HINTERNET handle returned by InternetOpen. Used by InternetQueryOption and InternetSetOption.

INTERNET_OPTION_PROXY_PASSWORD—Returns or sets the password currently being used to access the proxy. Used by InternetQueryOption and InternetSetOption.

INTERNET_OPTION_PROXY_USERNAME—Returns or sets the user name currently being used to access the proxy. Used by InternetQueryOption and InternetSetOption.

INTERNET_OPTION_READ_BUFFER_SIZE—Returns or sets the size of the read buffer. This option can be used on HINTERNET handles returned by FtpOpenFile, FtpFindFirstFile, and InternetConnect (FTP session only). Used by InternetQueryOption and InternetSetOption.

INTERNET_OPTION_RECEIVE_TIMEOUT—Returns or sets the timeout value, in milliseconds, to receive a response to a request. If the response takes longer than this timeout value, the request is cancelled. This option can be used on any HINTERNET handle, including a NULL handle. Used by InternetQueryOption and InternetSetOption.

INTERNET_OPTION_REFRESH—Returns or sets the value that determines if the proxy information can be reread from the registry for a handle. The value TRUE indicates that the proxy information can be reread from the registry for a handle. This option can be used on the HINTERNET handle returned by InternetOpen. Used by InternetQueryOption and InternetSetOption.

INTERNET_OPTION_REQUEST_FLAGS—Returns special status flags about the current download in progress. Used by InternetQueryOption. The flag can be one of the following values:

- INTERNET_REQFLAG_ASYNC—Not currently implemented.
- INTERNET_REQFLAG_CACHE_WRITE_DISABLED—The Internet request is not "cache-able" (HTTPS request).
- INTERNET_REQFLAG_FROM_CACHE—The response came from the cache.
- INTERNET_REQFLAG_NET_TIMEOUT—The Internet requested experienced a timeout.
- INTERNET_REQFLAG_NO_HEADERS—The original response contained no headers.
- INTERNET_REQFLAG_PASSIVE—Not currently implemented.
- INTERNET_REQFLAG_VIA_PROXY—The request was made through a proxy.

INTERNET_OPTION_REQUEST_PRIORITY—Returns or sets the priority of requests competing for a connection on an HTTP handle. Used by InternetQueryOption and InternetSetOption.

INTERNET_OPTION_SECONDARY_CACHE_KEY—Returns or sets the secondary cache key. Used by InternetQueryOption and InternetSetOption.

INTERNET_OPTION_SECURITY_CERTIFICATE—Returns the certificate for an SSL/PCT server into a formatted string. Used by InternetQueryOption.

INTERNET_OPTION_SECURITY_CERTIFICATE_STRUCT—Returns the certificate for an SSL/PCT server into the INTERNET_CERTIFICATE_INFO structure. Used by InternetQueryOption.

INTERNET_OPTION_SECURITY_FLAGS—Returns the security flags for a handle. Used by InternetQueryOption. Can be a combination of these values:

- SECURITY_FLAG_128BIT—Identical to the preferred value, SECURITY_FLAG_STRENGTH_STRONG. Only returned in a call to InternetQueryOption.

- SECURITY_FLAG_40BIT—Identical to the preferred value, SECURITY_FLAG_STRENGTH_WEAK. Only returned in a call to InternetQueryOption.

- SECURITY_FLAG_56BIT—Identical to the preferred value, SECURITY_FLAG_STRENGTH_MEDIUM. Only returned in a call to InternetQueryOption.

- SECURITY_FLAG_IETFSSL4—Not currently implemented.

- SECURITY_FLAG_IGNORE_CERT_CN_INVALID—Ignores the ERROR_INTERNET_SEC_CERT_CN_INVALID error message.

- SECURITY_FLAG_IGNORE_CERT_DATE_INVALID—Ignores the ERROR_INTERNET_SEC_CERT_DATE_INVALID error message.

- SECURITY_FLAG_IGNORE_REDIRECT_TO_HTTP—Ignores the ERROR_INTERNET_HTTPS_TO_HTTP_ON_REDIR error message.

- SECURITY_FLAG_IGNORE_REDIRECT_TO_HTTPS—Ignores the ERROR_INTERNET_HTTP_TO_HTTPS_ON_REDIR error message.

- SECURITY_FLAG_IGNORE_REVOCATION—Ignores certificate revocation problems.

- SECURITY_FLAG_IGNORE_UNKNOWN_CA—Ignores unknown certificate authority problems.

- SECURITY_FLAG_IGNORE_WRONG_USAGE—Ignores incorrect usage problems.

- SECURITY_FLAG_NORMALBITNESS—Identical to the value SECURITY_FLAG_STRENGTH_WEAK. Only returned in a call to InternetQueryOption.

- SECURITY_FLAG_PCT—Not currently implemented.

- SECURITY_FLAG_PCT4—Not currently implemented.

- SECURITY_FLAG_SECURE—Uses secure transfers. Only returned in a call to InternetQueryOption.

- SECURITY_FLAG_SSL—Not currently implemented.

- SECURITY_FLAG_SSL3—Not currently implemented.

- SECURITY_FLAG_STRENGTH_MEDIUM—Uses medium (56-bit) encryption. Only returned in a call to InternetQueryOption.

- SECURITY_FLAG_STRENGTH_STRONG—Uses strong (128-bit) encryption. Only returned in a call to InternetQueryOption.

- SECURITY_FLAG_STRENGTH_WEAK—Uses weak (40-bit) encryption. Only returned in a call to InternetQueryOption.

- SECURITY_FLAG_UNKNOWNBIT—The bit size used in the encryption is unknown. Only returned in a call to InternetQueryOption.

INTERNET_OPTION_SECURITY_KEY_BITNESS—Returns the bit size of the encryption key. The larger the number, the greater the encryption strength being used. Used by InternetQueryOption.

INTERNET_OPTION_SECURITY_SELECT_CLIENT_CERT—Sets the client certification. Used by InternetSetOption.

INTERNET_OPTION_SEND_TIMEOUT—Returns or sets the timeout value, in milliseconds, to send a request. If the send takes longer than this timeout value, the send is cancelled. This option can be used on any HINTERNET handle, including a NULL handle. Used by InternetQueryOption and InternetSetOption.

INTERNET_OPTION_SETTINGS_CHANGED—Informs WinInet that the registry settings have been changed so that it checks the settings on the next call to InternetConnect. Used by InternetSetOption.

INTERNET_OPTION_URL—Returns the full URL of a downloaded resource. If the original URL contained any extra information (such as search strings or anchors) or if the call was redirected, the URL returned differs from the original. This option is valid on HINTERNET handles returned by InternetOpenUrl, FtpOpenFile, GopherOpenFile, or HttpOpenRequest. Used by InternetQueryOption.

INTERNET_OPTION_USER_AGENT—Returns or sets the user-agent string on handles supplied by InternetOpen and used in subsequent HttpSendRequest functions, as long as it is not overridden by a header added by HttpAddRequestHeaders or HttpSendRequest. Used by InternetQueryOption and InternetSetOption.

INTERNET_OPTION_USERNAME—Returns or sets the user name associated with a handle returned by InternetConnect. Used by InternetQueryOption and InternetSetOption.

INTERNET_OPTION_VERSION—Returns the version number of wininet.dll. The lpBuffer parameter is the address of an INTERNET_VERSION_INFO structure. This option can be used on a NULL HINTERNET handle. Used by InternetQueryOption.

INTERNET_OPTION_WRITE_BUFFER_SIZE—Returns or sets the size of the write buffer. This option can be used on HINTERNET handles returned by FtpOpenFile and InternetConnect (FTP session only). Used by InternetQueryOption and InternetSetOption.

D

Appendix

Error Messages

The Win32 Internet functions return Win32 error messages when appropriate. The following error messages are specific to the Win32 Internet functions.

ERROR_FTP_DROPPED—The FTP operation was not completed because the session was aborted.

ERROR_FTP_NO_PASSIVE_MODE—Passive mode is not available on the server.

ERROR_FTP_TRANSFER_IN_PROGRESS—The requested operation cannot be made on the FTP session handle because an operation is already in progress.

ERROR_GOPHER_ATTRIBUTE_NOT_FOUND—The requested attribute could not be located.

ERROR_GOPHER_DATA_ERROR—An error was detected while receiving data from the Gopher server.

ERROR_GOPHER_END_OF_DATA—The end of the data has been reached.

ERROR_GOPHER_INCORRECT_LOCATOR_TYPE—The type of locator is not correct for this operation.

ERROR_GOPHER_INVALID_LOCATOR—The supplied locator is not valid.

ERROR_GOPHER_NOT_FILE—The request must be made for a file locator.

ERROR_GOPHER_NOT_GOPHER_PLUS—The requested operation can be made only against a Gopher+ server, or with a locator that specifies a Gopher+ operation.

ERROR_GOPHER_PROTOCOL_ERROR—An error was detected while parsing data returned from the Gopher server.

ERROR_GOPHER_UNKNOWN_LOCATOR—The locator type is unknown.

ERROR_HTTP_COOKIE_DECLINED—The HTTP cookie was declined by the server.

ERROR_HTTP_COOKIE_NEEDS_CONFIRMATION—The HTTP cookie requires confirmation.

ERROR_HTTP_DOWNLEVEL_SERVER—The server did not return any headers.

ERROR_HTTP_HEADER_ALREADY_EXISTS—The header could not be added because it already exists.

ERROR_HTTP_HEADER_NOT_FOUND—The requested header could not be located.

ERROR_HTTP_INVALID_HEADER—The supplied header is invalid.

ERROR_HTTP_INVALID_QUERY_REQUEST—The request made to HttpQueryInfo is invalid.

ERROR_HTTP_INVALID_SERVER_RESPONSE—The server response could not be parsed.

ERROR_HTTP_NOT_REDIRECTED—The HTTP request was not redirected.

ERROR_HTTP_REDIRECT_FAILED—The redirection failed because either the scheme changed (for example, HTTP to FTP) or all attempts made to redirect failed (default is five attempts).

ERROR_HTTP_REDIRECT_NEEDS_CONFIRMATION—The redirection requires user confirmation.

ERROR_INTERNET_ASYNC_THREAD_FAILED—The application could not start an asynchronous thread.

ERROR_INTERNET_BAD_AUTO_PROXY_SCRIPT—There was an error in the automatic proxy configuration script.

ERROR_INTERNET_BAD_OPTION_LENGTH—The length of an option supplied to InternetQueryOption or InternetSetOption is incorrect for the type of option specified.

ERROR_INTERNET_BAD_REGISTRY_PARAMETER—A required registry value was located but is an incorrect type or has an invalid value.

ERROR_INTERNET_CANNOT_CONNECT—The attempt to connect to the server failed.

ERROR_INTERNET_CHG_POST_IS_NON_SECURE—The application is posting and attempting to change multiple lines of text on a server that is not secure.

ERROR_INTERNET_CLIENT_AUTH_CERT_NEEDED—The server is requesting client authentication.

ERROR_INTERNET_CLIENT_AUTH_NOT_SETUP—Client authorization is not set up on this computer.

ERROR_INTERNET_CONNECTION_ABORTED—The connection with the server has been terminated.

ERROR_INTERNET_CONNECTION_RESET—The connection with the server has been reset.

ERROR_INTERNET_DIALOG_PENDING—Another thread has a password dialog in progress.

ERROR_INTERNET_DISCONNECTED—The Internet connection has been lost.

ERROR_INTERNET_EXTENDED_ERROR—An extended error was returned from the server. This is typically a string or buffer containing a verbose error message. Call InternetGetLastResponseInfo to retrieve the error text.

ERROR_INTERNET_FAILED_DUETOSECURITYCHECK—The function failed due to a security check.

ERROR_INTERNET_FORCE_RETRY—The Win32 Internet function needs to redo the request.

ERROR_INTERNET_FORTEZZA_LOGIN_NEEDED—The requested resource requires Fortezza authentication.

ERROR_INTERNET_HANDLE_EXISTS—The request failed because the handle already exists.

ERROR_INTERNET_HTTP_TO_HTTPS_ON_REDIR—The application is moving from a non-SSL to an SSL connection because of a redirect.

ERROR_INTERNET_HTTPS_HTTP_SUBMIT_REDIR—The data being submitted to an SSL connection is being redirected to a non-SSL connection.

ERROR_INTERNET_HTTPS_TO_HTTP_ON_REDIR—The application is moving from an SSL to a non-SSL connection because of a redirect.

ERROR_INTERNET_INCORRECT_FORMAT—The format of the request is invalid.

ERROR_INTERNET_INCORRECT_HANDLE_STATE—The requested operation cannot be carried out because the handle supplied is not in the correct state.

ERROR_INTERNET_INCORRECT_HANDLE_TYPE—The type of handle supplied is incorrect for this operation.

ERROR_INTERNET_INCORRECT_PASSWORD—The request to connect and to log on to an FTP server could not be completed because the supplied password is incorrect.

ERROR_INTERNET_INCORRECT_USER_NAME—The request to connect and to log on to an FTP server could not be completed because the supplied user name is incorrect.

ERROR_INTERNET_INSERT_CDROM—The request requires a CD-ROM to be inserted in the CD-ROM drive to locate the resource requested.

ERROR_INTERNET_INTERNAL_ERROR—An internal error has occurred.

ERROR_INTERNET_INVALID_CA—The function is unfamiliar with the certificate authority that generated the server's certificate.

ERROR_INTERNET_INVALID_OPERATION—The requested operation is invalid.

ERROR_INTERNET_INVALID_OPTION—A request to InternetQueryOption or InternetSetOption specified an invalid option value.

ERROR_INTERNET_INVALID_PROXY_REQUEST—The request to the proxy was invalid.

ERROR_INTERNET_INVALID_URL—The URL is invalid.

ERROR_INTERNET_ITEM_NOT_FOUND—The requested item could not be located.

ERROR_INTERNET_LOGIN_FAILURE—The request to connect and to log on to an FTP server failed.

ERROR_INTERNET_MIXED_SECURITY—The content is not entirely secure. Some of the content being viewed may have come from unsecured servers.

ERROR_INTERNET_NAME_NOT_RESOLVED—The server name could not be resolved.

ERROR_INTERNET_NEED_UI—A UI or other blocking operation has been requested.

ERROR_INTERNET_NO_CALLBACK—An asynchronous request could not be made because a callback function has not been set.

ERROR_INTERNET_NO_CONTEXT—An asynchronous request could not be made because a zero context value was supplied.

ERROR_INTERNET_NO_DIRECT_ACCESS—Direct network access cannot be made at this time.

ERROR_INTERNET_NOT_INITIALIZED—Initialization of the Win32 Internet API has not occurred. Indicates that a higher level function, such as InternetOpen, has not yet been called.

ERROR_INTERNET_NOT_PROXY_REQUEST—The request cannot be made via a proxy.

ERROR_INTERNET_OPERATION_CANCELLED—The operation was cancelled, usually because the handle on which the request was operating was closed before the operation completed.

ERROR_INTERNET_OPTION_NOT_SETTABLE—The requested option cannot be set, only queried.

ERROR_INTERNET_OUT_OF_HANDLES—No more handles could be generated at this time.

ERROR_INTERNET_POST_IS_NON_SECURE—The application is posting data to a sever that is not secure.

ERROR_INTERNET_PROTOCOL_NOT_FOUND—The requested protocol could not be located.

ERROR_INTERNET_PROXY_SERVER_UNREACHABLE—The designated proxy server cannot be reached.

ERROR_INTERNET_REDIRECT_SCHEME_CHANGE—The function could not handle the redirection because the scheme changed (for example, HTTP to FTP).

ERROR_INTERNET_REGISTRY_VALUE_NOT_FOUND—The required registry value could not be located.

ERROR_INTERNET_REQUEST_PENDING—The required operation could not be completed because one or more requests are pending.

ERROR_INTERNET_RETRY_DIALOG—The dialog should be retried.

ERROR_INTERNET_SEC_CERT_CN_INVALID—The SSL certificate common name (host name field) is incorrect; for example, if you entered www.server.com and the common name on the certificate says www.different.com.

ERROR_INTERNET_SEC_CERT_DATE_INVALID—The SSL certificate date that was received from the server is bad. The certificate is expired.

ERROR_INTERNET_SEC_CERT_ERRORS—The SSL certificate contains errors.

ERROR_INTERNET_SEC_CERT_REVOKED—The SSL certificate was revoked.

ERROR_INTERNET_SEC_INVALID_CERT—The SSL certificate is invalid.

ERROR_INTERNET_SECURITY_CHANNEL_ERROR—The application experienced an internal error loading the SSL libraries.

ERROR_INTERNET_SERVER_UNREACHABLE—The Web site or server indicated is unreachable.

ERROR_INTERNET_SHUTDOWN—The Win32 Internet function support is being shut down or unloaded.

ERROR_INTERNET_TCPIP_NOT_INSTALLED—The required protocol stack is not loaded and the application cannot start WinSock.

ERROR_INTERNET_TIMEOUT—The request has experienced a timeout.

ERROR_INTERNET_UNABLE_TO_CACHE_FILE—The function was unable to cache the file.

ERROR_INTERNET_UNABLE_TO_DOWNLOAD_SCRIPT—The automatic proxy configuration script could not be downloaded. The INTERNET_FLAG_MUST_CACHE_REQUEST flag was set.

ERROR_INTERNET_UNRECOGNIZED_SCHEME—The URL scheme could not be recognized or is not supported.

ERROR_INVALID_HANDLE—The handle that was passed to the API has been either invalidated or closed (Win32 error code).

ERROR_NO_MORE_FILES—No more files have been found (Win32 error code).

ERROR_NO_MORE_ITEMS—No more items have been found (Win32 error code).

INTERNET_ERROR_BASE—Not an error code; base value used for the Internet error codes.

E
Appendix

Recommended Reading

The following is a list of recommended supplemental reading material that I found especially helpful.

WinInet

- Microsoft Internet Client SDK Documentation at *http://www.microsoft.com/msdn/sdk/inetsdk/asetup/default.htm*
- Microsoft Visual C++ 4.1, 4.2, and 5.0 online help
- Microsoft WinInet newsgroup at *microsoft.public.inetsdk.programming.wininet.*
- *Microsoft Windows CE Developing Embedded Systems* at *http://www.microsoft.com/windowsce/embedded/default.asp*

Internet Protocols

- RFC web site at *http://www.rfc-editor.org*
- RFC Index at *ftp://ftp.isi.edu/in-notes/rfc-index.txt*
- RFC 959, *File Transfer Protocol (FTP)* at *http://info.internet.isi.edu/in-notes/rfc/files/rfc959.txt*

- RFC 1436, *The Internet Gopher Protocol* at *http://info.internet.isi.edu/in-notes/rfc/files/rfc1436.txt*
- RFC 1945, *Hypertext Transfer Protocol HTTP/1.0* at *http://info.internet.isi.edu/in-notes/rfc/files/rfc1945.txt*
- RFC 2068, *Hypertext Transfer Protocol—HTTP/1.1* at *http://info.internet.isi.edu/in-notes/rfc/files/rfc2068.txt*
- RFC 1738, *Uniform Resource Locators (URL)* at *http://info.internet.isi.edu/in-notes/rfc/files/rfc1738.txt*
- TCP/IP Tutorial at *http://oac3.hsc.uth.tmc.edu/staff/snewton/tcp-tutorial/index.html*
- W3C HTTP information at *http://www.w3.org/protocols/http*

COM and ATL

- *Essential COM* by Don Box (Reading, MA: Addison Wesley Longman, 1998).
- *Effective COM* by Don Box (Reading, MA: Addison Wesley Longman, 1999).
- *ATL Internals* by Brent E. Rector and Chris Sells (Reading, MA: Addison Wesley Longman, 1999).
- *Inside COM* by Dale Rogerson (Redmond, WA: Microsoft Press, 1997).
- "The Active Template Library Makes Building Compact COM Objects a Joy" by Don Box *(Microsoft Systems Journal,* June 1997).

Multithreading

- *Win32 System Programming* by Johnson M. Hart (Reading, MA: Addison Wesley Longman, 1997).
- *Win32 Programming* by Brent E. Rector and Joseph M. Newcomer (Reading, MA: Addison Wesley Longman, 1997).
- *Multithreading Applications in Win32: The Complete Guide to Threads* by Jim Beveridge and Robert Wiener (Reading, MA: Addison Wesley Longman, 1997).
- *Advanced Windows, Third Edition,* by Jeffrey Richter (Redmond, WA: Microsoft Press, 1997).

ISAPI and ASP

- *Inside ISAPI* by Jeffrey Trent (Indianapolis, IN: New Riders Publishing, 1997).
- *Professional Visual C++ ISAPI Programming* by Michael Tracy (Chicago, IL: Wrox Press, 1996).
- *Professional Active Server Pages 2.0* by Brian Francis, Alex Fedorov, Richard Harrison, Dave Sussman, Rob Smith, Alex Homer, and Shawn Murphy (Chicago, IL: Wrox Press, 1998).

Index

Addison-Wesley Computer and Engineering Publishing Group

How to Interact with Us

1. Visit our Web site

http://www.awl.com/cseng

When you think you've read enough, there's always more content for you at Addison-Wesley's web site. Our web site contains a directory of complete product information including:

- Chapters
- Exclusive author interviews
- Links to authors' pages
- Tables of contents
- Source code

You can also discover what tradeshows and conferences Addison-Wesley will be attending, read what others are saying about our titles, and find out where and when you can meet our authors and have them sign your book.

2. Subscribe to Our Email Mailing Lists

Subscribe to our electronic mailing lists and be the first to know when new books are publishing. Here's how it works: Sign up for our electronic mailing at http://www.awl.com/cseng/mailinglists.html. Just select the subject areas that interest you and you will receive notification via email when we publish a book in that area.

3. Contact Us via Email

cepubprof@awl.com
Ask general questions about our books.
Sign up for our electronic mailing lists.
Submit corrections for our web site.

bexpress@awl.com
Request an Addison-Wesley catalog.
Get answers to questions regarding your order or our products.

innovations@awl.com
Request a current Innovations Newsletter.

webmaster@awl.com
Send comments about our web site.

jcs@awl.com
Submit a book proposal.
Send errata for an Addison-Wesley book.

cepubpublicity@awl.com
Request a review copy for a member of the media interested in reviewing new Addison-Wesley titles.

We encourage you to patronize the many fine retailers who stock Addison-Wesley titles. Visit our online directory to find stores near you or visit our online store: http://store.awl.com/ or call 800-824-7799.

Addison Wesley Longman
Computer and Engineering Publishing Group
One Jacob Way, Reading, Massachusetts 01867 USA
TEL 781-944-3700 • FAX 781-942-3076

Learning Resources
Centre